Reflecting Back, Looking Forward:
Civil Rights and Student Affairs

Lisa E. Wolf-Wendel, Susan B. Twombly,
Kathryn Nemeth Tuttle, Kelly Ward
and Joy L. Gaston-Gayles

NASPA
Student Affairs Administrators
in Higher Education

Additional copies may be purchased by contacting the NASPA publications
department at 301-638-1749 or visiting http://www.naspa.org/publications.

ISBN 0-931654-33-5

TABLE OF CONTENTS

FOREWORD

H e must have been out of his mind, crazy, insane! Never mind that in 1950 Thurgood Marshall, attorney for the National Association for the Advancement of Colored People (NAACP) Legal Defense and Education Fund, challenged "separate but equal laws" in education. Never mind that the Supreme Court heard the case in 1952, and in 1954, Chief Justice Earl Warren's court unanimously agreed that "separate but equal did not belong in education." Never mind that in 1955 "Brown II" of the 1954 court case *Brown v. Board of Education of Topeka, Kansas* required all schools to desegregate "with all deliberate speed." When Clennon King in 1958, a professor of philosophy at Alcorn A&M, attempted to enroll in the graduate school at the University of Mississippi, he was arrested and committed to a state mental institution for 12 days. "He was declared insane on the premise that any Black person who would apply for admission to the University of Mississippi had to be out of his mind" (Branch, 1988, p. 524).

THE SCENE

In the early 1960s, when the first critical mass of Black students integrated colleges and universities throughout the United States, some students felt more welcome than others. For some Black students, attending a White university was like riding a segregated bus in Montgomery, Alabama—Black passengers paid their fare at the front door and exited and entered again through the back door so they could sit in the rear, leaving the seats up front available for White passengers. Black students were barely tolerated on many campuses and felt the sting of racism in class where they were simultaneously invisible and a spectacle. No one made eye contact, especially the teachers, but everyone was looking. Further, even on more progressive campuses, life was not structured to recognize and accommodate the needs and desires of Black students.

During these times of challenge and change, Black students, and their allies among White students, had numerous occasions to interact with administrators at colleges and universities. Most often the administrator responsible for speaking with students was the student affairs officer. Notwithstanding the advocates among faculty and staff on college and university campuses, the decade between 1960 and 1970 was a time when student affairs leaders were prominent and at the center of campus life. The role student affairs administrators played in keeping the peace and in maintaining an open dialogue has not been thoroughly explored, until this book. *Reflecting Back, Looking Forward: Civil Rights and Student Affairs* includes 18 stories from student affairs administrators during the civil rights era. Their stories do not represent all institutions or experiences but, taken as a whole, merely provide a small window into the role of student affairs in the civil rights era.

THE SPARK

With such a history around the freedom to participate in education, it is not surprising that college students sparked a revolution that forever changed the world. Historically, students have played a pivotal role in revolutionary change around the world. As part of their development, they want to see if their actions have power. Every generation seeks a cause.

Many students in the 1990s lamented that all the good causes were gone; they resented hearing about the civil rights era. They viewed reflection on students of the past as an indirect criticism of their present day "apathy." Likewise, students in the 1960s could have used the same argument. After all, the adults in the 1950s had already challenged and won legal battles against school desegregation, and the bus boycotts had successfully desegregated public transportation.

But instead of accepting the status quo, four Black students in Greensboro, North Carolina initiated what came to be called "sit-ins." These students witnessed the power of nonviolent protests when Rosa Parks refused to give up her seat on the bus. They witnessed that fighting for social justice not only made a difference in the dignity and lives of people but also provided the activists with hope for the future. These students in Greensboro, like their peers, were going to college, but they didn't feel the elation that is the result of accomplishment and triumph. They could only imagine the feelings renowned activist Bayard Rustin described when he said, "Martin (Martin Luther King, Jr.) makes going to jail [feel] like receiving a Ph.D." (National Civil Rights Museum [NCRM], 2004). These were students who believed that attaining a college education would do nothing for them if they continued to be treated as inferior beings without the right to participate in the minimal freedoms afforded citizens of a democratic society, such as sitting at a lunch counter at the local five-and-dime store.

On some level, conscious or not, students understood that being emotionally engaged in a common experience supporting humanistic values is an intrinsic part of the educational experience. Reverend James Lawson in 1960 said, "All the while American students were simply waiting in suspension, waiting for the cause, that ideal, that event, that 'actualizing of their faith' which would catapult their right to speak powerfully to their nation and world" (NCRM, 2004).

A New Era

Student affairs administrators understood that emotion and desire could not be turned off like a spigot. As uncontrollable as this flood of student energy appeared, it opened the gates to an era of responsibility for claiming their citizenship in this democracy. Students saw evidence that civil action could, indeed, bring about change. In 1960, the Student Non-Violent Coordinating Committee (SNCC) told students, "Truth comes from being involved and not from observation and speculation" (NCRM, 2004).

That small percentage of activist students who had seen how protest could bring about change on integrated campuses began to test their strength by organizing and demanding to be heard. Students who participated in on-campus or off-campus protests took risks and were often expelled. As Carl Anderson stated in the section Civil Rights at Research Universities later in this book,

> For example [at Howard University] students wanted to fly the Black liberation flag on a pole with the American flag. They wanted to put up outside speakers on top of buildings to allow them to speak almost to the entire campus from outside microphones that were placed on top of buildings, so that they could rally the students at a moment's notice. We had to find ways to support those aspirations that were legitimate, but at the same time, not compromise the university's basic mission—providing instruction and service to the students.

Racial justice was not the only civil right for which students protested. Lessons learned from the struggles for equal treatment and opportunity under the law were applied in the anti-Vietnam War protests that involved even more students and were often more violent. As a number of the interviewees in this book suggest, the issues kind of all blended together. Lee Upcraft in his chapter in the same section noted, "Black students were at the forefront of the antiwar movement because it was Blacks who were dying in the war more than anybody else." It was this reality that supports Dr. Martin

Luther King, Jr.'s assertion that "poverty, racial injustice, and war were 'inextricably bound together'" (NCRM, 2004).

STUDENTS AND ADMINISTRATORS REMEMBER

Student affairs administrators understand that student protesting, regardless of the cause, is one of the rites of passage in students' development of personal maturity. To support this part of the educational process caused some campus administrators to face moral contradictions as they addressed the constant and radical changes occurring on their campuses. In her interview in Civil Rights at Regional Commuter Campuses later in this book, Augustine Pounds described one particularly tense situation involving Oakland students and a demonstration around the university flagpole. As the student demonstration progressed, fears the students would burn the flag intensified. Pounds explained,

> Each step toward the flagpole brought me closer to the conflict in my role as an administrator and an advisor. I struggled with my internal conflicts over these roles. Could I represent the university and support the students without any conflict? Could I influence these students? Did these students trust me? Would they value my opinion? It would also be a test of my authority as an administrator to get them to disperse and return the flag. One of the most pressing questions was what would I do if I saw a burned flag?

In my work as NASPA's executive director, I've come in contact with other individuals who have unique personal perspectives from the civil rights era. I recently had the privilege to speak with Frank L. Matthews, publisher/editor-in-chief of *Black Issues in Higher Education*, who was a student at Clemson University between 1967 and 1971. He shared his outlook that during this decade of unrest, the senior student affairs administrator at Clemson was not a partner or educator for students. Matthews said that the administrator did not exhibit hostility toward the students but he was also not an advocate or resource either. Black students saw this administrator as the "cop on the block," and they knew to steer clear of him. Matthews and his peers had few resources to help them amplify their voices, as the highest-ranking Black employee at the time was the Black janitor who supervised the other Black custodians. Despite this lack of administrative support, Matthews and his fellow Black students staged a successful protest by officially withdrawing from the university and leaving the campus to stay in the community. Evening news anchor, John Chancellor, reported on the students' protest and their goal to have the university offer at least one course in African American studies. Even today, I could hear the pride in Matthews' voice when he said that this small protest of approximately 30 students finally grabbed the attention of the university.

Matthews' story portrays a negative picture of campus administrators. However, in listening to Matthews, it brought back memories of how a display of such a small amount of respect for students could make such a large difference. Students wanted an audience. They wanted to be heard. They wanted respect and to belong to a community. Matthews remembers one administrator fondly who, though he was not an overt advocate for student rights of any kind, did look at and speak to Black students, while the professors and other administrators refused to acknowledge their presence. While many in student affairs, regardless of their individual values, were intelligent partners in the civil rights movement, some were seen as a menace, a nonentity, or irrelevant to the success or failure of students. However, many administrators, such as those highlighted in this book, used these encounters as teachable moments, and in this way made important contributions to not only the education of students but also the civil rights movement. Student activists compelled student affairs administrators to become educators, as they learned to balance their actions and decisions on the scales of civil rights, institutional prerogative, and their personal and professional responsibility.

BUILDING COMMUNITY

Dr. Charles V. Willie, who later went on to become a tenured professor at Harvard for 30 years, started out as chair of the department of sociology, and subsequently the vice president for student affairs from 1970-72 at Syracuse University. Willie entered the student affairs profession because he had a strong belief in creating community on campus. In fact, almost every action he took was initiated with this larger purpose in mind. I recently had the opportunity to speak with him, and his understanding of the larger picture, during a time of great stress and action, astounded me.

Willie cultivated community in countless forums. He recalled frequent racial fights and flare ups in the dining hall. It became such a routine that he persuaded the psychiatrist in the Health Center to coteach a course with him called "Reducing Prejudice and Discrimination." All the students who had been in trouble on campus were required to attend. He also asked all student leaders, such as the president of the Student Government Association (SGA) and the editors of the campus newspaper, to attend the class as well. As a result, the class had rich discussions and the faculty was able to address student needs more effectively. Some time later, he saw one of the former students on the campus at Harvard who recalled those days as a time of deep learning.

Willie also worked with a school of journalism faculty member to begin a public opinion/affairs poll. The students conducted polls when there were major issues on campus that appeared irresolvable. One such issue was whether or not the Reserve Officers' Training Corps (ROTC) should recruit on campus. The assumption was that no one wanted the ROTC on campus in spite of the fact that some students depended on the scholarships to attend the institution. After the poll was completed, the results concluded over-whelmingly that the campus did support the ROTC presence. The "big controversial issue" immediately went away. Willie provided a forum where all interests were given equal opportunity and issues were eventually resolved in a peaceful manner. The poll was merely a medium to adjudicate difficult issues where each side had staked out incompatible positions. This was yet another way to build community on a campus.

Willie always defined the role of the senior student affairs officer as "marginal." Not marginal in today's sense of the word—such as being on the perimeter of the action—but instead in the sense of being in the middle or betwixt-and-between, where one stands with a foot on each plane, with knowledge that could help people with different perspectives find common interests. Willie had profound respect for students as constituents in the academic environment. Likewise, students responded to the respect Willie cultivated in his faculty peers. When students occupied/took over buildings, he would have faculty crawl into the windows to simply sit alongside the protesting students. Out of respect, when faculty was present, students refrained from vandalizing the buildings.

A Career Path is Chosen

Dr. Cynthia Smith Forrest, recently retired senior student affairs administrator at Framingham State College, Framingham, Massachusetts, was a second-semester student in her first year at the University of South Carolina when she witnessed the unthinkable on a university campus. She shared with me:

> I never will forget that afternoon in the first week of May in 1970 when I looked out of my residence hall's third-floor window to witness fully outfitted and equipped National Guardsmen unloading with great precision from buses parked in the lot across the street. I remembered thinking that they appeared to be prepared, and I wondered with great dread what would unfold during the night ahead. I

knew that protesters were holding "sit-ins" and were not budging from the student union. Additionally, I knew that in the administration building, there had been a series of confrontations. The Vietnam War protest and civil rights movement were central to the anger that was spilling out across my campus. Tear gas hung heavy in the air and people darted between buildings. A campus curfew was imposed. All of these tensions were swirling as exams loomed ahead. These days in May compelled me to face the world and its injustices and contradictions in ways that I never had experienced before. This microcosm was quite mild compared to many other campuses around the country, as complete buildings were destroyed and lives were lost. The tragedy at Kent State sent a message that serious leadership was needed to search for additional approaches to fight for change and justice. My university community faced these challenges directly, I believe, because campus leaders, faculty, students, and administrators came together. The leaders crafted opportunities to explore how we might think and work together for change in these complicated and tense times without violence and destruction (Smith Forrest, personal communication, February 2004).

Smith Forrest remembers this period as critical in her development. When University President Thomas F. Jones, along with Vice President of Student Affairs Charles Witten (who shares his reflections in Integration at Southern Universities later in this book), and Dean of Women Elizabeth Clotworthy, identified individuals who would serve on teams of faculty, administrators, and students, Smith Forrest was a student member on the team. Their task was to organize and facilitate campus conversations focused on the civil and student rights issues facing the university. Smith Forrest credits this introduction to higher education administration with helping her to identify her life's work. She said, "These powerful models of invitational leaders who dared to engage the campus during these intense times remain important figures in my professional life" (Smith Forrest, personal communication, February 2004).

LABORATORIES FOR DYNAMIC SOCIAL CHANGE

The civil rights movement has been a powerful model for how nonviolent, persistent, direct action for social justice yields positive change. Just as campuses in the 1960s were laboratories for activism, college and university campuses will continue to be cradles of unrest and laboratories of learning for future leaders of the world.

Walking with students as they take their first steps toward independence, toward taking a stand on principles and values, and toward being heard is a critical teaching and coaching role for student affairs educators in every position, at all institutions. The power of the Internet for communicating and organizing poses different challenges today that can also be overcome with appropriate professional skills and humanistic values so critical in a world that is increasing exponentially in diversity and in intolerance at the same time.

IT HAD TO BE WRITTEN

Because of the courage and conviction of many student affairs administrators, this book had to be written. It had to be written to preserve a rich history and to acknowledge the role of college students and their complex partnership with student affairs administrators; it had to be written at this time, upon the 50th anniversary of the legal denunciation of segregated schools.

Student affairs administrators of the civil rights era were functioning at various levels of experience and personal risk. While they don't want to be called heroes—as I referred to John Blackburn upon first hearing his story, which was the impetus for this work—the administrators interviewed for this book are indeed heroes to the students whose lives they touched during one of the most progressive and challenging times in the history of the United States. May these heroes be duly recognized for their contributions and critical roles during the civil rights movement and beyond.

On behalf of NASPA, I thank the interviewees who earnestly and candidly shared their stories from the civil rights movement. I am extremely grateful to the interviewers and authors for the many hours they devoted to this endeavor. A special thank you to Lisa Wolf-Wendel for her willingness and eagerness to take the lead in coordinating this publication. And finally, thanks to NASPA staff, Jesse Ward and Kevin Kruger, who worked with me to do the final shaping and publishing of a work that will be an invaluable resource for posterity.

PREFACE

Three years ago, Gwendolyn Jordan Dungy, executive director of NASPA, asked us if we would take on a project of collecting first-person stories of current, retired, and retiring chief student affairs officers who had occupied a student affairs role during the civil rights era. In addition to collecting the stories, we were to fashion the stories into a book. The idea for the project originated from conversations between Gwendolyn Dungy and a group of senior and retired chief student affairs officers, including James Rhatigan, James Appleton, David Ambler, and John Blackburn. They believed that their administrative experiences dealing with civil rights and student protest in the 1960s and early 1970s, and those of other individuals like them, have lessons to offer current and future student affairs administrators. Although basic issues of access to higher education for African American and other groups have been solved from a legal perspective, the challenges of creating truly integrated communities are still with us.

Because each of us is involved in preparing future student affairs administrators, we recognized the value that such stories could provide in informing the continuing struggle to create richly diverse campuses, and we agreed to take on the project. For many current student affairs administrators, higher education's struggle over civil rights is a distant memory and for our current students, most of whom were not yet born, it is textbook history. The project started small—we began with the purpose of capturing the stories of a few specific individuals—and grew as Gwen pushed us to include former student affairs administrators from different types of campuses in different parts of the country, and to include African American administrators. What emerged is both narrower in scope (it focuses primarily on civil rights) but more inclusive (it includes stories of more individuals) than the originators envisioned, but we hope it serves their intent even better than they imagined.

The specific purpose of the book is to present first-person accounts of the experiences of student affairs administrators in the civil rights era (1950s-1970s). Each of the first-person narrative chapters presents the memories and perspectives of a student affairs administrator, collectively representing an array of institutional types and geographic locations. These stories allow us to examine the role that student affairs administrators played in the civil rights era, and identify lessons that are relevant to today's campuses as they struggle to deal with issues of equity and diversity.

The importance of student affairs administrators in the lives of students in the civil rights era is undeniable—when universities were integrated, these administrators were the college officials who admitted, housed, and counseled not only African American students who faced hostility and prejudice, but also the White students who were often complicit or even supportive of the racism of their communities (Tuttle, K.N., 1996).

Colleges and universities have been the battleground for many important civil rights concerns and many authors have chronicled student social movements of this era (e.g., Adelman, 1972; Altbach, 1973; and Strauss & Howe, 1997). In both Northern and Southern colleges and universities, integration of African Americans into higher education was a slow and difficult process described in books such as *The Band Played Dixie* (Cohodas, 1997), *At the School House Door* (Clark, 1995), and *Paradoxes of Protest: Black Student Activism in a White University* (Exum, 1985). Once on campus, African American students had to deal with segregation in all types of out-of-class domains including housing, cafeterias, social activities, organized group activities including athletics and fraternities and sororities, availability of scholarships, on-campus and off-campus jobs, and access to barber shops and beauty parlors. Student affairs administrators played a key role in representing student demands to the administration, and sometimes advocating for change to occur (Clark, 1995; Laliberte, 2003; Tuttle, K. N., 1996).

Simultaneously, the presidents of many college and university campuses expected the student affairs staff to represent the institutions' views to the students and to discipline students who failed to follow the campus rules. These conflicting demands—the desire to support students and the desire to be seen as effective administrators and keep their jobs—put many student affairs administrators in precarious positions (Nichols, 1990). There has been very little written about student affairs in this era. One study of note by Crookston and Atkyns (1974) found that during the period of unrest in the 1960s, many senior student affairs officers left their positions. They also concluded that individuals in student affairs became known as crisis managers, and most colleges and universities elevated the chief student affairs officer from dean to vice president during this era. In recent research that examines student affairs during the turbulent years of 1968-1972, Laliberte (2003) confirms the crisis manager and student advocate roles.

Student affairs professionals served as crucial communication links between the administration and students and experienced enhanced status and advancement to higher administrative positions. The student affairs administrators of this era, whose experiences are chronicled in this book, became the icons of the profession and continue to have an influence on the direction of the field.

A NOTE ABOUT METHOD

The narrative chapters are the product of approximately one-and-a-half to two-hour interviews with individuals who were student affairs professionals during the civil rights era. We asked each person to describe his or her role in responding to civil rights concerns and to elaborate on his or her relationships with students, with other administrators, and with faculty members. We asked them to walk us through an event (or several events) to give us a sense of what their lives were like on a daily basis during this time period. Because much more has been written about other aspects of the protest era, such as anti-Vietnam War protests or fights to do away with restrictions such as parietal hours, we attempted to keep the focus on civil rights concerns. Although, as most of our respondents admitted to us, separating out these different issues was not always a simple proposition. A complete copy of the interview protocol is in the appendix.

As much as possible, we have tried to present the bulk of each chapter as a first person narrative account that is true to the voice of the interviewee. As such, one will note that there are a variety of styles and voices represented and we did little to unify them or force consistency, except through a somewhat common array of broad topics. To do more would have stripped the unique voice from the chapters. Some chapters include more supplemental material than others. When the interviewee provided written materials, we used them to supplement the interview and we cite them to distinguish written from spoken words. However, we did not seek out written documentation. The interviewee's words are indented.

We utilized a number of sources to find interviewees—including recommendations from NASPA members, referrals from those we interviewed, and by requesting "nominations" via the NASPA listserv. Because we were restricted to interviewing people who are still alive, our ability to fully capture the role of student affairs in the civil rights activities of the 1950s was somewhat limited.

Although we made an effort to attain diversity in terms of gender, race, institutional type, and geography, our goal was not to provide a comprehensive, definitive study of the role of student affairs in the civil rights era. Thus, we do not presume that the stories told here are generalizable to all student affairs professionals or situations experienced during the civil rights era. Instead, we see these stories as unique and as making a contribution to our understanding of what it was like to deal with civil rights concerns, often on a daily basis. That said, we do believe that the varied stories told here represent the experiences of many who served in student affairs roles during the 1960s and 1970s.

The stories told in these chapters represent the views, perspectives, and memories of the interviewees. We did not seek to verify the "truth" of their statements. Indeed, these chapters represent the participants' memories and impressions of the time as framed by their past and present experiences. As such, these depictions may not be 100 percent accurate from the standpoint of the historical record, but represent the perspectives and memories of the individuals involved. While some details may be lost, exaggerated, or obscured, the combination of these impressions and recollections offer the reader some common lessons and important themes that are applicable today.

ORGANIZATION OF THE BOOK

The first chapter of this book presents an historical overview of student affairs and of the civil rights era, providing a context for the remaining chapters. Following this historical chapter are 18 first-person narrative accounts of what it was like to be a student affairs professional during the civil rights era. We have organized the individual stories by institutional type and geography, though we found there to be striking similarities across these boundaries. The exceptions to this scheme are the stories of John Blackburn (University of Alabama) and Charles Witten (University of South Carolina), which are in a section of their own, because they assisted their institutions in the process of integration early in the 1960s. Thus their stories are unique and they generally precede in time period those of the others in this book. In some cases there is overlap among the interviewees, some even representing the same institution at the same time. This overlap offers an interesting perspective on some issues, as sometimes the same event was viewed in very different ways depending on the perspective of those involved.

The personal narrative chapters are presented in the following order. First, we present the stories of two deans at Southern universities attempting to respond to the integration of African Americans. The first story is told by

John L. Blackburn, who was dean of men at the University of Alabama from 1956 to 1969. The second chapter in this section is by Charles Witten, dean of students at University of South Carolina from 1963 to 1975.

The next three chapters represent student affairs administrators at smaller private colleges. The three chapters in this section tell the story of James Lyons, dean of students at Haverford College from 1962 to 1972; Mark Smith, dean of students at Denison University from 1953 to 1972; and Judith Chambers, dean of women at Mount Union College from 1960 to 1968 and dean of students at University of the Pacific, beginning in 1968, who recently became the special assistant to the vice president for university advancement.

We then present six chapters that represent the stories of student affairs administrators at various regional, commuter campuses. The first story is about Augustine Pounds, who held various student services positions at Oakland University from 1971 to 1975. Her story is complimented by the story of James Appleton who was dean of students at Oakland from 1965 to 1972. Harrison Morson is the subject of the third chapter in this section. He was dean of students at Union County Community College from 1969 to 1986, having served as a principal at a high school in the same community. James Rhatigan, dean of students at Wichita State University from 1965 to 2002 is the subject of the fourth story in this section. The next two chapters both present individuals who worked at Kent State University during the 1960s and 1970s. Ron Beer was assistant to the president at Kent State from 1961 to 1972. He then became dean of students at University of Nebraska at Omaha from 1972 to 1980. David Ambler was dean of men and later dean of students at Kent State from 1966 to 1977. He then became vice chancellor for student affairs at the University of Kansas from 1977 to 2002.

We include six chapters representing the experiences of student affairs officers at research universities. The first chapter in this section is by Carl Anderson, who worked in student affairs at Howard University from 1958 to 1990. He became dean of students there in 1968. The second chapter in this section is about Philip Hubbard, the dean of academic and student affairs at the University of Iowa from University of Iowa 1965 to 1991. Robert Shaffer is the subject of the next chapter. He worked in a variety of student affairs positions at the University of Indiana beginning in 1941. He became dean of students at Indiana in 1955. Harris Shelton's chapter discusses the period between 1968 and 1971 when he was dean of men at Florida State University. The next chapter features Jo Anne Trow, dean of women and associate dean of students at Oregon State in 1966. She eventually became the chief student affairs officer at Oregon State in 1984, where she served until her retirement in 1995. The final chapter is about Emily Taylor, dean of women at the University of Kansas from 1956 to 1975.

We view ourselves as both authors and editors of the book that follows. Clearly, credit for the heart of this book, the interview chapters, lies in the stories of the interviewees. The individuals featured here were at the forefront of the profession as its main role shifted from one of acting *in loco parentis* to one of viewing students as adults with rights and contributions to make. Moreover, although the context is thankfully more peaceful today and the issues often more subtle, we can learn from their lessons in struggling to deal with issues of access and climate for African American students and other students of color. Our contribution has been to provide a framework that more easily allows the reader to gain a sense of the themes and lessons that cut across the stories. In our concluding chapter we have done just that—we tried to identify the commonalities and differences across the stories and to distill the "lessons learned" in some framework that is easily accessible to readers. In this final chapter, while attempting not to oversimplify complex situations, we identify important themes that have implications for today's practitioners as well as for historians of the profession.

There are several ways to use this book. As noted earlier, the Introduction provides a historical backdrop to the role of student affairs and to civil rights. Chapters based on the individual student affairs administrators follow. In Reflecting Back: Themes from the Cases we look for and identify themes across the individual stories and in the final chapter, Looking Forward: Lessons Learned, we draw lessons from the individual stories, both personal lessons learned by the student affairs administrators themselves and lessons for the field. A reader can choose to read some or all of these pieces. For example, for a class on the history of the profession, one might choose to read the Introduction and closing chapters. By taking this path, the reader will obtain a summary of the contents of the individual stories set in an historical overview of the field and its role in civil rights. Another reader may choose to focus on the individual stories, which are interesting in and of themselves and may choose to skip the cross case comparison in Reflecting Back: Themes from the Cases. Or, of course, an individual may choose to read the whole book, cover to cover.

ACKNOWLEDGMENTS

We would like to thank Gwen Dungy for bringing an idea originating with a small group of NASPA members to fruition, for pushing us to be more inclusive, and for having the patience to wait on us to finish the product. We would also like to thank the numerous university and college archives for helping us collect photos.

Many NASPA members provided potential subjects for us to contact. Without their help we would have been lost. Most importantly, we want to thank the 18 individuals who spent a considerable amount of time talking with us on the phone or in person and editing text, and in some cases providing us with their personal papers. John Blackburn chauffeured us around Tuscaloosa, showed us "The Schoolhouse Door," treated us to dinner, and he even took us through the Paul "Bear" Bryant museum. We have each been deeply touched by the stories in this book and by the individuals who lived them. Singly and collectively, these individuals and their stories bring to life the crucial role of student affairs administrators as advocates for students and as the linchpin in the institutions' relationship with students in this crucial period in higher education's history. Many of the individuals featured in this book have left formal legacies on their individual campuses through which they have touched the lives of hundreds of students. These stories are for the rest of us. We hope they touch you the way they touched us.

Lisa E. Wolf-Wendel
Susan B. Twombly
Kathryn Nemeth Tuttle
Kelly Ward
Joy L. Gaston-Gayles

INTRODUCTION

When Augustine Pounds negotiated with the African American students who had taken over the Oakland University cafeteria in 1972, her main goal was to teach the students to protest effectively. She remembered:

> Integrity, fairness, equity, and hope are perhaps the words most often associated with my memory of the Oakland experience. We never lost hope that the increased activism and agitation by students would make the institution take a look at itself and change.

As director of the Student Center, Augustine Pounds played a crucial role in helping students formulate their demands to the administration, eventually forcing institutional change. Countless others in the student affairs profession played similar roles in the civil rights era from the 1950s to the 1970s, yet little is known about their efforts. This lack of knowledge is born both of the larger societal ignorance of the student affairs profession in higher education, and of the profession's ignorance of its own past. The past has the ability to inform both the present and the future. According to student affairs experts, however, "In our field, the present is a dominant preoccupation. The price of this preoccupation is the diminution not only of our predecessors but also of ourselves" (Appleton, Briggs, & Rhatigan, 1978, p. 9).

Student affairs administrators have a long history advocating for students' civil rights. In the 1920s, racial prejudice on campus was a topic at National Association of Deans of Women conferences. In 1941, Northwestern University charged Ruth McCarn, dean of women, with spreading "tolerance propaganda" and having the audacity to "foster social equality in race, creed, and color" (Tuttle, K. N., 1996, p. 144). McCarn's "crimes" were working with the student-led Interracial Commission to change policies toward African American students, including provision of on-campus housing and influencing the Panhellenic Council to recognize Alpha Kappa Alpha, a traditionally African American sorority. Northwestern was the second university in the country to charter an African American sorority, and McCarn's efforts were directed at solving the housing problem for African

American women students at Northwestern. In the 1940s, African Americans who attended Northwestern were forced to commute back and forth to Chicago in long trips on the "El" since there was no place in Evanston or on campus that would house them. McCarn was also an adamant supporter of Jewish students. An "international house" finally opened in 1947, but the next year McCarn was fired because she was "interested in the welfare of all students" (Tuttle, K. N., 1996, p. 154).

Protecting the welfare of all students has been a primary role of the student affairs profession for over a century. Since the 1890s, deans of men and women helped disconcerted college and university presidents deal with increasing numbers of male and female students and their housing, discipline, health, counseling, and social needs. Ruth McCarn's story illustrates why the student affairs role in the civil rights era was so predominant and crucial—student affairs administrators manage those out-of-classroom domains such as housing, food services, personal and vocational counseling, campus jobs, student governance, social activities, and organized group activities, including fraternities and sororities and recreation, that affect the daily life of students in fundamental ways. In Northern colleges, where classrooms had been integrated, in some cases for over 100 years, out-of-classroom activities were as segregated as they had been since before the Civil War. The civil rights era from the 1950s to the 1970s was a wake-up call for college administrators. In Southern colleges, where integration of the whole institution caused years of dissent and disruption, as it did at the University of Alabama, student affairs administrators were the ones called upon to negotiate with White students while supporting and housing disparaged and isolated African American students. And during the Black power movement of the late 1960s and 1970s, student affairs administrators were intimately involved with negotiations and support of African American students as they demanded not merely legal integration, but full acceptance and recognition in majority White institutions.

To provide a context for the important civil rights roles shared by student affairs professionals in this book, we review the history of the student affairs profession in relationship to racial concerns; the role of student affairs in response to student activism; segregation and integration as concerns for student affairs administrators; the response of student affairs administrators to Black power demands; and the inclusion of African Americans in student affairs professional organizations.

THE HISTORY OF STUDENT AFFAIRS IN RELATIONSHIP TO RACE

Student affairs work arose at the turn of the 20th century from the professional development of four main groups: deans of women; deans of men; personnel workers who utilized psychological testing; and vocational counselors (Appleton, Briggs, & Rhatigan, 1978; Tuttle, K. N., 1996). Historical roles that shaped student affairs professionals' relationships with students are crucial to understanding the profession's role in the civil rights era. Cowley (1940) outlined three types of administrative roles that arose in response to higher-education changes from 1870 to 1920 and each role extended to the civil rights era. First, the *humanitarians* arose in response to the depersonalized, research university of the late 1800s. This same thread can be seen in the deans who were sympathetic to students' claims of injustice and who saw the university as a part of the institutionalization of racism. The second group, the *administrators*, focused on administrative efficiency and supervision of a rapidly expanding campus early in the 20th century. It is these administrators who found themselves caught between the students and their presidents when protests escalated. And finally, the *psychologists*, who originally used the testing methods developed during World War I, expanded the counseling and the therapeutic model for students after World War II. It is this group who responded to the psychological impacts of racism, especially during the Black power movement (Tuttle, K. N., 1996). The threads of each of these historical administrative roles are woven into the complex professional roles that student affairs professionals fulfill today. Everyday they are called on to combine humanitarian, administrative, and psychological insights to respond to the needs of students, staff, and faculty.

The need for professional development for student affairs administrators surfaced quickly. Deans of women initiated the first national student affairs professional organization, the National Association of Deans of Women (NAWDAC), a precursor to the National Association for Women in Education in 1916; the first professional training at Columbia University Teacher's College in 1913; the first professional journal in 1938; and established the fundamental principles and practices of the field (Schwartz, 1990). Deans of men first met in 1919 and founded the National Association of Deans of Men (NADM), the precursor to NASPA, in 1929. Lucy Diggs Slowe, dean of women at Howard University from 1922 to 1937, started the National Association of Deans of Women and Advisors of Women and Girls in Negro Schools in 1929 (Tuttle, K. N., 1996). At their meeting in 1930, Marion Cuthbert (1930), dean of women at Talladega College, explained the importance of their role: "The dean in the Negro school must help students to fit into a world where they are neither socially welcomed nor economically secure" (pp. 21-22).

As the roles of dean of women and dean of men rapidly spread to most college and university campuses in the 1920s and 1930s, racial issues sometimes surfaced in professional meetings. Lucy Diggs Slowe addressed a professional group at Columbia University Teachers College in 1925 and made a plea for better race relations. She became the first African American NAWDAC member in 1924. At the 1923 NAWDAC Conference, Anne Dudley Blitz, dean of women at the University of Kansas, presented a program on social issues related to interracial contact on campus and described ways she was trying to reduce prejudice on the University of Kansas (KU) campus. Though KU had never restricted African American students from the classroom, its racial climate in the 1920s was dismal: African American students were barred from dormitories, the swimming pool (the student swimming requirement was conveniently waived for African American students), athletics, musical groups, debate, the Men's Student Council (but not the Women's Student Government Association) and even the YWCA and YMCA. KU's chancellor, Ernest Lindley, approved the segregation of the cafeteria in the new student union in 1927 on the grounds that White students would refuse to eat with African American students and integration would threaten the economic survival of the new venture (Tuttle, K. N., 1996; Tuttle, W. M., 2001). Dean Blitz stayed at KU only two years before leaving for the University of Minnesota, her alma mater. Disagreement on the issue of race was one of several conflicts she had with KU's chancellor (Tuttle, K. N., 1996). The racial climate and relationship between the dean responsible for student life and the president evident at KU is emblematic, not only of the tense racial climate of the 1920s, but also of the conflicts between deans and college presidents during the civil rights era of the 1950s through 1970s.

After weathering the economic turmoil of the 1930s, the student affairs profession faced new challenges in the 1940s with World War II and the return of phenomenal numbers of veterans to take advantage of the G.I. Bill after the war. It was the explosion of services established to handle the veteran glut on campus that forced student affairs into a new administrative structure, which eventually eliminated the roles of deans of women and men, and instituted a new bureaucracy headed by a dean of students, exclusively a man. The postwar era also presented a new racial climate, as both White and African American soldiers, who had fought for democracy and racial equality abroad, returned to the segregated and racist realities of the United States. These veteran students had little tolerance for discrimination at home. It was in this climate that Ruth McCarn fought for racial equality for the students at Northwestern and was fired. On other campuses, deans of students dealt with local chapters of the Congress of Racial Equality (CORE), National Association for the Advancement of Colored People (NAACP), and other integrated student groups demanding an end to racial segregation (Altbach, 1973). At Northern universities, one effect of these protests was the gradual desegregation of student housing, eating facilities, and student athletics (Tuttle, W. M., 2001). These postwar efforts set the stage for the activism of the 1950s through 1970s.

THE ROLE OF STUDENT AFFAIRS IN RESPONSE TO STUDENT ACTIVISM

Four themes that underlie the work of student affairs also influenced responses to this activism. These themes include: treating the whole student; the role of discipline; the rise of student rights; and the role of student affairs as a student advocate. The first theme is based on the Student Personnel Point of View, the founding philosophy of the profession first iterated in 1937. It calls on student affairs professionals to "consider the student as a whole...intellectual capacity and achievement...emotional make-up...social relationships...vocational aptitudes and skills...moral and religious values...economic resources...[with an] emphasis on development of the student as a person" (NASPA, 1989, p. 49). Student affairs deans could not consider only the classroom life of students, where most Northern colleges and universities were integrated, but were called on to consider all aspects of student life that included numerous realities of segregation and racism.

The expectation to consider moral values ties in with another traditional role of deans of men and women—that of discipline. While many, including James Rhatigan (Appleton, Briggs, & Rhatigan, 1978) and Jo Ann Fley (1963), who have studied the history of student affairs, challenge the stereotype of inflexible, controlling deans, the dean as disciplinarian is still a common image. But if this image is expanded to include the 19th century concept of moral discipline, then what deans attempted to develop was an inner discipline based upon moral and spiritual values. Marion Talbot, dean of women at the University of Chicago, described it as "unlocking the virtues found in every student" (Appleton, Briggs, & Rhatigan, 1978, p. 22). If discipline includes character building, moral and ethical training, and citizenship responsibilities, then the link to civil rights becomes clearer. But when student activism involved nonviolent protests, and later violence and destruction of property, it seemed to demand that student affairs administrators invoke discipline as control. Certainly presidents, boards of trustees, and parents insisted that students, even those involved in nonviolent protest, be controlled. Then, as now, college presidents depended on senior student affairs officers to handle student disruptions. Antiwar protests and the Black power movement intensified this concern and further challenged the student affairs profession to define its disciplinary role.

The broader issues of controlling behavior and the specter of *in loco parentis* highlight another theme that influenced student affairs professionals— the rise of students' rights. The revolution in the 1960s that ultimately affected the work of deans and the direction of student affairs much more than student demonstrations was the death of *in loco parentis* and the birth of students' legal rights. The changes in legal rights were strongly influenced by civil rights cases. Many deans cite the push for students' legal rights—in the areas of due process; free speech, including student free press rights; access to their own educational records; the rights to protest, demonstrate, and organize; and involvement with institutional governance—as having the most profound effect on the roles and activities of student affairs administrators. Students were no longer second-class citizens under the law. Again the civil rights movement provided the impetus for change. The key case in establishing students' new status was *Dixon* v. *Alabama State Board of Education* (Kaplin, 1986). This 1961 case involved students expelled from Alabama State College during civil rights protests in Montgomery, Alabama, and their Fifth and Fourteenth Amendments, due process rights to a notice of charges and a hearing in cases of expulsion, or other serious disciplinary action, for misconduct.

Responding, and in some cases anticipating these legal changes, a "Joint Statement on Student Rights and Freedoms" was created in 1967 by members of the American Association of University Professors (AAUP), the United States National Student Association, the NAWDAC and NASPA (*Student Rights and Freedoms*, 1992; Tautfast, 1969). Once again the civil rights struggle was a prime mover—the statement began as an AAUP effort in 1960 to address unfair treatment of students who had peacefully demonstrated against racial discrimination. The statement recognized students' rights to free expression and inquiry and also called for students' responsible use of these new freedoms.

These legal changes had a profound effect on the student affairs profession. Many deans not only welcomed the demise of *in loco parentis* but also supported the activism of students. Katherine Towle (1966), dean of students at the University of California, Berkeley, commented,

> From the silent generation of the 1950s, we have come full circle to
> the articulate and activist generation of the 1960s. The lesson of
> Berkeley is that the effect of student commitment to social justice and
> political freedom should never again be misjudged....*In loco parentis*
> has little place in today's institutions (pp. 101-103).

Robert Shaffer (personal communication, March 26, 1994) welcomed student activism at Indiana University, as well. "I would rather worry about demonstrations and issues than judge beauty contests," he declared in a 1967 *Life* magazine article. He wanted, "every leader and critic the campus could attract" (Moore, 1967, p. 90). His blunt liberalism attracted its own critics, however. He remembered, "Saying what Indiana University needs is more radicals here than less... got me in all sorts of trouble."

Finally, student affairs administrators' role as student advocates received a rigorous challenge during the civil rights era. Is their primary responsibility to students? Or is it to the president, to the parents, to the public, to the police, or to the National Guard? Is their fundamental role as a part of the college or university administrative leadership team? What is the obligation to professional ethics and professional standards? This is where the senior student affairs officer's fundamental vulnerability lies—between students and the administration (and, in some instances of student protest, violent or not, the police). From the 1950s through the 1970s, many student affairs administrators faced the anxiety of further violence and conflicts. This conflict was frequently mentioned by those we interviewed and in a NASPA survey conducted by Crookston & Atkyns (1974). At the 1965 NASPA Conference, marked by palpable tension, a dean remarked in the session on student demonstrations when an emergency announcement was made for a conference attendee to call his home campus—"The pitter patter of the hearts of many started to tick, 'Well, I wonder if it is me this time'" (NASPA, 1965, p. 186). The civil rights movement inspired the student demonstrations that deans worried about.

Early in this period, higher-level administrators seemed unwilling to trust the student affairs administrators' role as student advocate, and instead expected control and discipline. In the early 1960s, sit-ins and picketing, promoted by the Student Nonviolent Coordinating Committee (SNCC), spread throughout the South and led to voter registration efforts that sympathetic White college students joined. Many of those involved in the free speech demonstrations at Berkeley in the fall of 1964 had spent the previous summer registering African American voters in Mississippi; that was one reason dean of students, Katherine Towle (1966), recommended a reasonable outlet for student expression by allowing tables and leaflets on Bancroft

Avenue. Yet even Towle, who had served as the women marines director in World War II, and was named one of the first female deans of students in 1961, would not be listened to by male administrators in the fall of 1964 when she opposed the decision to ban student organizations from handing out literature and setting up tables on a strip of Bancroft Avenue just outside the campus gates. Students had used the area throughout the summer to garner support for candidates and civil rights activities, and Towle maintained that allowing students to continue to use the area provided a safety valve during a politically volatile time. Towle and many of her fellow deans wanted students to "be given responsibility for governing themselves, with deans acting as advisers only" (p. 102).

Antiwar protests became increasingly violent: State highway patrolmen killed three students and wounded 27 on the campus of South Carolina State College in 1968, a tragic event that became known as the Orangeburg Massacre. The violence culminated in the killing of four students at Kent State University and two students at Jackson State College in May 1970. The Jackson State killings, overshadowed by Kent State, occurred when city police and highway patrolmen fired directly into a women's residence hall. Student affairs administrators reacted with horror to the events that spring; they were "shattered" remembered David Ambler (personal communication, December 12, 1994), who was then dean of men at Kent State. He saw his boss, the vice president of student affairs, as "the one person trying to prevent what happened from happening" but higher-level decisions prevailed, and tragedy ensued. Student affairs administrators were doubly dammed during the political protests of the 1960s—by students, whose needs deans presumably represented to the administration, and by their administrative superiors, who often failed to take their advice but made them the scapegoats when things went wrong. "On campus after campus the chief student personnel administrator has become the 'whipping post' for students, faculty, and other administrators," complained Elizabeth Greenleaf (1968, p. 226) in her presidential address to the American College Personnel Association (ACPA) in 1968. "The dean is seen as responsible in some way for the student power movement, for the image of the university as seen by the public" (p. 226). Some deans avoided playing the scapegoat by leaving the profession; one dean described it as "the great exodus from what appeared to be the most hazardous job of all—the student deanship" (p. 226). "I didn't go into this business to be the enemy of the people," quipped Dorothy Truex (personal communication, March 4, 1994), then dean of women at the University of Oklahoma.

> I was the symbol of the rules at this point and that was not very pleasant.
> I didn't really want to change jobs until the students were all rebelling. I
> got blockaded in the office a couple of times—that was enough.

In 1969, Truex transferred to the faculty ranks for five years before returning to administration at the University of Arkansas, Little Rock, as one of
the first female vice chancellors for student affairs.

And many deans thought individually, and as a profession, student affairs
responded too slowly and then too ineffectually, to student demonstrations.
"We were very slow," said Robert Shaffer (personal communication, March
26, 1994), dean of students at Indiana University.

> I remember at NASPA, the head of the federal prison of California
> addressed us at a meeting. He said before you deal with anyone you
> reestablish your authority. That was the early response to demonstra-
> tions. You do not give in. The word among the deans was: don't give
> in under duress. It was just ridiculous because often the students were
> absolutely right in their protest against rules and the unenforceability
> of the rules that we had. We had just absurd rules...maybe it's because
> so many of our superiors, presidents, public relations people, trustees,
> thought the dean's job was to hold the line on behavior.

Student affairs staffs were challenged not only to respond to students' civil
and legal rights but also to their intellectual and developmental needs in a
new way in the 1960s. The publication of Nevitt Sanford's *The American
College* (1962) and *Where Colleges Fail* (1967) shook the foundation of student affairs work and provided, in Sanford's terminology, an environment of
"challenge and support" for the field's identity. This "psychological and
social interpretation of higher learning" was a watershed in applying these
approaches to research on colleges and universities, and particularly for student affairs, to research on the college student. Sanford's focus on college
student development, the culture of the campus, educating the whole student, and providing an environment with the appropriate challenges and
supports to encourage students to mature intellectually, socially, and psychologically was essentially what student affairs professionals had been doing
since the turn of the century. But here were psychologists, and a host of
social scientists, confirming this approach from their academic research.
College student development theories became the organizing principle for
many in the student affairs field in the 1970s and 1980s.

Even though the sense at the time was that student affairs did not respond
quickly enough to student disruptions, a recent study by Laliberte (2003) found
a positive long-term effect in the challenges student affairs administrators

experienced in the civil rights and student rights eras: College presidents would increasingly come to depend on deans of students to be the communication link with students, and this critical responsibility in a time of crisis soon elevated these deans to vice presidents of student affairs.

SEGREGATION AND INTEGRATION AS CONCERNS FOR STUDENT AFFAIRS ADMINISTRATORS

Prior to the civil rights movement, issues for Northern and Southern colleges were very different, yet each area of the country was plagued by deep and pervasive racism. In the South, higher education was clearly segregated. In 1930, the four Southern states with the highest percentages of African Americans—Alabama, Louisiana, Mississippi, and South Carolina—had only four public higher education institutions (none provided graduate or professional education) for African Americans while Whites had 23 public colleges and universities to choose from (Anderson, 2002). In 1940 in Alabama, which had a 37 percent African American population, for every $100 spent on education for Whites, the state spent $6 for African Americans (Clark, 1993). Not one four-year college degree was offered at any public African American institution. In the North, the institutionalized racism, while influenced by legal and social differences, was an effective barrier to African American student participation in higher education (Anderson, 2002). The few African Americans admitted had rights only in the classroom, and even then, some were segregated at the back of classroom (Tuttle, W. M., 2001).

In the 1930s and 1940s, important court decisions, led by efforts of the NAACP and Thurgood Marshall, resulted in some integration of graduate and professional education. In Gaines v. Missouri, 1938, the Supreme Court ruled that if states offered law schools for Whites, they could not force African American students to leave the state for their law education (Wallenstein, 1999). Another 1938 ruling banned segregation in classrooms and libraries once African American students were admitted. Then there was the immediate impact of World War II, CORE, and other campus efforts to end segregation late in the 1940s. West Virginia, Delaware, and Arkansas started admitting African American graduate students without court orders around 1950. The education systems of 17 states were legally segregated in 1954 when the Supreme Court decision *Brown v. Board of Education* irrevocably changed the racial landscape. Border state universities in Missouri, Arkansas, Oklahoma, Kentucky, West Virginia, Maryland, and Texas started admitting African American undergraduates in 1955. Alabama (1963), Georgia (1961), Louisiana (LSU-1964), Mississippi (1962), and South

Carolina (1963) were most resistant to desegregation. Mississippi State University was the last to integrate in 1965. The nature of the institution could also delay change: The University of Texas integrated in 1955, but the more conservative Texas A&M, with its corps of cadets, did not integrate until 1963 (Wallenstein, 1999). It took the 1964 Civil Rights Act for the federal government to enforce the comprehensive desegregation of higher education (Teddlie & Freeman, 2002).

In this chronology of desegregation are many poignant stories. For example, Irving Peddrew was admitted to Virginia Polytechnic in 1953 because there were no electrical engineering programs at Virginia State University, a Historically Black College. Virginia Polytechnic was the first White Southern school to integrate, and Peddrew was the only African American among 3,200 students. Peddrew had to live and eat off campus. "He bore by himself the full burden of desegregating a school, often felt wretchedly isolated, and left after three years without graduating" (Wallenstein, 1999, p. 134).

Stephan Mickle described his life as the first African American graduate of the University of Florida in 1965 this way:

> One of the reasons I was able to survive and eventually graduate was because I could withdraw from the university setting and go back home every day. I could revive my spirit…get some words of consolation, get cheered up the next morning, and go back out there and deal with that very hostile and frightening environment…..a wall of silence. Nobody spoke to you all day long…We were there and ignored (Wallenstein, 1999, p. 140).

Often, student affairs professionals limited the hostile environments endured by these pioneering students who helped integrate higher education. Dorothy Truex, dean of women at the University of Oklahoma (OU) from 1947 to1974, was asked by the president to assist with the African American female, high-ability student in pharmacy who integrated OU in 1955. Truex put her in a residence hall where the graduate counselor had worked with the YWCA and in other integrated settings. Truex decided to put her with other students, rather than to place her on a separate floor with only staff, as had been suggested. The students welcomed the African American woman, electing her hall president. She declined the position. To deal with parental concerns, Truex directed hall directors to ask that each student write her parents and tell them there was a Black student living in her hall (Truex, personal communication, March 4, 1994).

Deans of students also took roles in the community to improve race relations, such as Robert Shaffer (personal communication, March 26, 1994) at

Indiana University, who was the first chairman of the Human Relations Committee for the city of Bloomington. Sometimes the arena of integration would be in the area of services that students needed, such as restaurants and barber and beauty shops. As Shaffer recalled, "Barber shops would not cut Negro students' hair until President Wells and the dean of students' office worked with the union to hire a licensee who promised to cut all hair." Shaffer convinced Ed Correll, president of the barber's union, to become that licensee, and the union policy had an influence on barbershops in town. Shaffer also makes the point that involving local religious organizations and their ministers, including African American churches, was often part of the campus/community effort and offered an "aura of respectability" to protest efforts.

Students at Historically Black Colleges and Universities (HBCUs) played a seminal role in the civil rights movement sparked by the lunch counter sit-in by four North Carolina A&T students in February 1960 in Greensboro, North Carolina (Exum, 1985). Students from Fisk and Tennessee A&I found themselves leaders of the civil rights movement (Halberstam, 1998). The issues for deans of women and men at HBCUs must have been even more complex than they were for their White counterparts. They felt both admiration and concern for students who were protesting, and yet a need to maintain calm. The role of student affairs administrators at HBCUs has been insufficiently studied and is a topic ripe for further investigation.

One aspect of college life often charged with harboring stereotypes and prejudices—fraternities and sororities—was typically a student affairs responsibility. Fraternities and sororities continue to offer a particularly stubborn challenge to issues of integration. Today, on many campuses, fraternities and sororities are the last bastion of segregation, a point noted by most of our interviewees. The racial problems faced by fraternities and sororities have a long history. In the 1950s and 1960s, the crucial issues with fraternities and sororities were their exclusionary clauses that discriminated not only on the basis of race but also religion. Based on National Association of Deans and Advisors of Men (NADAM) conference proceedings, it appears few deans of men were progressive on this issue, but many more took a more conservative stance. In contrast, at the 1949 NADAM Conference, Everett Baker, dean of students at Massachusetts Institute of Technology (MIT) said fraternities need to "do a little house cleaning at the point of discrimination." He said that some fraternity charters that included phrases about only White or Christian membership, "read exactly like *Mein Kampf*. Colleges and universities should stand unequivocally against discrimination. We should lend every conceivable support to fraternities who are trying to change their charters against the opinions of their national fraternities" (NADAM, 1949, p. 38).

But most deans of men disagreed with active support of progressive fraternities. For example, an autonomy resolution passed at the 1954 NADAM Conference supported the National Interfraternity Conference's stance that member fraternities had the right to establish their own membership qualifications. The majority of deans of men seemed to feel that the 1949 Michigan Plan, which called for fraternities to remove selectivity clauses based on race, religion, and color, was coercive. Assistant Dean William S. Zerman of the University of Michigan called students who initiated the plan "rabble-rousing antagonists" who "infiltrated our student government" (NASPA, 1954, p. 191-192). The assistant dean was not alone in his unprogressive stance: Two University of Michigan Presidents, Alexander Ruthven and Harlan Hatcher, vetoed the Michigan Plan, an announcement applauded by the deans of men.

THE RESPONSE OF STUDENT AFFAIRS ADMINISTRATORS TO BLACK POWER DEMANDS

In the late 1960s and early 1970s, the issues changed from integration to Black power and separation. Changes in admissions policies and recruitment led to more African Americans on campus in both the South and the North. The dynamics of the1950s were different than the 1960s—after the Brown decision, very small numbers of African American students were integrated. They were seen as individuals and not as a group, and were usually very strong students academically. In the 1960s, larger numbers of African American students arrived on campus as the Civil Rights Act of 1964 systematically enforced desegregation. When African American students were seen as a group, they seemed more threatening to Whites (Exum, 1985). They were judged as not as strong academically as is mentioned at several of the institutions mentioned later in this book. In 1964, three percent of the college population was African American. From 1964 to1970, African American college enrollment doubled—mostly in White colleges. By 1972, 75 percent of all African American students were enrolled in White colleges—about the same percentage as today (Exum, 1985).

There was a significant rise in African American student activism after the death of Martin Luther King in 1968. In 1969, six percent of college students were African American, but "57 percent of campus protests involved Black students" (Exum, 1985, p. 3). Students were affected by the urban riots of the late 1960s and "loss of momentum of civil rights activities"

(Exum, 1985, p. 7). Students saw institutional racism in their colleges and universities, which validated Black power protests. There was a difference from earlier protests: students focused on the university, not society; it was not an interracial effort—African Americans were in their own separate group; they were not explicitly nonviolent; and they were not part of a national movement, such as NAACP or the SNCC, they were mostly independent student groups (Exum, 1985).

The story of the Black power movement as seen through the eyes of Harris Shelton, assistant dean of men at Florida State University (FSU) and Mark Smith, dean of students at Denison University, told later in this book, illustrates how two student affairs professionals responded to this new campus crisis of the late 1960s and early 1970s. The NAWDAC Journal printed several articles in this time period trying to help student affairs professionals deal with Black power issues and student protest. At the April 1968 NAWDAC annual convention, Jeanne Noble, an African American dean commented:

> Student personnel workers....lived through the "uncommitted, unsilent" student era. We sustained the student freedom fighter period that gave the civil rights movement its dramatic thrust. Now we face an era of activism characterized by demands for participatory democracy among predominately White student groups and for Black identity among African American student groups. On White campuses, students want to escape total immersion in White values they perceive to be alienating, materialistic, and racist. On Black campuses, students want to escape total immersion in "Black bourgeoisie culture" which they see as paternalistic and authoritarian (Noble, 1969, p. 49).

Noble called on deans to understand this as an identity crisis. "There is much to be said for the fact that one has to know who he is before he integrates" (p. 54).

Others tried to help administrators understand cultural factors, values, and the failure of schools to portray African American culture and history (Anthony, 1978). Anthony recommended that counseling issues focus on dealing with societal injustices and said administrators should not ask African Americans to adjust to societal or institutional dysfunctions.

> Avoid becoming hostile, defensive or frightened when counseling "militant" Blacks by recognizing that "Black consciousness" is related to healthy psychological functioning, to heightened self-esteem, to increased positive group identification, to increased feelings of control. Be prepared to support goals and objectives of Black students

which may clash with your own goals and/or goals of mainstream America (Anthony, 1978, p. 151).

THE INCLUSION OF AFRICAN AMERICANS IN STUDENT AFFAIRS PROFESSIONAL ORGANIZATIONS

There was a general sense that deans of women were more progressive on the issue of racial integration during the civil rights era than were deans of men. NAWDAC admitted its first African American member in 1924—Lucy Diggs Slowe—but the first African American member of NADAM was not until 1940s—Armour Blackburn of Howard University—and he was first officially listed as a member in 1952. Also, NAWDAC was the first personnel association to support the 1954 Supreme Court decision on school desegregation. As noted above, NADAM was quite conservative on the issue of removing restrictions on fraternity membership. Both NAW-DAC and NADAM had poor records of including African American members at conferences. Hotel restrictions were constant, and affected not only housing but also meals and banquets for conference attendees; sometimes African American members were required to use service elevators and the organization occasionally had to rent separate facilities for integrated meals (Tuttle, K. N., 1996). As late as 1969, at the NAWDAC conference in Atlanta, African American members were not allowed to attend the conference dinner banquet, a fact bitterly remembered at a NAWDAC history panel in 1979 (Brett, Calhoun, Piggott , Davis, & Scott, 1979).

But both NAWDAC and NADAM also tried to improve conditions for African American members. NASPA actively sought membership from Howard University in the 1940s. And when NASPA leadership learned that the Austin, Texas hotel scheduled for the 1952 national conference would not house African American conference attendees, they moved the conference to Colorado where the president of Howard University was the keynote speaker. Through the 1950s and 1960s, the NASPA national convention provided an opportunity for programs and discussion on racial issues. The rise of the Black power movement forced both NAWDAC and NASPA to take a closer look at their own policies and programs. African American membership grew slowly until the early 1970s, when NASPA took an active role in recruiting African American members, and in surveying the profession to determine the percentage of minority student affairs professionals. NASPA took a strong stance in developing groups within NASPA to support African American and other minority NASPA members and student affairs professionals (Meyers & Sandeen, 1973).

CONCLUSION

The importance, then, of student affairs administrators in the lives of students in the civil rights era is undeniable. When universities were integrated and the number of African American students increased, student affairs administrators were the college officials who worked directly, not only with the African American students challenged by prejudice and isolation, but also with the White students who were sometimes ahead of, but often expressed, the racism of the era. It was deans like John Blackburn who were there when African American students were integrated into the university and the residence halls, and deans like Augustine Pounds and Harris Shelton who led the negotiations when the Black power movement of the late 1960s led students to protest and demand reforms. Their stories are told here.

INTEGRATION AT
SOUTHERN UNIVERSITIES

JOHN L. BLACKBURN[1]
University of Alabama (1956-1969)

O n June 11, 1963, in one of the most highly publicized events of the civil rights movement, Governor George Wallace stood at the door to Foster Auditorium in an attempt to block the efforts of two African American students to enroll at the University of Alabama. The students, James Hood and Vivian Malone, were accompanied by officials from the U.S. Justice Department, National Guardsmen, federal marshals and state troopers. Historian Culpepper Clark (1995) describes the events that ensued:

> At 10:48 a.m., in roiling heat (the thermometer had already climbed past 95 degrees), the three cars containing Malone and Hood and Federal officials pulled up in front of Foster. From the shadows of the door, Wallace watched Katzenbach (Assistant U.S. Attorney General), Weaver (U.S. Attorney), and Norville (U.S. Marshall) approach. A year of pledges and promises, followed by months of planning, had come to this....
>
> With a copy of the president's proclamation in his coat pocket, Katzenbach strode forward, flanked by Weaver and Norville. Standing behind a shellacked-wood podium, with a mike slung around his neck, Wallace raised his left hand like a traffic cop to stop them. He said nothing....Finally, Katzenbach identified himself and said, "I have here President Kennedy's proclamation. I have come to ask you for unequivocal assurance that you or anyone under your control will not bar these students." Wallace said, "No."
>
> Katzenbach folded his arms across his chest to avoid awkwardness of gesture or signs of anxiety. "I have come here," he stated more confidently, "to ask you now of unequivocal assurance that you will permit these students, who after all, merely want an education in the great university...." (1995, pp. 225-226).

Wallace launched into his own five-minute denunciation of the central government....He closed with, "I hereby denounce and forbid this illegal and unwarranted action by the central government."

Having finished, Wallace cleared his throat, took a funny little "skip step backward" and "hopped into the doorway" as two burly patrolmen closed in beside him....With mounting exasperation Katzenbach grew more confident, "It is a simple problem, scarcely worth this kind of attention.... From the outset, admission of these students.... I ask you once again to reconsider"....Wallace stared straight ahead, chin thrust forward, refusing to say anything.... Thus denied, Katzenbach wheeled and walked toward the waiting cars.

Katzenbach poked his head in the car and said, "We're going to the dorm." James Hood was driven to the men's dorm about one mile away. Katzenbach had told Vivian "to go up to her room and come down and go eat by herself in the dining hall." In fact, things went better than expected. "She went [into the dining room] by herself, sat down at a table all by herself, and within thirty seconds, six or eight kids had joined her." The problem of Wallace still remained.

Brigadier General Henry V. Graham of the Alabama contingent of the 31st Dixie Division of the National Guard had been directed "to proceed to Tuscaloosa to assume command of operations in that city." While Graham was taking his place, Wallace ordered troopers to bar all windows to Foster Auditorium, except the north entrance. Wallace then sat down to a tall glass of iced tea and a medium-rare steak smothered in catsup, with french fries and lettuce.

Sizing up the situation at Foster, Graham sent 100 Guardsmen to the campus. At 3:16 p.m., three troop carriers escorted by motorcycle police roared up to the side and rear of Foster. Infantrymen, in green fatigues and carrying M-1 rifles formed a line up the west side of the auditorium. Another convoy arrived in front of Denny Chimes, across from the president's mansion on University Boulevard. General Graham arrived in a green, unmarked command car. With four sergeants in green berets, he donned his soft cap and moved toward the final confrontation. On the way, he huddled with Katzenbach, Norville, and Weaver, who fell in behind the General with the four sergeants bringing up the rear. They strode purposefully toward the wall of state troopers and reporters. The silence was eerie, disturbed only by the soft whirring of cameras and popping flashbulbs. Seeing their approach, Seymore Trammell, an assistant to Wallace, turned

toward the entrance and clapped on his straw hat as a signal for
Wallace to take his stand. At 3:30 p.m., General Graham, in combat
fatigues with the Confederate battle flag of the 31st Dixie Division
stitched to his breast pocket, came forward and saluted the governor.
Snappily Wallace returned the salute. Graham then said, "It is my sad
duty to ask you to step aside, on order of the president of the United
States." (1995, pp. 226-230)

Wallace asked to make a statement in which he railed against federal
interference, and at 3:33 p.m. he left, and Jimmy Hood and Vivian
Malone passed through "the schoolhouse door," registering in less
than 15 minutes. According to Clark, "Hood and Malone stayed in the
dorms that night, where student leaders had been assigned to make
them welcome" (1995, p. 231).

With the registration of James Hood and Vivian Malone, the struggle of
African American Alabamans to gain entrance to the University of Alabama,
which had begun with the unsuccessful efforts by Autherine Lucy in 1956,
had ended. But another battle to integrate the university was just beginning.
Young John Blackburn was dean of men during this dramatic period in civil
rights history. This chapter represents his views and experiences with civil
rights at the University of Alabama.

PROFESSIONAL BACKGROUND

I was a history major as an undergraduate at Missouri Valley College
and was offered a teaching job. When we talked about the pay, it was
so shockingly low. I was on the GI Bill and it was just slightly more
than I was making while going to school. So I decided that I needed
to do some graduate work. I went to see the dean of the college about
what I was going to do with my life. I told him I wanted to go to
graduate school somewhere and he said, "Where would you like to
go?" I said, "Well, I'd like to go to the mountains; I would like to go
to the University of Colorado." He said, "What are you going to get
your degree in?" I hadn't thought about it until I decided that I didn't
want to teach at the sort of salary they were offering. The dean was
the one who said, "You've been active in student affairs in college.
Why don't you do something in that area? Why don't you consider a
degree in counseling?" Counseling was the big thing then. They did-
n't have student personnel programs in those days. So, I got started on
my master's degree at the University of Colorado.

In 1951, Blackburn accepted a teaching post at the Air Force Personnel and Guidance School.

> I was teaching a course for reserve officers to update them on the new Air Force Classification System. One of the students was Otis McBride, the dean of men at Florida State University (FSU). He apparently liked my class so he came up on my last day with him, prior to their final exam, and said, "I need to talk to you." I said, "Well Colonel, what part of the course is bothering you?" He said, "No. I'd like for you to join my staff." I immediately accepted and we moved to Tallahassee in the summer of 1952. My first position at FSU was director of Senior Hall, a men's residence. With all my counseling training and experience, I sat in my office and waited for the students to come to me. I was ready to help them. "Hi, I'm here to help you. What's your problem? Tell me your problem." No one came, except to tell me that the stereo or the plumbing didn't work. I decided that Senior Hall did not need a counselor. It needed someone to make the place work and it needed someone to make the environment more attractive and educational. So, I'd go to the student rooms and I'd go down to the lounge. I started organizing some activities and getting things in line. When I asked the residents what they needed, they replied, "Pencil sharpeners." I said, "Well, I'll take care of that." They laughed. I went over to the housing office the next day and I said, "Look, I need six pencil sharpeners." They replied, "We're not going to put anymore pencil sharpeners in that building! We put them in there and every time we do, they're stolen or broken." So, I went down to the dime store, bought six pencil sharpeners and put those things up. The students said, "He's got those pencil sharpeners!" You would have thought I had created a miracle. I learned much by that experience. They'd been trying to get all the past directors of that hall to get pencil sharpeners and they couldn't do it. I never told them how I'd done it, but I learned that sometimes you have to spend your own money to get things done. It also made me move away from what I call the counseling syndrome approach to student affairs.

> Eventually I decided that I wanted to do further graduate work, so I planned to go to Columbia University for my doctorate. I received acceptance and housing at Columbia and we were ready to go when Dr. Corson, dean of men at Alabama and former dean who replaced McBride at FSU, called and offered me the assistant dean of men position at Alabama. I laughed because we had just watched on TV the demonstrations and the unsuccessful efforts to integrate the

University of Alabama in January of 1956. He said, "Well, John, I'm wrong I guess. I thought you were concerned about race in America." I said, "Well I am." He said, "So where else would you want to work?" I said, "OK, I'll come for one year."

PREPARING FOR INTEGRATION

From the time I arrived, the top administration would ask, "How are we going to integrate this university? How are we going to get through this with the conflict of the federal mandate and the resistance of the state governor? How are we going to make it so that when these two forces hit, they glance off of each other and the university becomes integrated without bloodshed?" That was the number one, overriding thing guiding everything we did then. The situation was this: The university president wasn't going to be out front. There was just no way. You're talking about a segregated society. What he was trying to do was take the university through that anger. The problem was there was no leadership anywhere. The governor wasn't going to help. The state patrolmen were all segregationist leaders. The university had no support system.

It was obvious that if the university was going to be successfully integrated then student affairs administrators were going to play a prominent role. The residence hall system at Alabama was poorly run. I spent my year as assistant dean building up staff and programs for the residences. A year later, Dean Corson resigned. He had become convinced that the university would not be integrated without bloodshed and he didn't want to be part of it. Of course, I was a young guy and the idea of bloodshed.... I said, "I'll just take care of that somehow." I was named dean of men by the new president, Frank A. Rose. Now, I was going to be in a leadership role during the integration to come.

When I looked at the failed 1956 attempt to integrate, I realized that the top student leadership did all they could to maintain a peaceful environment. They made the right speeches and did the right things, but there wasn't any system underneath that to support their efforts. What was missing was a supportive student environment from the leaders of the student organizations and student housing units, including fraternities and sororities. I started thinking, how could one address this? It wasn't just a matter of counseling individuals; it was much more complicated and intricate than that. I started exploring and searching even more deeply for models and conceptual frameworks.

Shortly after being made dean of men, I called in student leaders and I talked to them about moral leadership in this whole area of integration, and about what their legal responsibilities as leaders were. As I looked at it, I decided that we needed to provide a support system for the student leaders. There has to be a way for the student leaders to really lead this. There would be agreement on these subjects, but then I'd look out the window and see a student leader with a bunch of people who wanted to take the university in a different direction. I said (to myself), "You know, a person who wants to have a political career is /going to go where the voting power wants that person to go." Even though the student leaders were personally committed to integration, if they thought they could build their reputation politically upon segregation, they'd take that position. It was a shock to see that happen. The students weren't so much supportive of integration as they were for helping the institution. They weren't segregationists; let's put it that way. Even if they were for integration, they couldn't say it publicly at that time. That was when I decided to create a residence hall to nurture and support student leaders. Basically, we had this idea that we wanted to get student leaders together and put them in an environment in which we could provide certain experiences for them that would, in essence, integrate the university. We couldn't say that or we would've been fired and shot, so we discussed different ways to do it.

The "Men of Mallet"

The residence halls didn't have any programs back in those days. There weren't even intramurals and so forth, so we went about making change. I got rid of all these seventy-year-old housemothers. They were nice ladies, but it just didn't fit the situation that we had to have. I hired graduate students for the residence halls. About this time Phil Jacob's book, *Changing Values in College*, came out. I studied and restudied this book. Jacob came to the conclusion that colleges didn't do much about changing values. They didn't even have a plan. I thought, you know, "That's right. Colleges made certain value-laden statements in the introduction to the college catalog; but, once you were inside the offerings, you didn't see any real courses about values that students should embrace." We had to get students to start thinking about values. So, I created Mallet Hall. It was a relatively new hall at that time, and we decided that we were going to create a leadership sort of hall and invite freshman to come participate.

In the spring of 1960 just prior to final examinations, I invited 18 faculty members to my home to discuss the program for Mallet Hall. I had gone through the faculty directory and identified what I perceived as the faculty person's significant others. That is, the respected faculty person to whom the general faculty ran to discuss issues and ideas. I thought if four people came, I would go ahead with the program. All came, in spite of the fact that they were preparing final examinations. We discussed the Jacob book. I told them we were going to invite 110 students from the freshman class who demonstrated leadership ability to live in Mallet, which would have a special program that would support their objective for coming to the University of Alabama. I asked the faculty to assist by coming to the hall and discussing with the residents their personal values and their professional values of their disciplines, and how the two interacted in their lives. They agreed to do it.

The problem for us was how to identify these future leaders. At first we discussed the idea of having the principals and superintendents nominate students. We backed off from this approach when we realized that if a young person was an entrenched segregationist, a likely pick by local leaders, then we were not reaching the right person. Someone said, "Well, let's go on the assumption that the smarter they are, the more apt they are to be a leader." We took the top of the test scores of 135 men and I wrote them a letter. All my letter said was, "The university has identified you as having certain qualities which the institution values. [The university] wants to support you in what you want to do with your life." That's all it said, but some of these people had never gotten such a letter. In fact, they had been criticized because they were out of step in their community or in their school. So they'd never gotten a letter in which somebody said, "You have outstanding qualities." I think we sent out about 150 letters over my signature and we received about 108 acceptances. It was amazing.

The hall opened in the fall of 1960 and 30 some odd students ran for hall governor. We had never had a response like that before. In most of the residence halls, the staff would have to make somebody run to be president. The hall had a faculty reception at the beginning of the year and had a fine turn out of faculty, but the amazing thing was that the Mallet students had developed a system so that every faculty member met every student without the faculty realizing it. Dr. Jenkins, head of the philosophy department, said, "John, you have created a monster." Looking at all the programs in the hall, we averaged about 25-30 in attendance each week. You could feel and hear the students changing their views and, in reality, their values as each professor talked.

At first, other students tried to make fun of Mallet Hall. In fact, one of the halls across the street talked about the "Pansy Palace" across the way. Well, that made the Mallet Hall people mad; so they went out and organized themselves into athletic teams and beat the hell out of the rest of them in athletics, so they couldn't make fun of them for not being manly. Later the other halls started imitating Mallet hall.

In their sophomore year at Mallet, you'd have a scientist talking to them, and then you'd have the head of the philosophy department, and you'd have a lawyer talking to them, and you could see the students changing practically every week. Pretty soon they couldn't change anymore. They had become what they really were. They developed their own kind of philosophy. A lot of them changed. The dean of engineering got mad at me because too many of the engineering students were changing their majors to liberal arts, though a lot of them switched back to the sciences later on.

Nothing was said explicitly about race or segregation in these talks. If it had been said, it would have been killed. There was just too much resistance. But, you can talk about values. Nobody's going to have a problem with enhanced values. It's damned hard to argue about that. They had one discussion that went on for three weeks, on whether a conservative could be an intellectual. There are a lot of intellectual conservatives today, but back in those days there weren't very many conservative intellectuals. The intellectual community was dominated with a more liberal perspective than it is today. That was an exciting thing to hear them talk about. Of course, some faculty were unhappy because they hadn't been asked to be in it, but I would welcome them and they'd come sit in on the discussions.

One of the objectives in those days was that students came to college reflecting the values of their church, their Kiwanis club, and the YMCA. The role of universities at that time was to get people to challenge that and think differently, to see the world through new eyes. So, that is part of what we were doing in a well organized way. In their sophomore year, the student newspaper had been a segregationist paper, but the sophomore students of Mallet hall formed this kind of political unit and they elected the editor of the student newspaper. It became an integrationist sort of paper.

In the summer of 1963 when integration took place, the students elected Don Stewart as president of the student body. Don Stewart ran against the political machine, which was made up of fraternity and sorority leadership. He had been a member of it, but he turned and ran against it with the support of Mallet Hall and was elected president of the student body.

IMMEDIATE PREPARATION FOR INTEGRATION

We spent more than six months prior to the integration dealing with the parts of campus that we had some control over: the residence hall, food operations, and general campus security. We put together teams of administrators and faculty, and discussed possible scenarios such as, "What if a Federal Marshall pulls a gun? How should everybody else behave?" We did this because the thing that always goes wrong in anything, whether you are in war or anything like that, is the unexpected—that's what creates the disaster. So, we wanted everybody to know, if given this situation, what they should do. I had different staff members writing position papers about these different steps—they got all emotionally tied up in it.

We cleaned off the campus. There were no Coke machines on the campus, no bottle machines, and we put in paper cup machines. There were no rocks on the campus. There were no pieces of wood bigger than a toothpick that you could pick up. There wasn't anything that you could throw. We banned all cars on campus. If you ever want to know something that is serene, ban all automobiles and trucks from your campus. You heard birds sing; you felt like you could almost see the flowers grow—it was just unbelievable—doing away with the automobiles on campus. We had to park over on our northern campus. The students had to go there to get permission to come to the main campus, in order to control who could get onto the campus.

We had a detention center setup on campus so that, if we had to detain students in any sizable numbers before we could get them to the police, we could put them in there. I had authority to suspend a student and force them off campus, just by say so, and no hearing would be held within 24 hours afterwards. I had authority to breakup anything, and remove and jail any student that caused trouble.

During the spring of 1963, the dean of women and I met once a week with about 30 student leaders. During that summer period, we met daily. We had to prepare them for everything. When we were going through this and when we were putting these thirty students together, there was this one kid who had some real leadership potential. Many of the students thought he was probably in the Klan. I doubt it, but I told Don Stewart to get him in our group. I said, "Look, he's going to have some to say about the outcome." Well, I learned so much from that. The only opportunities he'd had prior to that time to lead were in a negative sort of way and when he had an opportunity he became a rabblerousing, liberal, far-left guy. Often when we see students behaving in ways that we can't quite understand, we need to realize that maybe that's the only opportunity they've got to demonstrate their leadership skills.

I realized in working with this group of 30 students that I had to prepare them for the idea that things would go wrong, because one of the things that often happens with a student or any young person is that, faced with adversity, they might say, "Hell, I did this and now this happens, so I'm through." So I kept telling them everyday, "There's going to be something wrong. We're doing well, but something will go wrong." For example, the U.S. marshals decided we needed a curfew and I had told the students there wouldn't be a curfew. They'd asked when we first met that summer. But the Marshals decided, and I went back to those students and I said, "I told you some things would go wrong and they wouldn't go the way we want them and we'd be awful disgusted." I said, "They've decided that we're going to have to have a curfew. Everybody has to be in by ten o'clock." You know, the students in our group went around and talked with the other students on campus and convinced everyone that this was necessary. I just couldn't believe how well they responded to that.

I always told the student leaders that they were teachers. "You're a teacher; you're a student leader and that has teaching responsibilities that you have to fulfill if you're gonna be a leader." I still believe that today, that student affairs people should work with the student leaders as though they were teachers and let the student leader assume some responsibility. It's great training. What I think I helped teach these people to do in that summer of 1963 was to form a community. I learned I can take any aggregate of people and I can make a community out of it.

June 11, 1963

First, I need to outline the scenario. A few days before the event took place, Governor Wallace brought in state police and National Guard who were reporting to the governor and had them circle the campus. He had the perimeters secured and controlled. Inside the perimeter, the federal authorities, everyone from the U.S. attorney general's office to federal marshals, were in control.

A few weeks before, President Rose told me that I was going to have to keep the students and other people away from Foster Auditorium where the two Black students were supposed to register for classes. We knew Wallace was going to be there. We had already had the damn thing marked off. The president asked me, "What are we gonna do about the students?" I knew that I was going to be blamed if there was a problem, so I said, "I'll take care of it." Dr. Rose said, "Well, John, I'm sure you will, but you tell me how you're gonna take care of it." I said, "Dr. Rose, I don't know how I'm gonna take care of it, but I'll take care of it." He argued with me until the administrative vice president said, "Well Dr. Rose, if John says he'll take care of it, you gotta listen and move on to something else. He'll take care of it."

So, I went to the thirty students and I said, "Oh, you won't believe this, but I promised that we could keep students away from Foster Auditorium." So the student group worked on it. On that day we just had a few students there and the rest of them were over in this residence hall, over in Paty Hall. I'd put together the idea that we would to get all the students, there were about 700 on campus, and we would have a presentation on civil rights looking at *Brown versus Board of Education* up until that day. We presented about the whole civil rights movement up to that time. We had Don Stewart and we had a vice president of the university give a talk to the students. We also showed a film by a graduate student named Mel Allen. It was a fund raising film called Eleven O'clock which talked about a university and what it's really worth. There was nothing said about fundraising in it. It said that there are times when people really have to make sacrifices and get behind a university. All during the film, Mel Allen is whittling a stick into a whistle and he ends the film with this statement, then plays Dixie on this whistle. I got the projectionist and I said, "Not one note of Dixie is to be played on the film." Well, I had phone contact with all the areas of my staff by a hotline which I had connected to my house. I picked up the phone and asked "How's the film?" My contact said, "Well, we've got a problem. That Dixie is still on the film—they didn't cut it off." I said, "You tell that projectionist that I'll kill him, I'll kill him!"

The program was being held in a big residence hall that housed about 1,000 students. It was catty-corner across the street from where Jimmy Hood was going to be in his room. We couldn't possibly have a big crowd rolling out of the hall when the marshals were out there trying to put Jimmy Hood in the residence hall. Somebody could have killed somebody, innocently. The timing had to work but it was screwed up because of the whistling Dixie thing on the film. The film finished early, so they made the students go through three or four different rooms and back out. By the time they hit the street, Jimmy Hood was in his room and everything was quiet, there were just some federal marshals standing out in front of the residence hall. It was an exciting few minutes. I learned later that the president of the student body, and several others, went around to every residence hall room the night before the integration occurred and went to each student's room and talked to them about their responsibilities. Luckily it was summertime so there were only about 3,000 students on campus—it wasn't like trying to see 15,000 students.

Meanwhile, when Wallace turned the students away from the door, he thought they would go back outside the perimeter where his forces were in charge and then it would be the federal government using force—the federal government would be the initiator. But, instead of that, we took them to their rooms and could announce that they were like other students who hadn't completed registration. That changed the dynamics because now, somebody else had to be the aggressor, not the federal government.

Later in the day, the students worked out when Jimmy would go from Palmer over to Paty to eat. When he left, a student leader would get up and get in front of him and another one would get right behind him so that when he went through the cafeteria line there wasn't anybody who could get to him and do something. The first meal he ate with a U.S. marshal at a table, just the two of them. At the second meal, the students had worked with the marshal and the marshal stood in the back and Jimmy ate at a table by himself. At the third meal, the next day I guess it was, the students filled up all the tables, so there weren't any empty tables. Jimmy came off of that cafeteria line and saw that there were no empty tables and Don Stewart stood up and said, "Jimmy, why don't you join me." At the same time that Jimmy was having a seat with Don Stewart, some little freshman was going across to take his tray back to the tray bin and he stumbled and fell and dishes broke and so forth, and the students roared and applauded, and the university was integrated at that moment. Now, I wished I could say I planned to have the student drop the tray, but the way it happened just broke the ice. Now that sounds strange today, but a Black eating with a White in Alabama in 1963, it was a big event and Don Stewart risked his life and his career.

Some say that Wallace did a great service to the university in the sense that he told the Klan and the White citizens groups to stay away from the university, "I'm taking care of it. I'm representing you there." Bobby Shelton who was head of the Klan said that George Wallace betrayed him. "George Wallace said he wouldn't let that happen; he told me he wouldn't let that happen. If he hadn't done that, we would have been there and it wouldn't have been integrated."

ONCE ON CAMPUS

Jimmy's first night on campus I went to visit him in his room. You had to go by a couple of marshals to get up to Jimmy's room, one on the outside of the building and then one that was in the corridor going up to his room. The director of the hall had told Jimmy that I was coming over so he was expecting me. We talked, and he sat on one bunk and I sat on the other and we talked about things. I had met him before, prior to their coming to the campus in the federal judge's quarters in Birmingham. I explained to Jimmy that I was available around the clock to assist him in anything, and that there were a lot of people that were there to help him, and he needed to realize that he could call on them if he had a problem.

One day Jimmy came in and asked, "Where can I get a haircut" I talked to my barber over in the student union and he agreed to do it. I think he did it just because of our friendship because he really caught hell from the rest of the barbers for cutting Jimmy's hair. I don't think he'd ever cut a Black person's hair before but he did. Burt Jones who was director of the hall took Jimmy over there.

Jimmy also came over and asked, "Where do I go to church now?" Why didn't I think of that? I wasn't a regular church attendee myself so I missed that idea. I said, "Don't worry about it. I'll take care of it." They had biracial meetings at the Episcopal Canterbury House, but I also called the Presbyterians and the Methodists and the Baptists. After I made about two phone calls, none of the ministers would answer the phone. I couldn't get through. The Methodist minister ultimately took him in. Five or six years later when integration was the popular thing to be for and the civil rights movement was developing, a couple of these guys from the churches came to see me about what the university ought to be doing about the race problem. I said, "You've come to the wrong person. When this university needed you, when the Black students that were coming here needed you, you wouldn't respond." I said, "Don't ever come in here and tell me about what the university ought to do in terms of race, because you had your chance and you flunked it." They never gave me any advice about race after that.

Campus was a little isolated environment. I think that Vivian Malone (the first Black woman student) probably had some people that made some nasty remarks to her. There was also a bomb thrown out by her dormitory somewhere in that first week. The police got a call in the middle of the night about it. Other than that, we thought of ourselves as an oasis of integration in an otherwise burning state. I go back to the idea that the students themselves were opposed to what was happening in these communities.

Still, I used to get horrible phone calls, threatening phone calls. The chief of police would tell me what the Klan was saying about me at the Klan meetings. It didn't really bother me. It would now. I don't know if I can take that now, but we didn't have a child. Our daughter was born in December of 1963. If we went out at night, we turned the light on and we looked around. Lots of times I'd go out and raise the hood of my car. I didn't know what the hell I was looking for, but I'd raise it, you know, trying to see.

In terms of other civil rights demonstrations, students at Alabama were involved in the integration of theaters. Jack Pallance, the movie star, he came in here, and you know students would love to go to jail with Jack Pallance. That became an honor—to get arrested with Jack and go to jail. In those days, when the police arrested students they'd put them in the tank down there and then they would call me and I'd go down and they would be released to me. I would promise that the student would show up in court and it just worked that way. So, I spent my weekends getting students out of jail. It's amazing how popular you become on Saturday night when they're in the tank down there. When I walk in they say, "Dean, hey do you remember me?" There's nothing like having a relationship with students like that.

The following summer, we had several Black students that were entering, which would have been the fall of 1964. Again in Paty Hall, we brought them in groups of 200 and went through orientation. During one orientation I found out on Sunday that on Saturday someone had taken a book of matches and made a little cross and set it out in front of a couple of Black students' doors, knocked on the door and ran. When I talked to the graduate assistant, he said he knew it had happened. I asked, "What did you do when you found out about it?" And he said, "Well I didn't do anything." He said he didn't want to affect his rapport with the students. I said, "What do you think about your rapport with the Black students?" We found out who had done it, and we called the students into the office before classes started and told them that if they condoned that behavior they were not to come to the university. They had to promise that they wouldn't do that if they wanted to stay. I'm not sure you could do that today; they'd probably have their parents show up with a lawyer, but we did it then.

As a footnote Jimmy eventually dropped out. He dropped out and I didn't want him to, but he got in trouble by writing a guest editorial in the student newspaper about a demonstration. He said that right at the time when demonstrations were the vogue across the country and his own family about killed him. So, it created some real problems in his life. He eventually earned his undergraduate degree from Wayne State.

FRATERNITIES AND SORORITIES

Reflecting on his experiences, Blackburn admitted that he could have done some things differently.

I think if I made one mistake, I should have integrated the fraternities and sororities, but there were so many other things to deal with at that time. But it was probably easier then than it would be now. It would make people feel a lot better. It's actually not that much of an issue for the students, but the faculty is going crazy about it. The faculty members, who haven't had a Black faculty member in their department, are making speeches all the time about integrating fraternities and sororities. Part of that is to keep the spotlight off of their academic unit, you know talk about somebody else. I think I should have done it. The current vice president's number one problem is the lack of integration in the Greek system. We have pressure from the newspapers to deal with it. Here we've got the Tuscaloosa News, they haven't got a single Black in the top leadership role at the paper, but they're writing editorials about how bad it is that fraternities and sororities aren't integrated.

What I would do, if I had their problem today, is I'd create a fraternity. If you wanted to get a national, I'd find a national one that would give me a charter, and I'd create an integrated fraternity. I'd go to that faculty senate and I'd say, "I want you to help us. You people have been yelling for all this. Here, we've got the students. I want you to reinforce them." They need to have their hand called and get them in there to do it, and I'd like to participate in that role. Once you make the breakthrough, it's not that difficult; but making the breakthrough and the fraternity sorority thing is complicated by the fact that you have many faculty members who don't like fraternities and sororities.

I missed the boat. If I had known then what I know now, I would have created a new type of fraternity and sorority that would have done this. I was like everybody else, thinking, "Let's just take what's here and we'll get them to do this." We should have created something new; we should have built it fresh. It's still not too late to do that. We've got to quit just doing something because it's tradition. You've got to save your traditions and your values, in particular if you come in new into an institution, you better be sensitive to those historical values. But you can take some of those values and recreate them in ways to achieve what the institution wants to achieve.

THE ANTIWAR MOVEMENT

The antiwar movement had started before I left to go to Denver and at the University of Alabama we had a silent vigil on the union steps everyday at noon. We had appointed a guy as the head of security, a retired army colonel, who would just as soon shoot everybody because he thought what these people were doing was evil. So, I had to go out everyday to kind of protect these students from people would like to do them harm, and Wallace had this undercover investigator who followed me around. I could see him following me around on those demonstrations and making notes on what I'd say and what I'd do. I kind of enjoyed that because I'd make statements that were ridiculous as hell just so he could get it back to the files.

Once, I had to go to make a speech at West Virginia Tech. I called in the two students who were leaders of this demonstration each day and I talked them into canceling the demonstrations while I was out of town. Those students did that and I've always had so much respect for those two people, because they knew there were so many chances for something to go wrong if I wasn't there. I probably exaggerated my value to their safety, but at least the students recognized that it was important that I be there.

The antiwar movement hurt the Black movement. It diffused it. The antiwar movement and the Black power movement were tied together in many respects at first. Then integration was no longer the key thing. I think the antiwar movement fueled most of the Black power. It forced Martin Luther King to change his strategy. He had to embrace the antiwar movement and it took the spotlight off of integration of the students. It took the recognition away from the Blacks and their bigger situation.

THE ROLE OF NASPA

Blackburn has been a very active member of NASPA throughout his career, and shared with us his views of the role played by that organization in facilitating civil rights.

That first year, 1953, I went to both ACPA and NASPA. Hell, it didn't take any time at all before I realized that the people at NASPA were the people doing the hiring, and the people in ACPA were the ones looking for a job. Over at the ACPA meeting, people looking for jobs were being interviewed by people looking for jobs. In NASPA, that's where the power was and that's where I wanted to be. So, I committed after that first meeting, and I've only missed two meetings in 25 years.

At that time, I was pretty much opposed to the regional vice presidents because the only chance we had of integration in the South was the pressure from the national scene. Those of us who were trying to make things happen down there needed that (national pressure). Regionalization scared me in terms of that because we were still not through this process; we were in it up to here. NASPA, fortunately, had gone on record in support of integration (even) with a number of Southern schools voting against it. I was strongly opposed to creating regional vice presidents because I thought we'd be getting away from what I felt were some national agendas. At the same time, there was a whole movement in everything on regionalization. I said, "When I die and go to heaven and am going in, St. Peter will say, 'I tell you what, we made a change and we have regional vice gods now. You have to go through them.'"

As director of professional development and standards for NASPA in 1967 when the antiestablishment movement was at its height, we did two things. First, we developed a policy on confidentiality of student records. Different institutions had policies and the federal government had some legislation and so forth but we developed a record on that and we suggested that institutions use it to prepare their records. The other thing we did was a program in conjunction with the Research and Higher Education program at Berkeley. It was on innovation and we had speakers from Berkeley. People that were selected to go this program had to prepare a paper on an innovation they were doing on their campus. I have those documents on innovations that were done by over 100 people. Most of those innovations were not really innovations as you or I would do it, but in their particular campus, it was an innovation. It was something that a lot of other people were already doing so, at first, I was kind of disappointed but then I saw how excited these people were to talk about what they were doing. That was the whole idea! We wanted to stimulate people to become innovators in higher education. I don't think we do enough of that now. People have to think more globally about the institution as opposed to single issues such as financial aid or diversity. They've got to think about the total institution and innovations that help the institution.

PERSONAL CHANGES

Events at "the Schoolhouse Door" and following have clearly had a major impact on Blackburn's life and career.

Being involved in the integration of the university was obviously the greatest experience of my life. It is the interaction with a lot of the alumni that carries it on and gives a kind of a rebirth to it. After having been through integration of Black students at the University of Alabama, I thought to myself, "You know, after what I've been through, there can't be a lot too exciting about student affairs for me in the future. Everything is going to be mundane and won't seem significant." But I've had a lot of good experiences.

Not too long ago, I went down to the Chamber of Commerce. I was walking down and was starting to cross the street when a guy in a big, white, pickup truck stopped in the middle of the street, jumped out, grabbed me, and said, "I am so and so." He said, "You kicked me out of school and it was the best thing that ever happened to me. I thought I could do any damn thing I wanted to do." He said, "I just want you to know that I have done well and l owe you a lot for that."

When I got involved in development and went back to these kids, even those with disciplinary problems, they were anxious to see me. One, they wanted to me to see that they'd succeeded and that they had done well. Secondly, they wanted to give something in order to be on record with the institution that they'd had good luck. I'll say this: In those days, I kicked a lot of students out of school, but I kept a good relationship with them. I even corresponded with them after they were out and encouraged them to come back.

In about 1992 or '93, the student affairs people called me and said that they wanted to name a room in the student union for me. I had been through this in business before. Pretty soon they hyphenate the room, a few years later they remodel it or the room's not even there so I said, "No, you can name it after somebody else." I said, "If you really want to honor me, I'd like for you to do something that I think is important. I'm concerned about leadership. We have these very bright students that have so much leadership potential but they don't run for public office. They don't exercise real civic leadership; they go on to do other things, i.e., they become outstanding lawyers."

I said, "We need to keep these student leaders together. As they're identified in a class, bring them in. The next year, bring some more in. Then, bring them all back each year so that, in twenty years, we'll have an organization of several thousand leaders that can address issues. We're not going to be democrat or republican; we are just going to address these issues—both sides of the picture are going to be discussed. We can't let it be a propaganda unit for any political party." And so, we were off. In fact, next weekend the institute meets for its retreat. It's one of the highest honors to be selected for the Blackburn Institute.

LESSONS FOR STUDENT AFFAIRS AS A PROFESSION

We asked Blackburn what lessons he thought his experiences during the civil rights movement had for the student affairs profession.

Looking back over these 40-something odd years, I want to say that everyone in this field ought to have a great sense of pride. I think that integration and the achievement of creating more of a society for minorities has largely been accomplished by student affairs in higher education. There is no other division of higher education that's had the leadership in developing diversity. Even in integration itself, there are parts of the country that were not integrated at the time. So, we have that very much to be proud of. I think the same thing about distance learning—you see student affairs getting involved in that now. When people ask, "What's the role of student affairs?" I say, "It is to fill vacuums that exist on the campus." That's the way to have an impact, to fill vacuums.

That said, one of the things about student affairs, and I think it's still true, nobody really gives a damn what you're going to do in student affairs. If you want to do something in the academic world, you've got to go through all these committees and the departments and approval, and by the time you finally get it approved, you've lost interest in what you originally were proposing. In student affairs and housing, if you can keep behavior to the point that it can be rationalized and don't lose money, nobody particularly cares what you do in housing. So, student affairs people have all this opportunity to do things.

Your job as a student affairs administrator is to listen to what the president is saying he wants to do and listen to what the vice president for academic affairs says that the institution is doing and listen to what the faculty is saying. And then you help create the environment that reaches those goals. Now a lot of student affairs administrators, their goal is what they picked up from some other institution that sounded like a good idea. What you really want to do is to pick out what is unique about your institution, and to find out what your president is really working for. What does he want? Now a lot of presidents have such limited goals, but occasionally you have one that is more creative. Of course, a president like that, if you succeed and make him look good, then he'll embrace the idea too. I've always thought that whatever we did in student affairs was an important part of the larger institution—I never put that isolation in it. And I thought that what we were doing should be fitting in with whatever the goals and objectives were at the institution; it needed to be consistent.

One of the things that I toyed with was creating a pharmacy of a social experience. This came from talking to the psychiatrist who headed up our student health. He said, "John, if a student has a medical problem, a disease or an infection, I can prescribe a medicine and feel reasonably sure that, if they take their medicine and do what I say, that they will get well. But if a student needs a social experience to get better, if the student knows that they've got the problem, but they don't have the skills or they're scared to move about joining a group, how can we help them?" That's where I came up with the idea of a pharmacy of social experience. The idea is that staff could write a prescription that says that the student needs to work in this center or this is the sort of organization this student ought to be in. They would make it happen. It would work.

I think one of the big changes I've seen is that we are still, to a certain effect, dominated intellectually by the influence of National Vocational Guidance Association which hasn't existed for 50 years, and also by the counseling and guidance people. We still use students as patients. We still talk to them and we counsel them. We really tell them, "Well, if we gaze at your navel long enough, the truth will emerge." As opposed to going out and creating a world that makes things better, creating a world for integration. After having my experience at Alabama, I knew that all my previous counseling experience wasn't going to be of any value in me achieving what I wanted to achieve in higher education. I had to be doing things: organizing students and creating sorts of (things), which now I would call communities, but at the time I just called it creating functions and so forth— achieving and doing things.

When I first went to the University of Alabama in 1956, the first student I talked to said, "I'll kill the first nigger that walks across the quadrangle." Now, was it my job to see that his needs were met? No, my job was to create a sort of environment where you wouldn't have people making crazy statements like that. I told that story in a speech once to some young student affairs people in Colorado Springs when they were talking about how they represent students. "You represent whatever the students want?" I asked and they said, "Sure." So I told them about this experience and I said, "Do you represent him? Are you going to help him kill?" I think the students' attitudes ought to be influenced and changed, and it is our job to work at making that happen.

The opportunities to innovate and to make change are greater today than they've ever been during my lifetime. There is more openness to new ideas. There are a lot of problems, I don't want to minimize that, but there are opportunities to do different things and with a different approach. Often, student affairs people don't take advantage of their opportunity to innovate and to make change at their institution. We tend to try to deal with whatever the status quo is and modify it, rather than really making change by restructuring student affairs to achieve the different goals which the institution thinks are important.

How to Build Community

I was now seeing student affairs from a community construct rather than from a counseling syndrome. I believe that, without community, man reverts to savagery, arrogant savagery. Community is the glue that holds civilization together. To build this community, you can take any residence hall, for example, and you decide in advance before you let anybody in what the environment is going to be and make sure that everyone understands that. So, when the student walks in you can say, "Here are things you may want to get involved in." In contrast, in a typical residence hall a staff person may say, "Well, what would you like to do?" Instead of asking the student what they want to do, you tell them what is available to do, and it creates a better environment for everyone. You give students a great deal of freedom, but you set the perimeters. Basically, if you want to bring people together you have to come up with a value that transcends those people. It needs to be some decent value and it has to have some intellectual content to it.

There were many criticisms of this concept. Some people thought that we should house students only on a random basis. When you house on a random basis, you affect people's lives. My response was that students deserved the right to know what kind of an environment they were going to live in. Having designed Mallet Hall on this concept, I knew I was on to something, but I wasn't quite sure how to conceptualize it. Then I read Robert Nisbet's book, *Degradation of Academic Dogma*. If you are building a community, you must have a transcending value over the aggregate. Nisbet's key elements of community formation are: (1) transcending value, (2) authority, 3) honor and status, (4) uniqueness, (5) hierarchical roles, and (6) solidarity.

In my community, everybody has a hierarchical role and that can change, but there are roles. Not everybody's making every decision. I learned that from watching the antiwar leaders. They'd say, "Well, we're having a meeting at the student union at seven o'clock — come." "Well, what are we gonna discuss?" "Don't worry about what we're going to discuss, just show up." "What should I be thinking about?" "Don't worry, just whatever you want to say that day." So they come, but the leaders have their agenda. They guide that thing and they make you think you're participating in it, but they're just manipulating it. Educators ought to be doing that. We say we have a drug problem in the residence hall but we don't know what the hell to do with it. Part of the problem is we're not doing anything to meet that person's needs in any way socially, and the drug people are saying, "Come join us. We'll have a party and you're one of us. We've picked you out, you're important." We need to do that.

I still get excited when I think about the potential of student affairs-created communities. But most student affairs people would have to be trained and have to become dedicated in ways that are not now expected. We're still making the same mistakes. I don't know what happened to the Mallet Hall program. The Mallet Hall men still exist and they have a program, but they have no recognition in the university. There's nobody from the staff that works with the kids or anything. They're over there and the student affairs staff have other priorities, and this isn't one of them. Mallet Hall doesn't exist because you hire somebody and they come in from Michigan State University and they want to make a residence hall just like the residence hall they lived in at Michigan State, or wherever they came from—not necessarily Michigan State, but any place they have that experience. To avoid this, higher education programs should offer community formation programs, teach students how to take an aggregate to make a community. I don't think we ever got the student affairs people involved in how you create community, how you design mosaics community, how you decide what it is the institution wants to do and then design communities based on that. We tend to take what's there and make do with it as opposed to creating new forces, new communities, and new organizations that achieve what the institution wants to achieve—not necessarily what the students want to achieve but what the institution wants to achieve.

Today, student affairs people operate on the assumption that everyone is equal in what they say, and of course it has got to be multicultural today. That's the number one priority. That's the buzzword. I go to these meetings and I want to vomit sometimes because that's the only damn word they know, and they don't understand what it means to be multicultural to start with. If you want to have a multicultural community, then sit down and design one and don't just preach about it. Sit down and design one so that you can have one that will work.

The university itself can't be a community, it is too large. I think we need smaller communities that interlock together to get one sense of a larger community. Obviously you can have an African American community. You can have all the ethnic kinds of communities that you want to have. I think that's a bad way to go. I'm not sure how they can all fit together some way where it's really valuable to society. I'm not talking about what's good for the individual; I'm talking about what's good for society. We need to think more about how important a community is to us, so that we don't dissolve into being arrogant animals that are independent but shoot and kill everybody else. You have got to get people to work together and I think you can design that, but you need to do it and you need to stick to it.

HIGHER EDUCATION'S CONTRIBUTION TO THE LARGER CIVIL RIGHTS MOVEMENT

In Blackburn's view, higher education played a pivotal role in the civil rights movement.

Since almost all of the leadership in our society comes from college and university graduates, one can assume that little could happen without graduates being involved in leadership. Could Martin Luther King have been such a leader without his higher education background? There is no doubt that the students making up the Freedom Riders and that thrust to desegregate facilities and to establish voting rights in the South had a profound impact. With the death of the students in Mississippi, the broad outcry of support from across this nation resulted in local, Southern business and community leaders stepping forward to challenge the Klan and the citizens council groups.

It might be interesting to reverse the question. What contribution did the civil rights movement make to higher education? Prior to the civil rights movement, higher education saw its role as independent and separate from the larger society. Most changes in higher education came from outside pressure and influences such as the training of engineers and the establishment of agriculture colleges. Although there was involvement by students in the antislavery movement prior to the Civil War, higher education was mostly an observer and recorder of the larger society. I believe institutions are much more involved in advocacy today. Without the example of the civil rights movement, I doubt if there would have been an antiwar movement. However, a case could be made that the antiwar movement hurt and diminished in many ways the civil rights movement for African Americans. The civil rights movement had as its objective the opening of opportunities for Black Americans. With the development of the antiwar activity, the original civil rights movement was pushed to the back burner.

THE RELATIONSHIP OF HIGHER EDUCATION AND SOCIETY

Since higher education produces the leaders for all phases of our society, then higher education must have a responsibility to prepare students to be leaders and to be change agents for the larger society. The academic programs of our institutions can provide the students with competence, skills, and the intellectual acumen essential to the professions, but student affairs and the student environment may be the best if not the only way to teach community and society leadership, as well as community building and community management. Student leaders in this environment should be considered as teachers, and should be so regarded by student affairs administrators. Student affairs administrators should be qualified to design and develop environments that carry out the mission and objectives of the institution which they serve.

Commenting on student involvement, Blackburn offered:

Student involvement in the early civil rights movement was dangerous and exciting. Participation involved a public commitment which could not successfully be withdrawn. Today's student participation is not only not dangerous, it doesn't even involve risking one's reputation or career.

EPILOGUE

John Blackburn left the University of Alabama in 1969 to become vice chancellor for student affairs at the University of Denver. He returned to Alabama in 1978 to assume the position of vice president for educational development (fundraising). Upon his retirement from the fundraising role in 1990, Blackburn had, in 10 years, helped the university raise more than it had in its first 148 years of existence (Morrison, 1990). John Blackburn has hardly retired. He and his wife, Gloria, live in Tuscaloosa. He remains involved in community activities and continues his commitment to leadership development for students at the University of Alabama.

---

[1] As dean of men at the University of Alabama, many of the experiences Blackburn relates in this chapter refer specifically to Jimmy Hood, the male student admitted on June 11, 1963. Sarah Healy, dean of women was responsible for working with Vivian Malone. Clark (1995) credits both with playing crucial roles in the events surrounding the eventual successful registration of both at the University of Alabama.

CHARLES H. WITTEN
University of South Carolina (1963-1975)

O n April 12, 1861, General Pierre Beauregard led Southern forces in a successful attack on Fort Sumter in Charleston Harbor, South Carolina. This began the United State's Civil War, otherwise known as the War Between the States or the War of Northern Aggression. South Carolina is the emblem of Southern plantation society. Charleston's stately plantations and museums do nothing to dispel the image of a place rooted in its past, a past based on slavery. The Palmetto, the palm tree that occupies center stage on South Carolina's flag and license plates, off which British cannon balls bounced without doing harm during the Revolutionary War, is symbolic of the state's stubborn resistance to change. Within this context, the story of desegregation at the University of South Carolina (USC) as told through the experiences of Charles Witten, former vice president of student affairs, comes as somewhat of a surprise. Certainly, General Beauregard could never have imagined that, 102 years after his victory, African American students, themselves likely descendents of South Carolina slaves, would enter the doors of the state's major university, which recently celebrated its bicentennial, and do so peacefully. It should be noted, however, that during the reconstruction the university had both Black faculty and students (Hollis, 1956). In fact, Witten recounted the fact that the first Black graduate of Harvard was a faculty member at USC during the reconstruction.

Witten shared with us several key written documents that we draw on in addition to our interview with him. When we use material from those written documents, we cite the document.

BACKGROUND: FROM THE U.S. NAVY TO STUDENT AFFAIRS

Charles Witten served as dean of students and as vice president of student affairs at USC from 1963 until he retired from that position in 1975. Until

1986, he stayed on at the university as a professor in the higher education program he founded.

Charles Witten was born in New York and moved to Columbia from his farm near Williamsburg, Virginia. He attended the University of North Carolina (UNC) at Chapel Hill where he majored in chemistry. In an earlier interview with John Lowery, a former student, Witten noted that, despite attending college during the Depression, he was actively involved in college life (Lowery, 2002). After working as a chemist in a pencil factory, Witten returned to UNC to earn a graduate degree in chemistry. After a short time as a research chemist, he was commissioned in the Navy in March 1941. He served on several types of naval ships and as commanding officer of a destroyer escort, two destroyer transports, and, later, a destroyer. After graduation from the Naval War College, he served several tours of duty as a planning officer for the U.S. Navy and NATO commands (Lowery, 2002). In 1960, he was promoted to the rank of captain and was assigned to head up the Naval Reserve Officer Training Corps (NROTC) unit at USC (Lowery, 2002).

Witten was appointed dean of students by the university's new president because, according to Witten's account, the new president liked the way NROTC was being run (Lowery, 2002). Soon after his appointment as dean of students, Witten helped to found the Student Personnel Services program in the college of education (Lowery, 2002). Witten explained to Lowery, "When I took the job of dean of students, I wasn't exactly coming in as a newborn baby without clothing. I had two pairs of diapers [his NROTC experience and his experience as a graduate student in the College of Education where he had earned a master's degree]" (Lowery, 2002, p. 3).

Witten made many immediate changes in the division of student affairs at USC. He appointed a dean of men, so that there were both deans of men and women. But his biggest concerns were for the residence halls. He explained:

> The people who ran the men's dorms were largely fifth year students—in those days football players came to get an education—athletes to whom the university owed a job. And the housemothers ran the women's dorms; they were nice old ladies who knew somebody in the legislature or on the board of trustees. When I took over in 1963, I said, "This will be no longer. I'm going to have a semiprofessional program." And to get people to be RAs and hall directors and what not, we had to have a graduate program. So that's why, when I was an assistant professor in the college of education, we started a graduate program in student personnel services.

DESEGREGATION

Witten was dean of students when the University of South Carolina was integrated. It was actually desegregation that brought Witten from a long and successful career in the Navy to what would turn out to be a very successful career in student personnel administration. Witten was careful to point out that the process of desegregation has not ended:

> You know, most people think that was when we admitted our first three Black students, but it's a process that's still going on today. Today there are almost 3,900 Black students at the University of South Carolina at undergraduate, graduate, and professional levels. Blacks comprise 15.4 percent of the student body, the highest percentage of any flagship state university.

Witten gave a speech to the ACPA in 1970 in which he described the context of the university as it faced desegregation:

> The University of South Carolina, founded in 1801, has for years been a "faithful index of the ambitions and fortunes of the State of South Carolina." In an agricultural state, it had educated those from the plantations, the towns, and the cities—the children of the aristocracy—who were to become the leaders of the state. And even after the state had changed, so that no longer did most of the population live on farms and 35 percent of the university's students came from the metropolitan area in which the institution was situated, it was still largely educating those who were to be the future leaders of the state.

> It was a segregated school, segregated by custom and by law: one law providing that its state funding would be cut off if a non-White student was admitted in response to court order. It was a school where, when faced with a federal court order to admit a Black student, the trustees felt constrained to issue a statement which said:

>> In the interest of the preservation of the dignity of the orderly processes of education at the University of South Carolina, the board of trustees is forced to direct compliance with the Order of Judge Martin, unless it be lawfully modified or rescinded....The board of trustees will not condone or tolerate any disturbances which tend to disrupt the intellectual and educational life of the university, nor will it permit the university to be exploited by special interest groups.

> We provided police protection for our first three Black students and we established special rules for their conduct. They were advised to,

"Conduct themselves in a manner which will not lead to criticism by other students of their dress, manner, actions, and public statements." They were told that the administration would make every effort to see that they were treated fairly. We requested, even though we knew it would be hard for them, that as much as possible they turn the other cheek to students who jeered or made fun of them. We were going to do what the law, as then interpreted, demanded and nothing more.

The first African American students at USC enrolled peacefully; there were no federal marshals, no riots, and no destruction of property. In the beginning, USC officials were merely carrying out the law. Witten explained how USC decided to approach the demand to enroll African American students:

Our Southern universities desegregated one by one, painfully: University of Mississippi, University of Alabama where George Wallace stood on the school house steps, and University of Georgia, where my friend, Dean Tate, made *Time* magazine with a performance that wasn't too sharp. Then we had Clemson University, in the state of South Carolina, which did a magnificent job of admitting their one Black student in January 1963. Governor Ernest Hollings had declared that it was time for segregation to end, and that South Carolina was governed by rule of law and not by rule of men. In the beginning of the spring semester 1963, two students (or would-be students) sued in federal court to gain admission to the University of South Carolina. Their attorney was Matthew Perry, a local attorney, who later on turned out to be a federal judge and now has a federal courthouse named after him. Anyhow, we saw the handwriting on the wall, and so the president of the university did what presidents always do when faced with a difficult decision: He appointed a committee.

He appointed a committee that he called the Ad Hoc Committee on University Affairs, or something like that, a totally innocuous title. He appointed as chairman of the committee the dean of the College of Engineering, who was a local boy who had been "ruined" when he went to Yale and got his doctorate, and gotten contaminated up there. But he was in a position of having a grandfather or great-grandfather who was president of the university, I think before the War of Northern Aggression, as some people call it. His appointment was a safe one.

And then he appointed, I really forget who the faculty members were, except two of them I remember. One was dean of the Law School (who years before had fought a case in the Supreme Court against integration of South Carolina schools), and the other was the head of the Navy ROTC. The president figured, since at least I was a federal officer, that if the federal government said, "Do something," I'd do it. I happened to be the commanding officer of the Naval ROTC, professor of naval science, at the time.

MANAGING THE REGISTRATION OF THE FIRST AFRICAN AMERICAN STUDENTS

Witten continued his story about USC's transition from a White-only institution to one that was desegregated.

One of the first things we did was go up to Clemson and visit the dean of students there. I remember it was a beautiful spring day– we visited him in his home because he was home recovering from a heart attack, which had nothing to do with the desegregation issue. Dean Walter Cox, who many years later was president of Clemson University for a year or two, a wonderful guy, went through the whole process with us, what they'd done and so on. We were sitting on his back porch amidst the blooming dogwood, a beautiful day. We came back to USC and we started to put a plan together. One of the troubles was that we were right in the middle of a city. Another trouble was that, in those days, not too far from the campus, well, adjacent to the campus, was a Black ghetto, which has since been removed as the university expanded. Beyond that, maybe a mile or so, maybe two miles from campus, was a Southern mill village. I remember this mill village very well because, about 10 years after we first desegregated the university, I was on the local school board when we desegregated the schools in the city. My children went to middle school in the mill village.

The men and women who worked in the mills lived in houses that were easily recognizable because they were erected by the mill company. But you'd drive in there, and you'd see posters on the lamp-posts: "Don't be half a man, join the Klan." This is ten years after we desegregated, so this is the kind of atmosphere that prevailed.

You know, we weren't too afraid of what our students would do, but we were worried about what some of the locals would do. So one of the first things we did was build a beautiful iron fence, which we said had nothing to do with the coming of desegregation, it just had to match the iron fence that was on the old part of the campus. And so the main part of campus was completely fenced off. One of the members of the committee was the public relations officer for the university. He made sure that we worried about keeping the media happy, because, you know, they'll stir up anything. So we had a good public relations annex to our plan.

The plan was to get these two students in. We were told to admit them, and we'd see that the media didn't interfere with what was going on, see that they had protection, and see that outsiders didn't come in and cause trouble. (Witten's August 1963 letter to incoming students explained that student leaders would be asked to carry a special ID card identifying them as leaders, whose instructions were to be followed in the event trouble broke out.) After I became dean of students, I wrote two letters, one to every returning student, and one to every new student. The letters said, "It looks like we're going to admit Black students. If you feel you would have trouble going to school with Black students, don't come." Further, the letter said:

> The students of the university, together with their parents, the faculty, the administrative staff, and the people of this great state must meet this situation in a manner which will reflect only the highest credit on the intellectual integrity of our university and the dignity of our state. The board of trustees will not condone or tolerate any disturbances which tend to disrupt the intellectual educational life of the university, nor will it permit the university to be exploited by special interest groups. It stands firmly behind the president of the university, who is charged with carrying out the policies set by the board, and intends that all necessary measures be taken to insure that disturbances and disorder will be prevented (Witten, personal communication, November 2003, from a letter dated August 1963).

It was a long letter, and it told the students if there was a disorder, this was the thing we would do: People would stay in their classrooms; the power plant whistle would blow three times; that sort of stuff.

THE ARRIVAL OF THE FIRST AFRICAN AMERICAN STUDENTS

Witten described the arrival of the first African American students as being peaceful:

> When the two students showed up, they wanted a room in a dormitory—we called them "dormitories" then. We got a room for the male in the men's dorm without a roommate, and the female lived in the women's dorm without a roommate. We had a dean of women then

who lived close by her female student, and we had a phone installed in the student's room. Students didn't have phones in their rooms in those days, but we had a phone installed in her room. I don't remember whether we had one installed in the male student's room, in case he needed to call for help. But then, lo and behold, when registration time came, a third Black student showed up. He was a graduate student, and wasn't living on campus. He had a graduate assistantship and was no problem to student affairs. Everything went smoothly about the registration process.

Before registration I had sent out invitations to about 100 or so student leaders, various student body officials, senior and junior class officers, heads of fraternities, sororities, various organizations, and I can't remember whether I invited them to supper or not. But we had a meeting in the cafeteria in the student union, so maybe we invited them to a meal. We talked for a long time about "this thing's [desegregation] got to go, and it's got to go right."

After outlining the plans the president's committee had made to insure peaceful entrance of the African American students, Witten appealed to the student leaders directly. He told them:

This is where you come in—I have faith in the majority of our students....We hope that you are the ones who will assume the responsibility for maintenance of law and order among our students. I am not going to ask you to patrol a beat or take any extraordinary onerous duties—but merely in your ordinary comings and goings about the campus to use your influence with the remainder of our students to preserve peace.

First—just in your contacts with your fellow students, I hope you can make them understand that whether we like this situation or not—it has been forced upon us and we have to live with it, and it will be much better to accept it with a manner that reflects credit upon our school than having it forced down our throats by federal marshals or troops. And the eyes of the world *are* upon us....People outside the University are continually asking me, "Well, are you all set for trouble down there?" But I tell them and I say it to you that with the help and loyal cooperation of our student leaders, we won't have any trouble (Witten, personal communication, November 2003 from a speech in September 1963).

I made it clear to them the quality of their degree, the regard people had for the degree they got from the University of South Carolina, depended on the reputation of the university. And if they wanted a good degree, it was up to them to see that things went well. It was for their own, selfish interests that desegregation had to work.

Well, the next thing that came up was we were concerned about our football stadium, which at that time was about a mile from the campus, and our games were played at night. We were worried we couldn't provide protection for these students if they wanted to go to the football games. I don't remember if there was a special section for seating of Black people or what at the time, or if they even went to the games; but we made appropriate arrangements with these students, and they agreed to not go to the games. Appropriate arrangements included giving them back the fee they paid for the tickets, which all students had to pay. So that crisis was over, and then, I don't remember all that went on, but from time to time incidents would pop up of outsiders coming on to campus and threatening trouble.

We began to get more and more Black students—I hired a Black member of my staff. Well, I had an intern, a graduate intern in our Counseling Bureau in about 1966, a Black student from Purdue University who was a local, who had gone off to Purdue to go to graduate school. I was impressed with the work he was doing and told him when we were ready to—and I remember standing on the steps and telling him that—when we were ready to take on a Black member of our staff, I'd certainly get in touch with him. Well, about a year later I thought the time was right and I got in touch with him. By that time we had maybe 10 or 20 Black students. I got in touch with him and he joined my staff—the student affairs staff. I gave Charles McMillian a title; I guess it was coordinator of minority student affairs. He was sort of an ombudsman. I remember very well one of my Black students came in to see me. In those days, I guess I was vice president of student affairs at that time, they changed the titles in 1966, but I still was accessible to students. He told me about his problem and I said, "Well, you go see the coordinator of minority student affairs," and he looked at me and said, "But I don't know him. You're my friend." He wanted to talk to me. He didn't want to talk to somebody he didn't know even though that somebody was a Black.

UPWARD BOUND

Another thing that happened was in 1966; I was up talking to the president about something, and he handed me a sheaf of papers. I guess it was a request for a proposal or whatever they call those things, from the U.S. Office of Education for something called Upward Bound. He said, "Look at this; I can't get any of the academic deans to touch it." When I looked at it, I could see why. And I said, "Well, if you really want it, Mr. President, I guess I can do it." And this was a Monday afternoon, late Monday afternoon, and I said, "When does the grant proposal have to be in Washington?" He said, "Friday." Well, we put it together, two of my staff did, the director and assistant director of the counseling bureau. I laid down some guidelines, and they put it together. One of the things was we had to take the students from two communities in the state, and we chose Columbia and Florence, and the students had to be in the same proportion racially as the general population below the poverty level. If the poverty level—well, I forget what it was, but it turned out they had to be about 50/50, Black and White. Believe me, there was no trouble at all recruiting the Black students, but recruiting the White students was a different story. We had to lay it on the line that half the students in the class would be Black. Donald Swanson, assistant director of the counseling bureau, who ran the program, had no difficulty recruiting an excellent staff consisting of both White and Black members.

We put it together, and it was the first Upward Bound program at any state university in the Southeast. Now, we kept it mighty quiet. We didn't go bragging. But when some of the politicians in the state found out about it, they raised holy hell. You know, here we were creating a program to assist African Americans get a college education, but the politicians were unreconstructed. We got through that.

I remember one very bright young man who, let's see, he was about six feet tall and probably about three feet wide, and had a neck like a—he had no neck. But I remember at Upward Bound graduation he gave a talk on Edgar Allen Poe that was just wonderful. He was great. He was recruited by Harvard. I said, "Look, you're going to be out of place up there; it ain't for you; why don't you come here?" But he went off to Harvard. He didn't even last a year. Here, he would have been great. But we took all the Black students who finished Upward Bound.

Then another program was started, I forget what that one was, but it was started soon after we got our first Black basketball player. Frank McGuire, a well known basketball coach, got our first Black athlete. Right in the middle of our campus was Booker T. Washington High School. One of the star football players from Booker T. Washington

High School back in the 50s went off to University of California, Los Angeles (UCLA) and made all-American, because he couldn't go to school at the place where his high school was, right in the middle of the campus. But we, I remember a lot of the faculty wanted to do something—I won't go into the politics—but we started a program where the president could admit 100 students a year who didn't come up to normal academic standards if they were outstanding in other ways. It came up for discussion at a faculty meeting, and the faculty was hesitant. They looked at it as a way for the president to admit academically unqualified athletes. And I got up and said, "Hey look, you guys wanted to do something. We got our eye on a bunch of kids who are artists, writers, actors, etc., really talented and we have a program for them." And so they passed it. As we left the meeting the president asked me what the program was, and I told him we hadn't designed it yet. And lo and behold, the president made me chairman of the admissions committee to admit these special students. We did admit a few athletes, and some we turned down. I remember one we turned down because he couldn't fill out the application blank, and he went off to one of the Big 10 schools and made all-American. But we got a lot of good kids who turned out well. Many of them were Upward Bound kids. In this special program they took five courses. They were in special sections of mathematics, English, history, and a science course under selected professors. As a fifth course they enrolled in a regular section of a subject of their choice, together with regularly admitted students. If these Opportunity Scholars got through the first semester, they undertook a regular program. Well, by about 1968 we had a sizable number of Black students—maybe, I don't know, maybe 100 or 200.

THE REALITIES OF DEALING WITH INTEGRATION

All was not entirely smooth sailing at USC, however. Witten continued:

An incident happened down at South Carolina State College, which was a predominantly Black institution, which is now known as the Orangeburg Massacre (February 8, 1968), where state troopers armed with sawed-off shotguns fired into a crowd of students and killed three of them. Finally, this past year, the governor of South Carolina apologized for that action. Well, our students were upset about that, especially, our Black students. Now, there was some reaction from the ultra-right wing and one of the things that one student group did, and I think it was shortly after the Orangeburg Massacre, they were going to have a grits sale in honor of something, I don't remember what.

They packaged up little bags of grits and wrapped them in a small Confederate flags and set up a table in the student union selling these packages of grits. Well, the Black students were irritated and they gathered a crowd. I was at a big luncheon meeting down at the other end of the campus when the head of the state constabulary (the State Law Enforcement Division) came in and told me, "You better come with me; something's going on." And I went down to the student union and there was this group of Black students and a group of White students, a large group, maybe a 100 to 150 on each side, facing off against each other. Not knowing any better, I walked into the middle of it. I got hold of the Black leaders, when I saw who was leading it, and we reasoned for a long time. There are two church-affiliated, predominantly Black institutions, Benedict College and Allen University, located nearby. Some of the students attending the demonstration were from those colleges. I walked up to them, I knew almost all the Black students on our campus, and I walked up to one hulk and I looked at him and I said, "You're not a student here." He said, "No, Sir." I said, "Get the hell off this campus." And he turned and left! And the head of the state constabulary later told me, he said, "I never saw a group of Black students talk to a White dean that respectfully as they talked to you." I said, "Well, these kids all know me." That was the important thing.

Student affairs was their friend. About the same time, they started something they called the Afro-American Student Association, or something like that. Well, we had a rule at the university that every student organization had to have a faculty advisor. That was normal, in those days. And of course, there weren't any Black faculty members. Well, what do you do? I got hold of Judge Perry, he was a judge by that time, I guess. He was the Matthew Perry, who had been attorney for the first Black students, and I said, "Hey, do you know anybody here who is in law school, a mature graduate student who could act as advisor to these kids?" And he found a third year law student, and he sent him to see me. Well, this guy didn't trust me, but when Matthew Perry said I could be trusted, he agreed to be invited to advise these students. And they formed an association. The association had two wings, one was the radical wing, burn the place down, and the other was the conservative one, all they wanted was to get an education, you know, just leave us be. They agreed on a compromise leader. The student's name was Harry Wright. Harry Wright is now a professor at our med school. Harry was the first president of the association.

AFTERMATH

Reading from an old file, Witten went on to talk about several incidents that occurred during the university's attempts to integrate its campus.

> Whoever took my place when I resigned or retired or something as vice president of student affairs to being a professor burned all the old files. But, luckily, I had copies of some papers in my personal files. This particular document is called, and it's not dated, but I imagine it's late 1968 or early 1969, "A Report by the Negro Students of the University of South Carolina," their words not mine.

And let me read it:

> Whereas we are Afro-American citizens in the United States with proud African and American heritages, whereas our fore-bears have helped build the American nation, especially the South during the past 249 years, whereas we and our ancestors have been categorically denigrated and persecuted by the American socioeconomic system for this period of time, where-as we have continually resisted this subjugation from the begin-ning and will steadfastly resist oppression in any form so long as it is necessary, whereas we are cognizant of the misrepresen-tation and gross ignorance of the true history and culture of Black people by the White citizens of South Carolina, whereas this ignorance has perpetuated distortions of the greatest magni-tude resulting in racial prejudice and personal injustice against Afro-American citizens of South Carolina, whereas we are bit-terly angered by the most recent manifestation of the evil inher-ent in the existing order, the needless and wanton slaughter of three Black students at South Carolina State College on February the 8th, 1968, whereas we are committed to build and strengthen the lives and institutions of Black South Carolinians in order that they may control their own destiny, whereas many inequities of the general society are manifested on the University of South Carolina campus, we the Association of Afro-American Students at the University of South Carolina do hereby resolve to eliminate racial injustices in all aspects of university life.

And it goes on.

Explaining the Relatively Peaceful Integration

Witten attributes much of his success—and the relatively peaceful integration of the USC campus—to several factors. First, he treated all students, both African American and White, the same way. Second, he knew students and students saw him as their friend. Third, given its history, it was important for South Carolina to do things –particularly integration of its university—with style. Lastly, student affairs was proactive, not reactive, in most of what it did. For example, an internal committee chaired by Paul Fidler, Witten's assistant, came up with what they considered to be the legitimate "demands" of the African American students. This list the student affairs division took as its plan for action. This was the proactive approach.

For Witten, the key was that he knew the students and they saw him as their friend. Given the nature of the times, we asked Witten if it was a problem for him to be seen as a friend of African American students. He simply replied, "Well, I was their [White students'] friend, too. Students are students, and everybody gets treated the same. I didn't go out of my way. None of us did." In fact, in his speech to student leaders, Witten cautioned them that being overly friendly to Black students could also cause problems (Witten, personal communication, November 2003 from a speech in September 1963). "We just treated everybody the same way."

It became pretty clear that Witten was tough on both groups of students. The Black students were often critical of him. Likewise, he was not afraid to confront White students. He recounted several examples.

> We had a White student who got a permit to hold a parade on the main street of the city in honor of something, waving a Confederate flag. You know, that's still an ongoing battle in this state. Well, I got hold of him in the Administration Building hallway, and I said, "Look, if you go through with this thing, there's going to be nothing but trouble." He said, "Well, we're going to do it." Well, I knew the guy and, as a matter of fact, his first cousin is my youngest son's godmother and I knew his mother, and I said, "Okay." I grabbed him by the collar and said, "Look. If this parade goes, you go; you're out of school." In those days, you could do things like that. The parade didn't go. The threat had been a last resort. We had tried reasoning with him but that hadn't worked.

> In the same way, some Black students were going to hold some sort of demonstration, a parade on Main Street. This is a city of 100,000 and when you count the metro area, it's like 350,000. I got a call from the city manager saying, "Look, we have given a parade permit to

some of your students, and it's going to be horrible if it goes." And I said, "Well, what do you want me to do about it? It's your city." He said, "I want you to get the parade permit back." And I said, "Hey, big deal." Well, so my assistant and I sat down with the five leaders of this thing and we negotiated and argued for I guess all of a Saturday, six or eight hours around a conference table in my office. Finally, they agreed that we were right, and they would call the parade off. So I called the city manager and said, "Come and get your damn permit." And he said, "Would you mind delivering it to me?" So, we did.

Regarding another incident, Witten read from notes of a meeting where the African American students were clearly denouncing him:

They had all sorts of grievances. Every meeting I went to I was presented with grievances. Well, here are notes I took at a meeting with Black students where one of the Black students was really raising hell with the racist vice president for student affairs. The father of this same student was an official in the state National Education Association (NEA), and when I saw him the next day at a meeting he told me how greatly his son respected me. And these were some of their demands; they dealt with everything. It says "Not equal treatment for Negroes in the courts, so we've got to start at the foundations: promotions in the police, no desk sergeants and no motorcycle cops, no respect for Negroes, jail while they're building up—oh boy—prevent violence from breaking out before it happens." All we had was White police. Now what were we supposed to do about it at the university? I don't know. "Biased reporting in the city newspaper" and "improve the youth centers in these Black communities. Give us some parks and playgrounds, unequal coverage on TV to Negro high schools. The housing is slums. Improve education for Negroes. Employ Negroes (now we get to the university), employ Negroes in administration. Abolish the dual system of education. Enforce compulsory attendance. Integrate the faculty."

Well, this goes on.

The first step toward the goal of avoiding resorting to extraordinary methods, we demand that the present administration of the university take immediate action to accomplish the following: establishment of a subcommittee of the university educational policy committee (which I never heard of) to review the curriculum; inclusion of books by Black authors on the freshman required reading list; increasing the proportion of Afro-American

> students to 40 percent to accurately reflect the general popula-
> tion; inclusion of Black athletes on major university sports teams
> (of course, right now in basketball and football, that's about all
> we got); increasing the number of Black teaching assistants, fel-
> lows, professors, and administrators; elevation of Black persons
> employed in services other than janitorial; establishment of an
> exchange of professional...

And the list goes on and on with that sort of thing. And that's what
this Black crowd was up to, you know. No, I didn't say we were
particularly friendly to them.

In yet another incident, White, reactionary South Carolinians tried to get
Witten and President Jones fired.

> In the town of Orangeburg, where the Orangeburg Massacre had
> occurred, there was an organization which was slightly to the right of
> the John Birch Society. And they had a radio station there called
> WDIX, and the radio station sent me a copy of an editorial dated May
> 26, 1968. They wanted to get me and the president fired, because we
> were treating Black folks like they were people, and one thing that
> brought this about was there was a recognized Black student group
> that wanted to go to a meeting down in Alabama or someplace. And
> they had the money in their budget, so they got a university car, but
> they had to have a responsible adult, and we permitted a Black gradu-
> ate assistant to go with them. Well, she didn't have good sense. She
> went down to Orangeburg to gas up the car and the people there saw a
> University of South Carolina car with no White people in it. I don't
> know why she went to Orangeburg; it may have been to pick up a stu-
> dent from South Carolina State. The editorial made the press all over
> the country. So, the Associated Press called me at home wanting me
> to make a statement. Well, I had had some oral surgery the day before
> on my tongue, and when they wanted to talk to me, my wife said,
> "I'm sorry, he can't talk; he's just had his tongue operated on." That's
> the best thing that could have happened.

Not a Hero

Despite his role in integrating the university, Witten does not see himself as
a hero or even particularly a civil rights activist.

> Well, I did it [integration] because the law said to do it. I was a retired
> Captain in the United States Navy, and when legitimate authority told

me to do something, I did it. Furthermore, I never called what we did the civil rights movement. It was something, just a segment of our population was undereducated and we had people paying taxes for state universities, the state university had a job to educate everybody in some way or another.

However, Witten does explain South Carolina's different approach to integrating its university by resorting to history.

You've got to go back in history. South Carolina was settled by aristocrats, and you've heard of John Locke, haven't you? Well, as far as I was concerned he wrote two important political documents—his words are in the Declaration of Independence, and also he wrote something called The Fundamental Constitution for the Carolinas. And it was set up as a feudal system, and it has got traditions. Okay. In South Carolina we do things with dignity.

In the books that have been written about integration of the University of Alabama (Clark, 1995) and University of Mississippi, (Cohodas, 1997), the presidents and boards of trustees are not portrayed as being particularly helpful to integration efforts so we asked Witten about USC's president. He replied:

Dr. Jones was a great president for the times. He was a good ol' boy who was born in Tennessee, raised in Mississippi, and educated at Mississippi State College before he went off to the MIT for graduate work. He was a politician and could not get out too far in front of his trustees. He was an engineer, but a humanistic and liberally educated engineer who was a firm believer in equal educational opportunity for all. He supported all measures that would lead to such a goal.

It is also clear from the letters written to students quoting the board of trustees, that the trustees were publicly committed to upholding the law and avoiding the disruption experienced by other Southern universities.

THE ROLE OF THE STUDENT AFFAIRS PROFESSION

Witten described student affairs as playing a key proactive role in the successful integration of the university, but this was not a particularly heroic role. When pushed to describe the role of student affairs he simply said,

Student affairs worked with all students. The Black students got a fair shake at student aid, student work study jobs, and other programs, but everybody did. We just carried out our policies and treated them like any other students. That's why I say it was nothing different. We had a Black student body president about 1970-71, which was amazing.

Perhaps as important as the student body president as a marker of success was the fact that there came a time when African American students didn't even know who the coordinator of minority affairs was.

Well, that was very, very important because when the time came, I remember one time I was walking across the campus with a couple of my staff, and past a couple of Black students, and they didn't even look at us. And one of those with me was the coordinator for minority student affairs. I said, "Well, things have really changed when we've got enough Black students that they don't know you."

It is difficult for Witten to separate civil rights from what he calls the cultural revolution or unrest due to the war in Vietnam.

Civil rights was running the same time as the general cultural revolution was going on, and holding the place together was our goal—and I don't know which of them got more time. I don't think I was consciously spending more time on the problem of peaceful desegregation than on providing for the education of all students. Well, we had a visitor, a vice president of Ford Foundation here one time, and the president was taking him around the campus; he called me in to meet him and said, "I want you to meet my vice president in charge of all education outside the classroom." That was very significant; the role of student affairs was to facilitate the education of students and provide for the education with such things that they didn't get in the classroom. I don't think it mattered whether the students were Black, White, Indian or Asian, or what.

The student leaders really played a significant role. For example, here's one note from his file: On noon Friday, February 1969, the student government of the university and the Afro-American Students Association cosponsored a memorial service for students who died in Orangeburg. The president of the student body, Sam Drew, (who was White and from Charleston) issued the following statement:

By holding this memorial service we are expressing our solicitude over the situation in Orangeburg and are paying our respects to those that died. The service is purely memorial in nature and is not intended to justify or condone any one faction. The service is made possible by the efforts of our own initiative in cooperation with the Afro-American Students Association and encountered no opposition from the administration. Many people have asked why student government is cooperating in this matter. The answer is simply this: It is too easy to hide behind stereotypes. It is too easy to advocate violence against the Negroes. It is also too easy to advocate violence against the White man. It is too easy to ignore that we have problems. What is needed is to step away from clash toward cooperation. Today we have this opportunity to take such a step, and we have begun to respond.

And this is the kind of thing we did; students were here to get an education. We didn't have one real revolutionary, we had several. But we had one Black real revolutionary who even altered his name. He assumed, he said his name was a slave name, and he took another name. I don't know if he ever graduated, but when I was getting out of the car to go to church a couple of weeks ago and parked right in front of it, I've got a handicapped sticker, a car going by jammed on the brakes. They squealed, and a man ran out, threw his arms around me and said, "Dean Witten!" He was that former Black revolutionary, now a respectable middle class minister.

Well, there were a lot of things that student affairs did. We set up something we called the Metropolitan Education Foundation. It was the brainchild of Robert Alexander, who at the time was our director of volunteer services. It brought together the city's business leaders, Black community leaders, and the university to work in the ghetto area adjoining the university, which has now been done away with. The foundation was to provide programs for the people of the area and develop community spirit and so on, showing them that the university cared. But it's all gone now. He worked directly with the student leaders. When they wanted something done they went to the top. You know, they were never satisfied to deal with subordinates. They wanted to know that things had the approval at the top.

When asked what lessons he personally learned through participation in the civil rights movement, Witten replied, "Oh, I didn't participate in the civil rights movement. I just did what the law said and the president said to do. It was what student affairs people had to do."

When asked whether he thought student affairs as a profession learned something about the role they played he responded:

Clemson and this place, in the early days, especially, and later I think every place—student affairs played a significant role in facilitating, and I hesitate to call it civil rights, in student rights on the campus. Do you remember something called a Student Bill of Rights? Well, one of the most successful lawyers in this city who, I don't know what his take-home pay is every year, but it certainly dwarfs mine, was president of the student body. And we hashed that thing out to make it applicable to this place, and it was adopted by the faculty and the student body and approved by the board of trustees. Facilitating student education takes many forms. There was something, it's a nationwide thing now; we called it University 101 or "The Freshman Year Experience." Well, student affairs played a significant role in getting the thing started and adopted. And it's just another aspect of what I call facilitating the education of students, and that's the important thing.

What student affairs at the USC did in the way of facilitating desegregation was to follow the old guidance set forth by the ACPA and NASPA many years before the problems of desegregation in the South ever appeared. It was the work of a team—the vice president, assistant vice president, dean of residence life, dean of student activities, director of the counseling bureau, coordinator of minority student affairs, foreign student advisor, their staffs and in fact, all the campus chaplains. They all played an important role.

Perhaps even more significant than any single program, Witten's 1970 speech to the ACPA also indicates a fundamental change in perspective:

As time passed, we began to reexamine our role in the education of the total population of our state. We had a growing influx of Black students who were largely the products of a segregated school system. A growing realization began to dawn that something more would have to be done for them if we were to do more than just admit them, let them flounder on their own, and then depart.

We began to realize that the first job of the student personnel staff in dealing with the problems of the culturally different was to sensitize ourselves, to sensitize other administrators, the faculty, and the students to the special needs and problems of the culturally different. We sent our staff to meetings. We had, and continue to have, in-service training dealing with the problems. We acted as a catalyst in forming a Faculty Steering Committee on the Education of the Disadvantaged, and an Ad Hoc Faculty Committee on the Problems of the Black Student. We began to realize that when you take a young person from a culture in which he is raised and set him down in another culture you cannot expect him to function efficiently in the second culture without a great deal more being done for him (Witten, personal communication, November 2003, from ACPA speech in 1970).

Another important aspect of Witten's contribution was his role in providing educational opportunities for students through the master's and doctoral programs in higher education administration at USC, of which he is very proud.

EPILOGUE

Witten admits that when he retired in 1986 he separated himself from USC. He does not keep current on what is going on at the university or in the world of higher education—except what he reads and hears in the news. He doesn't read as much as he used to and rarely watches television or listens to the radio. He is deaf because of years of exposure to the Navy's big guns and is losing his vision because of glaucoma and macular degeneration. He spends a good deal of time in front of his computer working on his autobiography and at his log cabin home in North Carolina's Smoky Mountains where he has an apple orchard and sits and watches the birds.

CIVIL RIGHTS AT SMALLER, PRIVATE COLLEGES

JAMES W. LYONS
Haverford College (1962-1972)

James Lyons was Haverford College's first dean of students. He served in that position from 1962-1972. From Haverford he went on to become dean of student affairs at Stanford University. Although this chapter is based primarily on Lyons' experiences at Haverford, he does occasionally refer to his Stanford days.

Lyons describes his entry into student affairs as, "the usual combination of accident, fortuity, interest, and affinity of experiences." He earned his undergraduate degree from Allegheny College in Pennsylvania in 1954. While there, he worked for the dean of students doing a lot of "odd jobs." He describes part of his job as mediating conflict, which he notes, "is a significant part of a dean's job." Lyons was also the second resident assistant in the college's history. While working for the dean's office, Lyons became a "water cooler friend" with the president, Louis Benezet. "Somebody gave me a paper Benezet wrote and I found it absolutely fascinating. I told him that, and then we started having discussions. He became my mentor. That was when I learned about higher education as a career." Eventually, Lyons was hired as a resident counselor at Indiana University and was admitted to a graduate program in the school of business. He later switched to the School of Education, where, in 1962, he earned his doctorate in higher education with additional studies in business and law. In that same year, he was hired as dean of students at Haverford College in Pennsylvania.

PERSONAL INTRODUCTION TO CIVIL RIGHTS

Long before he accepted the position at Haverford, Lyons had an early, and personal, introduction to civil rights.

> In 1953, when I was an RA, the dean of students with whom I worked was a highly principled man who acted on his beliefs. I remember as a

senior, I was being nominated for a Fulbright. The dean was writing my letter of recommendation. In the middle of the evening on a Friday night, the dean called me. One of the students yelled, "Hey, Jim, there's a phone call for you." It was the dean. He said, "Jim, I'm working on this nomination." I said, "Okay." He said, "Well, I've got one question here that I really don't know how to answer." He said, "What is your view on civil rights?" I thought to myself, "Geez, it's 9 o'clock on a Friday night." But I said, "Well, you know we've had all kinds of discussions about this." And he said, "Yeah, but don't you belong to the Phi Delt fraternity?" "Yes," I answered. He asked, "Are there any Blacks in the fraternity?" I replied, "There's only one in the college and he and I are good friends, but no, he's not a Phi Delt." "Why isn't he in there?" I answered, "Because of the clause." He said, "Well, how do I answer this question, then?" What a marvelous teachable moment he seized. It was powerful; he just drove an icicle into me and let it melt. That led me to organize a group of people to start a national movement and raise money to change the clause in the national fraternity. Our efforts got soundly walloped the first time it went up. The clause was eventually changed. That was my introduction to the sharper edge of civil rights.

THE CONTEXT AT HAVERFORD

Until 1962, Haverford had a dean of the college but no dean specifically assigned to carry out traditional student affairs responsibilities. According to Lyons:

> Haverford did not make the typical academic nonacademic distinction. Haverford then was small, approximately 780 students, and back then it was a men's college. When I began, there was a very small population of African American students, perhaps five or six. Haverford had rigorous academic standards and was highly selective. The other interesting thing at Haverford was that even though it was an expensive, selective, private college with the reputation of being a "rich kid's place," it was actually very economically diverse. This was, in part, because of the need-blind admissions policy. If you were admitted, we made sure that you could come. The campus culture was imbued with a Quaker egalitarianism streak.

> Haverford was highly prized for its sense of community and had a very powerful honor system, both social and academic. The honor system worked. The social part of the honor code played a key role in

Haverford's experiences with civil rights. The key operating word at Haverford was respect, respect for others. As a Quaker-related school, the institution had a highly ethical overtone to it, although less than 10 percent of the students and faculty were Quaker. The Quaker traditions, however, were strong and powerful. The school made decisions via consensus. In the history of the college, there has never been a vote taken. The basic philosophy at Haverford was that you put as much responsibility on students as they would take and then add some. You pushed them. We never had a smothering kind of *in loco parentis* at Haverford. We cared deeply but we taught and expected students to take responsibility for themselves and each other.

Haverford students and faculty were keenly aware of the civil rights movement, but they initially defined that movement as being associated with the situations in the South. Some faculty and students were involved in the Freedom Rides. They would go down South and help edit the publications, the freedom journals. The Quaker tradition that influenced the college included strong commitments to social justice and human dignity, so it was not surprising that Haverford students and faculty were involved in or supported civil rights struggles in the South. One of my associate deans was active down there. It was normal. There was always a group of students who were organizing something. They would simply say, "Some of us are going down." It was just a natural thing to do. It was part of the culture. We took that culture for granted.

CIVIL RIGHTS AT HAVERFORD

In 1963, when I first got to Haverford, one of the first of the social issues that year to come out was that there was a barbershop in the nearby town of Ardmore that would not cut the hair of Black students. Word got out about the barbershop and the students were absolutely incensed. I remember going to visit the barber shop and saying, "There are a lot of people concerned about this." I got the expected answer, "Well, we don't know how. Their hair is different." I said, "Is that a really serious problem?" Then they said, "We're really not in any position to change anything here." So the students, maybe a half dozen or so, picketed in front of the barber shop one day. Later I got a call from the barber shop, "Well, we'd like to talk some more." That was a case of very direct action. This situation was justified because it affected maybe some of our students, but it was more justified because it was wrong. Just like going to Mississippi, it wasn't our backyard, but it was wrong, and we felt good because we tried to help—and did.

Lyons explained that the experience at the barbershop led to a growing awareness on the part of the campus that there was a nearby Black community in Ardmore.

> Ardmore was a bedroom community of Philadelphia. It was not rich, but it was not poor. This do-gooder quality that was part of the Haverford culture quickly found an outlet when some students said, "Well, let's do something for the children of Ardmore." That led to the founding of a summer day camp called Camp Serendipity. The camp exists to this day. We got the local Friends Meeting involved in creating the camp. The creation of the camp was one of the most wonderful things that I have ever experienced, because it involved the coming together of two groups with great cultural differences—a Quaker Meeting and two local Black churches. We had all kinds of meetings and we needed to raise some money. We had the usual pitch-ins and gradually, over about a year, we all got to know each other a little bit.

> At that time, Haverford, very consciously, tried to get one or two people from the Ardmore community on the staff of the College. We wanted to create some bridges, a presence. We also established a little community council to improve communication. Eventually somebody said, "Let's get together and do a gospel concert." Quakers are not big on singing but they do a great pitch-in dinner. Ardmore had three little churches, and the choirs in each included maybe five or six people, but when you put them together you had something special. So, we had a rockin' gospel concert in the college auditorium to raise money. It is now a cherished annual event. Working together on those activities nurtured the day camp and improved relations. These experiences with Ardmore were successful in helping to build bridges and it wasn't long before more local African American students began applying to Haverford.

FROM NUMBERS TO CLIMATE

> In terms of access of minority students to Haverford, the issues were not only Black and White. At one point, the governor of Puerto Rico established a scholarship in Puerto Rico for two students to attend Haverford. That relationship was established by the admissions staff that traveled to Puerto Rico to recruit students. They met the governor and convinced him to help us recruit students from down there. The

scholarship was the equivalent of two full-time rides a year for Puerto Rican students. This allowed us to carve out a little recruitment niche in the early 1960s. When we tried to extend that niche by recruiting Puerto Ricans from New York we learned another lesson. There is a huge cultural difference between Puerto Ricans from New York City and those from the island. They regard each other as different, and occasionally with some animus. We didn't know that. That is when I learned something else—you should be careful not to fall prey to your own stereotypes. This was an early and a powerful lesson.

At Haverford, we had an abundance of discussions about attaining a critical mass of minority students. The term "minority" was unexamined back then. We didn't realize how limiting and dumb that term was. The other term that we would cast about was "disadvantaged." That became not only a useless term, but a destructive one because it equated color with disadvantage. We weren't defining things very well. We saw our main job back then as increasing the presence of students of color at the college. It was about access and numbers, it was an admissions issue. We didn't worry about climate because that was what we knew best, that sense of community that is a part of Quaker tradition. But we didn't know as much as we thought that we did about such matters. We all agreed that if we got a critical mass then it would work.

Well, one day we got a critical mass. I don't know how many Black students we had at the college then, probably 25 or so, which for Haverford's small size was a lot. The Black students were good leaders and they decided to invoke the most powerful tool in the Haverford culture. One day the Black student leadership announced, "The college is not abiding by its own honor code. We are not respected. And, until we are, we are not going to speak to anybody." Holding picket signs wasn't going to have the same kind of effect as calling into question the most sacred values of the college. The culture at Haverford was that you talk and talk and talk. All meetings at Haverford were designed to reach decisions by consensus; that meant extended efforts to speak clearly, forthrightly, and to listen respectfully and thoughtfully. All of a sudden, a group of our students said, "We're not going to play. We'll go to class. We'll take notes. But, we're not going to have any conversations." The faculty said, "What did we do wrong?" The White students said, "What did we do wrong?" We thought, "We have been working really hard to make it from five to 25." We felt unappreciated. This went on for a week. It was marvelous. Finally the faculty said, "We've got to have a meeting to discuss this." I remember walking into that meeting. All the Black students were lined-up, creating an aisle you had to walk through to get to your seat. They didn't say a word; there were no signs, posters, or handouts. At Haverford, this was devastating. That was the first time that the issue changed from admissions, from numbers, to climate.

We had spent all of our time talking about Black students. "Do they have the qualifications? Do they have the education? Do they have the money? What is wrong with them? How come he failed? What is it about his background?" As a college, we had asked all of those questions. The experience of the silent protest led us to hold up a mirror to look at ourselves and our college, and try to begin the much harder task of understanding how we appeared to Black students. "What is wrong with us?" We began to look much more clearly at what we were doing. For me, that was a major, yet humbling, moment in my professional career. If you think about it, this is what student affairs is all about. We should be sensitive to the need for nurturing learning environments. As long as we can get beyond regulating students and taking care of the bureaucratic trivia, we can move to creating an environment that supports learning. We should not be asking how to recruit more people; we should be asking different kinds of questions. We had made some progress in the community; the barbers were cutting hair now and we had the summer camp and all those things. We had turned the corner and I had expected to see the end of the street. What I saw was that the road goes to infinity, the job had just begun.

The Black students were saying to us "You haven't paid attention to what has been going on in our own backyard." That episode culminated in an all-night meeting with me, the president, members of our student government honor council, some faculty members, and representatives from the Black students. We met at the president's house, which is right on campus. The meeting went all night, and it was a hard meeting. All felt the need to come out of that meeting with a joint statement that would set the stage for future changes on our campus. We issued a statement and the college got back together. The College community realized that it needed to look at itself and all of its parts. That was an important turning point. I don't remember the specifics, but I remember that the meeting set up a whole new set of questions and the realization that the old agenda was not going to work.

THE CIVIL RIGHTS MOVEMENT WAS FUELED BY OTHER TIDES OF THOSE TIMES

The civil rights movement was just one of several movements of those times. It was clearly important and sweeping and was the movement with roots and techniques that remain visible today. But when we look at the changes that occurred on our campuses, we find that multiple forces were at work. What were some of those changes? Students were treated as adults and not as children. The days of the college assuming the role of parents were gone. The nature of many relationships that are fundamental to collegiate life changed dramatically. Examples include relationships between students and their college, students and their parents, the college and parents, colleges and the law, and students and the law.

Students, for example, ceased to be protected from "real life law" by their colleges. Rather, they were seen as having no greater, nor fewer, rights than other citizens. On the other hand, there were newly emerging rights for students such as earning the vote and having a major role in governing their own affairs. In addition, students earned the right to expect a level of fairness, privacy, and also reasonable codes of conduct. Sexual mores changed. There were major changes in the rights (and expectation of rights) for women. And, collegiate relationships with spouses and children became as important as relationships with parents.

What was behind these changes? Clearly the civil rights movement in all of its forms was a key force. But there were other forces too. This was the period when student populations soared. It was the time of the greatest increase in the provision of public higher education. The era was affected by the psychedelic movement, Vietnam, Cambodia, the Selective Service, and the peace movement. The voting age dropped from 21 to 18; students became enfranchised citizens. The "pill" became widely available and used. Efforts by civil libertarians in the higher education community led to the empowering policy statement, "The Rights and Responsibilities of Students." Cries for curricular relevance and reform brought about by the insistent nature of the times resulted in significant curricular and pedagogical changes.

All of these forces, and more, were active at the same time as the civil rights movement. Many were interrelated; most were both cause and effect. I think that the power of the civil rights movement on the American college campus is more thoroughly appreciated and understood by also knowing the context of those times. Those times were exciting, productive, troublesome, energizing, agonizing, socially powerful, and politically dramatic. They led to major changes in the culture and shape of the American college and university. They may have been the most exciting, opportunity rich, and challenging of times for those of us working in student affairs.

THE ROLE OF STUDENT AFFAIRS

Deans are on committees. Those are often domains where change gets crafted, priorities set, and policies studied. I was an advocate of knowing as much as we could about the movement and its ways. It was a time when many were unaccustomed to having students speaking up and being critical of the college. Hence, it was important to help colleagues and others understand that, in times of protest and advocacy, there is often a difference between what people say and what they mean. One of my roles was to help students communicate clearly—to make their basic points clearly. Another was to help others glean meaning from their words.

One of the great attributes of the small college is that the institutional arteries don't get so hardened. Everyone understands its mission. Everyone is driven by that mission. And the common cause is more easily found. Hence, small college deans (or at least this one) were free from the nitty-gritty expectations to "maintain order" and make sure that rules are followed. It was possible, therefore, to focus on the question, "What is the right thing to do?" and then do it. That approach was crucial to the times. The hardened roles and bureaucracies didn't get in the way.

When I was the dean at Haverford I was free to be myself. I didn't have to carry other people's water. I was lucky enough to get a job where the fit was just gorgeous. I also saw my role as shaping beliefs. My job was to help run the college, and my job was to be one of the president's men (being a men's college). The fact was that I knew I had no job guarantee, anyway. I always worked at the favor of the president. Only later did I learn that I was the only guy who resigned every time we changed presidents. I resigned once at Haverford, and I resigned at Stanford. One of my presidents laughed at me when I gave him a resignation letter signed but undated. I said, "I think I should do this because you should be able to pick your own people." He said, "You've got to be kidding." He wanted me to stay. The point is he made a choice. We agreed to work with and for each other.

I have a responsibility to argue with the president, to check the president, to disagree with the president, to inform the president. You don't disagree publicly, obviously, but behind closed doors, the president could count on me to challenge him. I could also count on the president to challenge me. I was really lucky to have situations during my professional time when I could help run the college. I felt a responsibility to help run the place, especially when I sense I knew something that was helpful.

THE ROLE OF NASPA.

There were times I felt like I was in a different country, because I always seemed to be having experiences ahead of other campuses. So many times at NASPA I felt like saying, "Just wait gang, you are going to get this stuff next." I would say, "You're going to get drugs next." Then they would get them. I would say, "You're going to lose *in loco parentis*." They would say, "Hell no." Then they would experience it. Still, NASPA was crucial during these times. There was no *Chronicle of Higher Education*. And you only tended to call and consult with colleagues that you knew. So NASPA's local, regional, and national meetings were where you got to know other colleagues and their situations. It was where information was exchanged. It was where issues and practices were analyzed and presented systematically. It was the vehicle whereby clusters of nearby schools facing new winds and tides could gather to learn from each other. This was terribly important because so much was new during those times.

HOW STUDENTS ARE DIFFERENT TODAY

There have been changes in our profession; there are some significant generational changes. The students coming in today have been affected by different life circumstances than in earlier times. This means they are behaving a whole lot differently than they used to. For example, conduct issues are more important now, in part because of the way we are treating students once they arrive. We are back to treating them like children again. The guiding principle seems to be "keep the waters calm, don't allow disturbances, and don't upset the parents." Parents are calling more often and now we actually accept the calls. Earlier, when parents would call the first thing we would say is, "Well, have you talked to your son or daughter about it?" We forced it back to the student to solve the problem. Now, we intervene. That's a change.

In terms of dealing with race and ethnicity, students may be less able to deal with conflict and differences than they were in the 1960s and 1970s. I'm quite unsure of this hypothesis because it seems so counterintuitive. But the general level of interpersonal skills and social sophistication may be less than the early and mid periods of the civil rights era. Perhaps students are spending most of their time on electronic keyboards, and not interacting with people. They are avoiding conflict because they can. They grow up with toys that bark, that play songs, that make funny noises, rather than using their imagination and playing with others. Play for a kid is highly organized. They are growing up in a much more programmed and structured environment. They show up in high school with day planners. Such input is bound to show up in some way. For one, it may just be that the students are unable to take advantage of and learn from the rich differences they now encounter in schools and colleges.

In many places in the country, the term, civil rights, is defined in Black and White terms. But this narrow view doesn't help when understanding the wide diversity that exists in California. There is an emerging category—one that may soon be significant in size. That is, students whose parents are ethnically different from each other. They don't fit the categories the government and our registrars impose on them. They have a different array of cultural roots to discover and embrace. They are often "recruited" by one or another group that doesn't really reflect the worlds of their upbringing. Curiously, they are like most all other Americans: a mix of ethnic backgrounds and culture. The labels of the past don't mean anything and they are no longer good guideposts for educational policies.

There is another interesting change in students, and the times. It is how students expect to be treated. Of course, they expect to be treated with respect. Beyond that, though, they want to be treated as individuals. They want to be known, not anonymous. Being African American, or Moslem, or the daughter of immigrants is important—but may be only one of hundreds of factors that shape an individual's skill, hopes, aspirations, interpersonal adeptness, and world views. The early theorists of student affairs preached the view that "students are individuals" and therefore should be treated as such. Furthermore, like snowflakes, no two students are alike. Our job is to understand what makes them distinctive. The early days of the civil rights movement, however, pushed other views. It was argued that because someone was Black or Latino or something else, they had certain individual and social characteristics. So we asked ourselves, "What does it mean to be this or that?" That's a good question—and it is no less important today. But today we need to be more sophisticated and ask questions like, "Okay, you are a son of an immigrant. What does that mean? How does that meld with your other life experiences? How does that shape you as an individual?" Everyone is special; everyone is an individual; everyone learns better when we treat them that way. But we cannot overlook race and ethnicity as an important factor in their development.

I suspect that stereotyping still happens. Perhaps it is best seen as a shortcut to understanding individuals that just doesn't work. So teaching better ways to understand difference remains one of the main missions of our informal curriculum. It is a growing-up skill with which most traditionally aged college students wrestle. We can all recall examples from the past. In the 1970s, a student came to me once and told me she wanted to go home. She was a Native American; a Seneca from western New York State. I asked, "Tell me why?" She said, "Well, my dorm-mates have called me a thief. They said that I was stealing." Then she explained,

> I'm having a very hard time. My family is poor and we don't have a whole lot of food. Here, at breakfast time I see more food left over than my family has probably ever seen at one time. So what I do is I take unused boxes of cereal left on trays and I take them to my room and once a month I just box them up and send them home. Somebody reported me as stealing food from the dining room.

So, what's wrong here? In a sense, this is a growing-up issue that has cultural and racial overtones. The real issue was that one group of students and an RA were unaware of someone else's life situation and were unable to keep open the possibility that there might have been alternative explanations of what was going on. They were unbelievably embarrassed and contrite when I got us all together to talk about that. Here is an example of how students have to become sensitive to others. This is a maturational issue with socioeconomic and racial overtones that could easily be confused with racism. It could be racism, of course. But social maturity includes, among other things, the ability to refrain from rushing to judgment in the absence of facts. It means knowing that behaviors of others are best understood in the context of at least a temporary willingness to suspend disbelief. Maturity means at least recognizing that human behavior is complex and that it isn't always what it appears to be.

Traditional aged students are still just 18 years old. They still don't know about difference; they have never shared a room with anybody before; they've never eaten food other than their mommy's meals. They still have a lot of maturing to do. We had a tendency to take ordinary growing-up situations and make larger hills or mountains out of them. Still, underlying those situations were some real issues that needed to be addressed. If student affairs people are teachers (and I think that we were, are, and should be), we should see this as a significant challenge for our informal curriculum.

LESSONS LEARNED

I think we probably learned a lot of humility about predicting success of our students. I would like to say that Stanford and Haverford didn't have to learn as much as a lot of other places because all along we have said that we are going to admit only students who we have reasonably good reason to think are going to succeed. Secondly, both Haverford and Stanford make it possible for students to return if they decide to leave. Once you join our club, you are a member, and you are always a member. If you go to Haverford or Stanford, and you say "I don't want to be here next year," then you can return whenever you want to. Once you have been admitted if you leave you can come back. You don't need permission. You don't need anything.

During one year at Stanford when we were trying desperately to do a better job recruiting and retaining Native Americans, we invited some guidance counselors from high schools in the West to come talk about how we could improve our efforts. I had a revelation when we were talking about dropout rates. One guy was an Alaskan Athabascan and he said, in a quiet but stern and persistent way, "Why is it that you think that if somebody was here only a year and left, that they are a failure?" That was a powerful question. I remember we stumbled through the usual answer, "Well, because they didn't complete the degree." Then he said, "You just finished telling me they can complete it later if they want. Well, maybe they learned enough in that year to become the treasurer of their tribe. Maybe to them that is success." I tell that story to illustrate what we have tried to learn about redefining success. We all know that somebody can zip through this place, get good grades and so on and so forth, and be an unmitigated disaster afterwards. We have had to look at ourselves to see if there is a good relationship between what we say and what we do, between our mission and our accomplishments.

The thing that hasn't changed about student affairs is that you are still dealing with trying to help individuals grow up and learn about themselves. You're still trying to craft communities that are supportive and nurturing. You are still trying to encourage some faculty colleagues to be effective mentors for students. You are still trying to humanize the situation. You are still trying to make the place less anonymous.

In the early 1970s at Stanford right after I arrived, I learned that the RAs at one of the houses had memorized the names of all the incoming freshmen. I thought it was a good idea, so I told all the RAs at the initial training meeting, "You know there are some things here that are just terrific, like this tradition of memorizing the names and two other things about every incoming student, and greeting them." It became a tradition right at that point, by declaration.

It was so important to have a diverse staff. It was especially important in student affairs because we could diversify quicker then the faculty. We started working toward that goal as soon as I got to Haverford. It was clear to me, for the wrong reasons I might add, that we should have staff of color. I always tried to have a presence in the room. One of the wrong reasons was for the good of others. That is, students need to learn to interact with people of color. Well, of course that's not a proper reason even if it is a welcome benefit. It is ultimately a destructive notion. It is a using notion; you are using people for something that you shouldn't be.

We are reaping some early investments, often painful investments, of maintaining standards by exercising judgment about what constitutes success and what constitutes evidence that we're pretty sure that somebody can succeed. It is an investment in ambiguity, because what we care about is not determined by what is coming in as much as what is going out. We have always tried to stand by that measure. It was not until recently that we would ever release even things like board scores for that reason. We admit on ability; we don't take the ability to pay into consideration when determining admission, and we maintain a financial aid program that assures that if you are admitted you can come. It becomes terribly important, the combination of making it possible for someone to come and also to maintain the standards. Now, when students get admitted here, there is simply no question other than the ordinary question that everybody feels, "Am I a mistake?" Factoring that out, nobody really thinks "I'm here because I'm Black or Asian or something." That is a factor in your being admitted, but it is not the only reason you are qualified to be here.

It is important to know that you are going to encounter a diverse environment. If you are valued for what you bring to the table, it means you are going to run into some strange people here, valued similarly from other places. I have always been looking for ways, different ways, to analyze, to answer questions, to start discussions about affirmative action, as one example. And the minute you mention affirmative action, somebody's going to assume you're talking about discrimination, and you're going to talk about quotas, usually. One is a concept; the other is a mechanical device. So how do you deal with the discrimination thing? This led me to believe that discrimination, on its face, is not a bad concept. We're discriminating all the time. We discriminate based on academic achievement, promise, and age; so it's not the fact that something's being discriminated. Rather, it's the basis for discrimination that becomes important. So I think this kind of series of thinking about men's college, women's college because I was in one, led me to think that way. Are there ways that would justify discriminating for men only, other than history and tradition? No. I couldn't think of any, really. It felt good to admit women to Haverford. It felt like, "Gee, we'd be losing something really nice here, like the old Stanford people losing their Indian." But the fact is it didn't fit; in my opinion, men's colleges are not a useful concept. This made me think analytically about "What do we discriminate for?" and on what basis, to what end?

EPILOGUE

James Lyons retired as Stanford's dean of student affairs in 1990 after 18 years in that post. Lyons continued his teaching appointment in the school of education where he taught in the administration and policy analysis program and directed a master's program in higher educational administration. He retired from that role in 1997 and still maintains connections with Stanford and his professional colleagues, and is active in community affairs.

MARK W. SMITH
Denison University (1953-1972)

Mark Smith's career in student affairs began at Denison University, Granville, Ohio in 1953. Initially, Smith was hired as an assistant professor of psychology and director of career services; shortly after, he was named dean of men. He was promoted to professor with tenure in 1959. Smith worked at Denison in student affairs until 1971 and until 1972 as a professor of psychology.

To contextualize Smith's story it might help to know a little about his personal background.

> I grew up in a relatively wealthy family with a lot of servants, many of whom were Black. I was raised by a Black woman, Mattie Moyer, in my home in Columbus, Ohio. In the late 1960s, when Mattie was in her eighties, she became the coleader of the Black-White coalition in Columbus. She was a great churchwoman, and her husband was the janitor at the downtown club where my father was president. She became a dominant force in Columbus' attempts to do what Nashville and other cities were doing to get Blacks and Whites together to deal with problems involving racism. I grew up both loving and respecting the Blacks who worked for us. Also, I've always hated any kind of cruelty or insensitivity, whether it is against animals or people. Our son is the same way, as is my wife. We detest racism, and everyone who knows us well knows that.

CONTEXT AT DENISON UNIVERSITY

The mention of civil rights at Denison in the 1960s and 1970s first calls for a portrait of what the private, coeducational, liberal arts college was like before the arrival of African American students on campus. Despite its use of the name "University," Denison is, by choice, solely an undergraduate university. Smith painted a picture of Denison in the 1950s:

> It had 1,500 to 1,750 students, many of them legacies, and a 97percent graduation rate. Most of the students were from affluent families; perhaps half were children of professionals. Probably 40 percent were going on to law school, medical school, or graduate school. SAT scores weren't very important at all. They are now. The students were really nice kids, with about 98 percent membership in fraternities and sororities. Almost all of the students lived on campus. I had no staff and the dean of women had two dorm assistants. The student head residents and junior advisers who ran the dorms, the fraternity and sorority presidents, and the student government leaders were the student personnel staff of the college. When I first arrived, there were rarely more than four or five Black students. There were no Blacks on the faculty or staff. The only significant Black presence was on the female housekeeping staff. There were more Blacks in the student body and on the faculty and staff in the early 1960s, but only a few.

THE INTRODUCTION OF MORE BLACK STUDENTS TO DENISON

The student population changed in the mid-1960s when Smith claims that the government imposed new policies on Denison, calling for the admission of significantly more African American students.

> The student body was essentially White until the arrival of the quota system. That immediately increased the Black student population to about three percent of the student body (the objective was five percent). This was less than a critical mass of Black students. We didn't choose the quota system, it was imposed on us by the government; we had to do it if we wanted student loans.

Smith, as a strong student advocate, worked closely with the Black students, and was intimately acquainted with their struggles to become a legitimate presence on an otherwise White campus.

> Initially the presence of more Black students on campus had little to do with civil rights as genuine protest against discrimination against Blacks. It was simply the result of a decision to cooperate with a governmental demand. Our situation had none of the emotions represented by the civil rights movement. There was no enthusiasm about what was being done, and those with truly racist objections kept them pretty much to themselves. There was no controversy. Civil rights meant

little more than bringing more Blacks to Denison through aggressive recruitment, scholarship offers, and compensatory admissions. The program was in no way tied to the college's mission or values, and we knew damn well that there were not sufficient numbers of Black students for them to have a comfortable, rewarding experience. The college did the minimum, and it did it without conviction or commitment.

Denison did the minimum and struggled to do that, mainly because most Black applicants were simply nowhere near White applicants in terms of measurable academic ability, especially with the racism of the Scholastic Aptitude Test (SAT). We were admitting Black students who did not actually qualify for admissions. I thought that was the right thing to do, still do. But we certainly had a bunch of trustees, parents, faculty, and others who said, "Do you realize that these students are taking the place of much more qualified applicants, including children of alumni." My answer to that was, "Tough. It's the right thing to do." But the easiest way to get rid of the critics was to suggest that they might be racist, if only by saying, "This is the right thing to do in terms of the kind of social conscience our college should have." You had to fight for that belief. The faculty was very twofaced about this, very two-faced. With all of their wonderful cocktail party liberalism, many still said, usually in private, "We can't educate these people." An English faculty member came to me once and said, "These people can't write." And I said, "Don't call them 'these people.' Why don't you just consider the way they write to be legitimate English?"

Black students came to Denison in small numbers and the supports weren't there to help them succeed. Granville, Ohio was White. Black students had to go 27 miles to see anything of Black culture. The college made no provisions whatsoever for the kinds of entertainment or activities that Black students might want and need. Everything just stayed kind of White. The Black students were uncomfortable, and they felt they had been brought in to satisfy the image needs of the institution and the image needs of the federal government. They felt used. I can remember saying to them, "You know it's kind of like you just got carted into the cotton fields." The Black student leaders and I were close from the beginning. A few of them didn't trust me at all, if only because I was White, tall, bald, and a psychologist. Unfortunately, because of my size (6'9" and 260 lbs.)

and assertiveness, and perhaps my friendliness, some Black students were clearly afraid of me.

The addition of more Black students just did not work. President Knapp agreed that the college was not doing the extra things that they should have been doing to make Black students feel like first class citizens. Other colleges like Denison had the same problem. We tried hard to make the situation better, but again and again the faculty would turn on us. If I would say in a faculty meeting, "I think we need to double the number of Black students." The faculty would stay, "Whoa, stop. Why double?" I might say:

> Well, I'm no better than you are at guessing what would constitute a critical mass, but it has a lot to do with how many other students like them Black students see on their way to class. If you are sitting in a class of 22 students and were the only White, how the hell would you feel? Maybe you should go to Black university and see how it feels.

And they would say, "Well, doubling the number is impossible." A science faculty member would say, "We have to have our scholarships, we can't give them away to Black students." We had to offer full-ride scholarships to almost all of the Black students regardless of academic credentials. Nonneed Black prospects, as well as those with strong academic credentials, were the most sought after prospects in the country at that time, and Denison wasn't about to attract very many. The faculty said, "We haven't got enough scholarship money now for effective recruitment of top-notch students." They were unwilling to give on that issue. But what hurt us the most was that faculty leaders who claimed to be antiracist and pro-civil rights wouldn't support us.

The faculty wouldn't budge, and the trustees, in general, felt that what we had done was sufficient. At that time, Denison trustees were anachronistic, as trustees were at most institutions, and anachronistic in those years meant de facto racist. It was a very bad situation both for Black students and for Denison.

THE BLACK STUDENTS MAKE DEMANDS

As was happening on other campuses, the presence of more African American students at Denison eventually led to their becoming angry about the lack of African American culture and a critical mass of African

American students. According to Smith, at the end of the 1960s, the African American students at Denison introduced a list of demands that included, among other things, 50 more African American students, $150,000 cash, a car, a residence hall for African American students, more African American professors, and extensive African American activity programming.

> Presenting a list of demands was a tactic used by the Black students to call attention to their needs and discomfort and to embarrass the administration; it was never expected that these demands would be met. While some things on the list were more possible than others, the Black students intentionally included things that we were unlikely or unable to do.
>
> The demands changed the game. Things got very political and very serious. I was in my office working one evening when Henry Holden, a Black student from Youngstown, Ohio who claimed to be a Black Panther, stormed in. He was a great kid. He was big and handsome and bright and loved to brag about being trained as a Panther when he was in high school. With one blow of his fist, he destroyed my dictating machine. He just demolished it, and it flew all over the office. Then he got down on the floor and with his ear against the rug, said, "I can't hear anything." And I said, "Henry, what in the world are you doing?" He said, "I'm trying to hear the man." I said, "Henry, I am the man." He said, "Ah, Smith, you're not the man. I'm trying to hear the man." And I said, "What do you want?" And he said, "Shut up! I'm listening for the man!" And I said, "Do you want the car?" (Another Black student had told me that the Black caucus was talking about pushing for the car.) "Do you want a station wagon?" He said, "What?" and I said, "Do you want the car?" He said, "How did you know that?" I said, "I don't know, I just guessed." And he said, "Yeah, we want a car, new and now." I said, "Fine. A station wagon?" He said, "Definitely. How did you know that?" I said, "It just came to me." I said, "You get only enough gas to keep you within the continental United States, is that okay?" He said, "Sure." I said, "Let me call the president." So I called the president's office and said, "Henry Holden's in here and they want a car and I've told him it's perfectly okay with us, and that we'll buy it at Walker and Battatt Motors in Newark and they'll have it tomorrow." Then I said, "Right" and hung up, just after President Knapp said on the other end, "What in the world are you talking about?" Then I said, "Henry." He said, "What?" I said, "You've got the car. You can go over and pick it up tomorrow. We will give you a gas card." And he said, "It's ours?" And I said,

"It's yours. Is White okay?" And he said, "That's the color we wanted." I said, "I knew it." He said, "How did you know that?" I said, "I just guessed." So he went back over to the student union where the Black caucus was meeting in the room next to the antiwar group (who were smoking pot), and he announced to the Black caucus, "I just saw Smith and we got the car!" They screamed "Henry, it's a demand. You're not supposed to get it!" And, they beat him up. Henry had given me an opportunity to call their bluff and I wasn't about to pass it up. The demands game and its purpose were unacceptable in a liberal arts environment. It was time for the college to stand up for its rights.

The demands came about because the Black students felt they had to become political in order to gain acceptance. There were other symbolic acts. For example, I will never forget the time the Black students put up their flag. They wanted the Black flag to fly on the flagpole out in the center of the quad in front of the student union, and they took down the American flag and the Denison flag and replaced it with theirs. This was in the middle of winter and it was colder than hell. They got a message from somewhere that a group of White students were going to come and take their flag down. So, a group of Black students gathered around the flagpole to protect the flag. I am sitting here with a picture in front of me that my wife gave me last night when she heard I was going to talk about this stuff. There I am with the Black students, out in the cold for 38 hours, protecting the flag— nobody came. Things were getting ugly, and it wasn't fun. Denison was no longer a lovely, peaceful, happy little college on a hill in a pretty little Midwestern college town.

Another incident was less political but much more incendiary. Around midnight on a weeknight, a White student driving by the student union leaned out of the window of his car and yelled a filthy, horribly racist insult at a Black female student crossing the road. She became hysterical and rushed into the Black caucus room, where a group of Black students were meeting. I was sitting in the family room of my home grading papers when about 30 Black students came through the back door. They filled the room, and their leader, Henry Durand, screamed at me, "Get the president, Smith; we're going to get a guy in the Phi Gam house." So I went next door and woke up our new president and told him his presence had been requested. He and I and the Black students went to the Phi Gam house to confront the racist student. I asked a Phi Gam officer to bring the man down to the living room, where the Black students had stationed themselves. As we were waiting, the president stood up and said to the Black students, "I feel your feelings." That was a mistake—Henry Durand leapt to his feet and said in a very sarcastic tone, "May I dance for you, master?" With which Henry and I got into a wrestling match, which essentially diffused the situation. The culprit was brought in, very drunk and scared to death. The Black students got up and left without a word, and I sent the young man home.

RELATIONSHIPS BETWEEN BLACK STUDENTS AND WHITE FACULTY

In reality, Smith explained, the Denison environment was not one in which students needed to make demands. "All they had to do was come in and ask." So the challenge was for Smith and other administrators to try to meet real needs in the midst of the political game of demands. To shed light on this nuance, Smith talked about some significant interactions he had with Black students.

> During a typical day, two or three Black students would come to visit me in my office for very legitimate reasons. A Black student would come in with a graded paper that had a statement by the teacher that said, "Good job, you're making real progress. D." And the student would say, "This says I'm dumb." It would almost always be written by a faculty member who unintentionally was racist, just totally uneducated in terms of realizing that the Black brain is not inferior. Few faculty members had experience with Black students from urban areas and most had no clue about Black feelings and sensitivities, not to mention the abilities of educationally underprivileged Blacks.

Smith, a dean of students and faculty member who indicated that he enjoyed unusual rapport with students because of his respect for them and his forthright commitment to their welfare, talked about how he handled such situations.

> In responding to these situations it helped that I was a tenured professor who had been at Denison for a long time. Most of the faculty members were good friends of mine who viewed my job as difficult and thankless and saw me as a teaching colleague. I lived on campus and many faculty members were neighbors and our kids were friends. I could call up or go see the professor and say, "Hey, do you realize what message this sends? Real progress, D? If you're going to say that, don't give a grade at all or make it higher. Do you realize what a D means? D means dumb to a Black student."

Another Black student would come in and say that the word "nigger" had been written on her door. I would usually go over to her floor that night, meet with all of the students, and say something like, "If I find out who did this, there will be one less student at Denison—and I will find out who did this." I almost always did. I was a very aggressive dean, especially when it came to racism. Three national fraternities found that out the hard way.

Aggressive responses to racist incidents were what the Black students needed and deserved. The demands were a political device, but when real needs arose, such as the need for someone to confront an insensitive White student or staff member, I responded immediately.

THE HUMAN BOMB INCIDENT AND OTHER "EFFECTIVE" TACTICS

In the spring of 1970, the spring of Kent State, things began heating up, but it all seemed more like mimicry of what was happening elsewhere than like something threatening. Black students would come into my office and spit out a few dirty words. There was clearly unrest, both among African American students and among students, mostly White, protesting against the war.

Smith recounted the "human bomb" incident as an illustration of burgeoning student unrest:

In February of 1971, I was on sabbatical and got a call at home on a Sunday from the interim dean, one of my best friends. He said, "We have a problem over here. As you may know, we had a fire bomb threat against the administration building and we have to close it and post it, or the National Guard will come (think Kent State). We have a student sitting in the middle of the upstairs hallway in front of the president's office who will not leave, and we cannot close and post the building until it is empty. We have to empty the building but he will not leave."

I said, "You've got a human bomb." And he said, "What's that?" I asked, "Is he small?" He said, "Yes." I said, "What's his name?" He said, "David Lowenstein." And I said, "Yep. Don't touch him." He said, "What's going on?" I said, "You're supposed to get frustrated because you have to close the building because of the bomb threat. You have to get that kid out of there. Because the building doesn't have an elevator, you are supposed to carry him down the steps." I asked, "How many students are out in front of the administration building?" He said, "About 300." I said, "Right. You're supposed to pick him up and carry him down the stairs. He will break loose and fall down the stairs. You will have brutalized him, and that will radicalize the crowd. That's the human bomb."

So he said, "What do we do?" I said. "Just stay there, I'll get him out of there." So I went over, went upstairs and said, "Hi, David, how are you doing?" And he said, "I must have a dialogue with you, Dean Smith." I said, "I can't, David. There's been a bomb threat. You have to leave." He said, "Unless we have a dialogue, I'm not going to leave." And I said, "Fine. I'll give you five minutes." He said, "Then we'll have a dialogue?" I said, "No, we'll have the dialogue outside." He said, "No, we must have it here, Dean Smith, you know that." I said, "Right, five minutes." So after five minutes, I said, "David." He said, "Yes." I said, "Unless you leave right now, I'm going downstairs to my office and I'm going to call your mother." With that, David stood up and left the building. As he left the crowd was calling him dirty names. "Oh, you chicken shit!" To which David replied, "He was going to call my mother!" That's exactly what he said, "He was going to call my mother!" He was a good son and his mother wouldn't have liked what he was up to. Two weeks later, my office was firebombed.

Earlier that winter, during a faculty meeting in the auditorium on the top floor of the student union, a faculty member had to go to the bathroom. He went to the door and it wouldn't open. He looked back, and I can remember it to this day, he said, "The door won't open." So several faculty members went over and tried to push it open, but it was blocked on the outside by bodies. The hallway around the auditorium was completely jammed with students. The faculty got very claustrophobic; everybody was saying, "What are we going to do?" Suddenly one of the doors opened and a small group of students came in with bushel baskets full of apples and threw them at the faculty from the stage, injuring several of them. They threw them point blank, as hard as they could throw them. "Apple for the teacher!" Whack! The bad dream had begun.

It was a demonstration and it was more about power than about rights. These were not Denison students who were angry about the war and no Black students were involved. These were students who were being coached on how to "de-dignify" the establishment and get all hell to break loose. It was about provocation. Confrontation and provocation were the weapons of highly organized protesters. The faculty member whose class was disrupted and couldn't teach because of the dirty words being yelled from the back of the room was supposed to yell and scream and kick the disruptive student out, thus inciting more unrest—so much for academic freedom. We were in trouble.

THE CAMPUS TAKEOVER OF 1971

One year after Kent State, I was returning from a fishing trip and drove up the front drag of the college into a nightmare. When I got to the top of the drag, I saw that there weren't any cars. It was a Sunday, but there weren't even any student cars in areas where students always parked. I walked up onto the quadrangle only to find that the buildings were wrapped in gray crepe paper with giant signs out front that said things like, "Arts/Crafts/Self-Discovery." The teaching departments of the buildings had been changed to a new curriculum. There was trash everywhere, but no human beings. It all had the feel of the morning after an enormous party with lots of lots of psychedelic drugs and a Woodstock atmosphere. I went to the basement room where the telephone operator worked and there she was. I said, "Mary Katherine, what happened?" She said, "Oh, Dean Smith, we were closed down." And I said, "Where is everybody?" She said, "They're out in the country at Professor Hepp's house. The protesters drove the administration off the campus; they drove the faculty off the campus; they beat up students who tried to go to class; and they really hurt Peggy (the president's secretary)! I don't know where the students are." All of this was done by a small group of students (about 40 White students and three Black students) working with professional agitators and a group of five White faculty members who had declared themselves the new administration of the college. One of the faculty leaders, Bill Preston, was a close friend of mine. The takeover was billed as a pro-Black demand, antiwar boycott, but a new issue had taken over—the issue of faculty power.

I then drove to my home on the edge of campus. My house was filled to the gills with dorm advisors, fraternity and sorority officers, the Black student leaders, and about a dozen faculty and staff. My wife and children were serving food and drinks. The whole group seemed to be having a ball. Everyone welcomed me with open arms. I said, "What's going on?" and Henry Durand, a Black student leader who is now a college professor, came up to me and said, "You lost your college, dean." And I said, "Who's got it?" He said, "Your faculty buddies and the dudes from Columbus." He knew two of the professional agitators, well-known, Black leaders from Columbus. I said, "I hear the president is out a Maylon Hepp's house in the country. And he said, "Yep, and the trustees are there, too."

So I called the Hepp house and said to the faculty member who answered, "This is Mark." And he said, "Oh, my god, are you back? Where have you been?" I said, "I've been fishing." He said, "Get out here right now. Joel (the president) needs your help." So I went on out. When I arrived, the president and the board chairman handed me a beer and took me into a bedroom. They had been drinking better beer than the people at my house, but weren't having as much fun. They were traumatized. They didn't know what to do and they couldn't understand how they had gotten thrown off the campus. Evidently there had been some real violence, but they weren't sure whether students had been involved or if it had been nonstudents from Newark or Columbus. They asked me to break the whole thing up, restore order. I asked, "Where in the hell are the students?" They said, "They're in Huffman Hall (the women's dining hall). They've been there for two days, and they are singing and yelling and making speeches and celebrating and developing the new curriculum. I asked, "Who's developing the new curriculum?" And they said, "Your friend, Bill Preston, is leading it from the faculty standpoint." They also told me that about 300 students had packed up and gone home. I said, "I'll take care of it." "What are you going to do?" And I said, "I'm going to break it up." "How?" I answered, "I don't know," and left for Huffman Hall.

When I got to Huffman, I walked up the stairs into the dining room and there they were. Hundreds of students were sitting on the floor. One of the students was yelling into one of the standing microphones scattered throughout the crowd. The faculty leaders sat behind a table on a platform facing the students. At another table were five Black adults and a White man I had never seen. Suddenly, Bill Preston stood up on the stage and said, "Hey, ladies and gentlemen, guess who has just joined us, the great Dean Smith." Then he yelled, "Mark, it's great to see you; why don't you just come up here and say a few words." At that point all of the students laid down on the floor so I couldn't get by. I walked over them and on them. I heard a few squeals, but I didn't stop. When I stepped up onto the stage, I was, of all things, sad. The thought that came to me was of the president's delightful secretary on the morning of the takeover being hurt by the protesters. Preston said, "Hey Mark, where have you been? We noticed that you weren't here. Kind of yellow, aren't you?" I said,

"I've been fishing, Bill, you know that." He replied, "Sure, fishing, fishing for a way out of trouble. You don't like trouble, do you, Dean?" I said, "No, I don't Bill; I don't like trouble." Then I turned to the students and spoke. I won't repeat here what I said, but it was harsh. I concluded by saying "You're nothing. You're just a bunch of mush. And every one of you is ugly." At the end of my statement to the students, I turned to Bill Preston and the other professors and again I said something I won't quote right now. It wasn't dirty, but it was very personal and very hostile.

With that, Preston and the other professors jumped me. I guess they didn't hurt me very badly, but they did knock out a couple of my teeth. I am, as Preston said, pretty yellow and I'm not used to getting hit, but actually, I was too unhappy to feel anything. The professional agitators ran out of there. They were absolutely the fastest humans I've ever seen. They were gone.

Then I just got up and left. The students separated to let me walk through. They were aghast. As I left, I passed the president and the board chairman who had come to witness the event from afar. I went home and had a beer. My wife came in about a half hour later and said, "You have a problem." And I said, "I know." She said, "You better look out front." Perhaps 200 students were sitting on my front lawn. They had come to say they were sorry. I told them they didn't have anything to be sorry about, to go back to class. Then the phone rang— it was the president. He said, "Could you come back out here?" And I said, "Sure." I went back out there and the president said, "Mark, we would appreciate your doing us one more favor. You've certainly done enough already, but we hope you will help us with one more problem. I said, "Sure, what do you want?" He said, "Would you meet with the Black students and tell them that we will grant all of their demands." I said, "Sure. I'd be glad to." The president and board chairman said, "Thank you, Mark, and God bless you."

When I got back to my house, the Black student leaders were still there. I said, "I've got great news for you about the demands." Henry Durand, the leader, said, "I bet you they told you to tell us that we can have them, right?" I said, "Right." And he said, "Okay, Smith, what's it going to be?" And I said, "You get shit." And he said, "I was hoping you would say that." I said, "You get nothing, Henry, and you know damn well why." And he said, "You're right." And we've been friends ever since. The Black students agreed. They no longer cared about the demands because they had been used. They had known for some time that their cause had been taken away from them by the faculty radicals.

After that, I didn't talk to anyone at the college for about a week. The next contact I had with the president was when I walked into his office and quit. One crucial but touchy point should be made. The takeover never would have happened if the top leadership of the college had been strong. I was on sabbatical because I had decided to move to full-time teaching rather than being part of an accommodative, image-conscious administration. Two years before the takeover, the marvelous president who had hired me in 1953 and made me a dean, one-time NASPA President, A. Blair Knapp, had died suddenly. He was replaced on an interim basis by his strong dean of the faculty, my close administrative partner for 14 years, who then returned to full-time teaching in the psychology department. The new President who arrived in 1969 was not what Denison needed at that time. He simply cared more about looking good, being popular, and making fancy speeches than about representing the rights of the institution. The new dean of the faculty came from the faculty, and was a problem avoider. The senior faculty leadership had been shoved aside as old fashioned by younger, more liberal faculty leaders. And the board of trustees, like many boards at that time, not anxious to get involved in the actual life of the college, didn't even know what was going on. Although the new president immediately became a close friend and made me his chief lieutenant, I was seen primarily as a usefully powerful holdover from a previous regime. Joining the weaknesses and naiveté of the top leadership in opening the door for the opportunistic protest leaders was the gullibility of students who wanted to feel they were making a difference in the causes of equality and peace.

Another advantage for the takeover leaders was the ever-present fear of institutional embarrassment. The president and his staff feared that any administrative aggression would lead to negative publicity. They needn't have worried. One of the most significant events in the history of higher education—the Denison takeover—was never even noticed. That tells us how wonderfully removed from reality that marvelous college was. I still hear from many of those students. They always say, "I have no idea what I was thinking." I remind them that they couldn't have known because they weren't thinking, they were radicalized by a situation, feelings, and techniques that were totally new to them. For perhaps the first time in their lives, they felt that they had a political cause worth fighting for. I tell them, "Don't worry about it. You didn't do anything wrong; you just got suckered." They did get suckered and it was too bad. When the whole thing finally congealed into a mass meeting with microphones and speeches, and everyone sitting on the floor with the faculty leaders sitting up on the stage with the professionals, it was glorious, just glorious.

I also hear from the Black students who were involved. They, too, look back with some regret and confusion, especially about how their cause was taken away from them. When I spoke with Henry Durand at a recent reunion, he said,

> We knew when school opened in the fall of 1970 that the play had been taken away from us. We were invited to none of the significant meetings. Our advice was politely listened to and then ignored. In the week prior to the takeover, we were sort of asked not to participate.

The reason the Black students lost control of their own movement and ended up at my house during the takeover was that they were never confident or secure enough in the Denison environment to really believe they had rights. The only Black leader who consistently demonstrated confidence was Henry Durand, and that was because he was a football captain. This theory is supported by the fact that the Black students from that time have never participated in alumni events. They formed their own alumni organization.

After the 1971 incident Smith stepped down as dean of students but stayed on as a tenured professor.

> I taught for another year. I stayed as a teacher because it was too late in the spring to hire a qualified replacement in the psychology department. I stayed and taught the next year, and then I left.

LESSONS LEARNED

What's to be learned from involvement in an incident such as the takeover at Denison? Smith's reflections focus on the personal and professional, as well as on the student affairs profession in general. When asked what effect the experience had on his life, Smith replied:

> I think the only significant effect was to convince me that it was time to move on. I had been president of NASPA in the year before the takeover, and that experience had essentially completed my development as an educator and student personnel administrator. I am a

"segmenter;" always have been. What I mean by this is that I've never allowed my emotions to hang around after a difficult experience or to interfere with my behaving rationally and confidently. Also, I've never wasted time on hindsight or regret. One of the reasons for this has been my accessibility. As a dean, I was always dealing simultaneously with a large number of emotional situations involving young people, and each situation demanded my undivided attention and clear thinking. Identifying a student killed in an automobile accident was emotional. Calling that student's parents required poise. Also, I taught almost full-time when I was a dean, and teaching, too, requires undivided attention and clear thinking. One of my former students who became a dean once referred to all of this as "Smith's telephone booth ability."

It may well be, though, that the takeover experience, like serving as NASPA President at a turbulent time for student personnel administration (many very fine deans were being replaced by clever individuals seen as more capable of helping institutions deal with radical faculty and unprecedented political/legal problems), left me with a feeling of completion. In any event, in my next 17 years as a chief student personnel officer, my style and principals remained essentially the same.

In looking back on his career at Denison and his work in student affairs in general, Smith reflected on some of the lessons learned, but he sees these matters more as things for the field to think about than as lessons he learned.

FAIR AND EQUAL PARTNERSHIPS BETWEEN TEACHER AND STUDENT

I am convinced that the key to education is a genuine partnership between teacher and student, dean and student, and institution and student, and I mean every student. In this context, accessibility and respect for students are more important than discipline, control, or services. Further, forthrightness, patience, understanding, and humor are more important than administrative strength, image, or stature. When I was talking to former students at a recent Denison reunion party for the classes of 1957, 1958 and 1959, they kept saying, "My God, we're talking as though we just talked yesterday and it's been 45 years." One would say, "Do you know me?" and I'd say, "Damn, is your dog dead yet?" or something like that. I knew every one of them. Genuine partnerships are ageless. I once asked my wife, who was a student at Denison in the late 1960s, "Why in the world did women students come to me with such unbelievable personal stuff?" And she said, "Because you couldn't be shocked and because we knew we could trust you completely and that you'd either help us or find somebody who could. Most of all, we knew you wouldn't be judgmental."

The reason such a partnership is essential is that, despite the student rights and freedom rhetoric of the late 1960s, students actually have only those rights that are intentionally and willingly given to them by the institution. The takeover was nothing but a hopelessly ill-fated spree. That's why it was so easy to squash.

HUMOR

Too few administrators today have a real sense of humor, or perhaps better, a real sense of the ridiculous. Jim Lyons, one of my favorite deans of all time, was always truly funny. Even when he was deadly serious or pissed off, he always had that marvelous sense of humor. If one has power, humor engenders trust and respect. Humor can create friendship between unequal people that isn't patronizing and can destroy counterproductive fear. Humor is too rare now, and I put much of the blame on drugs. In the first place, drug use was the first thing that large numbers of students did that was wrong for reasons other than that they weren't old enough. It was also, when it first arrived, the first unacceptable behavior that most adults knew little about. Throughout higher education, drug use has produced a watchdog mentality that precludes humor, as well as discipline without perceived understanding, which destroys trust. Throw in the arbitrary lowering of the legal drinking age and the arrival of the government's alcohol and drug-free environment law, and we have a result somewhat similar to what happened as a result of the Black student quota edict—colleges working so hard to implement programs not clearly related to their missions or values that students see themselves as victims of institutional expediency. The loss of humor is a symptom of a more serious disease.

THE IMPORTANCE OF COLLEGE STUDENTS

Clearly, Smith's relationship with students was unique. He was a chief advocate of students and he worked very closely with them. Smith played a key role in empowering students to take on vast leadership roles and responsibilities. Smith's ruminations about his career and about higher education express his regret that the time when students and their needs were more clearly the focus of campus life is long gone.

The wedges driven between students and administrators and faculty have created other problems. The people I know who are in the profession now, and many of them are former students, are more disapproving and distrustful of young people than they should be. For example, I think anyone who would say to a young person, "How in the world can you stand that rap crap?" makes a stupid mistake. As a rock historian, I know how shortsighted it is to disparage a young person's musical preferences (or appearance). Just as troublesome is a decline in respect for privacy. I think any dean who expects or allows professional or student staff members to invade a student's privacy with room checks or unannounced searches is irresponsible. I think there is a tendency these days to want respect from young people without giving it. If young people don't get the feeling that you respect them as much as you expect them to respect you, your credibility and influence are dead.

At the larger public universities, other than a few unique institutions, the only elements of the undergraduate programs that are anywhere near as important as research, graduate programs, fundraising, and institutional image, prominence, and influence are athletic programs that create alumni and community support and positive national publicity. Throughout higher education, the faculty and administration are not accessible. I talked to a young woman the other day who is a sophomore at a small liberal arts college, and she didn't even know the name of her dean. Faculty advising, once a major factor in faculty evaluation, is now too often a resented and neglected chore. Students are being given less—often only token—leadership and administrative responsibility. The RA position used to be the most coveted leadership position in the liberal arts college. Students wanted badly to be members of the administrative team. Much of that is gone, in part, because of the emphasis in student affairs on policing and discipline. Former students who were at Denison in the 1950s and 1960s marvel today at how important and respected they felt, how proud they were to be the primary citizens of the campus community (and they were). These feelings created high morale, intense loyalty, and strong identification with the institution. They also created a real sense of responsibility (students never littered or vandalized the way they do now).

These feelings were the heart of the undergraduate experience. They are much less common now because much of the emphasis has shifted to faculty recruitment and morale, the college's image and reputation, and the size of the endowment. It's almost as though the dean is told: "You take care of the students; we have more important matters to take care of and more important people to please. And make sure the students don't embarrass the college or upset the faculty." These are not easy times for college graduates; the twenties have become the toughest times of many lives. It is tragic that so few of those who have had the advantage of a college education have had an experience as dignifying and appreciated as the one enjoyed by the Denison students I knew.

FINAL REFLECTIONS

One very important thing needs to be understood: I never viewed the experiences described here as unfortunate or unfair. This is critical in terms of understanding my style and perspective. Jim Rhatigan has a story that he loves to tell. It's about a young man who was very mild and humble and somewhat shy who challenged Mark Smith to a skateboard contest. They went to the top of a very steep incline, and both got on their skateboards and took off. As they were careening down the incline, they suddenly hit a bump and flew into the air and crashed together. As a result, their personalities were intermingled. The result of this accident was two completely confident, outspoken, assertive deans. I did my job as well as I knew how. I stuck by my principles and beliefs, and a wonderful college with wonderful students and a great faculty was seriously injured. Fortunately, it recovered completely. I was embarrassed more than anything else. I was embarrassed about the way I talked to the students in Huffman Hall. And I was embarrassed that all of those students ended up so ashamed. I wasn't very proud of becoming the clever, powerful man who blew the lid off of the boycott rather than the helpful dean who was also a respected teacher.

I will always be proud of the final response of the Black students. They didn't want to win without earning respect for their rights. At that moment, the civil rights movement arrived at Denison.

EPILOGUE

After Smith left Denison in 1973, he was hired as a psychology professor and vice president for student affairs at Union College in Schenectady, New York. Smith was fired in 1978 after exposing a hockey scandal at the college. Smith then was hired by Eckerd College in Florida, and served as a professor and vice president of student affairs until 1990. When Smith retired, he began working as a rock historian, specializing in heavy metal. Smith has always loved rock and roll music, and it is one of the things throughout his career that has helped him feel connected to students. Today, Smith is now known by some as a "metal head on Medicare."

JUDITH M. CHAMBERS
Mount Union College (1960-1968)
University of the Pacific (1968-the present)

Judith M. Chambers was dean of women and director of the student center at Mount (Mt.) Union College in Ohio and then she returned to University of the Pacific, her alma mater, where she was named vice president for student life. Mt. Union is a small private college; Pacific is a medium sized private university with campuses in three California cities: Stockton, San Francisco, and Sacramento. Whereas some of the chapters in this book focus mostly on civil rights of African American students, Chambers defines civil rights broadly to include women's rights.

PROFESSIONAL PATH

Chambers described her career path.

> I went to the University of the Pacific, the school where I am now, and graduated in 1958, and then went right on to graduate school to get a master's degree. I had two assistantships in graduate school. Thanks to the president of Pacific, one was in the dean of students' office. He knew of my interest in pursuing a career in student affairs. The other assistantship was in the department of speech, which was my major. At the end of those two years (1960), I was certain when the president called unexpectedly to invite me to come over and see him it would be for the purpose of offering me a full-time job. I thought I had done a good job with the responsibilities I was given and I loved being at Pacific. But that was not to be. In his wisdom, he said, "I'll help you find a job some place else. You need to go away and grow up. If you don't leave here, you will always be a student." (And he indicated, "Oh by the way, when I think you are mature enough I'll invite you to come back!") It was very paternal. That's exactly what happened.

Many people including President Burns helped me find my job at Mt. Union College. It was a brave president, indeed, who hired a 23-year-old to be dean of women, as I was barely older than the seniors. I was turned down a lot. I probably wrote a hundred applications, and the response was always the same. They were looking for someone with more experience. In any event, President Carl Bracey hired me to be dean of women at Mt. Union College in 1960. I was there for eight years.

Mt. Union Years

I had never been out of California before. I really wasn't even sure where Ohio was. But those eight years at Mt. Union College proved to be very defining years in my professional career. I greatly admired the president I worked for and I found it to be an extremely rewarding experience. In the beginning, I had a lot of difficulty being accepted by the students. What I had not known was that the former dean of women was asked to leave. She was very highly regarded by a certain portion of the student body. In the beginning, it was very difficult for them to accept me. But eventually, it did happen. A very big part of my Mt. Union experience was the opportunity to start new programs, to change a lot of antiquated rules, and to have my first real professional experience working as part of the president's cabinet.

Chambers indicated that Mt. Union College was quiet up until about 1968 when she left. She noted that even Kent State, only 25 minutes away, was quiet in 1968. She did recall a couple of incidents that did occur during her tenure at Mt. Union.

Looking back on my years at Mt. Union, I can think of two or three things which, broadly stated, could fall into the category of civil rights. There were very few minorities at Mt. Union College. But in the late 1960s, I recall that a White woman and a Black man were dating. I knew the woman much better than I knew the man. You will recall that in those days jobs were divided by gender and not by responsibility. The couple was very well accepted on the campus as far as I could tell. The problem was with their parents. There was also a great deal of concern expressed about the possibility of their marrying and having children, and how difficult it would be for their children to find acceptance. I talked with the female student many times. I believe they got married but I have now lost track of them. There was some general acceptance of interracial dating in the 1970s, but not all faculty and students approved.

Chambers estimated that two or three percent of Mt. Union students were African American.

> I remember another incident, though I don't remember all of the details. The dean of men was out of town. One Saturday night, I received a phone call from the campus police. There was an incident between two fraternities. A cross had been burned on the lawn of one of them. I went back to the campus. I had absolutely no experience from which to draw any ideas about how to deal with this situation. When I got to the campus, the police had separated the fraternity men who were all standing in front of their respective houses. It was very noisy. As soon as the men saw me, you could hear a pin drop. The whole situation just seemed overwhelming. I didn't know what to do or what to say. I just knew I wanted a cigarette. Without thinking, I said, "Does anybody have a match?" And for some reason the men thought that was funny and they started to laugh and it broke the ice. Someone gave me a light and I then invited the leadership of each fraternity to my office to talk with me. The conversation continued for some time after that evening.

> Because there were so few minorities at Mt. Union, it was difficult for people of color to feel at home. Again, my recollection is that some of the offensive things that happened were just that. They happened. I don't know that they deliberately meant to incite a riot or cause trouble. Most students simply had no experience with sensitivity training or race relations. Even though Mt. Union was relatively calm, it was obvious that tension was building, because two years after I left, Kent State erupted.

We asked Chambers about parietal rules at Mt. Union.

> During my tenure I established honor dorms. I have no idea where that idea came from. I like to think that maybe it was my own, but maybe I had heard about another school doing it. Those students who lived in honor residence halls had no hours. They could come and go as they pleased. In the early 1960s, that was a lot of freedom. There were waiting lists for students to live in the honor dorms. There were several of them, but the rest of the women had curfews. It was also a time of panty raids, and we had lots of those. We knew they were coming, and most of them at least started out to be fun. But on some

occasions, particularly if the men had been drinking, they did become mean spirited.

At Mt. Union, one of the things of which I was keenly aware was that there was no sex education, and there was no place to go should a student think she was pregnant or in fact be pregnant. The pill was introduced in 1964, but it would be some years later before its use became accepted practice at Mt. Union. I was positive the pill would redefine the role of women in our country and I believe it has. I know there were some women's lives that were changed forever as a result of a lack of contraception. I know there were marriages that took place that should not have happened because of pregnancy. I felt very helpless. I did not know where to send women students except to Tijuana. I would never have sent anyone there. It was a very difficult time for men and women who were sexually active. I believe the availability of the pill hastened the women's liberation movement. It not only redefined women, but I think it redefined student affairs. We could begin to give students the opportunity they needed and provide the education that would help them make realistic, but responsible, choices.

University of the Pacific

When I came back to Pacific in 1968, I was not in student affairs. I returned to be assistant to the president, a position I held from 1968 to 1971. President Burns died in 1970 and a new president, Stanley McCaffrey, was named in 1971. President McCaffrey was a Berkeley graduate who had had a very successful student experience as a member of Phi Beta Kappa, the captain of the football team, and student body president. He had a deep conviction that life outside the classroom was a very important component of the student's educational experience. He quickly learned that my professional experience was in student affairs. He wanted to make a change in the dean of students' office and he asked me to become dean of students, a position I assumed in 1973.

Chambers explained her administrative staff structure at Pacific. There were two associate deans, one man and one woman, and the dean of students. One of the associate deans was the woman who had been dean of women when Chambers had been an undergraduate. The other associate dean was a man with whom Chambers went to school.

The former dean of students was moved to another position at the university. Some people in student affairs felt the male associate dean should have been promoted to dean of students. The president did not agree and thus appointed me. The male associate dean left at the end of the year to pursue a student affairs job in southern California. The female associate dean stayed, but there were many difficult months ahead trying to work together. In the end, we were able to do so with success. This needed to happen for the students' sake.

When my predecessor was dean of students, the situation was complicated by the fact that at that time we had three cluster colleges. Each one of the colleges had their own "preceptor" who functioned as the dean of students. Rules in the cluster colleges differed from one college to another, and then differed greatly from the rest of the university, over which the dean of students had responsibility. As I looked at this from the president's office, I thought it was a nightmare in the making. One of the first things the new president, Stan McCaffrey, did after his inauguration was to appoint a task force on student affairs. One of the most important recommendations they made was to centralize all of the functions of the dean of students' office, including those in the clusters. That happened in my early tenure as dean of students. Building a successful student affairs program could not have been possible without that consolidation. Not only did the consolidation provide an opportunity for better resource management, but programs became university wide in nature and all students played by the same rules. From that base, we could begin to build a first-class student affairs program.

When describing the person she replaced at Pacific, Chambers reflected more generally on some of the challenges facing student affairs personnel administrators during the 1960s and 1970s.

I think the former dean of students was in a very difficult position. He did not always enjoy the support of the president, and many of the faculty did not give him credit for understanding what students were all about. At Pacific, we had students clamoring for freedom, being against the war, and wanting controversial speakers on the campus. The president totally supported an open speaker policy. But in the early 1970s, Pacific was still a pretty conservative school with a Methodist heritage. We had a conservative board of trustees that did not always understand why the students had to hear from Angela Davis, or why there had to be nude dancers from Berkeley dancing on the chapel lawn. Supporters threatened to withdraw financial support. Both President Burns and President McCaffrey strongly defended the right of the students to hear from these speakers, to demonstrate, to cancel classes for teach-ins, and to generally keep the campus as open as possible. I fully believe that that is a primary reason we did not have as much trouble as other schools.

Even with the president's support, the job of the student affairs professional of the late 1960s and 1970s was extremely difficult. Like others, I wanted to be an advocate for students. I tried to support their points of view when they were reasonable. I thought it was important to provide venues for them to express their points of view, but the tension between members of our board, some of the conservative faculty, and even some of the conservative students also put the student affairs staff members in a position where they never felt they were either doing the right thing, or enough of the right thing.

Chambers characterized the student body at Pacific in those days as being 50 percent residential, mostly from California.

A strong contingent of students came from Los Angeles, the San Francisco Bay Area, Hawaii, Oregon, and Washington. I would say that there was some diversity, more than at Mt. Union, but not the diversity that we enjoy today. We had Blacks, Hispanics, and Asians; we had very few Native Americans. I do remember a very important incident that happened in 1969. I was still the assistant to the president but I was very much involved in the incident.

President Burns was very ill and the academic vice president, Jack Bevin, was running the university. He was very good at conflict management. A Japanese student by the name of Kelly Kitigawa, led a demonstration demanding that there be scholarships and support assistance for minority students. Out of that demonstration came what was called the Community Involvement Program. The program provided 200 tuition-free scholarships to minority students living in the Stockton community. The program also provided support services for those students, who at that time always met university entrance requirements. The program was originally housed in the School of Education and was later moved to student life. As the program grew and matured, the admissions standards changed so that, today, each student admitted to that program must first be admitted to the university. The program still provides tremendous support services for those students. It is interesting to note that in recent years the retention rate of students who enter and graduate from Pacific is higher in the Community Involvement Program than in the university at large.

As I reflect back on the creation of that program, I am reminded that an Asian student led the protest, but clearly in the beginning it was the Blacks who benefited the most. When I was vice president, there was a member of my staff who was part of that protest. She talks in a very positive way about the administrative response to the demands, but does remind me that it was a hard sell to a pretty conservative board of trustees. During the protest, the students took over the tower in which the president's office was housed. It was a good thing the president was not in the tower because there was only one way out. The president's office was at the very top of the tower. It was symbolic. The students occupied the tower all night. Early the next morning, faculty and staff brought the protestors coffee and donuts. The Community Involvement Program, which has turned out to be a star in the university's crown, was initiated by the students. Even though it is over 30 years old, I doubt that the university would have thought of it. Today, it exists as a tribute to the students, who in 1969 knew that there was a need to provide these kinds of scholarships and services to minority, first-generation, college students.

The Community Involvement Program was multicultural and multi-ethnic. There were people of all races involved. There were as many different points of view as there were races. We used to have a football team, and a lot of the football players were Black. One student that I got to know really well, who was not a football player, said to me, "You know, it is really hard for a Black man on this campus if you're not a football player." He told me that it was difficult because he was not accepted by the White students, but he also wasn't accepted by the Blacks either because he didn't play football. The Black athletes hung out together. When he would walk by where they gathered in the student center, he said they often made fun of him and he didn't feel comfortable. To a great extent, if you were not an athlete, Pacific probably was not a very comfortable place for you to be if you were Black or any other minority in the 1970s. Part of the problem was that we did not have enough ethnic representation in the student body. There were no role models for those minorities who were there. We had one Black faculty member. We tried very hard to recruit Blacks to the student life staff, but we were not very successful. It was tough.

Concurrent with the racial unrest, there was also a lot of change going on with regard to student rules and regulations. As I talked with my colleagues in the public sector, I came away with the idea that private schools often had stricter rules and regulations. As a great example, for the women we still had curfew hours. On a residential campus, you also need to deal with issues related to alcohol, drugs, and the abuse of both. If you are on a commuter campus, those things become nonissues. There were a lot of behavioral issues on our campus. At Pacific, the most abused drug was beer. There was a lot of pot smoking, but we never had large numbers of students on the more serious drugs: LSD, cocaine, heroine, etc. I don't recall students ever developing serious addictions at Pacific. I do recall their bringing serious addictions to Pacific. I remember one student in particular who had a very serious drug problem. Ultimately, he was sent to a treatment program and never was able to complete college. I asked him when he started using drugs. He said, "When I was 12 my father gave me my first marijuana cigarette." As one looks back on those times, one needs to realize, at least in California, that it wasn't just the students who were abusing alcohol and drugs.

The fact that our campus was heavily residential was a plus in many ways. If a student got into trouble, we knew about it very quickly. This was a good thing because there was also a lot of acting-out behavior as a result of both alcohol and drugs. One day I got a call from public safety that two of "my" students were out on the back lawn naked, making love. When I went out to check it out, I discovered that one was a student, but the other was a faculty member.

One of the factors that made the late 1960s and early 1970s a happy experience for Chambers was the president's support for students.

I was very fortunate to work with Robert Burns and Stanley McCaffrey during those years of student unrest. President Burns initiated the open campus policy and President McCaffrey continued it. During his early years as president, McCaffrey was very visible on the campus. He jogged through the campus every morning often stopping to talk to students. He was known as the "Student's President." Upon his retirement, the board of regents named the student center after him. During his era, a number of student life programs were developed and enhanced. With McCaffrey's support, soon after I became dean of students, I abolished the hours for women. We initiated an all-university orientation program, a student-advising program, a wellness program, and we greatly enhanced the residential life experience.

During the early 1970s, many colleges and universities were dispensing condoms from their health center. For some reason, there was no conversation about birth control pills. I spoke with the President about that, but he did not think that was a good idea. I am uncertain whether he personally did not think it was a good idea, or whether he felt there would be severe criticism from the board if he authorized it. I felt it was really important to make these condoms available to our students. So, very quietly, I talked to a few staff members and suggested that the condoms be put in the vending machines in the student center. So there they were, right between the Fritos and the potato chips. The students found out very quickly where to find them. And soon after that we very quietly put them in the vending machines in the residence halls. I don't know if the president ever knew. If he did, he never said anything to me. But then, later, as times changed, we distributed both birth control pills and condoms in the health center. On an annual basis for many years we have celebrated National Condom Week.

In those days, members of the Stockton community viewed Pacific to be an elitist school for rich kids. To some extent, there are people in the community who still feel that way. But, in recent years, Pacific has launched a very ambitious outreach program to connect students and faculty with the Stockton community. That attitude is significantly reduced. In the 1960s and 1970s, Pacific was greatly misunderstood by members of the Stockton community. They did not understand our liberal policy on campus speakers. Any controversial action on the part of a student or a faculty member found its way to the front page of the paper, and of course protests were also misunderstood and not supported by the community. As I look back on it, I am surprised that we didn't have more unrest, given our close proximity to Berkeley. It was very clear that we received the benefit of many of their radical speakers.

When asked whether Pacific's proximity to the University of California at Berkeley, had any effect on student activism at Pacific, Chambers replied,

I think it did have a definite influence on our campus, because it was in very easy driving distance. And so students could go over there and hang out on weekends and come home and raise similar issues. However, I don't know how much we learned from Berkeley because, by the time I got into student affairs at Pacific, the eruption had already taken place. Clearly one of the benefits of being so close to Berkeley and San Francisco was that we had access to all those good speakers.

I just remember when Angela Davis came to the campus, our students filled the chapel; but they started drifting out as soon as she started to talk, because she was making very little sense. I'm not sure whether she was tired, on drugs, neither, or both. But she did not hold their attention, because she was just not saying anything that mattered to them. There were a few students who stayed. Timothy Leary's visit to our campus was very much the same way. I went to listen to him and he was just so burned out on drugs. He didn't hold any one's attention. I always had a lot of trouble with the Timothy Learys of the world, who deliberately led naive college students down the primrose path, where they got involved in drugs, burned out their brains, and never got over it. Their lives were ruined by being followers of Mr. Leary. In those days, students thought he could save the world. I often wonder whether he did more harm than good.

ROLE OF STUDENT AFFAIRS AT A PRIVATE INSTITUTION

We asked Chambers to describe the role of a dean of students at a private institution on the west coast. She noted:

I am positive my experience in student affairs is very different than the experiences of my colleagues who work on campuses of 20, 25, 30 and 50 thousand students. I saw my role more as an advocate for students than as a police person. Once again, I need to point out the support the president gave to the student life division. In 1975, President McCaffrey proposed for the first time in the university's history that a vice presidency for student life be created. The board approved his recommendation and I was appointed to the position. As a result, I was now at the table with the other vice presidents. I was now in a position to advocate for students at the highest level. The creation of the vice presidency also sent a message to the faculty, and I think it sent a message to the student life staff as well. It was a message that students and student support programs are important.

At private universities, the parents of students are a very important constituency. Every time we made any major changes, we advised parents of those changes. Some parents thought we weren't being strict enough. Others thought we were giving away the store. Many parents were very vocal about their child's education. When they are unhappy, the sentence usually begins with, "We're paying $30,000 a year to send our..." When you work primarily with the 18- to

22-year-old age group, parental influence is a major factor in your ability to create social change.

I think most student affairs professionals would agree that the role of chief student affairs officer is probably fundamentally about the same in a private school as opposed to a state school. There are different constituencies and I think some subtle differences. But the general mission is similar. Student affairs professionals are not in the business to be police officers, even though at certain times we may need to act like one. We are there to be advocates for students. We are there to make sure the out-of-class life is a positive experience.

ROLE OF STUDENT AFFAIRS IN THE SEVENTIES

Being a student affairs professional in the 1970s had to be one of the most difficult jobs on any college campus. Day-in and day-out, if you were trying to do your job as a student affairs professional, you were making some group unhappy. It just seemed to be a time that, no matter what you did, you never won.

The job, on the one hand, was to help students be heard and to try to connect them with the people who needed to hear what they had to say. On the other hand, it was also our job to try to interpret the positions the university had taken on certain issues that were not what the students wanted. Often times we were explaining to students why change couldn't take place, even though we didn't support the decision that had been made. On a daily basis, I found myself in the middle of some argument. That was the result of feeling that I could be totally honest with the president in private, but I needed to be supportive of him and the actions that the board had taken in public. They were often exactly what the students did not want to hear. I would not have advocated for everything, particularly if I did not think it was reasonable. I would have been reluctant to support a battle I did not think we could win. One needs to carefully select the hill one is going to go down on. I often helped students from behind the scenes. I did not think it was my role to be out in front. I was happy to help students get what they wanted if it was reasonable and if it would benefit the student body. I did not help them build cases for underage drinking and the legalization of marijuana, even though I was invited to do so.

I can remember working with the students, helping them to frame statements and questions in such a way that the President or the board would not find them offensive. I can remember the many times that students advocated for membership on our board. The president supported it but the board said "no." After 25 years, it has finally happened. But it took a courageous chairman of the board to simply say, "This is what we are going to do."

I think one thing I have learned from the 1970s is to let the students speak for themselves. The president and the board want to know what students think and what they believe, and on so many occasions I think the students can sell their point of view far more effectively than any of the rest of us. I am frequently asked what the students think about this issue or that. I really encourage our board to ask the students rather than me. And now that there is student representation on our board, it can happen. I see my role as helping students, but behind the scenes. Empowering them to do what it is they need to do.

LESSONS LEARNED

Chambers expanded on the lessons learned from the 1960s and 1970s.

As I reflect back on those years in higher education, I am persuaded that the more open the campus, the less likely there will be trouble. Another way of saying it is that the more student-centered the campus, the less likely the students will feel disenfranchised. When there is a national crisis or there is an important issue, we learned it is important to listen. We learned it's important to have those open forums for students to talk and for us to respond. And if the requests are reasonable, we need to find a way to do something about it. If their requests cannot be approved, then we need to explain why. Even though students may not agree with us, they deserve to know why their request cannot be acted upon. I think we also learned there is no one point of view; there are many. And that you have to do what is best to advance the mission of the institution. There's probably no rule in the university that doesn't need to be reviewed at some point. There also need to be good reasons for not changing it.

I think one of the lessons we didn't learn from the 1970s is, if a student exhibits behavior that is not acceptable, then you deal with that student. If 10 students exhibit behavior that is not acceptable, then you deal with 10 students. The unacceptable behavior does not warrant a new rule for the whole community. I think we have a lot of rules we don't need because we don't deal very well with individual behavior. If one student does something wrong, it doesn't mean 6,000 others will do the same thing.

Students learned a lot from the 1970s: They learned how to protest and we learned how to listen. But sometimes we forgot the lessons we learned. I recall one example after President McCaffrey retired. A new president came to Pacific. Our tradition was to have one large convocation and small commencement ceremonies in each of the schools and colleges. The new president decided that all those commencements were unnecessary and, without consulting the people he should have consulted, i.e. the students, he announced that we would be changing from small commencement ceremonies, to one large one. He didn't do his homework. He simply announced that it was going to happen. Within several hours, there were a thousand students protesting this decision on the lawn outside the administration building. To his credit, he reversed his decision. The students respected him a lot for that. He never did admit that he didn't talk to the right people. I am sure he knew he was wrong, because he was willing to change his mind. The student who was student body president at the time is still a good friend of mine, whom I see regularly. We have often talked about that incident, and he is quite frank to admit that one of the lessons he's learned is that if you don't like the decision that affects you and you have not been properly consulted about it, you can protest. Somebody will listen. Somebody did and it worked.

DIFFERENCES BETWEEN CIVIL RIGHTS AND OTHER ERAS

The civil rights movement was unique and happened at a unique time in American history. It was a time of protest over many things, not just the inequities of the civil rights movement, but about a war nobody understood, as well as about an oppressive educational system that hadn't changed in more than a hundred years. It was a protest over rules that existed at the time of the founding of many colleges and were never looked at since then. It was a protest over curriculum that was not seen as relevant. It was a time of coming together over a general unhappiness about so many things. It was also the time the voting age was lowered. I do not remember anything like it before that time or anything like it since that time. It did forever change the way we view the world and the people in it.

THE ROLE OF NASPA

All of us in student affairs were searching to define our role during that time, and I believe NASPA was as well. As a professional organization, I think it was trying to provide what it could. But during those years, the paid staff was very little and it was not the sophisticated organization that NASPA is today. What I believe it did provide, which was most valuable, was a forum for us to get together and talk about how each of us was handling the problems we were dealing with. Through my involvement with NASPA, I was able to develop some very strong friendships with colleagues across the country who were an enormous help to me when I was dealing with very difficult issues. I'd like to think that the reverse was also true.

When I was president of NASPA in 1987, we moved our national headquarters to Washington, D.C. During the preceding years, there were endless conversations about the role of NASPA: How best to serve our membership, how best to serve students. During those discussions, we were able to articulate a clear position about our mission and vision for the organization. As the years have passed, NASPA has developed services, programs, and workshops that are of enormous help to its membership. The NASPA leadership has also been very thoughtful in addressing current issues that are important to the profession. Were we to go through another time of national upheaval, I believe NASPA would find itself in the position to be of enormous benefit and assistance to the membership because of the strength of the organization today.

EPILOGUE

After over 40 years in the student affairs profession, Judith Chambers became the special assistant to the vice president for university advancement at the University of the Pacific. She was president of NASPA in 1987 and continues to be active in the Association. She is also a very active member of the Stockton community, serving on several local boards including the United Way.

CIVIL RIGHTS AT
REGIONAL COMMUTER CAMPUSES

Augustine W. Pounds
Oakland University (1971-1975)

In the late 1960s, Augustine Pounds began her career in higher education as an administrative assistant to the vice president for urban affairs at Oakland University in Rochester, Michigan. At that time, Pounds, a young, single mother of two small children, decided to work full-time and simultaneously pursue a bachelor's degree from Oakland University. In 1971, she was appointed assistant director of commuter services, and by 1973 she served as the assistant director of Oakland's student center. In her administrative capacity, Pounds also served as the advisor to Oakland's Black Student Association. As the advisor, she helped the students plan activities and attended most of their events. As an African American woman on a predominately White campus, Pounds' experiences with racism and her strong sense of injustice helped her to develop a special connection with the African American students at Oakland. Pounds often saw herself as a buffer and mediator between African American students and the university. She determined early in her tenure at the university that her energies would be dedicated to enhancing the positive aspects of diversity and improving the racial and ethnic climate at the university.

It is from these vantage points that Pounds presents her views and experiences of how Oakland University responded to civil rights concerns and student unrest in the early 1970s. As she explained:

> It was a time when educational institutions were under attack. Higher education was on the brink of change. This was a time when institutions were also resisting these changes. Colleges and universities were trying to hold on to the discriminatory practices of past years. At the same time, students were demanding equal opportunity and access. At Oakland, students were demanding that their histories, their cultures, and their experiences be included in the curriculum. This was a time that reinforced my dream of a future beyond the segregated Pontiac,

Michigan community that I called home. Professionally, it was a time that challenged both my role as a university administrator and my role as advisor to students. It was also a time when upholding my responsibilities for student conduct and personal growth would be in conflict with upholding my role as advocate, supporting the students' right to demonstrate for change. It was a time and place that shaped everyone who lived through it. Those were challenging times for the student development profession.

In this chapter, Pounds shares her memories and perspectives of her time at Oakland, highlighting a particular student sit-in and how it changed the nature of the institution. It also provided valuable training for her as she advanced in her career to positions of dean and vice president for student development at other institutions.

CONTEXT AT OAKLAND UNIVERSITY

Pounds described Oakland University in the late 1960s and early 1970s:

> The university was quiet, rural, and isolated from surrounding towns. The closest store was at least 10 miles from the university. The campus was comprised of 10 to 12 buildings, including the residence halls that housed about 2,000 students. The majority of students commuted to campus daily and went home in the evening. It was a school where White, middle class students from the northern suburbs of Detroit enrolled to receive an elite education. The university was located just 10 miles from Pontiac, Michigan, home of a General Motors plant and working class families, many of whom were African American. By late 1960s, Oakland enrolled about 5,000 students, about 40 of whom were African American, mostly from the Detroit area. These African American students were quick to feel like outsiders, lonely and alone, if not unwelcome on campus and in the surrounding area. The campus population also included several groups of politically active, liberal, White students, mostly from the East Coast.

Pounds recalled a young, creative, and energetic faculty who expressed concern for student complaints, but who seemed reluctant to enact institutional change. In some ways, because of the young faculty, Pounds expected that Oakland would be open, supportive, and responsive to students.

> While many faculty members considered themselves to be liberal, the conservative faculty seemed to be more powerful and influential. It was the conservative faculty who refused to respond favorably to

students' criticisms. Oakland was one of the first campuses to have a unionized faculty who chose to exercise their right to demonstrate their dissatisfaction with a contract. The faculty refused to teach one fall semester in the early 1970s, causing the campus to delay the opening of school.

The staff and faculty at Oakland University in the early 1960s and 1970s were not very diverse. There was only one African American secretary. In addition to Pounds, there were few African American administrators—the director of urban affairs, the director of Upward Bound and freshmen services, and the director of campus security, and only about four African American faculty members. President Varner created the Office of Urban Affairs in the 1970s in reaction to community pressure to serve as a link to Pontiac's African American community.

Pounds recalled the major incidents that lead up to a student protest at Oakland.

On many campuses around the country, students were protesting against the war in Vietnam and South African apartheid. Women were demanding equality of the sexes. At Oakland, students were demanding curriculum changes. They wanted an increase in the enrollment of African American students and the hiring of more African American faculty and staff. They also wanted the campus climate and institutional policies to be more welcoming to African American students. The students wanted Oakland to institute changes in the name of justice. Further, they wanted to bring attention to the larger community that the administrators at Oakland were not responsive to their needs.

Students were struggling to understand and survive the tumultuous times. Tensions in Pontiac added to the tension on campus. Two specific incidents triggered awareness of racial inequalities among the students at Oakland. The first incident occurred when the first African American graduate from Oakland was killed by a gas station attendant who mistakenly believed that the graduate was armed. At that same time, the Pontiac public school system was ordered by the courts to desegregate. Several school buses were bombed to demonstrate opposition to the desegregation of the schools. Supporters of desegregation countered this violence with several community marches. Students at Oakland were active participants in these prodesegregation events. This setting provided the backdrop upon which the most memorable protest occurred at Oakland University.

THE PROTESTS AND TAKEOVER

In the early 1970s, the students decided that they would take action to improve Oakland's campus climate by demonstrating for change. In less than 24 hours, Oakland students attempted three different actions to bring attention to their demands for change. They first scheduled an appointment to meet with the president to discuss their concerns about the curriculum and the campus climate. When these students arrived at the office and learned that President O'Dowd had left his office, they became suspicious that his absence was purposeful. They marched to the center of the campus, meeting at the flagpole.

From the student center window, I could see a group of students gathered around the flagpole chanting freedom songs and making speeches. Some administrators were overwhelmed by the demonstration and began making phone calls to the African American staff to ask for information and advice. One administrator asked me, "What are we going to do, the flag has been removed?" My response was that we allow students to express their views. The students had a right to gather around the flagpole and demonstrate. I would later receive a phone call from the director of security, an African American man who had once been a police officer in Detroit. The security director informed me that the flag was missing from the flagpole. Knowing that I had a close relationship with the students, the director asked me to tell the students that if they had burned the flag, they would be arrested. I was also asked to monitor the situation and report back to him if the demonstration became disruptive to the campus. Initially, I was concerned about how the students would view my presence at the flagpole, and how I would respond if I observed any violations of the campus conduct code. What would I do if I learned that the flag had been burned? Each step brought me closer to the flagpole, the group of students, and a higher level of stress. Each step toward the flagpole brought me closer to the conflict in my role as an administrator and an advisor. I struggled with my internal conflicts over these roles. Could I represent the university and support the students without any conflict? Could I influence these students? Did these students trust me? Would they value my opinion? It would also be a test of my authority as an administrator to get them to disperse and return the flag.

One of the most pressing questions was what would I do if I saw a burned flag? I took the short walk to the center of the campus, toward the students at the flagpole, and called one of the student leaders aside to inform him that, if a flag had been burned, the police would have to be notified. There was no flag flying nor burned pieces visible, but I told the students that I would leave, and that they must produce a flag by 3:00 that afternoon or the university would assume it had been burned and have them arrested. At the end of the workday, the students had disbursed and the flag had been raised on the flagpole. We never knew whether it was a new flag, or the old one. We did not ask. I left campus for home that evening and assumed that the students were satisfied with their expressions of protest.

Thus, I was surprised upon my arrival the next morning that I had to push through a group of students gathered in the lounge of the student center. It struck me as odd that so many students were gathered in the TV lounge at that early hour. Standing near my office door was one African American student in a sea of White students. It was not unusual for me to arrive at work and have students standing near my office waiting to see me. It was also not unusual that all of the students were White, as the campus was majority White. I did not anticipate that anything unusual had happened but I was prepared for an update on the latest rumors. I later learned that the students were there to have breakfast in the student center because they did not have access to the cafeteria.

"Students have taken over the cafeteria," was the African American student's first comment to me. I asked her to come to my office and as we entered, the phone began to ring. It was the director of campus security. Without the usual greetings, he blurted out, "We don't want to arrest the students who have taken over the cafeteria. Do whatever you can do to get them to leave." He continued, "We don't want to arrest them, but if they destroy anything, there will be consequences." Within the next few minutes, I found myself transformed from staff person to mediator. My first priority was to call my supervisor to inform him that I was going to meet with students who had taken over the cafeteria. He told me to inform the president of my plans. The plan was to go immediately to the cafeteria to ensure that there was no damage. I wanted to protect the students from arrest.

I assumed that the president would give the order to arrest, so I called him to inform him that I would be meeting with students within the next few minutes. I informed him that I was in touch with security and wanted him to know that I was going to talk with the students. The president sounded almost desperate in his response, "Augustine, do whatever you can." I knew from that short conversation that I had his support. After hanging up the phone, I walked from the student center, crossing the bridge over a small artificial pond that connected the seven-story residence hall to central campus and the student center. The five-minute walk seemed to have taken an hour. I arrived at the door of the cafeteria where hundreds of students came each day for meals. Instead of the usual clerk checking IDs, there was one student standing inside the door at the entrance. Without having to knock, he opened the door and smiled. He was the same student who had led the demonstration at the flagpole the day before. His first comment was, "Don't ask us to leave." I wanted to know why they decided to take over the cafeteria. He said it was to get the university's attention. He continued to explain that they were denying student and staff access to the cafeteria as a means of getting the attention of the university administration.

I then asked to speak to all of the student leaders. We moved to the kitchen and the student left someone else at the door. Several students were in the kitchen preparing food for the students sitting at the dining room tables. The cooks were mostly men. Many of the students sitting at tables in the cafeteria were not African American. In fact, the group was racially mixed and working together to prepare food for those who had gathered. All of the students in the cafeteria appeared to support the take over.

My initial question was, "Tell me exactly what you want." At that point they had not formulated their demands. Instead, students gave me a list of criticisms and demanded a meeting with university administration. They had not made the demands known to administrators at that time. My plan was to help the students move from criticism to request. It was amazing how calming that process became. The leader of the group was instructed to write down each demand. I suggested the name of administrators—those who had decision-making authority related to the area of concern—who should be included at their meeting. My instructions were to look at the concern and identify an appropriate solution. The second step was to identify who could make the decision.

I tried to help the students understand that a successful resolution did not mean that they would get everything they wanted by the end of the meeting. Instead, I explained that successful negotiations are likely ongoing, and that there is some give and take throughout the process, but that they did not have to give up because they did not get what they wanted that same day.

Once the list of demands was complete, the students contacted the administration and arranged a meeting. President O'Dowd, James Appleton, and other significant administrators agreed to meet with the students and review their demands at the close of the business day. They met at the agreed upon time. The meeting between the students and the administrators went on for hours. The students' demands involved issues of recruitment of minority students, scholarships, curriculum revisions, food/menu options, and campus climate.

That day was a new beginning. It was the first time those students sat with the university administration to work together for change. There were ongoing requests and updates on the issues and demands identified by these students. There were celebrations of victories and compromises between students and administrators. The students continued to work on these issues throughout the next year.

The cafeteria take-over was a learning experience for all of us, but especially for the students, and the university administrators. The students learned how to develop a set of demands and to negotiate a favorable outcome. The university learned to listen to its students and respond to a changing society. And I learned how to be a better administrator and advisor. The experience was valuable to me in other campus experiences and in relationships with students.

OAKLAND'S RESPONSE TO THE SIT-IN

In response to the cafeteria sit-in, some changes were seen immediately.

The most important change, according to the students, was that students became more directly involved in the decision-making process at the institution. Students felt they had more of a say in decisions that affected their lives. In particular, a student committee was formed to make suggestions about food. As a result of this committee, once a week, the cafeteria offered a soul food meal option. In terms of curricular changes, the most immediate outcome associated with the sit-in was the creation of a for-credit speaker series that focused on civil rights issues. The lecture series was deemed a success, as both African American and White students regularly attended the events. The purpose of the series was to expose students to different ideas about race and civil rights. A second purpose was to help the different groups of students and the faculty and staff understand and accept diversity. African American students wanted the entire campus to see how much richer the community would be if it were more accepting of differences and more inclusive in teaching. At the same time, many in the administration feared that the lecture series itself might bring about more civil unrest. Some feared that lecturers might present ideas that would upset or incite the students. As a result, after every lecture, students, faculty, and administrators would meet in small groups and talk about the lecture in order to make sure that all issues raised were addressed. The lecture series was well attended and very popular. The fear of inciting a riot never materialized. A well-liked, White professor, who was committed to equality, chaired this effort.

Prior to the sit-in, housing rules were an explicit concern of the students.

While campus housing was integrated; if a White student was assigned to room with an African American student, all he/she had to do was complain and the student complaining could choose to move. By the end of the year, most African American students lived either with another African American or in a single room. This room change policy was eventually changed. Further, the housing department hired an African American couple, John and Patty Guthery, to serve as hall directors. They were both alumni of Oakland and served as a valuable resource to the students and the administration.

The Office of Admissions was another area perceived as needing to change. In addition to hiring an African American admissions counselor, the institution set goals to enhance the diversity of the student body.

Each year goals were set regarding minority recruitment. Initially, the goal was to recruit 100 African American students. When the goal was reached, the excitement was palpable. In terms of representation on campus, African Americans probably were as high as 10 percent of the student population by the middle 1970s.

Perception and image played a role in the institution's response to the sit-in.

In general, the administrators at Oakland appeared more concerned about the institution's buildings than the students. Looking back at its written history in the library confirms that the focus was on growth and development of the campus buildings. They were more concerned about the reputation of the institution than about the safety and development of the students. Still, because Oakland was a very young campus, founded in 1959, and the faculty was quite young, it was assumed by many of the African Americans that the administrators were probably more open to change than older, more-established campuses. We tried to bring about change without success. It was the students who helped the administrators see that it was to their advantage to be open to change. Deep down, those in charge knew that change was going to happen, and so they adopted an "if you can't beat them, join them" attitude. Even with this attitude, not everyone got what he or she wanted. The students did not get all that they wanted, nor did the administration hold onto everything that they might have treasured before.

PERSONAL LESSONS LEARNED

To understand the personal lessons learned by Pounds, it is helpful to know a bit more about her personal history.

My story, in some ways, is the story of many African American students on a predominantly White campus in the 1970s. The exception might be that I graduated with the honor of being the most outstanding student when I earned my first degree and was recognized by Oakland for my contribution. However, when I gained employment at Oakland University in the early 1960s, it was not easy or pleasant. Coming to Oakland changed my life forever. The belief and value system that I had grown up with was challenged daily. Racism was visible daily, but I had to decide what I could live with and challenge what was unacceptable. I had to decide how I would support students and how I would support my job responsibilities in order to keep my job. I knew, early, that I could not be a part of a system that denied me freedoms.

I had graduated from Pontiac Central High School and tried to gain admission to Oakland University several times and was rejected, even though I had excellent grades. Eventually I decided that I would get a job at Oakland in order to learn how students gained admission. Once hired as an employee, I learned the sad truth. Few students from Pontiac went to Oakland. My high school counselor never discussed college with me, and I never knew there were loans or scholarships available. Instead, the most common career plan for African Americans in Pontiac was to gain employment at General Motors.

After I had worked at Oakland for a couple of years, I asked my supervisor if he would allow me to take classes during my lunch hour and when I had free time. He granted permission and the admissions director approved with the condition that "you can only take this one course." I continued to sign up for courses in subsequent semesters using vacation hours and lunchtime for class and study time. I also took courses in the evenings. In three and a half years, I had accrued enough credits to graduate. When the other secretaries learned that I had completed most of the required course work for my degree, they filed a grievance against me for being a full-time student who received a salary rather than earning student wages. The personnel office examined my work and academic record and ruled in my favor; I was allowed to continue to earn my full time salary and complete my last semester. I graduated with the Matilda Wilson Award, the highest honor a student can receive upon graduation.

Those experiences kept me centered and focused on what was important and the challenges African Americans faced on campus. I always tried to transfer my strong beliefs in equity and fairness to the students and help them build a core that would influence their actions. I also stressed that they should not let the negative campus climate alter their dreams.

When I reflect back on the time at Oakland, I am disappointed that more of the faculty did not work for change. I often questioned why change was so difficult, but when I recently saw the film produced by Michael Moore, Bowling for Columbine, I understood. According to Moore, a White Michigan resident, Whites are fearful of African Americans. There was one experience that confirmed this belief. Shortly after the cafeteria take-over, students had approached my supervisor for support of an event. The supervisor and I had several discussions about his apparent lack of support. Since he did not support them, I wanted him to face the students and verbalize his lack of support. He wanted me to be the messenger. I went into his office and closed the door. He reacted to me entering the room by throwing his hands up and saying, "Augustine, wait just a second now—don't you to do anything that you will regret." I had gone into his office to tell him, "You must support the students. You must meet with these students." I wanted him to be the one to tell students he supported them and not send the message by me. I told him that I would not defend him to students. After several exchanges, he would not change him mind, so I agreed that I would not publicly state his position but I would be silent when asked about it and students could draw their own conclusions. At the last minute, he changed his position and supported the students. Years later, I learned that the administrator thought I had entered his office that day to strike him. I am still shocked at his belief that I was going to hit him. He had never seen me act in a violent manner, so why would he assume that I was going to be violent and hit him? My assessment of the meeting was that he had thought that I was going to resign, and he was warning me not to resign when he said, "Don't do anything you will regret." His reaction to me was an example of the silent fear that existed during those years as African Americans struggled to be a part of the campus, to get an education, and to have a better life.

The administration never asked me to betray students. In fact, a few days after the sit-in, the president called to thank me for getting the conversations started. After that, whenever there were racial tensions on campus, I would have the students come to my home in Pontiac to meet and talk and have a good meal. I usually informed President O'Dowd when I was meeting with students in my home and invited him on several occasions. He never joined us. The meetings were to continue the dialogue. Even if I had not had the support of the administration, I was comfortable with the off-campus meetings with students. The administration never asked me about the content of those meetings, and I never shared our discussions with them.

There were times when I had discussions with the administration about students and I knew that they wanted to know more than I was telling them, but I guarded my relationship with the students. The administrators knew that I shared some of the same concerns that students raised, such as justice and equity and the civil rights movement. They also knew that I wanted the best for all students. Although I felt at times I walked a thin line, I was comfortable in my position. I do not think that the students ever requested anything from me that I could not deliver. At times, when I was with students, they would ask me to leave their meetings. I respected that, but often reminded them that I could only support their behavior if it did not violate campus codes.

My experience with the sit-in at Oakland was useful years later. In 1984, I was a visiting faculty member at the University of Zambia in Africa and the students organized a strike. I met with the president of the university and offered my support. He accepted and the rest is history. Students were back on campus within the week after negotiating a settlement between the students and the administration. The president supported the intervention. After classes resumed, I continued to work with the dean of students' office in Zambia to respond to student concerns. It was a successful resolution and a positive effect on my year of teaching in Africa.

Integrity, fairness, equity, and hope are perhaps the words most often associated with my memory of the Oakland experience. We never lost hope that the increased activism and criticism by students would make the institution take a look at itself and change. I remember those years often and always feel a combination of joy and sadness—joy that I could be at the institution to support the students, joy that I was able to manage my life and receive my degrees with honor, but sad that I could not do more to improve the climate for students earlier.

THE ROLE OF NASPA

While at Oakland, I attended most NASPA conventions. I cannot recall coming away feeling empowered to handle a campus disruption. I do not recall being provided information that would help a university take steps to prevent a disruption. If there were "how to" guides or resources on how other campuses handle their issues, I don't recall ever being provided with that sort of resource. If it is true that life repeats itself, we will have disruptions again, and need to prepare future leaders on how to handle them. One idea might be to develop a system of collecting data and archive the data to learn from others' experiences. We might use models that are already being used with government collection of data, to chronicle events and issues on campus so, when they occur, administrators will have access to a body of information to assist them in handling the event. If events are chronicled, issues identified, and the process of resolution collected, universities would be better prepared to respond. It is not too early to review the major events around the world to see if there are current issues that students are concerned about and patterns that are emerging. This compiled data would give administrators a heads-up for responding to campus issues.

LESSONS LEARNED FOR STUDENT AFFAIRS

Reflecting back on the role of student affairs administrators at Oakland, I viewed student affairs more as a support system for the police than as an advocate for students. My views were confirmed when I returned to campus recently and reviewed several documents about life on campus in the 1970s. I learned that the campus police were a part of the division of student affairs. The vice president for student affairs was also responsible for buildings, maintenance, and judicial affairs. Those in student affairs were clearly the enforcers of the student conduct code. There is little in the history to show our role as advocates. When students were upset about the campus environment, the student affairs administrators expected them to manage their anger and deal with the issues that they faced. Our role was more to maintain order and serve as judges rather than focus on student development. It is surprising that students trusted and worked with us as well as they did.

Educating students must go beyond classroom learning. We need to provide well-organized activities where students can debate issues, hold forums, participate in student organizations, and provide feedback to the campus leadership. The campus unrest at Oakland provided an opportunity for students to develop leadership skills and become engaged in the life of the campus. It was an opportunity for campus administrators to recognize that students can contribute and make the environment better. Racism still exists today, although subtler and more silent, it is still as hurtful as it was in the 1960s and 1970s. Students need to be encouraged to talk about race and diversity, and institutions need to go beyond a surface kind of understanding about difference; they need to embrace difference.

As we look at campuses today, the residence halls, the Greek system, the representation of African Americans in the faculty, and campus social groups, it is clear there is still plenty of work to do. Today, however, we offer students diversity training just to meet a requirement. After the training is over, the commitment to diversity seems satisfied and the program plan moves to the next topic. When more is expected to eliminate the isolation, the response is often, "We had our diversity month, so we don't need another one." Rather than this approach, we have to do more to help students include in their core belief system a sense of fairness and respect for people who are different.

When I reflect on what institutional leaders learned, I am not sure if we changed that much as administrators. We need to embrace difference, because that is what helps build that core of who you can become. We need to provide both information and experience to bring about change. I believe this is where our students, both Black and White, were, and still are, shortchanged. In those days, and even more so now, we learned things from our students that we should have already known. We should have recognized that things were not right. Why did we have to wait for students to call our attention to the issues? I am proud of those students and what I think they learned from the movement, because they learned that they could influence change. The students were focused straight into the future. "We have our future to be concerned about," they used to say. The students' priorities were to make their environment better. This was and continues to be a worthy goal.

EPILOGUE

Augustine Pounds left Oakland University in 1975, after earning a master's degree in guidance and counseling from Oakland in 1974. She served in several student services positions at Iowa State University from 1975 to 1989, including serving as dean of students from 1984 to 1989. Pounds earned her doctorate in education administration from Iowa State in 1980. After leaving Iowa State, Pounds became vice president for student development and associate professor of education leadership at Murray State University in Kentucky, and then vice president for student services, athletics, and college development at Anne Arundel Community College for five years before retirement in 1995. In 1996, she became an executive consultant, focusing on fundraising, diversity, and leadership training. Among other honors, Pounds served as the president of the American Association of University Women—Legal Advocacy Fund, received a governor's citation for outstanding service and distinguished leadership, had an appreciation day named in her honor by the mayor of Annapolis, Maryland, earned both an Outstanding Leadership & Contributions to the Profession Award from the National Association of Women in Education and a George Washington Carver Memorial Award from Iowa State University, was awarded the Outstanding Contribution to Quality of Life of All Students at Oakland University as an alumnus and administrator, and was named Citizen of the Year from Oakland County in 1970.

JAMES R. APPLETON
Oakland University (1965-1972)

L ooking back on his career, James R. Appleton noted, "The most
difficult and challenging time in student affairs for me was from 1969
to 1972 at Oakland University. Fortunately, I had good mentors."
Appleton came to Oakland University in 1965, having just earned a Ph.D.
from Michigan State University. His first title at Oakland was dean of students. He later became the vice chancellor of student affairs. This chapter
represents Appleton's perceptions of his experiences with the social
revolution movement of the late 1960s and early 1970s while he was an
administrator at Oakland University.

CONTEXT AT OAKLAND UNIVERSITY

Appleton's descriptions of Oakland do not differ greatly from those offered
by Pounds (see prior chapter). When he arrived in 1965, there were fewer
than 10 African American students at the college, in an environment that
was primarily rural and suburban White.

> Within a period of three or four years, African American students
> from urban areas grew to represent about 15 percent of the student
> population. At the same time, Detroit and nearby Pontiac (the center
> of the busing crisis) were literally blowing up. The text under a news-
> paper photograph from 1971 read, "Pontiac firemen work to put out
> the flames in a school bus after opponents of forced busing destroyed
> 10 buses and damaged three others with dynamite." The crises on the
> Oakland campus should not necessarily be blamed on the new stu-
> dents, but on the situations that resulted from the rapid changes occur-
> ring within the academy itself and in America, and the inability of
> institutions of higher education to understand the full meaning of
> such changes.

Campuses erupted as a result of so many important events happening simultaneously—the Vietnam War, the civil rights movement, the women's movements, and massive social and personal value changes occurring in society. Furthermore, higher education itself was perceived by students as having both close connections with what they called the "military-industrial complex", and a general education curriculum and pedagogy that was not sensitive to the learning needs of the new generation of students. Institutions were rethinking their responsibilities in relationship to *in loco parentis*. Students of color, admitted for the first time in any significant number at many campuses, felt disenfranchised. The issues were real and the campuses became the focal point for dissent and protest. It was a very explosive time; nothing like it had ever been experienced in American higher education.

THE SIT-IN

As in Pounds' account, the most dramatic civil rights event at Oakland, according to Appleton, was the build up to and the execution of a sit-in at the campus cafeteria in the early 1970s. A number of incidents that occurred over a period of several years might be recounted, but this was one of Oakland's defining moments. According to Appleton:

> Representatives of the Black students decided that there were changes needed at the university and, after failed attempts to gain the necessary attention from faculty and administrators, they initiated a sit-in at the dining facility. Close to a hundred students, mostly African Americans with some supportive White students, occupied the dining room one early morning. The students developed a set of demands. They were wise in not publishing them, because this gave all of us negotiating room. When groups published their demands, and most did, there was little room for compromise. On this occasion, the demands were not outrageous. Instead, they were focused on student recruitment, support services, the curriculum, advising, and campus climate issues.

> The students submitted their demands to the chancellor. He asked me to meet with their representatives and so, in a residence hall office, if my memory serves me well, we met throughout the afternoon and the night. We left the room only for food and restroom breaks. To read Pounds' more detailed account of the events that surrounded this sit-in and these dialogues provides an intriguing picture of the commitment of several

staff and faculty members, and the importance of complementary roles and responsibilities among administrators and faculty.

In the end, we came to what I thought were good resolutions. Some of the immediate changes involved diversifying the food choices in the cafeteria and creating a speaker series to bring diverse perspectives to campus. Other demands, such as those involving recruitment of Black students and faculty, and changes in the curriculum, were designated as long-term goals. The student concerns were really items that any rational person would say, "If we had the resources to do that, we ought to." When the negotiations were concluded, I met with the chancellor and said, "If we can agree to get these things done, we've got a deal." He did agree, and then he met with the faculty. Some faculty members were displeased with both the process and the results, but we had come to an agreement. Some of the items we could implement immediately, some we could not accomplish, some of them we said we would consider further. It is significant that once it was clear that we, as well as the students, were serious, the student representatives went back to the dining room. Students cleaned up the dining room so that it appeared better than it was when they had entered, and then they walked out.

This recital does not portray the emotional drain and anxiety that accompanied these events of the 1960s and 1970s. And this by no means brought to a conclusion the tensions or occasional outbursts of violence among students, but credibility had been established and a context for further work was intact.

Credit should be given to Chancellor O'Dowd, now retired in Santa Barbara, California, for enabling us to engage in the process just detailed and not requiring us to remove the students from the dining room. Rather, he confronted those who might have clamored for a more forceful response and said, "Start working on this and see what we can do." The colleges and universities that moved too quickly had more problems. I think it worked at Oakland because it was clear we were willing to make progress in meeting reasonable needs for all students, even if these needs were expressed as demands.

THE ROLE OF STUDENT AFFAIRS IN RESPONDING TO CIVIL RIGHTS DEMANDS

Student affairs professionals across the country were the persons who were at the intersection between the students, faculty, and the administration. Many of us were searching for ways to manage a new subset of issues not previously faced in American higher education. There were few good models. The faculty members were no better prepared then we were. Their ideas about students were often a generation or two old. Their ideas about curriculum and pedagogy had worked for them in the past, but it was a new era in the academy. In the classrooms, when students would clamor for more relevancy, faculty members easily translated this into students questioning their authority and wisdom. When students said, "There is no relationship between what is being considered in the classroom and what is happening out there," this was not understood very easily by a faculty somewhat insulated from the "out there." The students, especially upward mobile Black students, wanted their classrooms to be much more relevant to them. The faculty was not resistant, but had difficulty understanding what this meant. There were occasions when students would stand up in class and loudly proclaim, "This doesn't mean anything for us. You've got to do it differently." The faculty was sometimes confused and often quite alarmed by such strong behavior. So, the best of our student affairs professionals became resources for faculty as much as for students. Part of our job was helping the faculty understand the meaning and reasons behind these disruptions, while we also tried to convince students to be more patient and understand some of the traditional values of the academy that could make a difference in their ability to succeed in the years ahead.

Student affairs professionals were in a difficult position because students expected us to be their advocate, but the presidents and chancellors also rightfully expected us to be on their team. My perspective about this was clear from the outset. I was not an advocate for students, but I was in a position where I ought to be most sensitive to students and their needs and perspectives. Further, I ought to help them know how to advocate effectively for themselves. There would be times when, because I was not their advocate and because I was a member of the administration, we would be at odds. I would work very hard to understand their perspective, and then determine an appropriate course of action as I took into account this perspective as well as the mission and objectives of the institution itself. I think this way of thinking about our responsibilities was absolutely essential for those of us who survived those tumultuous years.

THE ROLE OF NASPA

NASPA was viewed as having played a helpful role in responding to the realities faced on campus.

> When I was a member of the executive committee of NASPA or sitting around hotel rooms with colleagues (I admit I hardly ever went to the formally scheduled conference sessions), I gained immeasurably from some of the brightest and best. I suppose the names of Mark Smith, Tom Dutton, Peter Armacost, Carl Anderson, John Blackburn, Alice Manicur, Alice 'Tish' Emerson, and Jim Rhatigan are hardly household names now, but they were my mentors and professional colleagues. Without being critical of our colleagues at Kent State or Jackson State, we would pick each other's brains about why Kent State blew up and why Denver did not. NASPA was very important, actually essential, because it was a place for important dialogue among a group of talented administrators. There is no better educational environment than experiencing the refiner's fire of criticism and exchange with professional colleagues. We were not simply trying to "keep the lid" on the campuses. Of much greater concern was how to enable our colleges and universities to become more effective in educating a new student generation. Many became effective educators as well as adroit crisis managers, and we assisted our colleges and universities to become better institutions of higher education in part through the influence of NASPA colleagues.

PERSONAL LESSONS LEARNED

When reflecting back on his experiences at Oakland, it was clear that the social movements of the 1960s and 1970s not only had a strong effect on Appleton's current views and ideas about campuses and leadership, but also on his personal outlook. He explained:

> I was very much affected by those experiences. In the short run, there were days when the situation was almost overwhelming. They frequently drained all the energy and emotion that was available. In the long run, however, I certainly became more racially and ethnically aware. I guess it may also be accurate to say I became more self-aware.

> "The best of days and the worst of days" also brought a sense of humility. An example may suffice. After the sit-in just described, I sat, exhausted, in my office. Manuel Pearson, a dean at Oakland who was African American, came in, closed the door, and said, "How do you

feel?" I said, "I feel really good." He said, with compassion in his voice and not meaning to criticize me, "Well, nobody's going to thank you." I asked him what he meant, to which he replied, "This kind of attention should have been given 100 years ago. Why should you get credit for it?" Those were important lessons. I was forever changed by that.

I became more "allocentric," which I define as the opposite of ego-centric. A person who thinks this way can have well-established beliefs and ideas, but is able to understand and value the beliefs and perspectives of others. I am not pointing to myself as a paradigm of virtue in this regard, but I do believe understanding this and trying to live in this way is important. I am still pretty conservative, and many of my values are based on religious thought. Yet, I have a deep appreciation for the beliefs and perspectives of others. Much of this comes from those Oakland years.

I also think it is quite easy for me to admit I make mistakes, because I sure made my share in those years. This contributes to not taking oneself too seriously. In the most stressful times, one has to maintain a sense of humor. So, a story may be in order. Huey Newton, defense minister of the Black Panther party, was scheduled to speak at Oakland University the day after his presentation at Michigan State University. The Michigan State administration had agreed to let Huey's bodyguards search all those attending the event, and had barred all news media personnel. We were obligated to follow suit. So, when the news media arrived at Oakland midday with notebooks and TV cameras in tow, I had the "pleasure" of announcing the closed session that was being held in the gym. I thought I had convinced Mr. Newton's entourage to have him meet with the press following his presentation, and so I promised this to the media. They waited patiently, and not so patiently, as I remember, in a classroom in the building while Huey Newton raged on. He was a very rambling speaker and often went on for a couple of hours. This was our experience that day.

Anticipating the conclusion, I encouraged the press to exercise patience if they wanted to talk with the speaker. However, upon finishing his lengthy performance, Huey Newton wished the audience well and was hurried out the back door of the gym and into a waiting car, to be whisked off campus without any intent of meeting what I had promised. I do not think it is necessary to describe the scene that I faced upon informing the press with their late afternoon deadlines that my promise could not be met.

I also learned that it is okay not to be liked. It is quite nice to be liked but, in an organizational sense, it is not necessary. These are important lessons. Part of my mindset in everything I do within an organization focuses on how what I do might help others in the organization be successful in what they do. So, many of these attitudes about administration and the application of one's unique style of leadership come out of that era.

LESSONS LEARNED FOR STUDENT AFFAIRS

When I was the president of NASPA in the early 1970s, I took the position that student affairs had to snuggle up much closer to academic affairs. In fact, I thought that on some campuses the chief student affairs administrator ought to report to the academic vice president or the provost. I still think this creates a symbol of the importance of faculty and student affairs personnel serving as partners in creating healthy learning communities. Good personnel can work in any organization, but good personnel can work better in good organizations. While we made progress in the 1970s, I think student affairs professionals still have not linked as effectively with the academic enterprise as should be the case.

We also learned that "competency power" can always trump "bureaucratic power." The breadth of one's administrative portfolio, often a measure of comparison among budding student affairs professionals, should fit the individual institutional situation and, in the end, is no more important to one's influence within the organization than simply being competent in completing the tasks at hand and having a vision of the possible.

I try to emphasize the value of student affairs personnel being resources for faculty—no less important today than in the era being described. Recently I taught a class that focused on critical issues in higher education. One of our good young staff members in student affairs was in the class. She did a fine paper on the Generation X students. I encouraged her to present these ideas to groups of faculty to assist them to be more effective in their work with today's students. This is a throwback to my early experiences, and the lessons learned then.

There is a very old story about a person looking at another person and saying, "My, you exercise such good judgment. How did you get such good judgment?" "Well, I've had a lot of experiences." "Well, how did you get all those experiences?" "Bad judgment, man, bad judgment." Most of what we did in the 1960s and 1970s was by trial and error. We made a lot of mistakes. We were not as sensitive as we should have been. Yet, the colleges and universities benefited from the exercise of leadership by student affairs professionals across the country. We were among the first members of the higher education community to recognize the changes that were in the wings.

In addition to the lessons already mentioned, many of us learned to give students an escape route, and I do not mean just physically. You always gave students a way to save face because, in spite of the bravado, these were fairly inexperienced leaders. Of course, it is easiest to illustrate this value by referring to physical sit-ins or the closing of buildings. It was necessary to make clear that if an illegal protest continued, the university was going to act to clear the blocked hallway and the disruption of business. On frequent occasions I can remember stating, "If you continue to block this hallway, we will take action in five minutes." In five minutes, I might come back and say,

> I said you had five minutes, and I just want to tell you that I'm willing to work on this, willing to ask faculty to get involved if you'd like, but I also want you to think again about where this is headed; so I'll give you another five minutes.

It was made very clear that, in representing the institution, I could not let this continue indefinitely, but there were lots of "five minutes." The fact that this situation was a violation of law or regulation was made clear. The consequences of behavior were articulated. Sometimes the process resulted in dialogue and resolution, sometimes disciplinary action had to be taken and, on some campuses, civil action was necessary. However, if at all possible, we were also not going to back students into a situation where they had to defend a position that could lead to police hauling them out. There is a huge amount of space between being laissez faire saying, "Oh, what the hell, let them sit in" on one hand, and on the other end of this continuum calling the police. Patience to establish the dialogue, if possible, and in implementing sanctions paid off.

One of the very important things that had to be learned was the difference between institutional racism and individual racism. Individual racism might be described as consciously or unconsciously treating another individual inappropriately because of race or ethnicity. Institutional racism might be understood as continuing patterns of the past that no longer fit the present situation. To disenfranchised persons, these patterns appeared to be racism. By way of an example, we found at Oakland that for many years when we redid the orientation brochures, we tended to simply update the text. Well, when we went from less than 10 Black students to 15 percent of the enrollment, we had a whole new population not represented in these materials, and this to a disenfranchised student was translated as "I don't count." Another example of inadvertent institutional racism came from the standard practices that might be employed by someone hiring a residence life staff. In the old days we would do group interviews. When you have a homogeneous group of people, group interviews help you understand who might be a better head resident, for example, because of the way individuals respond in that group situation. When you have a racially heterogeneous group (in those days at Oakland only Black and White), people who had different attendant skills or were in the minority find themselves more threatened or awkward being the only Black student in a group of seven or eight White students. This group procedure was considered by the minority person to put them at a disadvantage. So, the process itself had to change.

How Higher Education Is Different Today

The 1960s and 1970s were a unique period in history so it is very difficult to make comparisons. Today's students almost ask for permission before protesting. They are very engaged in community service, but they are not politically active. While I am not a good prophet, it is my opinion that this could change quickly if the United States is engaged in a war or if the world situation continues to spin out of control.

At most colleges and universities we think more about learning than teaching and we are the better for this. Pedagogy has changed; syllabi look very different. Once some of the professors in their disciplinary meetings had to talk about texts and the issues that they were facing in their own classrooms, change began to occur in the disciplines. Liberal foundations programs began to include race, ethnic, and gender as legitimate topics of discourse. We are paying more attention to interdisciplinary programs; we are more aware of the need to measure how effective we are, how well we do what we claim to do.

We certainly are more ethnically diverse and have learned that this has enriched the education for all students. I agree with the University of Redland's Vice President Phil Glotzbach who states:

> All of us who live in the 21st Century—from young persons just entering adulthood to those with a bit more life experience—need to be adept travelers in a multiracial, multiethnic, multicultural, global milieu that scarcely could be imagined even a decade ago. Moreover, given the now widespread recognition that increasing the diversity of a university community brings it new vitality, it is important to be clear about how concerns with diversity fit into the university's fundamental commitment to the values of liberal education.

That period of the 1960s and 1970s did not change us for the moment; it changed us forever.

HIGHER EDUCATION'S CONTRIBUTION TO CIVIL RIGHTS

Higher education's impact is not so much through the national bully pulpits afforded to a few high- profile leaders in higher education, but is more indirect, through the students we graduate. While we are highly respected institutions in this society, and academic leaders can exercise significant influence in local regions, our direct political clout is typically not very strong. Indeed, there are many educators who will argue that we ought to stay outside of the political fray unless the issues directly involve the academy.

We have made a contribution to civil rights through our admissions and financial aid policies, our individual and collective support for increasing the diversity of the campus, modifying curricula, creating policies and procedures that ensure fairness and justice, and increasing the support for multicultural centers. This then leads to what is our greatest contribution—informed and aware graduates.

We have had an enormous effect on the changes that are taking place across the country and the world through our graduates as they take their place in their communities and professions. If our students learn how to live fully and effectively in a multiethnic and global milieu as a result of the lessons from the classroom or laboratory, through study alone with a book or a computer, in rap sessions in their residence hall or chat room, or through the lessons available though the out-of-class curriculum of the campus, then we have made a most important contribution. The success of our graduates should become the measure of our success. In this regard, I think our influence has been rather dramatic, not only in helping to heal the ruptures of the 1960s and 1970s, but also in perpetuating legitimate good changes in society that were prompted by those difficult but wonderful times.

EPILOGUE

Appleton left Oakland in 1972 when he took a position as vice president for student affairs at the University of Southern California (USC). He remained in that position until 1982, when he became vice president for development at USC. In 1987, Appleton was named the eighth president of the University of Redlands. He remains in this position today.

J. HARRISON MORSON
Union County College (1969-1986)

I n 1969, Morson became director of student activities at Union County College, located in Cranford, New Jersey. In 1971, he was appointed as the first dean of students at the college and held that post until leaving in 1986 to accept the dean of student services position at Mercer County Community College in Trenton, New Jersey. Morson described the professional path he took to his first position at Union County College:

> I started my career teaching and coaching in the New Jersey public school system in 1956 and completed my master's in 1960 at Rutgers University. After completing my masters, I moved into high school administration, serving as a high school principal from 1965-69. Thereafter, I accepted an offer to join Union County College, formerly, Union Junior College, a two-year, private, transfer institution accredited to offer the associate in arts degree. Union College had only two principle administrative officers at the time of my appointment, the president and a dean of the college. My titled responsibility was director of student activities, reporting directly to the dean of the college.

Morson noted that, at the time he accepted his appointment, Union County College had been designated as part of a network of 16 statewide, county-based community colleges. In this chapter, Morson walks us through his administrative experiences at Union County College and gives a vivid account of the civil rights movement from a community college perspective.

THE CLIMATE AT UNION COUNTY COMMUNITY COLLEGE

> The climate at Union Junior College, which later became Union County College, was fairly receptive in terms of students of color. The climate, as I would describe it for students of color, was that you had

a cadre of faculty members who, before the elements of remedial kinds of services, anticipated dealing with a student body competent in managing college-level work. Minorities in some cases were falling through the cracks because they came ill-prepared. Although there were some programs, there was not an organized system to allow them to be successful on a consistent basis.

One of the exceptional statewide recruitment programs was titled the "Education Opportunity Fund" program. As a part of this program, the state funded students from diverse backgrounds who could be classified as educationally and economically disadvantaged. It was essentially a population profile of minority students, but deliberately not promoted as a minority student recruitment effort. Essentially, I found the college campus to be a receptive place for any student who had an interest in moving forward in his/her pursuit of career and life goals. Many faculty members went well out of their way to support the fundamental needs of those who came to campus lacking basic college survival skills. Study groups and related support services were established within the classroom and through the professional counseling department. Early in the program, remedial programs had not been institutionalized, but faculty members were dedicated to maintaining the long-established image of the former junior college title.

Union Junior College had previously been referred to as a flagship institution because of the high graduation and transfer rates. The transfer rate had been approximately 85 percent and faculty did not wish to see it diminish significantly. Therefore, everyone worked with great deliberateness to retain these lofty standards. However, within the first five years, as Union County College recruited a broader profile of students who did not need to submit SAT/ACT scores as an admissions requirement, the transfer rate fell sharply, but held around 65 percent. All of the support and remedial programs that subsequently became an accepted and approved part of the community college sector were positioned at Union. As a result, both faculty and students were better served and the community at large was reassured of the college's new direction in serving a more diverse population.

The Hispanic population, in particular, grew so dramatically in the city of Elizabeth that the college found it beneficial to open an inner city site. In its third year of operation as the county college, an extension campus had been opened in the city of Plainfield, which addressed the appeal of many African American residents. Both the

Elizabeth and Plainfield campuses were justified in terms of the absence of public transportation directly to the primary campus in the suburban community of Cranford. It was widely advertised, during marketing and recruitment efforts, that the two extension centers would provide only freshman level academic and selected certificate courses. The administrative expectation was that all students would need to attend the Cranford campus at some juncture to complete degree requirements for graduation. It took almost fifteen years to negotiate the extension of direct public transportation services to the Cranford campus from the cities of Elizabeth and Plainfield.

A Quick Promotion

As a part of my duties as director of student activities, I served as advisor to our Student Government Association. I found that this organization was lacking in its understanding of the mission of community colleges and a vision of how they could best serve their peers. I suggested to the student president that we formulate a statewide student government network at the community college level. My counterparts at most of the community colleges favorably received this proposal, since we were all struggling with similar issues. The first meeting of student government representatives was held at our campus. Thereafter, we agreed to meet twice each semester, rotating the meetings at four colleges selected primarily for logistics near the center of the state. This exchange process was instrumental in formulating a sound structural base for our student government body. It also provided an occasion for students to observe the facilities and organizational operations at sister institutions. The interaction among participating students was phenomenal and a number of positive ideas surfaced.

One concern picked up and launched by our student leaders was the absence of a student advocate spokesperson in the administrative organizational table at our college. It was near the close of my first year that the student government petitioned the president and dean to consider the establishment of a new position, dean of student affairs. Ironically, they also proposed to the administration that I be invited to apply for the new position. As a result of this student initiative, one of my biggest challenges at the conclusion of my first year was convincing the president and dean that I had not spearheaded the student petition.

141

The issues were there, but the reason, in part, why I became a dean for student services was the absence of a principal student advocate position within the college's organizational table. Nor were there any Blacks on the president's cabinet. Thus, part of the issue was visibility—someone students could recognize on campus that presupposed that they had a voice inside the system.

THE BLACK PANTHERS COME TO CAMPUS

We had pressing problems. Remember, this was 1968, 1969 so a lot of things were happening on college campuses that made national news. The Black Panthers came on campus and I had a discussion with two of the leaders representing that group. It turned out that one of their leaders, who insisted that they be afforded an approved location on campus to engage students, was a former student that I had encountered when I served as high school principal. I assumed he felt that he knew me well enough to think, "I can reason with this guy/brother," and we had an engaging discussion.

I acknowledged the need for his group's desire to be visible and present their message to those who felt moved to listen. However, I insisted that they could not in any manner interrupt or disrupt the traditional educational atmosphere. I explained, "We have a broad base to work with and there are many people who need to have access to your message. However, disruption of anything related to the classroom activity would not be tolerated." I also said to him:

> On the other hand, it would be acceptable if you wish to set up a table to offer information on your views of the shortcomings of minorities. You are invited to join the other, approved, student groups that had been authorized to use the student center facility hallways or designated walkways between buildings to solicit fellow students.

The time allotment was restricted to two days per week, Tuesday and Thursday, when we held college activity period from noon to 1:30 p.m. I invited the leader to select a location for their table and made it clear that working the crowd was only to be done from behind their table. Students should not be coerced if they failed to display interest in their message or materials. I reminded him that I was minority and in fact had been exposed to many more instances of racial prejudice than he had likely experienced. I told them, "You know where I come from. Therefore, you can have that access of visibility and communication on campus under the conditions outlined." He and his group accepted these terms.

Nothing occurred that prevented students from attending classes. Those who felt drawn to stop and chat did so without incident. Within a month, the table designated for coverage by Black Panthers was devoid of representation. I attempted to reach their leadership at the telephone number provided but was unsuccessful. We left the table in place for the balance of the second month and removed it when no one appeared or offered an explanation of their intent by the end of the second month.

MINORITY STUDENT UNION

Just prior to the appeal by the Black Panthers, several of the African American students recruited through the Educational Opportunity Fund program, approached the student government association with a petition to form a minority student union. Some faculty members, who were clearly sympathetic to the civil rights movement and diversity in general, actively lent their voice of support for recognition of such a club. On occasion, these faculty members created some disdain among their peers when they redirected classroom discussions and, in the opinion of their colleagues, usurped hours required by the subject area syllabus. I did have conversations with faculty chairs to enlist their support by discussing with faculty meaningful approaches for infusion of the diversity theme whenever they found this topic compatible with their program of study. At the same time, I insisted that my office had every intention of standing steadfast upon the principle that our primary communications in the classroom follow the prescribed course approved outline. The academic area chairs found no reason to reject my request.

THE STUDENT NEWSPAPER INCIDENT

Morson spoke of another incident on campus that occurred during this period of unrest at Union County College.

There was an issue with the student newspaper. An underground publication emerged and we could not track down the author(s). The declared scandal sheet was naming a lot of people, creating tension, and causing concerns for the possibility of legal action on the basis of libel. Despite the circulation of this underground newspaper, the one person who was made to feel very humble as a result of one of the articles came in and asked me, "What are you going to do about this?" We talked through the available options. We were already investigating the incident but could not track down the publisher. We did not think it was a group of any sort, because it did not appear as though what was being said was done from a group perspective. It appeared more likely to be a single individual with a personal vendetta. They were dropping and posting flyers around campus. As the flyers were observed, the majority were almost immediately removed and destroyed, but the campus community was very upset.

What upset people most was the use of the "n" word and other ethnic slurs that the authors came up with. Again, this publication was in the form of a scandal sheet. In an effort to confront the perpetrator(s), the editor of our legitimate campus student newspaper invited this mystery person(s) to write an article and become a part of the regular student newspaper staff. Although the approved student newspaper did not always make comments that the college administration and faculty found positive—charges of administrative oversight and resurrection of issues assumed to have been resolved—the publication was subsidized and supported by the college. Generally, key issues raised were addressed or left to simmer until the energies on either side of the equation abated. However, on this occasion, the effort to legitimize the derogatory comments did not bear fruit. No response was forthcoming from the mystery writer. Thereafter, the student newspaper took pains to point out the fallacies of the slanderous publication on the premise that, if it were a true voice, a voice of accuracy, and a voice of integrity, it would become a part of the larger unit and legitimatize itself.

I thought that was unique in the sense that here is a group of students saying, "We're not going to say exactly what you want us to say all the time, but we want to say what is accurate and right. We want to respect the newspaper's image of being a publication of merit." An interesting fact was that the students involved in writing the student newspaper were not tied to a journalism class. They were working on their own with student funding and other related funds, but they were wise enough to understand how this underground rag sheet was impacting their image. As a result of their efforts, the underground paper disappeared within two months.

Even though the illegitimate paper had disappeared, students were still hurt. Although a lot of people suffered indignities, I think most felt less discomfort and disenfranchisement knowing they had support from the vast majority of the college community. I said, publicly, we would support anyone who wanted to bring civil suit. The college would support them as well, which at least gave the students a sense we were not condoning this behavior, nor were we going to turn our backs and walk away politely. The students recognized the legitimate newspaper, as legitimate as it could be, supported the notion right is right. The students also understood if the person really wanted to say these things, within the cover of legitimacy, they were given the opportunity to do so in print and the legitimate newspaper was willing to take responsibility for any rebuttal.

The organizers of the newspaper were students who had an interest in writing articles on campus. Some of them were journalism students, and some of them were not. Some of them were involved in publications in their high school experience and wanted to continue that kind of career direction or presence on campus. Usually, as clubs develop at community colleges, they develop as an outlet for students. One of the most difficult tasks is to keep two critical groups—student government association and student newspaper—operational and sensitive to issues within the campus community. Remember, most community colleges are comprised of a commuter population. It is not practical to expect that students will hang around the campus after completing scheduled classes. Nor do they tend to arrive with time to spare before class commitments. Only the dedicated few will give up an evening or weekend to return to the campus to work on a newspaper or government-related task.

AFRICAN AMERICAN HISTORY COURSES

At the time, a sensitive issue at many colleges was the absence of a formal course in African American history. Fortunately, this topic did not bring about much debate to our campus. The college had introduced a course offering without prompting when the topic peaked at the national level. Both the president and dean of the college were sensitive to local and national issues. They impressed me from day one as being humane in the truest sense of the term. The attitude and posture of these two principal leaders was a critical factor in my decision to give up my high school principal post to join the county college. When the former Union Junior College president said to me,

> We don't have any Black administrators at the college; would you consider leaving the high school to become a part of what we are attempting to do in higher education? We need you to help others appreciate the new mission and role of our college in this community...

I sensed his invitation was more than just a gesture of tokenism. I read it as advanced thinking about the atmosphere and overall image needed to extend and renew the educational opportunity for many residents who may have previously felt unworthy. In reality, the college was engrossed in changing its mission from serving predominately degree-seeking, transfer students to paving access for the broader needs of the community at large.

RELATIONSHIP WITH THE STUDENTS

I think my relationship with the students at Union County College was unique. We were able to make significant changes and adaptations to the issues confronting us at the time, changes instrumental in fostering a shifting of attitudes towards improved tolerance and patience. When I mentioned to my colleagues that we were hosting the Black Panthers on campus, their responses were generally couched in terms such as, "Are you kidding? That would mean war on my campus. How did you get the administration, faculty, and staff to buy into that decision?" My response suggested a strong dependency upon "negotiation" and the alternatives of taking a confrontational stance. Of course, in my case, the blessing in disguise was my previous relationship with a key player in the Panther organization. We positioned ourselves to talk about the reality of what had to happen, or we could easily have had a riot on campus and there would have been no gain for anybody. Only increased ferment and lack of trust would have resulted. The stronger message could be sent by a cooperative effort moving both the Panther and college agenda forward in a nonviolent, disruptive environment. We worked collectively in appreciation that changing attitudes is much more difficult than simply shifting policies, procedures, and regulations. Much of our labor was directed towards individuals who held key positions that were essential to altering the course of sentiment for change.

I participated in student-led marches from campus through our downtown area, and slept over night in our gym with those who had a strong desire to demonstrate their support for the national civil rights movement. We never had any form of disruption or confrontation that turned violent on campus or during our treks downtown. A large number of students seemed to feel more comfortable operating on the fringes, observing, writing stories for the student newspapers, or volunteering to be interviewed. Thank goodness, no one among the student body felt anointed with leadership spirit sufficient to step forward as the outspoken spokesperson for a cause. Again, the commuter campus profile tends to find difficulty in producing students who are comfortable enough to choose the college setting as a forum to openly express vested interests. People came to campus and I sense that they felt reasonably safe. Some may have felt safer on campus than in their local communities, but I have no way of being certain of this assumption. We did deliberately plan activities that would retain students on campus for longer periods of the day. This was one reason why the administration acceded to the sleepovers in the gym.

Conflicts occurring in several sections of the county and nearby large cities (Newark and Plainfield) were also factors in our strategy for selective activities planned for campus. Some presentations were force fed by faculty assignments tied to classroom discussions. It is my belief that students who were being exposed to violence and intolerance in their communities did not return to campus feeling a strong need to vent in a negative, confrontational manner. They were afforded plausible outlets by means of our sensitivity and planned activities.

One of my foremost concerns was that of maintaining the integrity of my title as dean of students. The titled office and not the person holding the title, who happened to be an African American in this instance, must be viewed as consistently egalitarian in reaching decisions affecting the welfare of all students. Admittedly, I was more visible in my response to the Black Student Union, placing emphasis upon the need to develop leadership skills, take advantage of readily available resources on and off campus, and building trust and respect. I pressed members of the organization to spread there talents and influence by joining other student organizations that already had a strong voice on campus, as opposed to working in isolation. The motto became, "infiltrate the system and seek positive venues that would move your issues to the next level: consideration, acceptance, and incorporation."

The personal gratification that I have experienced from interacting with students and lending them support while they were enrolled inside the system was often realized years later. When a former student achieves a recognized position of political leadership within the

county or state, graduates with honors from undergraduate and graduate programs (I was extended a personal invitation to these events on
many occasions), or takes time to stop by for a brief visit to express
appreciation for the positive effect my guidance has made in their life
choices, you can feel that twinge of pride swell from within. We all
need some sort of stroking to keep us committed and focused upon
the tenants of our profession. I had conversations with a number of
students, privately, just to point out the values of employment in an
educational setting. This environment promotes one of the richest
opportunities to influence others, especially those seeking direction
and clarification of life's issues. The higher educational setting also
provides a concurrent arena for personal growth and recognition by
other professionals who have chosen careers beyond the field of
educational service.

One of the things that I encouraged was leadership development. Few,
then again maybe not so few, were willing to get up and shout about
their sense of indignity for being excluded from the table where major
decisions are made; decisions that affected their livelihood. Many students were unable to present their views in a manner that avoided
being received as confrontational by those already operating from a
seat of power. True, those on the control side of the table may have
felt challenged and possibly personally threatened, but we needed to
move the agenda in any event. Mediation became the behind-the-
scenes point of reference. I urged student spokespersons to present
themselves in a posture that promoted a search for positive outcomes
through mediation and tolerance. I advised them to think through their
presentation, as opposed to letting it seem like a spontaneous, spiritual, and/or emotional outlet. I urged them to consider what is it and
how is it that you want to draw a reaction, taking into account the
environmental setting in which you present this topic. I talked to them
about whom to approach first using the chain of command. I
explained to them that you do not always want to skip people
because, if you do, then you alienate them in the process of getting
what you want done. So, even if it is just the courtesy of going up to
someone and saying, "What do you think about this?" at least you
have alerted them to the issue that students view as part of the agenda
that deserves attention and action.

The Black Student Union often served as the vehicle for discussing change
issues. Morson stated:

Sometimes the Black Student Union was the forum and I frequently invited myself to their table, trusting that I would not be received in my titled role as dean of students, but merely as another witness. Indeed, as I look back, I was fortunate that they were agreeable to my presence. While at the table, I would offer suggestions as to optional approaches for taking action. Their selected advisor also played a vital supportive role and was extremely insightful. Thank goodness, the two of us shared rather similar counseling theory in dealing with students. My suggestions were couched by the fact that my words are not absolute—They are not God's. "I'm simply giving you some points of view from someone who has been through the system." I told them quite frankly,

> There are characteristics about my decision-making style that I would not want you to accept unchallenged. I have had to equate the priority of my objectives against anticipated outcomes, where you may find reason to assess the balancing act differently. However, I can offer sound advice related to the absolute need to developing a plan for action and devoting great care to avoid taking steps that may lengthen, delay, or defeat achievement of your intended goal, unless that outcome is a perceived part of your deliberate action plan.

Occasionally I would deliberately shout out (a bit of planned theatrics on my part) to make my point at a meeting. And then follow my outburst immediately with a critique of my behavior, asking club members to evaluate what it may or may not have accomplished, and how they internalized the episode. This behavior enabled me to stress that there are times to sincerely demonstrate anger, but generally one needs to be selective to obtain the desired results. I told students they may not want to play their trump card too soon and that it is not generally in their best interests to go to the wall on every issue. They should save their strongest efforts for the major events. Acting is indeed permitted in the process of seeking change. This was the best advice I could pass along at the time.

I was not the only one invited to the forums; there were other administrators invited as well. The students were encouraged to invite anyone that they felt needed to hear the message, or could be a part of helping proceed with how that message might better be delivered. It became quite apparent as the group moved forward that they were doing positive things. Some of the faculty who were of the same persuasion asked, "Is it okay if we attend one of your meetings?" Of course, the invitation was always open to anybody anyway.

One of the other things about the notion of having campus clubs and activities was that the student government, from the very onset, made it clear that any student group formulated on campus, receiving approval and funding, must open enrollment to any current student who wished to join. When the Black Student Union formed, they said, "Oh we're not going to do that." And I said, "Now wait a minute, are you going to ask for funding, are you going to ask for any kind of support from student government?" They said, "We don't need it." And I said, "Well think about it for a second." I was trying to help them understand and appreciate that having a Caucasian student sit in during one of their meetings would accomplish the same thing. I asked, "How many of you have, are willing to admit having, a Caucasian friend?" because, by such an admission you are ultimately stating that there are lots of *okay* people out there—people with whom you have confided. Moreover, the numbers are not in our favor. Thus, we should take full advantage of any support from those displaying empathy or concern for our cause. Acquiescence to this theory paved the way for acceptance of open club enrollment. In actuality, there was little need to be exercised, as I do not recall any White student who sought admission to the club, and only one Hispanic signed on. Considerable attention was devoted at the first several meetings to an appropriate title for the organization. The African American student organization title was the second choice and was defeated principally due to the intent to appear more inclusive by appealing to those international students of color who presently were not represented in sufficient numbers to establish separate racial, ethnic clubs.

I envisioned my role as a facilitator—someone to assist students in developing an understanding and appreciation of the available opportunities for personal growth that were within their grasp. This commitment was the bedrock of my extension of service to students, and any other responsibility that I can think of held a lower priority. This meant that any time I witnessed or someone called to my attention a student struggling with some aspect of the educational process, I felt moved to intervene. There were sessions with groups as well as one-on-one. Often we came together as a direct result of decisions and statements associated with my office. Sometimes, I was the culprit and sometimes not. I took the most heat when justly accused of issuing ultimatums devoid of sufficient consideration. Admittedly, there were times when I was reacting to personal pressures assuming that expeditious resolution was necessary. Students can be extremely instrumental in pointing out inequities, especially when college campuses are so burdened with professionals who play it safe by following long-standing traditions. In all honesty, administrators and faculty must be willing to address student concerns. It is so easy to react with your personal basis and belief that you possess greater intellectual insights, given your tenure inside the educational bureaucracy.

Such was the test of my integrity, endurance, and professional commitment when a small group of part-time, evening students appealed to my office a need to establish an independent student government organization, with student funding support. They argued that part-time, evening students did not share the same interest in sponsoring activities as their full-time counter parts that attended classes during the day. As more mature enrollees, they essentially viewed the present student governance body as one for the high school kids who had just transferred in. Although they were able to make a sound case on several fronts, the last thing I sincerely believed that the college needed was two student governments—one pulling against the other for power to do whatever; a marriage doomed for dissention and probable failure. I took pleasure in pointing out all the hurdles and pitfalls—election regulations as students shifted from part-time to full-time status, determining funding support with equity, setting priority use of our limited facilities, duplication of so much at unnecessary cost increases. I even directed the core leaders to track their idea with other community colleges in New Jersey, trusting that they would discover for themselves what I already knew—no other college hosted two government associations. Their findings did not serve as a deterrent. To make a long story short, we worked out a model to support their primary wish –the freedom to plan activities of special interest to part-time students enrolled predominantly in the evening. They also wanted to promote events that extended to their family members.

LESSONS LEARNED

One of the major lessons learned and carried forward from this experience was you have to listen and do not expect to have the answers in your hip pocket. You cannot pretend to be listening. You really have to make a concerted effort to focus upon what students are saying. Like it or not, you have to hear them. You cannot tune them out. They are on campus for some reason, good or bad, positive or negative, but you have to listen. You really have to open your ears and pay attention to them. Often we struggle with this notion, and sometimes we buy out by saying we do not understand. Sure it is difficult to understand where they are coming from and why they are there. It sometimes takes more time, certainly more time than we think we have available, as we factor in the host of other responsibilities calling for our attention. Sometimes you can delegate and turn to an assistant or someone else and/or point the student to the right person to hear the particular grievance or the message. There were times when I said,

> I'm hearing what you're saying, but I don't think I can really convey it to the president with the same kind of empathy that you feel I need to, in bringing it to his or her attention. Would you be willing to sit down, with the three of us, and talk about this?

And again, you may be providing another opportunity for expression and consideration.

THE INSTITUTION'S RESPONSE

Union County College invited me to join their team. I did not approach them; they solicited me. They were already open to the notion that "change" was a major objective in their mission. During my first conversation with the president, I commented that it was my assumption that I was the only Black administrator being brought aboard at this time, and would be reporting directly to the dean of the college. The President asked if I found the reporting sequence an issue. I responded that I had no basis to question the present organizational structure. Later the administrative reporting lines did change and I reported directly to the president. Before this realignment, I was assured that any time I sensed a need to speak with him directly, he would honor my request. I was never moved to pursue this option; as the relationship developed with the individual serving as dean of the college, I found him quite sincere and sensitive to my concerns. He often sought my opinion on student-related issues before they came to my attention. We developed a solid working relationship. The dean of the college was a true visionary with a sincere interest in student development and service. Improving services for students was at the center of my universe as well, paving the way for my meaningful orientation to college-level administration. The dean exhibited enormous patience with me as well as students I brought to his attention. At such gatherings he frequently might say, "What do you think?" As though I had the right solution tucked away and just needed his endorsement. I often think that he used me as a kind of sounding board for their administrative direction when I was not really asked to be so. There simply were things that I needed to learn about the whole experience because it was not exactly something to which I was accustomed.

I was a high school principal when Kennedy was assassinated. Our high school was in chaos simply because this drastic thing happened. Some people were numb or walking about like wounded folks. They could not quite figure out what was going on. It took several months to get our system back in place. Then, when Dr. Martin Luther King was assassinated in '68, the pent up emotions that had been smoldering beneath the surface erupted. Everybody, every day, was waiting for the dam to burst or a situation that might give license for the release of frustrations. Secondary schools, in particular, were vulnerable and often impacted by disruptions. Administrators worked diligently with faculty and staff to quell emotions and keep the lid on. But, many students were angry, venting their feelings openly with the hope that they might incite others leading to physical confrontations.

It is important to mention again that Union County College was located in a small, suburban, racially mixed community. Most African Americans resided in several small enclaves, but not exclusively. None, to my knowledge, owned downtown businesses, but many worked in these enterprises, held responsible positions in government and public service, or were employed in professional posts as teachers, lawyers, etc. Some commuted to New York City jobs. The college was certainly sensitive to the degree of ferment taking place locally. We were close enough to feel the heat when major violence took place in nearby cities.

I think that the college evidenced a great deal of foresight by acknowledging an absence of minority representation on the administrative team. First, they invited me to join the staff. At the same time, they contracted another African American as director of the educational opportunity fund, a program for recruiting economically and educationally disadvantaged persons. Second, the college placed an increased emphasis upon recruiting minority students and attempted to make some preparations to assure their presence on campus would be welcomed. Two African American counselors were employed. These professionals were charged with assisting students in their adjustment to college expectations and the exploration of career goals. In summary, these were specific and deliberate commitments to building a foundation for diversity and the extension of services leading towards student success.

The college also made a valiant attempt to forestall grievances arising from environmental decisions with regard to branch campuses and their logistics. We had established a branch campus in one of the hotbeds of unrest, Plainfield. Considerable energy was directed towards making sure that people working and enrolling for classes at this campus felt safe and treated as equal members of the college in its broadest definition. When we opened a similar branch campus in Elizabeth, the assumption arose, led by several self-perceived community spokespersons, that there was sustained effort by the college to isolate minority populations.

I think, in light of the local and national challenges confronting us during the late '60s and early 1970s, the college was well managed. I attribute much of our stability to the character and political astuteness of the president. His immediate cabinet was flavored with a supportive, team attitude. There were a significant number of faculty members who were "positive activists." I was fortunate to have had a mentor (dean of the college) within the hierarchy who was sensitive, willing to bend, take risks, and challenge faculty leaders to view change as growth. I think that a commitment to open enrollment cannot be shallow. You need to know that many students will enroll with excess baggage, negative attitudes, and a chip clearly on their shoulder, unprepared to make a serious academic commitment since some other agent is financing most of their costs. This represents a challenging agenda on both fronts. In many ways, it was an exciting personal growth period for me.

At least once week, I extended the invitation to have students visit my office for "open discussion" on any topic of choice related to campus life. Our student activity schedule was comprised of two one-and-a-half-hour blocks—Tuesday and Thursday—when no classes were scheduled. This time was set aside for student organizations and clubs to conduct business, presentation of guest speakers, or events intended to engage the campus community on a single topic. The allotted time also freed up faculty and staff advisors to assist their respective student groups. The fact that we reserved prime time—12 noon to 1:30 p.m.—created some annoyance among faculty, who would rather have held classes, and also gave ground to the notion that the time selected was the best time to hold students on campus. We knew that once they left for the day, they were less apt to return just to attend a student-organized event or meeting. I used the open activity period to sit in on various student clubs and observe the work of the student government association. This was another venue where I could announce and give witness to my interest and availability to address student concerns. I stressed the invitation to talk one-on-one when they were feeling pressured. I also emphasized the value in bringing personal concerns to the table for discussion and direction, rather than venting in virtual isolation or in peer groups that have limited insight, if any at all, as to the deployment of options open to positive resolution. In some instances I was able to offer formidable solutions, while others required referral or further mediation with involved parties and outside agencies.

THE ROLE OF NASPA AND OTHER SUPPORT GROUPS

The deans of students at community colleges throughout New Jersey formed a special action group comprised of selected members of the overall contingency. We called this smaller segment the dean's council. At the time, only 16 of 21 counties in New Jersey had community colleges. Five deans were selected to serve as the "special council" with priority given to the location of their respective institutions. There were only two African Americans on the council and I was one of them. The other held the dean's post at Essex County College in Newark. Council members spoke with each other frequently and I had many conversations with my counter part, as Newark was a hotbed of disturbance and violent crime in the wake of the civil rights movement. Council activity was predicated on the "hotline" approach to communication. We could reach out, any time of the day or night, for immediate discussion and feedback. This became a vital tool in quelling concerns arising at our campuses. I could not have brought back vital information for dissemination and discussion by our campus leadership had it not been for the conversations with council members, particularly the deans in Newark and Camden.

Through the dean's council, I was able to receive authentic information in a timely manner as opposed to reliance upon tabloid and television reports that may have been distorted. I had a critical edge. I could validate rumors and head off the spread of misinformation. Moreover, participation on the council in no way altered our professional obligation and loyalty to our home institutions.

As a result of creating the community college dean's council, an effort was made to form a similar component among the chief student affairs officers at statewide four-year colleges and universities. The effort never really came to fruition, as the vast majority of our colleagues at the baccalaureate level saw little in common with our two-year campuses. They were called upon to manage a much more complex set of variables—residential halls, student unions, fraternal groups, Division I, II, and III athletic programs, and larger, full-time enrollments in most instances. There were two four-year college deans that I had frequent conversations with. One was a natural, as he was positioned at the public state institution within the borders of Union county. A majority of our graduates sought transfer to his college—Newark State College. The other contact was a friend who served as vice president of student affairs at Seton Hall University. Because his institution was located near Newark, the campus experienced disturbances on a larger scale. Networking among professionals was invaluable to improving communications and the campus atmosphere, enabling us to better serve students.

I did not really know much about NASPA during my first few years as a dean of students. And mention of the association did not come up when the community college deans met. It did not appear to be a professional group interested in reaching out to two-year colleges. However, as conversational ties strengthened with my friend at Seton Hall, I was introduced to NASPA. My colleague had been active at both the regional (Region II) and at the national level, serving on the board. With his orientation and encouragement, I became active in Region II and later served on the planning committee for the national conferences in New York and Boston, as well as a delegate and, subsequently, member of the board of directors. Once "inside" the association, I found numerous support components, especially the promising network of veteran peers. I found new resource publications that became an integral part of my graduate studies at Rutgers University. NASPA became my professional home and I counted heavily upon the friendship ties. I also spent an inordinate amount of energy encouraging fellow community college deans to consider joining the association.

I would be remiss if I failed to mention the support from two mentors encountered while pursuing my degrees at Rutgers—Dr Samuel D. Proctor, who was my professor and chaired my doctorial studies committee, and Jeffrey Smith, who taught me how to manage statistical research and also served on my dissertation committee. These two gentlemen went well beyond introducing me to educational theory. Also worthy of mention was support from my parish rector from the 1960s through the 1980s. His spiritual advocacy seemed to appear when my soul was in most need of renewal. Finally, the affirmations by my wife and two sons who made untold sacrifices granting me the freedom needed to deal with issues arising from the workplace. They were instrumental in helping me sort out the baggage I unloaded after a difficult day in the trenches. I have probably omitted someone or group, but I have mentioned the most influential parties.

ACTIVISM TODAY

I base my response upon the community college students encountered over the last 10 years (1990-2000) of my campus experience. During this period, students appeared to possess greater self-assurance, rarely initiated counsel with assigned academic advisors, or pursued personal health information. Generally, they were bright, resilient, and aggressive when defending their perceived entitlements, such as availability of financial aid packages. Their sense of social service and civility appeared muted or at least diminished, a sort of, "what's in it for me?" attitude. I temper these comments by the fact that my meetings with parents often helped me appreciate why a particular student might adopt a contrary point of view when interacting with others. Essentially, today's students are astute, yet they are no less susceptible to the very same entrapments that are the nemesis of our society. That is not a bad position to be in as long as we learn from our mistakes and we don't make huge mistakes.

EPILOGUE

Harrison Morson left Union County College in 1986 to become dean of student services at Mercer County Community College.

I do not regret for one moment, one hour, or day of the 31 years devoted to "deanin" in higher education. My career was launched at a challenging time, and yet I found that new challenges continued to emerge as the semesters and years slid by. National and international crises arose that forced higher education to rethink traditional approaches to delivering educational services. Students came to our campus with broader high school experiences and extensive expectations from colleges. New technologies forced us to regroup, retrain, and pick up the pace to stay in touch with shifting communication methodology. The campus scene was always in a state of flux, and each day brought some new concern or a twist on one that we had previously put to rest. I genuinely looked forward to being present to cover the assignment of the day with the ego-fed belief that my voice and presence could, by being a positive force in attaining the mission we espoused, offer students the opportunity to improve their chances to become a productive member of our society, while reaping the personal gratifications that should accompany this goal.

Today, Morson is still very active in higher education and student affairs through service initiatives. He continues to work with Mercer County Community College as a consultant, and has been called back for two visits. In July 2001, he was asked to lead orientation sessions for new student services staff members. He was also involved in a self-study at Mercer to prepare for the accreditation visit in 2004 by the Middle States Commission on Higher Education. Recently, Morson was asked to serve as a part of a three-member team to review the self-study document prepared by the Department of Education on the US Virgin Islands for the Middle States Association of School and Colleges Commission on Secondary Schools. Although the assignment was voluntary, it was critical to the educational funding status of secondary schools on the Virgin Islands. Lastly, Morson was honored in 2003 as a Pillar of the Profession by the NASPA Foundation

JAMES J. RHATIGAN
Wichita State University (1965-2002)

In 1965, after earning a doctorate in student personnel from the University of Iowa, James Rhatigan was hired as dean of students at Wichita State University (WSU). At the age of 30, Rhatigan was the youngest dean in the country for a university of that size. In 1970, his title was changed to vice president for student affairs and dean of students. This chapter represents Rhatigan's perspectives on how Wichita State weathered, survived, and thrived during the civil rights era. Rhatigan is an amazing storyteller who believes strongly in the strength of a well-told tale. In conducting this interview, he noted,

> Storytelling is not about looking backward, even with the perspective that lengthening time provides. We use stories to convey bemusement and frustration in our work when we have to face issues that are damaging in the world of right relationships.

The following narrative represents the stories of WSU during the civil rights era as viewed through Rhatigan's eyes.

AREAS OF CONCERN REGARDING RIGHTS

When you look at the 1960s, you have to understand that there was excitement and hostility from different fronts, even though half of the country was just doing business as usual. For me, the two great issues of the 1960s were the Vietnam War and the civil rights movement. The Vietnam War was an urgent issue for students because there was a military draft for men. In terms of civil rights, during the 1960s, the word Negro, which had been used for decades in the United States, within a span of months became unacceptable on the American college campus. It was a symptom of the times. Indeed, the use of the term was practically an invitation to violence. The new term was

"Black" and there was an insistence about its use from activists. There were strong feelings at this time, particularly after the death of Martin Luther King in 1968. This is the period in which the Black "National Anthem" surfaced, often creating hostility among contending groups. The campus Black power experience was particularly volatile because Black students were not experienced in campus self governance. They had not been in the center of things. Now they were franchised in a hurry, but they didn't always know what to do with this power, so they squandered some very good things that they actually started. In the Black community the question was, "What's the university doing?" and we had to be responsive. By the mid 1960s these issues occupied a lot of my time. I remember saying to my staff, "You know, I think we can pretty much throw out our strategic plan. We are just going to have to admit that the only plan we are going to worry about is the plan for the day." People will just keep bringing you surprises all the time if you're responsive.

We had four or five other extremely important subthemes to contend with. We had the beginning of the women's movement, with the obligatory braless women on campus who are now the stereotype for the early days of women's issues. The birth control pill came out in 1960 and what we now call the sexual revolution was in fact another counterculture phenomenon of the time. On some campuses "sex, drugs, and rock and roll music" were all rolled up into one thing, and this was a huge problem when drugs got into the mix. Finally, there was a group on our campus involving some very aggressive students with physical disabilities who were demanding change. We had the onset here of some organizational awareness to the needs of students in wheelchairs that within a decade resulted in federal legislation covering a wide range of disabilities.

In the area of governance, we were talking about the standard parietal rules; too many restrictions in the dormitory, not enough say in the use of student fees, generally a need to restructure our whole system of governance as related to students. Parietal rules were created for a residential campus of another time. The students said, "I want more control of my life." Finally, there was the free speech movement that began at Berkeley and spread throughout campuses in this country and abroad. The civil rights and the free speech movements were two things happening simultaneously, coming together in some ways but separate in other ways. The intersection of these two major movements caused student affairs people unbelievable problems. Let's say you were a Black student and you had just been told you could no longer pass your "Save the Whales" pamphlets out; well what do you have on your hands? It doesn't have anything to do with race, but the person being denied is a minority. These were confusing issues with many permutations. We also had ordinary college students who were acting out their immaturity, who used all of these "causes" as vehicles to act out. They were just there to jerk our chain. They had delicious fun at our expense.

These many issues made campuses all over the United States very volatile. Bear in mind, the different groups didn't wear signs. Advocates would come together on some issues, or act separately, then come back together again. You saw different people at different events. There was a lot of cross-fertilization, which created a very difficult problem for administrators. We were just concerned about getting through the damn event of the day. I wasn't even sure there was ever going to be an end to it all, frankly.

The civil rights issues were unique because there was a subpopulation of the student body, in its entirety, that was affected. We had a whole population of students on our campus who, as a whole, wanted to succeed, but didn't always know how. They knew that if they studied hard, maybe some good things would happen, but how could they gain greater acceptance? Deal with the prejudice? How should they behave in places where they were the only one? How should they handle breakthroughs with no mentors to guide them? These questions were numerous, and each one came up in my office or in other offices where people cared very much. This led to some questions being asked on the university's part. "Well, here's Joe Blow, a minority student; he's got the grades for medicine, but frankly, hasn't got the money. What can we do?" Well, we all went to work until, by God, Joe Blow was up at KU in the School of Medicine. That's just it. There isn't any question about "Well, darn, I wish we could…" No, we don't didn't say that. There were no excuses. It was exhilarating at times, exhausting at times.

THE CONTEXT AT WSU

Wichita was just a typical campus politically. We were not a hot bed by any stretch of the imagination. The issues at WSU were raised on every campus in America of any size. At Wichita our issues were very focused on problems within the institution. We had the only "urban" campus in Kansas, and this descriptor was seen by many citizens in very pejorative and negative ways at the time. This is where, for many small-town Kansans, the "bad stuff" happened.

When I came to the university, there were 400 African Americans out of 10,000 students. There was a good relationship between the minority community and the university, but it was limited. In many ways there might as well have been a big wall around the university for the number of African American students who enrolled here. By 1970, there were about 800 African Americans. Today there are probably 1,100. We haven't grown radically, but there's a big difference between 800 and 400. Having a critical mass of African Americans made a big difference in terms of campus climate, a feeling of belonging. Most of the students at WSU, whatever their race, lived off campus. Student athletes were an exception; many of them were from out of state and many lived on campus. This created some interesting scenarios. I distinctly remember Blacks from Kansas City living in the residence halls saying, "Thank God the campus was friendly." Apparently the local Black community was not friendly. When these students went to the local Black church, nobody even spoke to them. People weren't mean to them, but they just kind of ignored them. They didn't really feel particularly welcome. Eventually, we tried to get the Black churches in town to have a fall picnic for minority students. I remember two or three years they did that it was very successful. I think maybe we picked up the tab for that, I'm not sure. That was a way to help those students find some adjustments from being away from home, using people in the local Black community.

The general perception from lots of people in our community was that Wichita State didn't have any problems of student unrest in those days. They would say, "There was no problem there because they had commuting, older students." It made me laugh. I told my wife, "Well, that's the greatest compliment I could ever get, because boy, my days are full of Alka-Seltzer." The older students of that era had huge problems. Older students were a lot savvier to the world's workings, so having them on campus was not particularly a blessing if you were looking for control. They knew their rights and they were more mature and could easily call your bluff.

The city of Wichita had some racial issues of its own. After the assassination of Martin Luther King, the city established curfews. Some of the racial problems in town were coming off our campus, created by the energy of our students, which was reaching energetic high school students who saw those Wichita State brothers and sisters out there raising hell with their administrators. They figured, why wouldn't that work for them too? One manifestation of civil rights was a whole series of either community legislation or community pressure in the area of housing, because we were a very segregated nation and city. One year, our entire basketball team went to the city commission meeting to demand fairer housing for Blacks in Wichita. They said, "This is not a protest, but we are all here to argue for a fair housing ordinance in Wichita." We also had a small cadre of liberal faculty who did a lot to help integrate the neighborhoods and front for minorities in housing situations. WSU was right in the middle of all that.

Our older students at WSU were all working people. They were trying to finish their baccalaureate degrees, coming out here at a later age to finish what they started earlier. They were looking for job promotions, or in some cases, they were retired. All these people came to the campus with different agendas and we tried to help them all. The older students were less likely to protest except for a few who asked, "How come you don't offer more courses in this or that at more convenient hours?" The younger students, however, were confronting personal identity issues, typical of the college experience.

In addition to Black students, we also had a handful of Native American students, but they never demanded anything because their numbers were insufficient. We heard complaints that we didn't have as many of them as we should have. Hispanic students were also on our campus and they made some demands, but they weren't nearly as well organized and did not have the inclination to be as aggressive as the Black students.

No one wants to come to college unprepared. No one wants to be set up to fail, but institutions have done that. At Wichita State, back in the 1960s and 1970s, we spent an inordinate amount of time and energy on our least prepared students, the bottom 25 percent. Many of them took only a few courses and they were insecure, which made them defensive, less open to help because help was always in the faces of White people, and might be the very White people who would turn around and betray you later. There was a lot to be overcome here. When you provide access to a Black student, you've got pay your dues first, then work hard later.

RELATIONSHIP WITH STUDENTS

I was advisor to the student senate, the Greeks, and I met with ad hoc groups when unrest began to surface regularly. I was out there on the front lines with them like many deans of students. For every issue that came up that had a name and more than one follower, I was there. I was in communication with them almost daily. We had a pledge with student leaders, "Don't surprise us and we won't surprise you either." The students' response to this approach was very positive.

I worked to establish credibility with the students. Once you have that credibility, you can say what you need to. I might tell them, "Well, that is the most stupid damn thing I've ever heard of" in relationship to a request the students had made or a position they had taken. If you didn't have a relationship with them you couldn't say that because it would just make them angry. I spoke my mind to them at all times, but not brutally or condescendingly. I was there with them everyday and many evenings. Occasionally, they didn't want any administrators hanging around. But, in general, I felt very well informed. I would take that information to the administration when I needed too, but I never saw myself as a lackey of the administration. A Black student once said to me, "Why you're the lackey of the administration, serving as their mouthpiece." I had my own worries, and that wasn't one of them.

I made it very hard to be a person they disliked, because even when I would go and say, "Look, I can't; I understand what you're trying to do, but I just can't do that." And they would say, "Well, Dean, we're going to do it anyway." I could counter with, "Well, I know you're going to do what you got to do, but I'm just saying that right now I can't help you there." So when the thing went sour, at least I had never lied to them.

In connection to requests for fewer parietal rules and more student rights, I tended to yield because I wanted students to live in the residence halls and some rules were unnecessarily discouraging. I believed you had to have some basic rules though, because students don't always exhibit common sense. We helped get rid of the excess baggage. Before, students spent too much time wondering, "Where does it say we can't do that?" When we reduced the rules, I would just say to the students, "We don't have that in the rule book because we assumed that you had a brain." I found it totally appropriate to challenge students. They didn't mind challenging me.

I believed that you should look for ways to say yes to students, not ways to say no. Finding ways to say yes to students has been the theme song of my entire professional life, really. When you can say yes, then students will recognize that they are being heard. Now they could turn to making their ideas work. "What the hell are we going to do?" That often was a little bit of a problem, because the organizational skills of some of the student groups weren't very good, particularly minority groups who had never had a chance to practice their skills. We had to look out for the fact that they would commit money they didn't actually have, or didn't make the arrangements they needed to make an event successful. They were very sensitive about supervision or suggestions from administrators, so that had to be handled delicately. You just had a leadership issue there, something that eventually they would overcome through experience. It was no different from any other issue, except when you added color as a dimension of any American higher education agenda during that period, it was immediately important.

The response of White students to civil rights on our campus was never hostile. As a matter of fact, they got secondary benefits from the unease of administrators. The attack on parietal rules was heavy during that time because of the influence of older adult students on the campus. I was protected because all the rules of WSU could fit comfortably on one page of the catalog. I had very basic rules: Don't misrepresent yourself. Don't ever hurt anybody or coerce anybody or mistreat anybody on the campus. I was very seldom disappointed, facing very few disciplinary cases of this sort.

CREATION OF TRIO PROGRAMS AND OTHER INSTITUTIONAL RESPONSES

In the 1960s, Blacks were apprehensive about coming to WSU. People I talked to said that a lot of Black people would never send their children to Wichita State because it wasn't seen as a friendly place for Blacks. I had to counter this belief, provide evidence to the contrary. When people rail against an institution, what it really means is they don't have any confidence in it. To combat this, I documented, in proportion to their numbers, how well we were doing with students of color. I also increased scholarship support for Blacks, not loans but free dollars to off-set the concern, "Yeah, the White kids get the scholarships and the Black kids get the loans." This documentation helped.

The best thing that happened was receiving funding for the federal TRIO programs at WSU. Through the TRIO programs, our at-risk students got a lot of one-on-one help. We needed to present and provide a more caring culture for those students coming in. For us, TRIO was a substantial answer. Our goal was to help make Black students feel welcome by providing good services, good programs, good activities, leading to good results for them. My plan was to help students be successful. Nobody wants to fail, so let's find ways to help people succeed.

We got into the first cycle of the federal TRIO programs by offering Upward Bound, whose aim was to recruit first generation kids to college. In fact, it wasn't even called a TRIO program back then. We eventually had one of the largest Upward Bound programs in the country. We had Upward Bound at WSU as early as 1964. I was surprised when I heard criticisms from the Black community about how little the university was doing. That got me to thinking, "Well, what else is available out there?" So then the university applied for and was granted Talent Search and Special Services. We called our special services program "Project Together" and that interfaced with Upward Bound. Special Services was meant to handle the problems of new freshmen and sophomores who didn't have a support group, to help them get through the maze of activities one had to go through to succeed around here. Later, we added Talent Search and the McNair Scholars program. We centralized these programs in student affairs. I argued that we should not have an Office of Minority Affairs because I felt that would become our ghetto office. I said, "Look, we need to enlist the support and loyalty and confidence of our Black students, and we're not going to do that by saying, 'Well, call minority affairs and they will take care of your problems.'" We needed a broader commitment.

I knew all of us in student affairs needed to build our relationships with the Black community and that was my message to our staff. I hired some really great people from Wichita to work in the TRIO programs. I hired an African American man to be assistant dean of students. His job was to help me work with the African American students on campus. Together we preached:

> Help students succeed. Find ways to make them successful because that is what they want to do. They don't want to be angry. They don't want to drop out. They want to amount to something, like everybody else. They want to have families.

They want to be successful, go to the church, school, and job of their choice, and be free of race as an issue.

We worked to incomplete success, of course, in the end, but we at least had a cause and a direction, which I thought was very exciting.

One of my messages to individual students was to get them to aim as high as they could. When someone would say, "Well, I've always wanted to be a nurse," I would look at their 3.8 grade point average and say, "You know, nursing is a tremendous profession. It's very good for women because, of course, you can go part-time while you are childrearing." I would add, "You know, though, as I look at your grade point average, you would be a shoe-in for medicine. Have you ever given any thought to becoming a doctor?" They often responded like they had just been shot. Never in their wildest imagination would they have thought of medicine as a career. It would be inconceivable. Nursing was a tremendous aspirational gain for them. "I'll be the only nurse in our whole family." So, I came to realize that, in a way, it was a problem for me, as in a way it was an insult to imply that nursing was not a worthy goal. On the other hand, I thought, what if one day that student thought, "I could have been a doctor if anybody would have ever encouraged me, or pointed it out." So, I always went that way. I always made sure I praised nursing and pointed out the values and the opportunities there, but then I did introduce this other idea. Would they like to talk to somebody? Sometimes they did, but more often they didn't. It was too intimidating.

It was hard to counter the feeling in the Black community that, "Well, what's Wichita State doing? They're not doing anything for us." Every time I had a group meeting with Blacks, they responded this way. They were not hostile but, "Well, we don't see anything. So what are you doing?" I remember the director of Upward Bound once said to me, "Jim, just quit worrying about that. The thing is if you take the pressure off a White guy he'll quit trying." He laughed at his private joke and said, "If we start giving a White administrator a lot of praise, you might just go sit right on back on your laurels." That was a help-ful perspective. Within the office my staff would tell me, "We're doing things. We are making progress." The thing I liked about dissent of this sort was the goal was not to raise hell, protest, or be mean. No, the goal was inclusion; the goal was fairness, being provided a chance to level the playing ground. In spite of our efforts though, there were many student academic casualties. There were some students who just could not make up the dreariness of their inadequate preparation. We had our success stories. We had a lot of failures, too.

FRATERNITIES AND SORORITIES

We had no luck desegregating fraternities and sororities in the 1960s. Some eventually had nondiscrimination clauses but they were not effective. Early on I tried to reason with some Greek leaders but their beliefs about social relationships were pretty firmly held. I remember asking the fraternities, "If Jim Rhatigan was Black and he was worthy, would you pledge him?" They responded, "He could be St. James, if he were Black we are not going to pledge him." We worked very hard with the Greeks on this issue. Eventually we had some success, but only with the men. The women were more resistant. Today you will see some Hispanic and Asian women in predominantly White sororities, but you can count on one hand the number of African American women who are in those sororities. For the men, to their credit, about 10 years after I started hounding them, some began inviting people of color to join. Times were changing. But by that time, the Black students weren't interested. They had their own social organizations. So, the Black students didn't want to join a predominantly White fraternity. Our timing was miserable. First the men didn't want Black members and then, when they did want them, the Blacks didn't want to join. This situation exists to this day. You can't count this one as a success, even though there are statements of nondiscrimination on the books everywhere.

THE IMPORTANCE OF TOP-DOWN LEADERSHIP

At WSU in the 1960s, student affairs was on the front lines. It was easy because we had the blessing of two outstanding and socially conscious presidents of that era. We had one president from 1963 to 1968 and another one from 1968 to 1983. In my opinion, you can try to resolve problems from the top down or the bottom up. I'm a bottom up believer. It takes longer, but I believe that bottom-up problem solving is more enduring. Still, you need a few top-down people, and our presidents were exemplary when it came to racial issues. I remember being at a meeting with some high-powered executives from Wichita and President Emery Lindquist. After President Lindquist was done making his presentation, he opened the floor for discussion. One of the executives was asking something about racial relations on our campus. But he asked it in a very pejorative way, and while the word "nigger" wasn't used, it didn't sound to anybody in the room that he used the word "Negro" either. Whatever he said sounded a little bit more like the former than the latter, and whatever he said didn't sound right to anybody on our team. President Lindquist blanched when he heard this, and I found myself wondering whether I should say anything. I decided it was the president's call.

When the event was concluding, President Lindquist summarized our visit, thanked everybody, and then he gave a very eloquent monologue with a moral in it. He said, "We have found on the campus how appropriate it is to use positive and affirmative language and regard each other ...." I can't remember everything he said now, but it was a noblesse oblige effort to nonpainfully but directly instruct all of us about the importance of right relationships. I really admired that approach because he didn't resort to any cheap tricks or anything like that; he just demonstrated his own compassion for young people of color and explained how the university was excited to be able to meet this commitment. Lindquist was really mad that this guy behaved so abominably, as he told me later, but on the scene he was much more of a teacher. He used the incident as a teachable moment. I thought to myself how much better that was than I would have done, which probably would have involved losing my cool. The president was very effective in this area, and it is one of the reasons why I think we made progress during this era.

DESEGREGATION OF HOUSING

In the 1960s, we had about 450 students living on campus, about 15 to 20 of whom were African American. It wasn't a huge number. Shortly after I arrived on campus, I was approached by one of the Black students who said, "Dean, we're all living together in the same few rooms." I went and asked, "How did that happen?" I learned that the secretary in housing was putting the Black students together. We used to ask students to send a photo with their application, which was pretty typical back then. A lot of the Black students would say, "What do you think they want my picture for? Well, I'll tell you why they want it. They want to stick me in the ghetto." Surprisingly, this was not a front-edge issue to the students. But in our department task force groups, we identified this as something that needed immediate attention. The woman who did it said she had put the Blacks together because she thought they would prefer it, be more comfortable that way. I believe this was an honest perspective on her part, but symptomatic of larger problems. Rather than berating her, the task force said, "Well, look, let's give some students some options." We didn't ask students whether they had racial preferences, but we tried to have students identify interests and then we tried to match students based on those. We also liberalized our room transfer policy for the first two weeks of school. If we had a roommate situation between Black and White students that was going to be problematic, then we allowed them to make a change. Sometimes that change was toward resegregation because I figured it was not my job to say, "Well, you can't live with Fred Jones because he's Black. If that's what you chose to do, well, who am I to say that's wrong?" We let the students decide who they wanted to live with, and if Black students chose to live with a Black friend that was fine. As a result of this policy change, the Black students became less segregated but not at the expense of their personal decision making.

THE CHEERLEADER INCIDENT

The most volatile issue I had to face during any of that time was over the selection of a cheerleader. You can think of all the great issues of the world—job discrimination, housing discrimination, and all the financial inequities—but what event caused the greatest uproar? It was the selection of a cheerleader. The Black students were well aware of the existence of racism in many venues, but that isn't what exploded, at least not on our campus. At WSU, the students tended to get most upset about issues they saw as direct personal slights. It may seem funny to say that today that picking a cheerleader presented a crisis, but it was not funny at the time. It was very tense.

In the 1960s, the cheerleader selection problem was an illustration that an issue doesn't have to be a world-class problem if the conditions are just right. This was the case with the cheerleaders. Wichita State had a coed cheerleading squad of 12 students. This particular time, two extremely attractive African American women—you know, the cheerleaders were selected in part on appearance—who had excellent high school experience tried out for the squad. Supposedly, of the six openings for the women, the African American candidates finished seventh and eighth. When the two women found out, they claimed it was no coincidence. "This is racist. It isn't fair." They were really angry and upset about the decision. They felt a tremendous personal sense of abuse on this one. As a result of their upset, the incident got the attention of our Black student community who became quite upset. As dean, I could see how volatile the situation was, especially as I had dealt with these students before on different kinds of issues. The African American students organized several large demonstrations claiming that the cheerleading selection process was racist and needed to be reversed.

I remember meeting with the president of the university and discussing this issue with him. We agreed that these two women were not just pouting, that their sense of injustice was very likely justified, though not directly provable. Given the look of these two women, their cheerleading ability, and their experience, they had a good claim that race was involved. We agreed, however, that, if we tried to override the selection committee, we were going to produce resentment and hard feelings. We needed another way to deal with this. It was President Lindquist's idea to expand the cheerleading squad. He said, "Let's just make the squad larger, and add two more women and two more men." We put a spin on our message saying:

> We have such a good cheerleading turnout, and we have enough money now, and we are entering into a larger sports arena as part of the state system, that it just makes sense to expand our cheerleading squad. It will make our squad more comparable in number with other schools at our level of competition and so we are going to be able to have eight men and eight women and expand to an exciting 16 member squad.

Since the selections were already over, we convinced the selection committee to add the individuals who scored seventh and eighth as the completion of the extended squad. This decision seemed to satisfy everyone. Once the squads became integrated, the members just became cheerleaders, and race seemed to disappear as a factor. Minorities have been well represented on the cheerleading squad ever since.

HUMAN RELATIONS COMMITTEE

The president established the university's first human relations committee in 1965 and named me the chairman. The committee looked at institutional policies, procedures, and practices. We spent a long time doing that and we introduced numerous recommendations. One thing that came out of the human relations committee was a new look for our university publications. Up to that point, there were never (or rarely) minority students in the pictures, except perhaps a minority student on the receiving end of some tutoring by a White counselor. Most of the pictures had been Nordic men and women with perfect teeth. Other students including minorities, those in wheelchairs, etc., were invisible in our publications.

Based on the work of the committee, I was able to sensitize the division of student affairs to the culture of diversity. We began to ask questions like, "Were the activities that we generally offered mostly interesting to White students aged 18 to 22?" "What would make us feel that students of color might want to participate?" "How would we have to change those programs to broaden their appeal?"

RELATIONSHIP WITH POLICE

We had our own campus police force, and that relationship was not always good, especially in the 1960s. We worked very hard at improving student relationships with the police. When I was hired, I made sure that we always had students on the committee when hiring new police officers. The first chief of police that I encountered was not a bad guy, but it was difficult for him to adjust to the idea of letting students in on the hiring process. The next chief met with students regularly. He listened to their complaints and there was a decline in racially related incidents.

We also got the police to go through "sensitivity training" through the counseling center. A lot of people thought that was a joke initially. That phrase has been diluted and doesn't mean anything anymore, but this sensitivity training was important. We brought in minority students to those sessions to say, "Yes, you have to protect our campus, but try to see the world the way I see it." Their examples were stunning. I think we made great strides. For example, at one of the protests against the war, we had over a thousand people participate. The protesters asked the chief and me to follow their parade, because they had confidence in both of us. They were more concerned about the reaction of our city police. At that very event, I got a call from the chief of police in Wichita, and he said to our chief, "Where's Rhatigan?" Our chief said, "Well, he's right here in the car with me." "Well, put him on!" I got on and the city chief said, "Dean, we're getting a lot of complaints that these marchers are using profanity and we're just not going to put up with it." I said, "Well, what are they saying?" He said, "Well, I don't want to get into that." I said, "Well, I

continued on page 185

In 1969 at Kent State University, the administration had received advanced word that students planned to take over the administration building and occupy it until their demands were met. Assistant Vice President for Student Affairs David Ambler and Dean of Student Group Affairs Gordon Bigelow attempt to negotiate with students. Ambler and Bigelow relay that a delegation of only three students will be admitted to the building to talk with the president.

Students protest the University taking action against seven students who had disrupted a disciplinary hearing and refused to leave the hearing room. The seven were arrested, convicted, and sentenced to six months in jail. They were released from jail on Friday, May 1, 1970, the weekend students protested the invasion of Cambodia on the Kent State Campus, which lead to the tragic killings the following Monday, May 4, 1970. Some believe that the convicted students instigated the resulting protests but there was never any evidence or proof of such.

Photo courtesy of David Ambler.

Police drag a dissenting protestor on the University of Iowa campus in 1968.

From the 1968 Hawkeye annual, Special Collections Department, University of Iowa Libraries, Iowa City, Iowa

Students gather at Dunn Meadow on April 21, 1971 at Indiana University.

Indiana University Archives

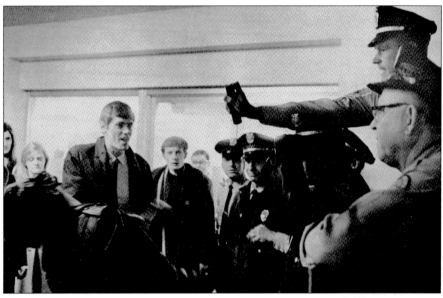

Taken in 1967 in Iowa, "mace foils protestors' attempts to break into the Business and Industrial Placement Office where Dow Chemical representatives were recruiting on December 5."

From the 1968 Hawkeye annual, Special Collections Department, University of Iowa Libraries, Iowa City, Iowa

Black Student Union Walkout at Oregon State University in 1969

Oregon State University Archives, P57:2301

Wichita State University students march along 17th street (south edge of the campus) in reaction to previous day's events at Kent State University.

The first black students since reconstruction on the day they registered at the University of South Carolina administration building. Left to right: Robert Anderson, Henrie Monteith, and James Solomon.

University of South Carolina Archives

need to know." He said, "They're saying, '1, 2, 3, 4, we don't want your fucking war.'" I had an awful time taking this seriously but I said, "Okay." I went to the head of the line of the protesters and found the organizer of the event and I said, "How's it going?" He said, "Oh, Dean, it's just great, look at these huge numbers; everyone's mellow; we're going to the park in 30 minutes and everybody's holding up just great." So I said, "Good, well, stay with it guy."

I reasoned to myself how long can a group of adults say, "1, 2, 3, 4, we don't want your fucking war?" I figured at the outside they could last maybe one minute. And so I went back to the car and called the Chief, "Well, I've taken care of it." From then on, I was a hero to our Wichita chief of police because he thought, "Boy, Rhatigan has absolute control over those students."

TENSION BETWEEN ADVOCACY AND SERVING THE UNIVERSITY

The position of vice president for student affairs was created in recognition of an increasing number of functions and services for students on the American college campus that were increasingly complex and expensive. The student affairs division was expensive and had to be managed successfully. I was a vice president for student affairs AND dean of students, in contrast to today's arrangements. In my role as dean of students, I was an advocate. I wasn't a patsy, but I was an advocate. I went to work when others said no to a student. When people said no to a student, this was often infuriating to me. Usually I took the view that the student's issue was legitimate, unless proven otherwise. Maybe we were not accommodating the student because we were just too damn lazy or set in our ways. Now occasionally, of course, I was conned, and I always let the students know, "You got your dean. Congratulations. But you didn't achieve a damn thing." Generally, I didn't get a lot of that. What I got was honest expressions of unbelievable discouragement, caused in some cases by campus staff! I got this insight from many international students of color, as well as from local students of color. Of course, I got it from White students, too.

Any student who came to see me got the full benefit of my passion, my knowledge, my full effort. I am, by very nature, a patient, kind and very gentle person. That is a key to working in a civilized way, especially when a lot of people are angry. If I was having a bad day, I would talk to my wife about it when I got home. But, at work, I had to provide a reliable image of stability. Upending an expectation is a very effective tool, so occasionally I would pop off. But this usually was calculated, and I did it to make sure that students understood that the old dean might bite back if pushed too hard. Still, I tried to resolve problems without the person on the other end paying a high cost. For example, a student might be denied the use of space. The reservation secretary might say, "Well, you can't have this activity on Sunday because we're closed." Okay? So I'd talk to the president. I would say,

> Clark? This is Jim. They won't let students use the interdenominational chapel on Sunday for their services because the facilities are closed and we can't get a key. But, we just have to open it, and this just isn't right.

And so then I'd hope the president would say, "Well, Jim, whatever you think you got to do, you go ahead and do." If so, I'd hang up and say, "Well, the president is really upset by this, and he said we are going to change that right now." So, often I got a triple win out of it. The president got his win, I got my win and the students got their win.

There were demands we could not meet. Students would say, "We want to have this issue addressed and resolved and you have until September of next year." So I'd say to those students, "Well, throw up the barricades because I can't meet that kind of deadline." And they'd say, "Bullshit, dean, we're not playing that game, you're conning us." And I said,

> Well, fine, do it your way, but you're not going to get anywhere. You're just going to get angry. But go ahead, because if your aim in life is just to get mad, rail, and thrash around, fine, you're on the right course. Now if you want to do something, if you actually want to be accountable for what you've done, sit down; let's talk about it.

Usually I got them back to talking, and I would see what I could do. The president was always supportive.

Not everybody was supportive of Black students. People loved them in the abstract, but didn't want to give them a position of influence because they were hard to deal with. I often felt that these students didn't know how to conduct business as the academy does it, so I had to show them how. I also had to make sure while they were trying to achieve their goals that they didn't trash a bunch of midlevel administrators who were victims because they did not have the authority to be helpful. They couldn't agree to do the things that they were being asked to do. So I often went along to be helpful, using whatever I had. This is all about advocacy.

Students knew I worked for the university. All I ever told them is "look, you're not going to hear me say, 'Yes I can do it,' and later on find out I've told somebody else, 'We can't do it,' but I'm holding you off and hoping you'll all graduate or go away." I said, "The only standard you can hold me to is that what I told you I would try to do." I used that for years, and I think that's all any human being can do.

Chief student affairs officers do not always have the luxury of knowing what exactly they are doing. Sometimes one has to go without proven knowledge, making one reliant on general skills and the skills of others. One thing I did learn was not to overpromise. I did promise to LOOK at things that we never did deliver, but I always made that clear at the beginning. "We'll try it, but I think your prospects are slim." To dink them around and to pretend that you had made an effort—now that was dangerous.

As an advocate for students, it was important to note that not all students saw things the same way. I had students in student government who were conservative and wore three-piece suits. My job was to try to get those student leaders to communicate with less traditional student leaders. I didn't see myself as the font of all knowledge and goodness. I was a facilitator in many ways. "You two talk about it. Don't tell me there's no resolution there. The reason you can't find one is because you're yelling at each other." Then they would calm down, maybe. Admittedly, our White students from western Kansas often did have a bit of a problem with the tough-talking dude from Wichita who was Black. In those cases, I would have to jump in and try to get the Black student to modify his anger a little bit so that the White students could be permitted to do the right thing, not look like they'd just collapsed like a deck of cards. I didn't want that to be the outcome. I'd try to tell Black student leaders, "Look, allow those White students to do the right thing. Let's see, if you give them a chance, what they are going to do." "Ah, dean, we've got to push a little bit; you know they're not going to do anything. They have had 200 years to do the right thing. They're not going to do anything." I said, "Yes, but now we've got a specific thing that's on the table; let's just see what happens." Then I might go over to the student government and say,

> Look, talk to the Black students frankly. Do the right thing. They're waiting to see what happens, so let's put your best foot forward. Let's frame that in such a way they can see that we're trying; even while we have our values, we're trying to help them achieve what they would like.

Students, almost without fail would say yes to that approach.

ROLE OF STUDENT AFFAIRS

When I left student affairs in 1996, the names and content of almost every program had changed since 1965. Then there were no TRIO programs, except for Upward Bound. The organized orientation office was not even invented by 1965. Academic advising had no coherence as an entity. We experienced enormous change in 30 years, including learning how to deal with diverse, diverging, and sometimes antagonistic populations of students.

Our field has been preoccupied by a concern for professionalism. We have thought of professional recognition as coming from outside, certified by others, a top-down proposition. I hope that one day we come to realize that professionalism comes from the bottom up, is based on the perfect mix of competency and caring, and can neither be given to us by others nor taken from us.

The main issues deans face today are so much different. Rather than lament about what we have lost in our budget cuts, deans should be asking, "What can we accomplish with what we DO have?" Let's not continually bemoan our fate. "We're unloved; oh my, oh my, if only I had more money I would be so great." I just don't believe it. I believe in adversity. You suck it up. What can you do that doesn't cost any money? The list would be long. Some people give up just when others get warmed up to carry on.

The 1960s were a transformational period for student affairs. We were working in an exciting time. The period of unrest changed the whole nature of student affairs forever. No one ever went back to the way it was. Students from that period on had a lot more of a voice in their affairs. I think that inclusion was the right thing for us to do. Deans of students coped either extremely well and prospered because they were out there on the front line, or they were totally ineffective. I've often said, if you want student affairs to prosper in the future, we need problems like the 1960s!

THE SITUATION FOR STUDENTS OF COLOR IS BETTER NOW

With the doors of opportunity open, students of color are in a better position today. Bear in mind though, the issues today aren't only about African Americans. We now have Asian-Americans and Mexican-Americans with pressing needs. Race is still an issue. It is the great unresolved issue of our country. Still, only the most die-hard would say we have made no progress. We have minority students who have graduated from WSU who are now doctors, lawyers, and professors. In terms of absolute numbers, the changes are phenomenally good, in percentages not so good. We went from about 400 African American students in the 1960s to about 1100 today. In terms of the percentage of students who have prospered, we haven't achieved what I'd have hoped for. We still have too many casualties. I can't account for this in any precise way. We need to do a lot better to increase the academic success of minority students.

In spite of it all, we are making progress in the United States, and unless you're an extremist on the right or the left, you know that this is true. We have something to build on. We don't live in a perfect world, but we can move toward better behavior. I don't mean just better rhetoric but by actually doing things that help students succeed.

Access was greatly improved in the 1960s. The numbers of minority students increased and the "specialness" of being a minority began to fade away. Having a critical mass of minority students decreases campus problems. Small numbers are what cause problems because students are sensitive, not enjoying their "exceptional" role and status. Students told me that it felt like somebody had their eye on you all the time. It was uncomfortable.

The development of leadership skills is an area where we still need improvement. A lot of minority students do not have leadership skills because they haven't had a chance to exercise those skills in high school or they didn't have a parent to show them how. We teach leadership development, but are still surprised that students are so primitive in their skills. This is something they have had to learn.

LESSONS LEARNED

Protest works. Students today do not realize the power of protest. Institutions are so afraid of public controversy. Universities will go to great lengths to accommodate students to avoid controversy. My rule was: "Don't get pushed around. At first students will only want your shirt. But then they will want your tie, your belt, your trousers and your shoes." When dealing with students, especially on an issue that cannot be resolved in the way they want, one sometimes just has to say, "Guy, do what you've got to do, but this time the answer has got to be no. We cannot do it."

Unrest got student affairs' people off the dime. It forced us to respond. It is very important to be able to respond the right way given the situation one faces. What we learned was that protest works. It worked then and still does today. Protest is better than trying to negotiate your way along; it's a shortcut because the university is so slow. Even when we had good intentions, change seemed to take too long for students. We have all kinds of time barriers, but when there is somebody occupying the academic vice president's office, well, students definitely had your attention.

One should have a strategy on dealing with protest, and that strategy, first of all, should never be to quell it. The first strategy should be to understand it. If you can't respond to it positively, fine. You want to go barricade yourself, fine. But you just don't react to protest, them and us, right and wrong, villanize your opponent and all that stuff. Those responses are immature and won't solve problems. One should never respond in fear, apprehension or surrender. The only thing that I yielded to was when their arguments were better than mine. And there were many such occasions. One cannot just yield out of fear, though, because once you are on the run you are a dead duck. There is just no hope for you after that. Still, I was not a fan of advocating "tougher than thou" behavior either.

I learned that planned change can happen! Not the passive change that one is simply watching, but change that you helped engineer. When this happens, you have helped engineer the future. When you change even one person's life, you've changed the future. This is a dramatic lesson. You change a life, you've changed it forever and perhaps the life of everybody in that person's environment—maybe their children, and their children's children—and you've done it even though your name, face, and voice will long since be forgotten. Now that is something you need to know as you work in this field. Work is the greatest opportunity that we have to be effective, so if you're sucking your thumb and lamenting, you are wasting the greatest gift that you've ever received. You can be an agent for change.

Another lesson I learned was when people are reeling and angry and mad at you, often it is only because they want so badly to succeed. They just don't know how. They have no experience. They didn't have an older brother, a sister, an uncle, an aunt, a father, a mother who ever went to college, so they didn't know what to do. You are seen as a hindrance not a helper. Passive students always fare the worst. They come in the front door and go out the back door, and no one knows or cares. In the 1960s, these students needed the people in the power structure to grab them by the lapel and say, "You're not going out the back door. C'mon back. We'll work this out." Aggressive students know what to do. They weren't the ones I worried about. The ones I worried about were the ones that came to us pretty much defeated and all we did was fulfill their worst expectations. They are the ones we might not see, but I made a point, the longer I worked, to remember that people who are hurting sometimes are invisible, so you better find them. It's up to YOU to find them, not up to them to find you.

In number, student affairs is a small band of warriors. If one wants to be successful in student affairs, one needs to find ways to work with the academic community, because they are people who generally have the same instincts that you do. They have to work for tenure, to write their books, do the other things that the game requires. In the end, though, if they are asked to do something, in my case, over 90 percent would say yes. Faculty has always been eager to do the right thing, to be of help, to do the extra bit of tutoring or whatever it took.

I learned the lesson that it is not them or us. When I talk about the complementarities of student affairs, I'm not talking about us as second class citizens, which some of my colleagues in ACPA and some in NASPA seem to think. There are those who argue that unless we are "returning to the academy" we are missing the boat. My view is that by diluting and misunderstanding the idea of service, we have lessened our effectiveness unnecessarily. Student development is a subset of service to students. We don't have to posture and claim exclusive rights in student development. Nobody wants to be "developed." People want to be successful, and you do this first of all through a genuine ethic of caring. If caring isn't there, you're doomed. If it is there, you've got a chance to succeed. You need skill to accompany it; you just can't care and leave your brain at home.

What really counts in my view is the single student, sitting in front of you, with a single problem, issue or hope, and you have one chance to do something. You succeed with that student or you don't. It doesn't require knowledge of theory. What is required is sound judgment and total commitment. When you do that, your chances of succeeding are good.

Most of my life experiences have centered on the small picture—one student, one issue. Rarely did I have a long history with students who came to see me. They appeared at a point in time; our lives converged perhaps only that one time. I learned a long time ago that it was not the depth of those encounters that made a difference, it was the timing. In helping a student, I would evaluate what he/she needed to do and then we would do it together. Development is a byproduct of what you do with students; it isn't a strategy and goal that you do to students.

When staff was impatient with students, I often said, "Think of that kid's father or mother as the governor of Kansas." Now you don't see that pain in the ass; you see that well-connected pain in the ass, and you're going to respond differently. So when you're turned off, that new attitude will encourage you to act with a little more energy.

Concluding Thoughts

Often in the heat of the 1960s, it was one day at a time, one hour at a time, one incident at a time. You didn't think strategically. You didn't have time to think reflectively. Maybe you thought tactically, if you had a week ahead of time to know that something was coming, you'd all get together and say, "Well, now, should this happen, who's going to handle that and how?" I call that tactics.

There are times when answers elude us. I remember a Monday morning when I was talking with an African American student I knew fairly well in an arranged meeting on a routine piece of business. He seemed distracted. I asked what the matter was, but once he'd offered his obligatory "nothing" in response, he changed his mind. He told me that on the previous Saturday he and two of his friends decided to go to the 9:00 movie at a large shopping mall near the campus. They parked their car, but in rounding a corner toward the main building, a White woman, elderly, they said, was walking toward them. When she saw the three of them, she froze in her tracks. The three men all saw her fear, and they knew that they were the source of it. Silently, they changed the angle of their path toward the building to walk obliquely away from her. But the movie they saw later was a waste of time. They had been judged and found guilty in an instant. Guilty of what? The bitterness was palpable. When he left my office I was as dispirited as he was because I neither had the ability to change what had happened, or even the words that would have offered comfort. We want to tie the best effort of our mind and spirit to solving issues and to reveal the immense possibilities for good that rest in each of us, but sometimes we just do not have the resources we need, and that incident is such an example in my own experience. I didn't know what to do. What would you have said to this kid, "Well, it might have been something else?" That would have been bullshit. There is no point in trying to talk your way through that issue. He was wounded! Better to be dumbstruck with him. I lamented, but on that occasion it was all the good that I could do.

In any given encounter you either come through or you don't. There is no hoping and wishing that students are going to talk about what you want to talk about. That is why experience helps with student affairs, because the longer you are at a place, the more relationships you've built, and that makes any particular issue with any one student easier to address. I argue not for power, but for influence. Influence is everything. Power comes and goes. People want to take power away from you, but influence is enduring. It allows you to do things. Longevity is one thing that helps establish influence. It either helps you or kills you. [LAUGHS] It helped me, I know that much. My life has been a series of small wins, and one hopes that when you put those together one can say, "Yes, what I've done is good."

EPILOGUE

James Rhatigan was the vice president for student affairs and dean of students at WSU from 1965 to 1996. In 1996, he was named senior vice president of the university, a position he maintained until he retired in 2002. Today he works half-time as a consultant for the WSU Foundation. Rhatigan has received numerous awards for his service to the student affairs profession, including the Fred Turner Award for outstanding service to the profession in 1980 and the Scott Goodnight Award for outstanding performance as a dean in 1987. He is still an active scholar, writing articles and essays in numerous refereed journals.

RON BEER
Kent State University (1961-1972)
University of Nebraska, Omaha (1972-1980)

O
n Monday, May 4, 1970, the shooting at Kent State occurred at about 12:30. The president and the four vice presidents and I were at a lunch. We went to lunch at a restaurant that was not far from the campus, after having spent the last 48 straight hours on campus. We had slept there. Appeals to the National Guard on Monday morning and to the governor were rejected, they would not leave, which was our request. We went to lunch. Maybe we went out about quarter to 12 because I remember some reference to a meeting on the commons at about 12:30, which was probably a class change on that hour. The commons, where all of this occurred, was a cross-roads from residence halls to classes, so a lot of people passed through that area. We went out to have lunch and while we had ordered, the food had not yet come. I took a phone call from the president's office that said that there had been a shooting, and the person thought that a policeman had been killed, shot by student rebels. I didn't even get back to the table before another call came in from another person to say that students had been shot. I ran back to the table, explained what happened; we just all got up and left. We had to settle with the restaurant later. We got to campus in about two minutes and the place was just pandemonium, absolute chaos. The vice president for student affairs immediately went to the site and the president went to the guard command. I started to help get students' information. The executive vice president of student affairs and the assistant vice president all got a hold of their staff as quickly as possible. We wanted to clear the campus, to just let the students go. Wherever, however we could, we wanted to let them go.

The mere mention of Kent State brings to mind the events of May 4, 1970, the day four students were killed and nine others were wounded when National Guard officers opened fire during a student antiwar demonstration.

As the executive assistant to the president of Kent State University at the time, Ron Beer was intimately involved in the student demonstrations and the tragic aftermath.

Beer's professional career in higher education began in 1961 at Kent State University. In his 11-year tenure at Kent, Beer worked in the president's office, alumni relations, and student affairs. This chapter describes his experiences with civil rights at Kent State as well as his subsequent experiences at the University of Nebraska at Omaha.

CIVIL RIGHTS AT KENT STATE

While the mention of Kent State conjures images of the student shootings in 1970, the campus was also long active in the struggle for civil rights. In the early 1960s there was a small group of African American students on campus. These students were described by Beer as being "fairly docile" and as focused on getting a degree.

> They always had financial aid problems. I do not think there was a lot of harassment before the early 1960s when the civil rights movement began. The Black students saw their leaders in society as a whole as models and said, "We need to try this at the university as well. We don't want to be second class citizens. We want the same kind of assistance as anybody else." In making their case, the students used athletics as an example. The students noted that the institution made all kinds of special services available to athletes, as they do in a lot of institutions. "If that is the case, why can't they do this for Black students, acknowledging what's happened to us historically: poor school systems, poor teachers, inadequate environment overall, and a lack of reading generally." I think the students were very sincere and honest, acknowledging, "We need help and we want you to provide that at no cost." National civil rights activities, as well as related activities in the nearby metropolitan areas of Youngstown, Cleveland, and Akron, influenced and shaped civil rights activities at Kent."

Student involvement in civil rights activism was the precursor to the antiwar demonstrations that led to the tragedy for which Kent State became infamous.

> I recall a prelude to the shootings, which was in reaction to the Vietnam War, and in large measure prompted by 'peaceniks,' students, and nonstudents. These peaceniks were certainly antigovernment and antibusiness, people that truly and honestly believed that we were the aggressor nation and that we should not be involved in that war, that

Nixon was wrong. Before the antiwar demonstrations, there were a lot of demonstrations by the Black students, particularly from the Cleveland/Akron area. There were some very, very vocal Black students. We had a number of the organizations—Black Panthers, Black Student Coalition—various organizations of that nature on campus. I cannot remember how many organizations there were. They held sit-ins. We had a number of sit-ins where Black students were trying to say to the university that we were not doing enough to recruit more Black students, provide financial assistance, and acknowledge that they came from school systems that did not prepare them adequately to compete. This was reflected in test scores, reflected in grades, institutions had a formula to say, "We will accept X number of Blacks," I have forgotten how many, some percentage, probably somewhere between five and 10 percent of people who show promise in other ways if they did not meet the entrance requirement.

Students typically met directly with the president. There was the sense on behalf of some student affairs administrators that "They are students. Don't listen to them. Don't do anything," leaving students adamant about wanting to meet with the president instead of the student affairs personnel, as was the norm on many campuses. The president tried to be responsive. He was sincere, wanting to make their pursuit of the degree successful, making the environment reasonably comfortable for African American students. He was not one to push students off on staff saying, "You go meet with them."

As the executive assistant to the president, Beer met with students and the president.

Usually I was responsible for creating the meetings, establishing the time. At times, Black students tried to take over buildings and we called in the Ohio State Patrol because the students were interfering with the normal functions of the institution. We had a highly professional highway patrol. I think records show that there were never any complaints about students being mistreated when they were physically removed from buildings.

It was my job, along with the student affairs staff, to make sure there was not any clubbing, or any maceing, or any unnecessary force. We asked the patrol to provide clear instruction when they walked into the classroom or office. They said, "Here's what you're doing and it is unacceptable. You've got five minutes to move. Failure to do that will result in the following." When we articulated that, we were gently firm, if you know what I mean. We did not mess around. But, the patrol did not kick people. They did not wrench their arms behind their back. They handcuffed them and they escorted them to a bus, and then took their mug shot. The students sat in the bus until they went to jail. I think the Black students thought that was a part of the civil rights movement. It was the only way, short of violence, to drive home the point, and it worked.

Student calls for civil rights on campus were the precursor of antiwar activity at Kent. The antiwar, women's, and civil rights movements were all intertwined.

The antiwar movement learned from the civil rights movement in using tactics and strategies that Martin Luther King and others utilized, though some did their own thing. The consequences of the antiwar tragedy had an impact, I think, because, after that, Kent created a Black studies program and they also had an institute for nonviolent activity programs. They also had, and I think still have, a major Black studies program. But the Black student leadership felt that if they were sucked into the system of protest in general that they would be lost, that they would be overwhelmed, and that people would lose what they were all about.

CIVIL RIGHTS AT UNIVERSITY OF NEBRASKA, OMAHA

In 1972, Beer moved to the University of Nebraska in Omaha as the vice chancellor for educational and student services, a position he maintained until 1980.

The University of Nebraska had been a municipal institution until 1968 and the citizens paid a tax to support that institution. I think it had fairly good contact with the Black community. North Omaha was predominantly Black. The university had a fairly good relationship with the school system. The university also had a fairly good number of Black students, some regular students and some commuters, as we would say. There was no university-owned housing, but there were day students who came to campus to take regular 12- to 17-hour loads, and there was a fairly sizeable number who came in the evening and weekends. I think the relationship was pretty good. In fact, after I was there about four years and was recruiting a lot of Black students as well as Native Americans, we had an incident with a board member. At a meeting, this board member from the western side of Nebraska, Scotts Bluff, an attorney, challenged the chancellor and myself—I was the vice president of student services, responsible for admissions and registrar—and accused us of lowering standards to allow all these Black students to come to the campus. He did not know what he was talking about. The trustee said,

> We ought to fire half the faculty and give the money from those who are fired to those who stay. Pay 'em. Keep the good people, but pay 'em properly. We need to develop standards. We have far too many incompetent students who are diminishing the standards of performance.

He had no basis to make that comment. The president of the university asked the chairman to stop the meeting to allow him to say something. The president said, as he had a wonderful way of doing,

> Mr. Chairman, all you have to do is adjourn this meeting for five minutes and allow me to go to my office in time to pen you a letter of resignation. I will not tolerate that kind of diatribe from this man. If he has factual information to support what he is saying, I want to see it. But we will not proceed.

And of course the trustee shut up. It turned out the president sufficiently embarrassed the trustee and we proceeded with the meeting.

The University of Nebraska at Omaha was very responsive to diversity and worked really hard at trying to engage the community. We had a good mix, a diverse staff. The woman who is now vice president of student affairs is an African American woman who worked in the counseling center in the 1970s. She came up through the system. Another African American woman joined my staff and eventually became assistant to the chancellor. We also had Hispanic and Native American staff in the financial aid office and the counseling center.

Issues of civil rights often bring to mind race as a "Black and White" issue, but at institutions like University of Nebraska, the civil rights discussion also included Native American students. Beer noted that at the University of Nebraska:

> The Native Americans were a bigger challenge. The younger Native Americans were coming to campus and were always frustrated with the challenge of "do I finish the degree and go back to my people to help them, or do I, in essence, enter the White man's world?" We worked really hard to include Native American students as well as Blacks in the student government.

We held a lot of conversations with business people, including the presidents of Mutual of Omaha, State Farm, and the Union Pacific Railroad, all of which were headquartered in Omaha. We would have their CEOs frequently to the campus for dinner and conversation with 10 or 15 students. I remember one Native American student, a very, very talented guy, who had said nothing during the dinner. One of the CEOs said to the Native American, "Now, I've been observing you all evening, and you've been a very intent listener, but you haven't said anything for about two hours."

The Native American dinner participant went on to talk about Native tradition and how it can conflict with corporate culture. Beer recounted what the student said to the CEOs in the room.

He told them what legend, culture and tradition meant to Native Americans, and how very difficult it could be in the business world, because when a tribal member dies, his family is in ceremony for four days or five days, whatever is the custom. There must be nothing more important than "ceremony-ing" this person to the Great Sky. Virtually every CEO present acknowledged their lack of knowledge about Native American customs and the impact of such in operating a business or, as far as that goes, the likely effect their beliefs had in causing few Native American citizens to apply for work in traditional businesses. The Indian student surmised that few businesses, if any, would allow sufficient time off work to attend a traditional Native funeral or other significant celebrations; therefore, few Native Americans would even bother to apply for work in such businesses. It was an "awakening" to the CEOs, all of whom became more highly sensitized to the differences among the work force and pledged to develop policies with greater understanding and tolerance for these differences in their hiring and operational practices. The student was stoical in his response, expressing appreciation for hearing him out, but quietly skeptical about the extent to which there would be "real" change. I personally believe that discussion did lead to changes in at least some of the hiring practices at these companies.

The student also explained that Native students did not like to leave the reservation. They would not leave the reservation. The university actually sent faculty from the college of education to the reservation. I remember distinctly a group of about 15 Native students who graduated with teacher certifications and, of course, they remained on the reservation and taught school there. The Native Americans would not come to us, so we went to them. We paid the way to transport classes and teachers to the reservation.

The struggle for civil rights at Nebraska was process oriented. Beer gave examples of how some of this process took place.

> I do not ever recall any demonstrations, any conflicts between youths and police officers, as was the case at Kent State. The president and I went to their turf. We met with a group of Black students down at a Black bar. It was a matter of acknowledging that you don't always have to come to our place. The meeting was with student leaders who wanted us to come to their community and meet with them and some of our people. The bar was the place that they thought was the most appropriate to have a meeting. We arrived before the students. We walked in and all these people had no idea why we were there. They could not believe that we were there. But we went in and went to the back room. We had a good discussion, about support, about how the institution could do even more in terms of financial aid. Students see their biggest problem as financial aid and maybe longer hours at the library because most of them didn't have a place to go to study. We were fairly responsive to that. We acknowledged it; we didn't argue.

Similar processes and conversations took place with other communities as well.

> We went to a lot of Black churches as a part of recruitment because that is where the focus of the Black community was. With Hispanics, we went to social functions, some celebration in their part of town, with dances and much gaiety. That was where you met parents. And that is where we spent our time in trying to recruit Hispanic students. We went to powwows to convey information about the opportunities at school. We wanted to assure community members, especially the tribal councils, that this was not a lot of talk, which was always a fear. We were not just White men making a bunch of promises that we were not going to actually provide. As a result of our efforts, the Native community accepted our offer when we said we would go on the reservation to offer classes. They conveyed the information to the people. The reservation responded well; the tribal leadership came to the campus and created scholarship funds. We spent a lot of time on that.

> I appointed a female coordinator for Native American student affairs. I thought she was highly qualified and the best candidate. Unfortunately, the male students would not go to her. It was a shame.

They wouldn't go to her. Students' lack of willingness to meet with her pointed to civil rights issues associated with gender in addition to race and ethnicity. We told the students,

> We don't understand. This is the lady you are going to have to deal with. She is fully qualified; she can assist you as well, if not better, than any man that would be in that position. It all has to do with education and the support systems available to you. I'm not making decisions about Native American tradition or customs or tribal matters. That's for you to determine. But she is the person you come to.

They finally did.

The process orientation and proactive stance of the administration at University of Nebraska in Omaha made for a "very dynamic, very vibrant place, and it just grew wonderfully in so many ways."

THE PERSONAL IMPACT OF CIVIL RIGHTS

I became much more sensitive to what the marchers in the South were doing and what it meant. I gained a better understanding, certainly, of the plight of many African American communities, where many youngsters were raised in a single-parent family. There is nothing necessarily wrong with that, but it placed a demand, an extraordinary demand, on the mother to sustain the family financially, and then to care for their family needs in the evening and weekends with meager or minimal, and in some cases no, resources.

Being raised in a White community in Illinois, we had no Black families in our community. I am embarrassed to say it, but when I left home I did not understand issues of race. When I look back on it in retrospect, I recall that there was an unwritten rule that no Black was allowed in town after sundown. We were on a major highway from Chicago to St. Louis, so a lot of people would come through. They could stop and eat. They could buy gas. Our town was so small; we didn't even have a motel. But, I was just unaware. I came from a very protective background. So, I learned a lot and I really came to know Black men and women. I knew that Black people could not get a drink out of the fountain, eat in a restaurant, or stay overnight to rest. But it wasn't until later that I realized they couldn't do that because they were Black. I think that there was empathy on my part to work hard at trying to convince other students, with whom I worked day-to-day, about the inequalities that we perpetuated.

Perhaps as much as any movement, civil rights called for an awakening and provided real-life experiences to make clear that every individual needed to be treated with dignity and to be respected, and not chastised, or repressed, or oppressed because of a particular belief and attitude. Certainly, individuals have no control over their ethnicity. I think that I changed dramatically as a person once I got into the profession of student affairs, just because of the exposure and the day-to-day interaction with students, including the confrontations with them. I think Kent State and Martin Luther King had a dramatic impact. These events say to folks that we can speak forcefully and change patterns of behavior, not only in our community and within ourselves, but nationally, if we do it properly and nonviolently. I think that Kent State was a turning point. The nation finally said we cannot solve our problems by shooting the young people because of what they are saying and what they stand for. It was going to happen someplace, given the pattern of activity related to the war in Vietnam.

THE IMPACT OF CIVIL RIGHTS ON BEER'S CAREER

Beer's most direct involvement in the civil rights movement was at Kent State and in the early years of his Nebraska tenure. The lessons learned from this involvement would go on to shape the rest of his career at Nebraska and at Oklahoma State, where he moved in 1980 and remained until 2000. Beer's involvement in civil rights issues created an empathic stance that often led him to taking on the role as a defender of student's civil rights.

There was one spring at Kent State when we were selecting staff for the next year's resident assistants for the undergraduate residence halls. We had selected several young men who were openly gay, and the contingents of one of the halls came running over one afternoon and were just absolutely urgent to speak to me. They came in and I said, "What is your concern?" They said, "You can't authorize or approve the appointment of those two, gay RAs because one of them will be in our hall, on our floor. We are not going to move and we are not going to have that person." I said, "Well what's the problem?" They said, "How are we going to go to the bathroom?" "Like you normally do. You know there are bathrooms down the hall." "Well what will we do if he comes in?" "Do whatever you've been doing." The point of it all was here were a group of young men that were obviously homophobic or perhaps didn't understand. I said,

> Well, gentlemen, you've got a choice. You can either live in the hall where this person is going to be your RA or you can leave. I don't think you have to worry about any of those things. He is not going to come in and molest you. If there should be an experience in the hall, we've got a procedure to handle that.

So they left with considerably different views. The students came back the next fall; they were on the floor with the gay RA and, as far as I know, they all got along okay. It is that perception, the misunderstanding that causes problems. I just think that the task is never ending to confront people when there is some indication that they are discriminating against someone because they are different.

I made it very clear with my professional staff that we just would not tolerate sexist jokes. In fact, I threatened them. Once, I made it very clear that I would fire an administrator, who was also a practicing physician in the health center, if I ever heard a sexist joke come from his mouth while he was on university time. The same is true about telling jokes about putting Blacks or Native Americans down. Another example is that as vice president at Oklahoma State and at Nebraska, I created an advisory group of students that included the presidents of the Black Student Association, the Native American Association, the Hispanic Student Association, and the International Student Association. A number of people did not understand that. They asked, "Why are you including these people when their groups represent a very small minority of the campus population? Everybody else is president of the senate, president of other, more traditional, larger groups." I said,

> Because they are a very critical element, small in number, but important, to be informed about what is transpiring and, most importantly, to have an opportunity to provide input from a perspective we're not going to get in any other way.

We made very clear that their voice was equal; we made sure that nobody was put down when they made comments. You can attack an idea, but not the individual making that statement.

Beer's close involvement with students from different minority groups made him very aware of the importance of leadership in higher education.

I'm talking about department heads, deans of academic units, directors of whatever program and above, which means vice presidents, assistant vice presidents, whatever title is given to them, they need to be vocal. I can remember many times at Oklahoma State going to the honors program for minority students, because it used to be under the division of student affairs. I was frequently one of the handful of vice presidents who were present, which I think is a travesty, because it says that faculty and staff really do not care enough to come to watch the students receive recognition. I think we need to put our feet and our presence where our mouths are.

Based on his involvement in civil rights activity, Beer is particularly emphatic about the need for presidents to take a stand on issues related to civil rights and diversity.

I don't hear many presidents, nationally, and I don't pretend to know about all of the institutions, but I hear very few who speak out as they should. Presidents need to speak out for these issues. I know of one person who is very courageous. He speaks candidly about the need for the institution to be more responsive. This guy is vocal and he speaks out with some regularity and frequency. If presidents aren't saying it, then who will? My professional staff probably got tired of hearing me say that, but it is just one of those things that needs to be repeated over and over, reminding them that you are here to serve students, and sometimes you can lose track of that.

THE IMPACT OF CIVIL RIGHTS ON THE STUDENT AFFAIRS PROFESSION

Kent made a big difference in saying we have got to be more responsive to our young people. It may sound like a cliché but, nevertheless, students are the leaders of tomorrow. I think it helped me at least to say to the leadership of student government, elected officers who run on a lot of local kinds of issues, I promise to do this and do that. I promise to get more tickets for the football game and better seating at basketball. I also promise to broaden their horizon and to be a teacher. I have used a saying for years that helped to guide me: "All that we are, all the while we are teaching," meaning that whether we are on the job, in a social setting, at the store, in a bar, wherever, we are always teaching. Even our nonverbal behavior says something to those who know us or know of us. Many times we are models to people who we may not know personally, because of our position, but who look up to us or model their own behavior after us. Our influence on students and others extends far beyond the office or the campus. What we say, how we say it, how we act, how we look/dress, all influence—one way or the other—those who know of us. This anonymous quote helps me to remember that it doesn't make any difference whether you are in office, whether you are in an official student organization, whether you are attending a function, or at the barbershop. I think we, who are in the profession, have an obligation, a responsibility, to practice that over and over and over.

Student affairs professionals face some limitations. I do not think that when you are in a leadership role on campus that you have the freedom that other people have. You have the right to speak your piece—one's first amendment rights should never be violated. But what you do, and how you do it, and where you do it, are subject to limitations. As leaders, our job is to show others what you should and should not do. I don't have the right to go out and be inebriated and act like a fool. Not that people violate the law in doing that, but I think it is a professional obligation to be a role model. I also think that there is nothing more important than to help young people understand that they need to treat their colleagues, regardless of color, regardless of beliefs, respectfully. We need to continue to work with students to help break down barriers by exposing students to different cultures. I think it is a never-ending task and ought to be done whenever the opportunity presents itself. The civil rights movement was perhaps as significant as anything else in this country, in the decades which I've been alive, in helping me to grapple with these issues.

The civil rights movement was as consequential as anything I know. I think that everyone has a responsibility to work for change. It is important for people to carry the torch or carry the banner and sound a trumpet, to say, "Wait a minute folks; you do have a racist faculty and you need to address that." In my experience, not always, you can bury stuff in committees and in the bureaucracy forever. Somebody has got to be really vocal. I think the leadership of the university, more so than anyone else, has to be vocal about these issues. Many students just need encouragement. They need to know that the vice president and the dean know them and respect them. I always make a strong effort to learn names and to say, "Hello Felicia," "Hello, Marcus," as students are passing by on the campus to make sure that they understand that I know who they are.

THE ROLE OF NASPA

I gained a lot from people in NASPA. They were a professional family and network that were just awesome to me. I would encourage anybody to join because they are so sensitive and responsive. I think NASPA has a long-standing philosophical base to be open, to be representative, to be responsive. I think their structure is the best. NASPA provides incredible opportunities, through its networks and through the regional system, for people to be involved. Candidly, while the national convention has an open microphone on the floor, and always has, the membership used to be more vocal. People used to be a lot more vocal than they are now about some of these issues. I was the chair for one of the national conventions and was responsible for the speakers. We made a significant effort to be inclusive of diversity, women and African American primarily. I think that is one of NASPA's strengths. I like to think that I was supportive for that along with a lot of other people.

LESSONS LEARNED

Beer learned many things from his experiences at Kent State and at the University of Nebraska at Omaha. He divides these in to two categories. When faced with incidents as pivotal as the May, 1970 incident, he observed:

One of the most significant lessons learned from the May 4, 1970 incident was the importance of developing and clearly articulating the chain of command in the institution. Any chief student affairs officer (CSAO) should insist on knowing the chain of command for whatever set of circumstances may arise. The Kent State experience and a number of incidents since (e.g., fires, bomb threats, serial killings, murder on campus, etc.), should make clear the need for a thorough but succinctly written policy for evacuating buildings or a campus. Every effort should be made by upper level administrators, always including the CSAO, to develop an open and candid relationship with key authority figures in the community—police, fire, mayor, city manager, sheriff, district attorney, constable, state police, national guard, etc. Student government officers should be fully informed about such policies, procedures, and practices, with a good understanding about their role in such matters; where their participation is expected, and where it is not, with what authority—if any—do they, can they, act? Each campus should identify a place, known to all administrators, faculty leaders, student leaders, and community authorities, where the person(s) in charge would be located once immediate or critical contact is judged to be important to the safety and welfare of the campus community. Phone numbers reserved for the purpose of contacting this place should be known to the same individuals. All such policies, procedures, practices, and written materials should be thoroughly reviewed and communicated anew every year.

Beer's experiences with civil rights led him to identify the following lessons:

Written policies should be in place to clearly articulate expectations of student, faculty, and staff behavior related to the fair and equitable treatment of all members of the academic community; in the classroom, in campus housing, in approved student organizations and activities, in employment at any level, and on the properties and at events of the university. All parties should know to whom to go to register what is thought to be a legitimate complaint about another's behavior directed against them, and policies should state what procedures will be enacted, by whom, to bring the issue to resolution within the university community. Accusations should be spelled out as clearly and in as much detail as possible. Racially based (also gender, sexual orientation, ethnicity) slurs, threats, or physical attacks should be addressed specifically.

In addition, my work with Black and Native American students led me to believe that student personnel staff members (and, hopefully other employees) need to make every effort to be as open, receptive, inviting, responsive, accepting, and interactive with minority students as they are with student leaders of major or large organizations. Student leaders of minority student organizations should be "at the table" where important information is disseminated to student leaders, where counsel is sought from student opinion makers, where recognition is given for accomplishments, and where policies and procedures are reviewed and promulgated. Their names should be known with a familiarity that allows one to address them specifically when meeting by chance on a walkway or in the cafeteria.

It seems obvious now, but I learned that special holidays, celebrations, unique customs and important events need to be acknowledged as happenings or occurrences, not necessarily by canceling classes or excusing attendance, but to say that we know that these things are important to your history or culture. We share in your sorrow or wish for you a happy celebration. I'm not sure this is something I fully understood before my experiences at Kent State and Nebraska.

Likewise, student affairs administrators need to seek out the individual or group that expresses anger, bitterness, urgent concerns, or reports threatening action from others, to talk directly and candidly about the issue, the circumstances, the time and place and date, and "who", when known. I learned that I couldn't wish for the incident to just pass by or think it was not really that important.

I also learned that addressing an incident efficiently, with fairness and integrity based on facts is critical in maintaining a trust, a confidence, and a belief that "I am, indeed, a fully accepted citizen of this community." When students saw that they were all treated fairly, they were reasonable. On the other hand, trying to placate a group by implying that something will be done or promising whatever is being requested, or in some cases demanded, when, in fact, you do not know that to be true or that it will happen, did not work.

Finally, I learned to be as attentive to attending functions, events, or activities sponsored by or held to honor minority students, as I was to majority students. I learned to make a special effort to invite minority students to an event or activity with which I knew they might be uncomfortable or unsure about their presence, or whether they are "really" welcome. However, once I did that, I had to accompany them, introduce them to others, and help to engage them.

EPILOGUE

In 1972, Beer took the position of vice chancellor for educational and student services at the University of Nebraska in Omaha, a position he continued until 1980. In 1980, he moved to Oklahoma State as vice president for student affairs, where he served until his retirement in 2000. Upon his retirement, Beer served as an assistant dean on a "Semester at Sea"—a voyage that took him and his wife, Cara, to Cuba, Brazil, South Africa, Kenya, India, Malaysia, Vietnam, Hong Kong, and Japan. He continues to be an active volunteer in Oklahoma and abroad.

DAVID A. AMBLER
Kent State University (1966-1977)
University of Kansas (1977-2002)

D avid Ambler earned a doctorate in educational administration from Indiana University while he served on the dean of student's staff as an assistant director of residential programs. He was selected to be an assistant dean of men at Kent State University in 1966. From 1966 until 1970, he held several different positions in the student affairs division at Kent State. In 1970, he was named vice president of student affairs, a position he held until 1977. He was then appointed vice chancellor for student affairs at the University of Kansas, a position he held until his retirement in August 2002. He is now vice chancellor emeritus. In this chapter, Ambler relates experiences from both Kent State, where he served during the tragic events of May 1970, and more recent events from the University of Kansas that illustrate the ongoing struggle that majority White universities continue to face in their quest to become truly integrated institutions.

PERSONAL EXPERIENCES

I grew up in northwest Indiana, which was one of the true "melting pots" of America. Long before it was called "integration," we had it there. Even though housing was segregated, both my grade school and high school were integrated. My parents were not wide-eyed liberals, but they did invest me with a respect for the rights of others and a sense of fairness and justice. It served me well in developing a commitment to civil rights which was an issue throughout the 40 years of my professional career.

An example of my early experience with this issue occurred in high school where I belonged to a small singing group, and three of the members were African Americans. One evening we were invited to sing at a country club but we were turned away at the door. We were told that the three members of our group who were African American would not be allowed in the club. I was shocked. Not only could five of us not do the program without the other three, but also I remember the five of us said, "That's crazy. We're out of here." That was my first involvement with racial prejudice and it deeply affected my commitment to this issue.

My adolescent experiences set some values in me so that, when I arrived in Bloomington (Indiana) to attend the university, the level of prejudice and segregation I observed really hit me in the face. Lake County, Indiana, where I grew up, was 95 percent Roman Catholic and 95 percent Democrat. The rest of the state and Bloomington were just the opposite: 95 percent Republican, 95 percent Protestant, and 99 percent White!

I came from a working-class family, so my motivations for going to school were primarily economic and social mobility. But early on, those motivations clashed with my moral values. As a freshman, I was asked to join a fraternity. But racial segregation was a reality in Greek life and was tolerated by the university. I simply could not join such a group. As an undergraduate, I also participated in a protest and boy-cott of the barber shops of Bloomington. At that time, the only place Blacks could get their hair cut in Bloomington was at the shop in the Indiana Memorial Union. I wouldn't describe myself as a radical per-son on racial issues; it was just a "this is not right" kind of attitude that led me to be involved with civil rights issues at an early age.

Entrée into Student Affairs

Being from a blue-collar family, I was highly motivated to do better economically than my father had been able to do. So, I planned on going into business or industry to make big money. However, my undergraduate experience—particularly my interactions with the Indiana student affairs staff—turned me 180 degrees in a different direction. Jim Lyons and Bob Shaffer, two of my most valued student affairs mentors, saw me struggling with my career choices towards the end of my undergraduate career and suggested that I consider a career in higher education. Not fully convinced, I began with a master's degree in public administration. I also had an ROTC commission, and my time on active duty gave me the opportunity to sort out what was important to me. In 1961, I returned from military service to the Indiana University with a strong commitment to go into higher educa-tion. I completed my master's degree and then the student affairs division offered me my first full-time, professional job. I ended up earning all three of my degrees at Indiana University, because they allowed me to work on my doctorate while I was working as an assistant director of what we now call residence life. When I finished my doctorate in 1966, Bob Shaffer, the gentleman that he was, said to me, "Now, Dave, we'd love to have you stay at Indiana but, if you do, you'll probably always be 'Dave Ambler, the student' to a lot of people." That was his gentle way of saying "You have been here long enough. Go get a life and a career!"

In 1966, I was hired to be assistant dean of men at Kent to replace Ron Beer, who was going to be working with the president's office part-time so he could complete his doctorate. By the time I arrived at Kent, I was named acting dean of men. Later that year we reorganized and they eliminated the dean of men and the dean of women positions, and I was named associate dean of students. I was in charge of residence life. At that time, it was a real buyer's market in this profession, and opportunities were many and promotions came fast—much too fast.

CONTEXT AT KENT STATE

Kent State was an "up and coming" regional public university that had initially been a teacher's college, then a state college, then a state university, and finally designated to be one of the big research institutions in the state. All of this occurred in about a 20-year span. The institution had experienced rapid change. It was heavily commuter when it first was established and did not have a strong student affairs program. In 1965, the new chief student affairs officer, Bob Matson, was brought in to quickly build a comprehensive student affairs program to meet the rapidly growing and changing student population. Kent had about 6,000-7,000 students in 1960. When I arrived in 1966, there were 18,000 students. About 30 percent of the students were commuters but they were rapidly building residence halls to accommodate this changing student body. We didn't have a large fraternity-sorority program. Most of the fraternities and sororities lived in old, single-family houses. And, most importantly, there were not a lot of established traditions in student life. At that time, Kent had very few African Americans on the staff and did not have an office of minority affairs or any programs to serve the growing minority population in the student body.

Kent is located in the northeast quadrant of Ohio, which includes Cleveland, Akron, Canton, and Youngstown, and was the most heavily populated and industrialized part of Ohio. I would guess that we had over 10 percent African American students. We had a large contingent of foreign students, and a smattering of other minorities. At that point, Kent was about 80 percent first generation students, mostly coming from industrial families in that part of the state. The African American students were equally represented in the commuter, resident and off-campus populations. As Kent attracted students from mainly first generation industrial class families, there was a lot of tension between Whites and Blacks. Many Whites saw Blacks as an economic threat. So the two groups were fairly segregated on campus. Ohio was an open admissions state at that time, so being admitted to a state university was not the issue; the issue was being accepted and treated with respect for your culture, your values, and your needs.

When I arrived, there were limited facilities for campus life and a student affairs program designed for a different age and student population. The new dean of students was committed to the transition from the old dean of men and dean of women model with a heavy emphasis on behavioral control and social monitoring, to a comprehensive set of student affairs programs to respond to the contemporary needs of the new Kent students. The excitement for me and the other new student affairs staff was that we were going to be involved in developing them.

FIRST PROTEST

In 1967-68, I dealt with my first student protest as a student affairs professional at Kent State. The protest centered on the Oakland (California) Police Department, which was invited to campus by the university placement center to recruit students. The Oakland police were notorious in their relationships with minority groups. Yet, Kent State had a nationally recognized law enforcement program that was very popular, and many police departments came to recruit its students every year. When the Oakland police came to campus, the Black students decided that they did not want their university to be compliant with a police force that they believed to be racist. The appearance of the Oakland police on campus became a focal point for all of the concerns and feelings of minority students about the city of Kent, the university and society in general.

The Black students blocked entrance to the placement center to prevent students from holding interviews with the Oakland police. This resulted in several of the students being told that they would be subject to disciplinary action and suspension from the university if the continued to interfere with a legitimate university program. Police were used to break up the blockade, though students were not arrested.

I watched the dean of students handle this protest. His basic message was "We can't tolerate this kind of behavior where you're interfering with the rights of other students and the rights of the institution." While he and many of us in student affairs were committed to the civil rights movement, the university, like most universities at that time, was not an active participant in the movement for fear it would "politicize" the university. At the same time, most universities, including Kent State, were not prepared to deal with major student protests regarding many societal issues including racial equity. We were "flying by the seat of our pants" in dealing with this issue.

When the university indicated they would proceed with disciplinary hearings for the students charged with violating university regulations, the Black students organized a march off campus. They demanded that we drop the charges and address the concerns of minority students by employing more minority faculty and staff, creating a minority affairs unit, and devising an African studies program.

They organized, probably, one of the most effective protest tactics I've ever seen and that was the walk off campus. They packed their suitcases and marched through the campus and out through the front gate. They went to a predominantly Black church in Akron and announced that they would not return until their demands were met. Their protest received much publicity and placed a lot of pressure on the university. The protest lasted four or five days, but it seemed to me like an eternity at the time.

I remember there was an African American psychology faculty member named Milton Wilson who walked off campus with the students. Many of the staff members were upset when they saw Milt walking with the students, but I knew him well enough to know what he was doing. He was looking beyond the immediate issue and saying, "When this thing is over, we still have to have some credibility and communication with the students." His actions made it possible for him to help us resolve the issue peacefully, and later he moved into student affairs and became the first director of our minority affairs programs.

The president eventually agreed not to prosecute the students, and to establish a commission to investigate and respond to minority student concerns. The students came back to campus and we began to develop what I considered a very progressive, creative, and effective program in student affairs for minority students. All of this was an important "learning experience" for me as a young professional in dealing with student concerns and campus protest.

This is where Dean Matson first demonstrated his skill as a student affairs leader. When the president decided to take another approach to resolving a crisis, Matson responded creatively by establishing the commission to hear concerns raised by the African American students. With his leadership, we developed one of the country's first human relation centers, or what would now be called a multicultural affairs office. When the students asked for one thing, the dean responded with even more. If they wanted "a," he also gave them "b," "c," and "d." He gave them not only a minority counselor, but also a whole program of human relations. We provided services and educational programs. We brought a number of offices into that human relations center, so it was not just African American and international student programs, but it was also a very comprehensive program that went far beyond their original demands. This was another important lesson for me in dealing with student issues.

CREATION OF THE BLACK CULTURAL CENTER

Creation of a Black cultural center was not really one of the demands stemming from the Oakland police protest, but it came about as this population of students gained more clout.

Eventually a group of students expressed an interest in creating a Black cultural center. To accommodate them, we found an old house that the university owned right near to campus and established it as a Black cultural center. The problem was we didn't think the issue through as well as we should have. We didn't ask, "What is the purpose of a cultural center? How will it be used as part of student life or an academic program?" As a result, it became a clubhouse that soon was viewed as a hotbed of radical and criminal activity. The police raided the center several times in the belief that is was harboring criminal activity. We learned a valuable lesson in establishing a new program: Make sure it has a legitimate purpose and that you staff it and fund it appropriately. It was an example of good intentions leading to a bad outcome because of poor planning—another important lesson learned by this young professional.

THE 1970 TRAGEDY

The May 1970 shootings at Kent State have been widely analyzed and memorialized in print. Consequently, Ambler focused on the intersection of race and the 1970 events.

Across the country in the 1960s, a number of different movements existed on college campuses including Kent State. There was the student rights movement, the counterculture movement, the civil rights movement, the women's movement, the environmental movement, and the antiwar movement. These were interesting movements in that some of them shared memberships, while others did not. There were, for example, distinct lines between the civil rights movement and the antiwar movement. Black students were very much opposed to the war in Vietnam, but they did not participate in the antiwar movement, generally populated by middle class, White students. They always expressed fears that they would be the ones subject to arrest and police brutality if they joined forces with the White, antiwar students. Their protests were always separate and with different issues to address.

Because of what we had done in the late 1960s in making Kent a more positive environment for racial minorities, we maintained good communications with the Black student leaders. As we approached those ugly days of 1970, I felt good about our ability to work with Black students compared to our relationships with the White student protesters. I am convinced that this good working relationship with Black student leaders was a major contributor to the fact that no Black students were arrested, injured, or killed in the protests of May 1970.

By the end of Monday, May 4, Kent State University was closed by a court order. Four students had been killed, nine injured, and the education of thousands of others permanently disrupted. The campus remained closed for the balance of the summer. That summer was the worst summer of my life. We had a variety of state and federal investigations, including a state grand jury, the FBI, the President's Commission on Civil Disorders, the Civil Rights Commission, and our own efforts to determine the cause of the violence on the campus. Additionally, we were preparing to reopen the campus and fearful of additional violence that might close the university once again and, perhaps, permanently.

By late summer I was exhausted, so I took my family to visit my parents in northern Indiana, some 400 miles away. While I was there, I received a phone call from the assistant to the president saying, "Bob Matson has resigned; the president intends to take your name to the board of trustees next week as acting vice president. If you disagree with that, you better get your butt back here pretty quick." So I rushed back to Kent. I was 33 years old; I was trying to decide what all this meant for me. I wasn't even sure I wanted to stay in higher education, let alone student affairs, and besides, I had never given thought to being a vice president! But the president pleaded with me that he needed my help. I knew I would feel guilty if I said "no." Yet, I was feeling totally inadequate for this challenge at such an early time in my career. With only a few hours to decide, I finally said "yes," but only on an acting basis. That was in August, and school opened up in late September. In November, the president asked me to take it on a permanent basis and I agreed. And the rest is history. I stayed there until 1977, and I would say between 1970 and 1977 we made continual progress on minority issues, but the campus was so dominated by the aftermath of the 1970 incident that everything else seemed less critical and had to take a back seat to the continuing saga of May 4th.

I never thought about it at the time, but I now believe that at least some of the credit has to go to the student affairs staff for the fact that no minority students were injured or involved in a major way with that tragic event. It might have been different had we not built good relations and communications with our minority student populations. I think a lot of the things we did at Kent in the years I was there were truly "cutting edge" in terms of making the campus climate better for African American and other minority students.

After the 1970 events, there were not, as I recall, any major incidents where minority students and the university came head to head. The students did not want the police brought in at the risk of provoking violence as we had experienced in 1970. The minority students were able to press their point without causing dangerous confrontations. As my tenure at Kent concluded, a protest against the construction of a new gymnasium on the site of the May 4th shootings developed, but it was resolved peacefully and without violence. I left Kent with a heavy heart but with pride in the progress we had made in student affairs in building a more diverse and peaceful campus environment.

After 11 years at Kent State and seven years as its senior student affairs officer, Ambler decided it was time for a career change. In July of 1977, he accepted the position of vice chancellor for student affairs at the University of Kansas. During his 25-year tenure in that position, he faced several major incidents relating to discrimination and civil rights on that campus. Indeed, his involvement with racial matters began before he arrived on the Lawrence campus.

THE UNIVERSITY OF KANSAS SORORITY INCIDENT

Before I left Kent, I started dealing with the racial climate at the University of Kansas (KU). I accepted the position of vice chancellor in February 1977, but did not assume the position until the following July. But the phone started ringing early on! The spring before my arrival, KU had a race-related incident during sorority rush. At that time, sorority rush was held at the beginning of the spring term in January. I received a call in early February from the young woman who was the president of the Panhellenic organization. I had met her during the search process. "I need your help! I need your counsel!" she said. It seems an African American woman from Wichita had gone through rush and was not pledged. The young women made no public comment nor did she file any complaint with the university. But two sorority members came out publicly to make an issue of the matter: "This woman was a perfectly acceptable candidate but she was rejected for one reason and one reason only, and that's because she's Black." Well, the whole campus was enraged and as you might suspect; faculty and student leaders were demanding punitive actions. At that time, national sorority offices were not encouraging racial integration and were of little help to those on the campus who were calling for change. The courageous Panhellenic president wanted the sororities to confront themselves and this issue, and devise a plan to diversify the Greek community. Since the rushee had not filed a complaint, the university could take no official actions and, with little support from her peers, she turned to me for advice and counsel. I was in a difficult position, but suggested to her that she address the issue publicly by announcing that the matter would be investigated by the Panhellenic judicial board, and that she was establishing a committee to determine ways that the sorority system could diversify its membership. No real actions came out of her efforts, but it bought me some time to get to campus and to determine how the division of student affairs could encourage the integration of the Greek community.

During my tenure at KU, some progress has been made on this issue, including the establishment of a permanent, joint fraternity-sorority commission to encourage racial integration and awareness in the Greek Community. Periodic progress can be noted, but both the predominately Black and White Greek groups have backed away from this issue. Fraternities and sororities organized around minority racial groups have decided that strengthening their own organizations is the better avenue to travel in improving the undergraduate experience for their members. I remain, however, committed to the idea that student organizations that are racially diverse make a significant contribution to achieving a truly integrated global society.

THE PIZZA INCIDENT

Several years later, another racial incident occurred when an African American woman was delivering pizzas to a fraternity. When the delivery person arrived at the house, she encountered a fraternity member who was drunk. Surprised to see a Black woman in the house, the young man verbally assaulted and physically intimidated her. Other members of the house came to her defense and she was able to leave without being physically harmed. However, as word of the incident reached minority student leaders and groups, a major protest erupted on the campus.

That incident affected the whole environment of this campus. There was a sit-in in the administration building and Chancellor Budig came and talked to the students. He promised appropriate disciplinary actions and, more importantly, greater efforts by the university to increase minority enrollments and to improve the racial environment on the campus. Eventually, it was determined that no disciplinary actions were warranted against the fraternity and, when the individual students involved voluntarily withdrew, tensions eased on the campus. One important byproduct of this incident was the hastening of the transfer of the office of minority affairs to the division of student affairs. Initially, that office reported to the executive vice chancellor, the chief administrative officer of the Lawrence campus. Its transfer signaled to the minority students that the office would be directly involved in student life programming, and would serve as an advocate for minority concerns within the student affairs division and the university administration.

THE MULTICULTURAL RESOURCE CENTER

Even though we had an active minority affairs office, the student senate initiated an effort in 1993 to establish a cultural center on campus. Drawing on my experiences with a similar project at Kent State, I pushed the student sponsors to define the mission for such a center. It became clear that they had little notion or concept for what a center would contribute to campus life. With the help of a creative director of the office of minority affairs, we convinced the students that such a center should serve as an outreaching resource center to the entire campus as a way of infusing the concept of multiculturalism in all aspects of university life, including the curriculum in the classroom.

The students became enthusiastic for this model and even agreed to provide 50 percent of the funding for the center. In its 10 years of operation, the center has made a significant contribution to improving the racial and cultural climate on the campus. Staff members from the center serve as resource personnel for campus housing units and student organizations; they promote training in cultural sensitivity, and advise faculty through The Center for Teaching Excellence on ways of improving the learning environment in the classroom. The establishment of the center was a cooperative adventure between the division of student affairs, student leadership, and minority students to improve the campus environment. It was a modest effort to be sure, but it represented a change from the days when the establishment of any such programs to assist minority students grew out of confrontation and controversy. For me, it was a symbol of how far we have come in addressing these issues from the earlier days of my professional career.

THE LOUIS FARRAKHAN AND THE KU KLUX KLAN INCIDENTS

The Louis Farrakhan and the Ku Klux Klan (KKK) incidents were separate events a year apart, but they had similar repercussions for the university, and represented the two most difficult racial experiences I had at the KU. They were difficult because both incidents placed the university's commitment to free speech and academic freedom at loggerheads with its commitment to racial equity and improving the multicultural environment on the campus. As these incidents came later in my career, I felt comfortable in dealing with both issues and keeping both concepts viable at the KU. Once again, student affairs were in the middle of the controversies over the invitation to both Mr. Farrakhan and the KKK to speak on the campus. It was our responsibility to protect the rights of groups to invite speakers of their choice to the campus. Equally, protecting the integrity, and providing for the safety of all the students is a major student affairs function. I was determined to fulfill both responsibilities.

In 1987, Louis Farrakhan was invited to campus by an African American student organization under the university's code that grants the right to students and student organizations to invite speakers of their choice to the campus, subject only to regulations regarding time, place, and manner. Nevertheless, it fractured the relationship between the Jewish and the African American populations, a relationship that had been deliberately nurtured over several years by both groups.

People who normally were unconditional in their support of free speech on the campus started backing off; the Jewish community was stressed in maintaining their traditional allegiance to free speech, but feeling deceived by the invitation to Mr. Farrakhan.

With much good work by the campus security forces, university relations, and the student affairs staff, the program came off with no violence or serious confrontations. A large protest in front of the campus auditorium was peaceful and kept in order by the large number of faculty, staff, and campus religious advisers who volunteered to be in the crowd to help keep the peace.

Meanwhile, over 3,000 students and others filled every seat in the auditorium to hear the views of Mr. Farrakhan. When it was all over, I took some small pride in believing that all of the legitimate purposes of the university were well served that evening. Many students had a genuine "learning experience" that evening that extended through the rest of their days at the university. That is student affairs at its very best.

A year later we had a different set of circumstances when the KKK was invited to speak on the campus. A faculty member in journalism who wanted his students to have the experience of interviewing some extremists extended the initial invitation. The issue then was not free speech on the campus, but academic freedom in the classroom. It didn't make much difference to those offended by the Klan; the protest was immediate and intense. The initial response was delicately directed by the vice chancellor for academic affairs and the dean of the school of journalism. Knowing that when "push comes to shove," they would have to allow the interview, they convinced the faculty member to hold the class in an off-campus location for the safety of all interested parties. This resolution seemed to lower the protest, even though some still called on the university to prohibit the appearance.

Those of us in student affairs thought we had escaped this issue as it was a "faculty matter" and seemed to be resolved in a skillful way. Wrong! A small group of students who maintained an organization titled "Not so Young Americans for Freedom" decided to test the commitment of the university by sponsoring a free speech forum and inviting the Klan to be a participant. They were a registered student organization and, even though the group was usually dormant, they had a right to the privileges of being a student group, including inviting the Klan to the campus.

Once again, student affairs was called upon to defend an apparent confrontation of university values. We worked with the sponsoring group to insure that their event could take place while at the same time asking them to understand the consequences of their decisions for the university and many of its constituent groups. We met with representatives of many community groups who could not understand or appreciate why the university felt obligated to let the Klan speak on campus. And we did our best to convince those students and student groups who were deeply hurt by the Klan coming on campus that it in no way altered the values and commitments of the university. And we did our good work with campus security, faculty, student leadership, counselors, and religious advisers in soliciting their involvement to help us maintain the integrity and the peace of the campus.

I was particularly proud of the role of the student body president in this incident. Himself a Jew, he never wavered in his support of the university and its commitment to free speech. I had several conversations with his worried mother to try to assure her that her son would be safe; yet I knew the dangers were there. He was an inspiration to me for his demonstrated maturity, strength, and commitment at a very young age.

Many who opposed the Klan, and even those who opposed the Klan but supported us in our commitment to allowing them to speak on campus, wore red lapel ribbons to clearly state, "I protest. I disavow the Ku Klux Klan." I, myself, and almost every other student affairs person wore one of those red ribbons. I don't usually like to wear my values on my lapel, but it was a way of saying, "I'm out here defending the right of free speech, but that says nothing about what Dave Ambler personally values." In the end, we prevailed in keeping the peace and upholding the values of the university. And, once again, 3,000 students in the auditorium and thousands more outside had a "learning experience" that went with them into their lives beyond the university. But the damage to the image of the university in such incidents is incalculable. It is one of the prices we pay for those things we hold sacred in the university community.

THE STUDENT BODY PRESIDENT INCIDENT

In 1990-91, the students at the KU elected their first African American student body president. The young man had been involved in a group called the "Black Men of Today" which was formed around the time of the pizza incident at the fraternity house and gained much campus visibility from that incident. It was formed primarily because its members thought that the Black Student Union was not very strong and not forceful enough in pressing issues within the university community. Their viewpoints had become popular enough to elect several student senators and now to place one of their members on the ballot for student body president. His vice presidential running mate was a Japanese-American, making this a truly diverse political coalition. They won the election and the university touted its first African American student body president in all the media.

Late that spring, however, some student leaders learned that their new student body president had been earlier arrested for physically abusing a woman. A movement immediately began to remove him from office. It was a frustrating time for student affairs as we could not intervene in what was essentially a student matter and a process established by the student's own governing codes. All we could do was to attempt to insure that the process was fair, and to raise questions regarding motivations, fairness, due process, and the integrity of the student senate and its members.

The student senate began the impeachment process in the fall semester and it was the most heart-wrenching thing I had ever experienced. As I do with so many of the student leaders, I had become very fond of this young man. I knew the story of his life and this incident, and I felt comfortable with it. I did not believe it warranted his removal from office when the facts were all known. Demonstrating a great deal of personal courage and humility, he stood before the student senate meeting and told his life's story and explained this incident. His was a typical story: his father abused his mother, and the cycle of violence was passed to him. He had gone into counseling after this incident. He had done all the right things to make his amends to this woman and to her family. In fact, her father came to testify on his behalf.

I was extremely frustrated by this incident for the outcome seemed to be foreordained. I had to remain neutral; yet I wanted the students to examine their hearts and minds before taking any actions they might later regret. I took the approach of talking informally to many of them and asking them "to look yourself in the mirror and tell me that, if he was a White person, this would be going down the same track as it is now." It was my way of suggesting that there might be some racism at work here. Doing that cost me some relationships with some of my other student leaders, but I really felt strongly that we needed to try to get the students to take a good look at this before they did something that was going to be very devastating to this young man, and to the university.

Eventually they did remove him from office. I remember thinking, "This young man will hate this university; he will probably leave here and go back home and this devastation will plague him and will plague us for a long time." Fortunately, I was wrong. He took an extra year before he finished his degree. He went back to Kansas City and eventually was accepted to the University of Missouri Law School, finished his law degree in good order, clerked for a county judge and became a practicing attorney. He's now in his own successful real estate business and he still loves KU. A few years ago he came back for a student leadership conference and was one of the featured speakers. We asked him to talk about dealing with adversity as a leader and he got up and told the story of what happened to him here at KU. He said, "You know, sometimes you have to go to the bottom of the valley before you can climb to the top of the mountain. And I've done that, and you can do it, too!" This is what student affairs is all about!

REFLECTIONS ON STUDENT AFFAIRS

The last article I wrote before I retired was in the NASPA Region IV West newsletter. I called it "Unconscious Resentment" which was a term coined by Jim Rhatigan in *Pieces of Eight* (1978). Rhatigan talked about how student affairs creates an unconscious resentment within the faculty, because we are a constant reminder to faculty of their failure to cope with the lives of students. Rhatigan said that student affairs was born on the periphery of the educational establishment. Where we should be located in the establishment, Rhatigan suggests, has been a perpetual question since our founding. If we become too embedded in the establishment of higher education, we might compromise our values and our commitment to "cope with the lives of students."

My article in the newsletter represented my reflections on whether or not I, personally, and we as a profession have been co-opted as we became part of the higher education establishment. We became executive officers of our institution during the campus protests associated with all those student movements of the 1960's and in doing so we became part of that establishment, that hierarchy. I believed there were times I had to compromise the values of the profession to be part of the establishment. I know there are times when I wanted to argue stronger with the presidents and academic officers with whom I worked, and maybe I didn't argue as strongly as I should, because I didn't want to jeopardize my position in the hierarchy. I think that is something the student affairs profession must continue to examine. Our location in the educational structure must permit us to play out the values so basic to our profession: "Each student is unique...Each person has worth and dignity...Bigotry cannot be tolerated, and...The freedom to doubt and question must be guaranteed" (NASPA, 1989, pp. 9-10). Without these values operating on our campus, there would have been no progress made during the civil rights era.

TREATING STUDENTS AS ADULTS

When the courts declared *in loco parentis* invalid, I was one of the first to cheer, for I saw the emancipation of the student personnel worker as a byproduct of that decision. As a profession, it allowed us get out from under the stereotype of being the keepers of student morals and manners or the "gatekeepers" of university standards. Others did not see us at the university as educators or as part of the educational process. That plagues us yet today. We must continue to work to establish our role first and foremost as that of educator.

One of the results of the legal demise of *in loco parentis* was the lowering of the age of majority from 21 to 18, which I believe was one of the best things that could have happened to our profession. I think the major right of passage in our society is when you graduate from high school. You are through with compulsory education; you can marry, and you can go to work, do all these adult things. Or, you can go to college and in many ways continue to be treated as a child. I was hoping that, when the age of majority was lowered, we would see a shifting of the responsibility of student behavior from the parents to the individual.

If there is a philosophical point that's a hallmark of my life, it is the belief that we need to quicken the process of maturation in our society so that an individual is virtually ready to assume the role of adulthood and take responsibility for themselves upon graduation from high school. I believed that this would put higher education, and particularly student affairs educators, in a different and a more educational relationship with students, for it means that, regardless of your age, behavior has consequences and you will be held accountable for your behavior.

LESSONS FOR STUDENT AFFAIRS

I learned very early in my career that there is no such a thing as too much communications in our professional work. When I became the senior student affairs officer at Kent State, I knew that reaching out regularly to students and student leaders was a prerequisite for successful student affairs work. I learned, early on, that you can never overcommunicate when you are dealing with a crisis like an antiwar protest or with racial conflicts. Communication is important, but you also have to have something to communicate. You have to have demonstrable values. The values I am speaking of are embedded in what student affairs is all about. You have to act on these values personally and professionally. You have to demonstrate that those values are operative in your life and in your organization. If you don't do that, then all the communication in the world won't mean anything.

Finally, I hope we learned through the era of campus protest that students must see student affairs as change agents. If we do not make it possible for change to occur in our institutions, then students will once again use inappropriate methods to achieve justice and equity. It is a fundamental responsibility of student affairs to make the processes of change in our institutions work for students. I do not wish the future members of my profession to experience what I did early in my career when students found the avenues for change untenable and unworkable.

EPILOGUE

Ambler retired from his post at KU in 2002. Throughout his career he served in national leadership posts and received numerous awards, both national and from the University of Kansas. In 2000, he was designated a Pillar of the Profession by the NASPA Foundation and he received the Fred Turner Award for Outstanding Service to NASPA. He was also recognized in 1987 by Indiana University when he received the Robert H. Shaffer Distinguished Alumni Award. In his honor, the University of Kansas established the David A. Ambler Leadership Development and Programming Fund, which will be used to support leadership development for University of Kansas students. Ambler continues to reside in Lawrence with his wife, Mary Kate.

CIVIL RIGHTS AT
RESEARCH UNIVERSITIES

CARL E. ANDERSON
Howard University (1958-1990)

Carl Anderson had a remarkable career in student affairs administration. As a young man, he was destined for leadership. Anderson completed his undergraduate degree in political science at Southern Illinois University at Carbondale. As an undergraduate, he was very active in his fraternity, residence life, and the homecoming committee. Several administrators took notice of Anderson's leadership qualities and encouraged him to pursue a career in student affairs. Upon completion of his bachelor's degree, he was offered a hall director position and enrolled in the new master's program in student personnel at Southern Illinois. Anderson was one of the first graduates of the student affairs program at Southern Illinois University.

After completing his master's degree, Anderson accepted a position at Howard University as a residence hall director. Anderson recalled,

> I went to Howard in 1958 as director of one of the residence halls. In 1960 I became the director of student activities. I served in that capacity for four and a half years until 1965. I then became the associate dean of students for administration and student life. In this position, I had responsibility for the general overview of the departments of student activities, financial aid, student employment, career planning and placement programs, and some aspects of the student judiciary. In 1968, I became acting dean of students after the dean of students suffered a stroke—I was his replacement.

> During that same period, I managed to complete my doctorate at the University of Maryland. My dissertation was *Selected Psychosocial Correlates of College Student Protesters and Non-Protesters at Howard University*. In 1969, when the new university president arrived, the dean of students retired, and I was named to the newly created position of vice president for student affairs. I held that

position for 21 years until the time of my retirement in June of 1990. I was at Howard for 32 years.

This chapter focuses on Anderson's career at Howard University during the civil rights era. Howard University was unique during this period because of its status as a historically Black university in the heart of Washington, D.C., where a number of marches and protests took place. Moreover, a number of major civil rights activists were graduates of Howard University. Anderson provides a vivid account of his role as a student affairs administrator during this period of unrest.

HISTORY AND CLIMATE OF HOWARD UNIVERSITY

The original mission of Howard University was to provide broad education for free men and women. Howard was founded in 1867, right after the Civil War, to provide higher education opportunities and ensure professional discipline for freedmen. Historically, some of the first students at Howard were actually White students who were children of the founders. Howard has traditionally served the African American population, even though it was integrated from the very beginning.

Howard has enrolled White students throughout its history. In addition, for many years, Howard had the largest percentage, in terms of total population, of foreign students of any major university in the nation. Up through the early 1970s and 1980s, Howard had that distinction. Back when I was there, the White enrollment was probably no more than four percent. The foreign student enrollment was probably between 10 percent and 15 percent, and the rest were African American. There were a number of White students who occupied leadership and active roles in the civil rights movement. Some held positions in student government and on the student newspaper and yearbook staff. There appeared to be little hostility between students of diverse colors and cultures.

Students at Howard always prided themselves on being what they called "activists." In fact, a review of the college's history would reveal that a number of prominent civil rights leaders either attended Howard or were somehow connected to the university. Civil rights leaders, such as John Jacob, Stokely Carmichael, Vernon Jordan, Courtland Cox, Anthony Gitters, Lawrence Henry, Ed Brown, Phil Hutchins, Michael Thelwell, and H. Rap Brown, all had a connection to Howard. During the 1960s and early 1970s, when new students came to Howard, the student association showed a video at orientation. This video exhorted them to be revolutionaries, and this was how they viewed themselves—they took great pride in social activism.

OFF-CAMPUS PROTESTS

Students at Howard protested segregated street cars and buses in Washington, D.C. back in the late 1920s and early 1930s. They also protested the segregated restaurant situation and the movie houses. In the early 1960s, they were in the forefront of efforts to integrate what was then known as Glen Echo Amusement Park. The park was exclusively White, located just outside of Washington, D.C., and operated under the National Park Service. The students organized picket lines and went out there practically every day for close to six months. They protested until the discrimination was discontinued in that park.

The students at Howard participated in all kinds of protests such as the South African antiapartheid movement, which of course came a little later. They participated in the sit-ins down South, and cooperated with Dr. Martin Luther King, Jr. and the Reverend Ralph Abernathy in the March on Washington. Student leaders at Howard joined in and supported, and sometimes actually provided the overall guidance for, any number of major events and activities that focused largely on Washington, D.C. There was no effort on the part of the university to stop students from demonstrating off campus. In fact, such efforts were tacitly encouraged.

STUDENT DEMONSTRATIONS ON CAMPUS

I can recall one incident where students took over an administrative building at Howard. This was the second massive take over (the first take over was in 1967-68, when students held the building for over five days). There was a meeting of the administrative officers that were trying to address problems and communicate with the students. The decision was made to bring in the police. I remember from this meeting that I objected to this approach. I explained that we did not want another South Carolina State, Jackson State, or Kent State situation here at Howard University. We did not want tear-gassing or that sort of thing either. If the police came to the campus and one student was injured, maimed, or killed, Howard and its administrators would be remembered as the ones in charge at that time and nothing else that we did would ever matter. But, my colleagues voted to recommend to the president that we call in the police.

I went to the president's administrative assistant and told her my feelings, and she said to me, "Why don't you call him?" He happened to be off campus when I called, and he invited me to his home. I went and told him my views and my perspective, and he told me that he would not call in the police because he was not going to be responsible for the aftermath. The president had worked all of his life in civil rights. He said he was not going to do it, and instead decided to resort to the courts to seek an injunction to resume control of the building. We engaged in marathon sessions, which led to agreements and the end of occupation of the building. Each demonstration (i.e., take over of buildings) ended with an agreement on a number of issues and a decision regarding the procedures or process to be used to deal with unresolved issues.

Students brought charges of racism against certain professors. Some students demanded certain kinds of courses be instituted in the curriculum. The Black studies program was formalized for credit and became a requirement. Students wanted certain parietal regulations relaxed, such as the demand for coed visitation and the demand for the consumption of alcoholic beverages on the campus. There were a number of issues and items engaged in that I think largely came out of two major protests: (1) the protest generally and morally associated with the whole system of discrimination—that is racial discrimination and race relations, and (2) the concern about the Vietnam War and the prospect that some of our students would be drafted and could be shipped off to war. I think those two things coming together made for a very, very heated kind of environment, which made it rather easy, frankly, for students to enlist in that cause.

Another incident occurred where students disrupted a speech given by General Hersey, head of the Selective Service Commission. These students, who were against the Vietnam War, jumped on to the stage to prevent him from speaking. That led to the development of charges based on violations of certain campus rules, which led to the expulsion of some students. The expulsion of students led to more protests and court proceedings, which ultimately resulted in a reinstatement of those students. It was like a tug of war.

Many years later, in the 1980s, we had a similar situation and my colleagues wanted to call in the police. I again went directly to the president, but the police had already come to the campus and were marshalling their forces in an attempt to resecure the building for the university. The president of the university rescinded the request for police action and stopped it. Then we started the process of negotiation.

HOWARD'S RESPONSE TO PROTESTS

At first, Howard made an effort to suppress the protests, which led to the expulsion of 38 students. The case eventually came to campus hearings that were disrupted, which led to court cases, and eventually the students were reinstated. I think eventually the university came to the recognition that somehow they had to find a way to mediate in order to be able to conduct the basic mission of the institution, namely, teaching, research, and service. But, at the same time, the university had to recognize that these dynamics were not going to go away. For example, students wanted to fly the Black liberation flag on a pole with the American flag. They wanted to put up outside speakers on top of buildings to allow them to speak almost to the entire campus from outside microphones that were placed on top of buildings, so that they could rally the students at a moment's notice. We had to find ways to support those aspirations that were legitimate, but at the same time, not compromise the university's basic mission—providing instruction and service to the students.

Meetings with students and protests occurred simultaneously. Sometimes we thought we had reached an understanding; however, that was not reflected in the next move that the students made. There were protests, seizures of buildings, and sometimes the university went to court seeking injunctions to get the students to relinquish the buildings. When the students refused, the courts sent marshals in and students were carried out. We had one building that was burned. There were many things that we had protests about. We had people who had come up through an educational system, who were running an institution, who had not experienced this kind of disruption or challenge to authority. Yet, it was clear that telling people to stop was not working and was not going to work. Somehow, we had to establish a relationship that allowed us to communicate with the young people, and for them to communicate with us, even though we may not have seen things eye-to-eye.

CHANGES THAT RESULTED FROM PROTESTS

Some of the changes that took place because of the protests were:

- a Black studies program was formalized,

- the ROTC was no longer to be compulsory,

- coed visitation was instituted,

- the consumption of alcoholic beverages on university property was approved,

- students were placed on the board of trustees, and

- students were, by definition, to be placed on and appointed to all university-wide committees. In some instances even the faculties of the several schools and colleges decided to have student representation on certain faculties.

At one time, around 1968-69, the university published a document after the first big take over of the administration building. It was called, "What Happened at Howard University: A Chronology of the Events."

THE ROLE OF FRATERNITIES AND SORORITIES

Fraternities and sororities were the most organized blocks of students that we had on campus. But, initially, students in sororities and fraternities were "suspect" within the student movement itself. In other words, many of the student leaders referred to Greeks as elitist. They were not open to everybody, they picked the people they wanted for membership. Fraternities and sororities were some who thought these organizations should not even be allowed on the campus to begin with, because there was an element of discrimination. As a result, they were thought of as bourgeois. But the Greeks demonstrated, anyway. They could command blocks of students when they committed themselves to a movement. They would show up in all of their paraphernalia and give, if you will, "color" as well as voice and expression to the movement. So they were part and parcel of it.

One of the things that I discovered while writing my dissertation, which focused on the psychosocial correlates of the protestors at our university, was that the majority of the protestors came from homes that were representative of higher socioeconomic categories than the average Howard student. They were in the social sciences and classics, and tended not to be in the hard sciences, like engineering, chemistry, or physics. They were in political science, sociology, law, and psychology, and divinity as well. They tended to come from families that supported their activities. In other words, they were not discouraged by their parents from being involved. They were idealistic, for the most part, in terms of their outlook on society and life in general. There were a number of things that separated them to a significant degree from the typical student. I think that Greek students wanted to be involved from the jump, but the problem was the perception that they were an elitist, bourgeois group that could not be trusted.

THE ROLE OF STUDENT AFFAIRS

Howard University has a unique relationship with the federal government. Congress provides a substantial portion of the university's financial resources. Therefore, you had to be careful with independent initiatives, and initiatives that were university sponsored. In my role, I tried to help students and administrators understand the nuances that were required in order not to jeopardize either one of those interests and efforts. Let me give an example. The religious organizations or denominational groups wanted the university to take positions on this, that, and the other, and they wanted official office space and residency on the campus. One of the things that I tried to do, and was successful at doing, was help them appreciate the fact that their independence and separation from the university provided a natural outlet for the students to engage in those activities without having to seek the blessing of the university. I tried to help students understand that they could maintain their independence and deal with, in their own terms, the moral issues. The university did not have to be thrown into the political dynamics in order to show sympathy toward certain efforts.

For example, for the March on Washington and the Poor People's March, people wanted to use university facilities. How could we do it and at the same time not give official endorsement? Well, we had a blanket policy that university facilities were made available to groups irrespective of political affiliation, as long as their sponsorship was legitimate. Therefore, we were able to assist in that regard. The religious groups opened their houses, which were one or two blocks from the campus, to those organizations for their use. The students invited guests to share their dorm rooms; but it was done under the broad, basic policies which were in existence that allowed for nondiscriminatory participation when there was no conflict.

We had to deal with everything that Berkeley, South Carolina State, Jackson State, and Kent State dealt with, including mass marches and arson. But we had certain objectives. One of them was to, in a sense, support legitimate aspirations of the students while at the same time, protect the university's mission. That was very difficult—very, very difficult. But I think that we managed to do it because there were several administrators who came around to the point of view that it was absolutely worth doing. If it meant making some changes, then they were prepared to do that.

Part of the role of student affairs administrators was to help faculty and staff understand the students, and interpret their views, perceptions, goals, and aspirations. We tried to help them appreciate the fact that not every demand was intended to be a challenge to their authority. Instead, it was a challenge to their way of thinking.

My role was to essentially help them find ways to bridge the problems—the potential problems. What could the institution officially condone? What could these organizations, operating within the university environment but not being university sponsored, do to facilitate objectives most of us shared? Every now and then we got some flak from the federal government where someone asked, for example, whether or not the university used federal funds to provide assistance, in terms of housing accommodations, for some of these groups. In reality, you had people who were trying to stop the protests and many of them were people who were politicians on Capitol Hill. Therefore, the university had to walk a tight wire. If the money was appropriated for educational use at the university, and somehow it was revealed that somebody was using the money to help pay for protests, which were directed largely at the policies of the government, then you had an inherent conflict that would cause a problem. The university was careful in its efforts to make certain that none of its financial resources were spent for those purposes. But that did not prevent the university from making available facilities on a nondiscriminatory basis just as it does for any group anyway.

One of the advantages that we had was that the student leadership never totally disconnected their communications with the student affairs personnel. I could communicate with the head of any of those activities at any time that I desired, and they could communicate with me. It was an open and free two-way exchange. Many students who were involved would try to understand the university's and the students' points of view and served as conduits for communication that allowed information to flow back and forth.

We met with students on a regular basis—almost constantly, it seemed. We set up all kinds of forums and had leadership-training programs. We had debates between faculty members, and integrated that as part of a freshman assembly program where several outstanding faculty members who had opposing points of view would debate an issue before the student body. We brought in speakers of all persuasions. In fact, the students themselves had a very elaborate speakers program. For a time, speakers had to be approved by the administration. We relaxed that rule and got out of the business of having to approve speakers. As a result, students brought in whoever they wished.

I came to Howard as a relatively young man, at 23. Frankly, I supported many of the students, both in their objectives and aspirations. I was firmly convinced and wanted to see changes in terms of the parietal regulations and procedures that we had at the university. For example, freshmen women had to be in the dorm at seven o'clock. Freshman women could not go downtown or far off campus until sometimes two months into the first semester. There were a lot of things that I felt were rather archaic and needed to be changed. The students had as much to do in bringing about those changes as any of the student affairs people.

We supported the students, but at the same time, it was the student unrest that led to the point where change actually occurred. We were sort of like mediators. We helped the students to maintain balance, and communicated with students with respect to what the university would or could not be expected to do. At the same time, we communicated to faculty and administrators that it was essential for them to listen and respond to legitimate concerns. I think we played an extremely pivotal role. In fact, if I may say so myself, I am extremely proud of the changes that were made. For example, we removed faculty control over the student newspaper. We placed the students in charge of student activity programs. In other words, we were still there as advisors, for guidance and support, but at the same time gave way to the interests of young people to experiment and make decisions for themselves. That is a role that I think we played rather successfully.

THE ROLE OF NASPA

NASPA and all the other student affairs organizations devoted considerable time and effort at national and educational conferences to these issues. I think that those organizations served as a forum for such expression, and the opportunity for many professionals to feel that they were not isolated and alone. There were places that they could turn to for assistance. I would get many calls from colleagues, all around the country, asking me how I might respond to one thing or another, just as I would call and say, "You went through this...What did you do? How did you handle this?" So, I think we served as sounding boards—as catalysts for sharing strategies to respond to these issues and concerns. I think it was very positive.

NASPA and other professional organizations were definitely support systems. I think it represents student affairs' greatest period. Frankly, if you notice, that was when we changed the title from dean of students to vice presidents. I do not know that there was a direct connection. I suspect there was some, because university administrators recognized the importance of the student affairs professionals. Even though the campuses were on fire, at the time, they knew. It was just like the response to 9/11. They needed someone to deal with homeland security, and it seemed that student affairs had more of a sense of what was going on and how to respond to it than most people.

LESSONS LEARNED

I do not know that I would really change anything. It is easier said than done. I found that it was almost more difficult to persuade the administrators toward a different way of thinking than it was to persuade some students to appreciate the necessity of the university to maintain an element of integrity, without prostituting its programs to accommodate whatever whim that came along. It was very difficult— very difficult. But I do not know that I would change anything. It was invigorating, challenging, exhausting, and threatening, but I think we all learned as a result. I think American higher education has changed dramatically because of the civil rights era. It is more of a partnership now. There is less authoritarian leadership within institutions of higher education than you had before. I think there is a greater sense of freedom that permeates higher education now than was the case back in the 1960s.

As a postscript, I think that student affairs professionals have to realize that in the higher education community, they are not going to be thought of as the most important element on campus—that is, first and foremost, the province of academic programs. To the extent that student affairs professionals align themselves in supportive relationships to that basic mission, they will be successful. There are some who still fight for faculty rank and let such side issues distract them. They are still fighting for a seat at the table for everything—just as the students were insisting on being in on everything back in the late 1960s, early 1970s. I think that is a waste of energy. I think that it is up to student affairs administrators to, in a sense, help the presidents, faculty, and students understand what their roles are, and to actually practice those roles, and do it better than anybody in that community. Just because you have a title, office, staff, and a budget does not mean that that you are going to be thought of as equal when it comes to academic matters. I think that is whistling in the wind. It is a battle that does not even have to be fought. What you should do is understand your role, get the president and others to appreciate that role, and do it the best you can.

Epilogue

Anderson retired from Howard in 1990 with the title vice president for student affairs. When he began working at Howard, the enrollment was 3,000 students; when he retired the enrollment had grown to 13,700 students. During his time at Howard, Anderson was responsible for transforming student life and for creating opportunities for students to fully participate in the life and governance of the institution. Anderson has received many honors and awards for his work, including the Scott Goodnight Award for outstanding performance as a dean from NASPA in 1990, and distinguished alumni awards from Southern Illinois University and the University of Maryland.

PHILIP G. HUBBARD
University of Iowa (1965-1991)

Photo compliments of Tom Jorgensen/
University of Iowa.

P hilip G. Hubbard served as dean of academic affairs at the University of Iowa from 1965-1972, when his title was changed to vice president for student affairs. He served in this position until his retirement in 1991. His story is somewhat different from that of the others in this book for several reasons. First, he was a mechanical engineer and, as the first African American professor at the University of Iowa, he moved his way through the faculty ranks, establishing himself first as a teacher and researcher. Second, during the period of student unrest, he administered student affairs from the position of dean of academic affairs, a position created by president, Howard Bowen, in 1965. Thus, he occupied a different position during the turbulent 1960s than did most of the other contributors to this book. However, much of his direct civil rights work occurred while he was a faculty member. Fourth, Hubbard wrote a memoir of his life published by the University of Iowa Press in 1999. Therefore, we know more about his life than we do about the lives of the other contributors.

EDUCATION: "THE OPEN PART OF A HALF-OPEN SOCIETY"
(Hubbard & Stone, 1999, p. 17)

Philip G. Hubbard was born in central Missouri, one of five children. His father was a craftsman and his mother a teacher. Following the death of Hubbard's father, his mother decided to give up her job as a teacher and move the family north to Iowa to take advantage of the "unsegregated" schools. As a result, Hubbard spent the better part of his youth in Des Moines, where his mother moved with a new husband. She remarried for the third time when the second husband died. Although schools were not segregated, almost every other aspect of his family's life was. Unable to resume teaching, his mother worked as an elevator operator and dressmaker. Hubbard excelled in school and, following one of his older brothers, he entered the college of engineering at the University of Iowa with $252.50 in his savings account, earned from a shoe shining business (p. 40). In fact, Hubbard continued the shoe shining business while in college. Following a stint in the Navy during World War II, Hubbard returned to the University of Iowa and earned his degree in mechanical engineering in 1945. He stayed on at the university and earned a master's and then a doctorate in 1954. He was offered, and accepted, a tenure-track appointment in the University of Iowa's department of mechanics and hydraulics. Thus, Hubbard's career at Iowa was established as the first African American professor at the university.

For Hubbard, education was "the open part of a half-open society" (p. 17). School was a place where he felt accepted and could excel on his own merits. In contrast, his life outside of school was shaped by the limitations imposed by a segregated society. For instance, "red-lining," the practice of identifying neighborhoods where Blacks could live, hounded Hubbard until the day when as a university professor, a departing professor, sold the Hubbard family a house in the White section of Iowa City. Hubbard writes of having to live in a private home during college because African American students were not permitted in student housing; of joining Kappa Alpha Psi, a Black fraternity; and of being subjected to practices such as assigned-seating for Black students. In the face of no city or university guidelines safeguarding rights of minority students, Hubbard writes, "we were at the mercy of the least tolerant person in the area of concern: if anyone objected, then the student's request was denied" (p. 45). Hubbard makes it clear that his engineering classmates "treated his enrollment as a normal event" (p. 43). He also remembers that the instructors were unbiased in their teaching and grading (p. 46).

In his memoir, Hubbard ponders the question, "Why did African Americans endure unfair treatment without protest or petitioning for reform?" He answers the question by suggesting that the response would be to offer the complainant the opportunity to go elsewhere. Furthermore, he argues, "we took the view that our misery was transitory—we could endure it for a few years because an education was seen as the way to a better future" (p. 42). All along the way, Hubbard was lucky to have had mentors who supported him and who made sure that he was given opportunities to succeed and to have the courage to persevere despite persistent unfair treatment.

EARLY INVOLVEMENT IN CIVIL RIGHTS

Hubbard's involvement in civil rights at the University of Iowa began while he was a professor in the quest to end discriminatory housing practices.

> In the 1960s there was still an undercurrent of resentment about Brown vs. Board of Education. It changed some people's attitude, but not everyone's attitude. There were some people who felt we were getting too brash, trying to go too fast, and expecting full treatment under the law. The vestiges of the earlier exclusion were still there in some cases. We had trouble getting service in certain restaurants; there were certain landlords who did not want to rent to people of color; and the realtors, they still had red-lining for property acquisition. Red-lining is the name they gave to the practice of realtors, homebuilders, and bankers of determining which areas of the city were suitable for people of color. They would circle those areas with a red pencil and, if you tried to buy property in that area, you would not be allowed to do it. The realtors would not show it to you; the homebuilders would not build for you; and the bankers would not lend to you. That is red-lining.

Hubbard went on to explain that the same was true for the students of color as far as the apartment buildings they could live in.

> It was up to the individual apartment owner; there was a great deal of individual discrimination in that regard. Some property owners would rent to people of color. Others might, if the students impressed them with their manner. There were others who would just say, "No, I've already rented that apartment.'

Hubbard became involved when the fair-housing initiative was taken up by the city council.

> Iowa City has the reputation for being a rather liberal community in spite of what I have been saying. And they did take the initiative in proposing a civil rights ordinance. I did not care much for politics. I had not been in politics and I had a rather dubious opinion of politicians, but political action is where things come to a focus. You express your philosophy in different ways, but the way that really matters is through politics. I had a good reputation in the community. I was active in the church, taught Sunday school, helped with the Scouts in various ways. People knew that I understood many of the important things in the community. So when the fair-housing ordinance came up, I was invited to speak to all the civic organizations

like Rotary, Kiwanis, the Optimists and so forth to help acquaint people with the issue. I leaped at the opportunity because I knew that those were the organizations to which these bankers, builders, and realtors belonged. So I spoke to them and I did not want to simply please them, so I laid it on the line, And at one point I said that home builders make money by building homes, not by refusing to build. Realtors make money by renting and so forth. A lot of the people did not really take it to heart, but there were some who did. Realtors and home builders have a lot of respect for bankers. They have a lot of respect for leaders of big businesses because these are hard-headed business people who are not soft-headed liberals. They want to make money and they want to have a compatible community for their employees, especially for the executive employees they hoped to hire. So, when the bankers came out in support of the things that I was working for, I think they turned the tide.

Iowa City passed a fair housing ordinance in 1964 and, according to Hubbard, was one of the first cities to pass such an ordinance.

Hubbard credits his involvement in the Iowa City fair housing debate as being the beginning of his administrative career. While serving on this commission in 1963, he was invited to sit on the university's committee on human rights. This committee was charged with promoting a newly revised human rights policy that sought to ensure the equal treatment of all citizens of the University of Iowa community.

CHANGING A SYSTEM BASED ON AN OBSOLETE CONCEPT

In 1965, Hubbard was appointed to the position of dean of academic affairs. From his new position, Hubbard supervised all of the offices we traditionally think of as being a part of student services: admissions, registrar, residence services, student financial aid, university counseling service, examination and evaluation service, Hancher Auditorium, Iowa Memorial Union, university placement service, Women's Resource and Action Center, campus programs and student activities, dean of students, office of cooperative education, special support services, and the Old Capitol Museum (Hubbard & Stone, 1999, p. 123).

In his memoir, Hubbard refers to the principles guiding student behavior at the University of Iowa as being obsolete by the time he assumed the deanship. As dean, he was constantly concerned about changing the nature of the university-student relationship to one in which the student was treated as an adult. When asked to explain what he meant by an obsolete concept he replied:

> Well, it may be the concept that I was referring to was *in loco parentis*. The president looked to student affairs to keep things under control so that the students did not embarrass the university or college and did not offend the trustees. That was the perspective and it showed up in many ways. It was evident in the restrictions placed upon the students' movements, such as when they had to go to bed. The foreign student advisor behaved as if she was more like an agent of the Immigration and Naturalization Office, keeping track of the students and keeping the authorities notified if there was anything she did not approve of regarding the student's behavior. Her other role was to acquaint international students with American culture, especially her perspective of what the American culture was.
>
> The most important things were the relationships with the general community. The dean of students looked upon himself and his associate deans to be hard on the students. If the student got into trouble off campus, the dean of students would intervene and assure the police that the university would take care of it. The police were happy to do that because they did not want to get a reputation of being hard nosed. The dean of students would threaten the students with expulsion if they did not straighten up and fly right. The dean was even known to pay the rent to an off-campus landlord in some cases. Such behavior seemed completely wrong. That should not have been the function of the dean. The landlord ought to take care of it himself. Then I found, indirectly, because one of the deans mentioned it, that there was an abortion fund. He said, "Oh, all the deans have one." I do not know whether that was true; it was probably an exaggeration. Nonetheless, it was the way in which the student affairs personnel helped to keep unsullied the reputation of the institution. If a student got into trouble, the dean would bail him out, even if it took money. Usually it did not take much, just the assurance to the police that the dean would keep the student under control. Further, it was known that if you displeased the dean, he could call you into the office and tell you that you had to be on the five o'clock train; that you were out of here. The dean of students was not the only one who could do that. So could the student's health physician. If the campus physician thought that a student's conduct or something was wrong, he could recommend that the student be removed from the university. That did not seem to be right

either. It was not right that the people in the nonacademic area could administer such discipline.

In contrast, Hubbard believed that students should be treated as adults.

A student's continuation as a student should depend on his academic performance and, of course, paying his bills. The exceptions would be if the student was a hazard to himself or to other people or to property. We did not want any firebugs running around. That was the philosophy on which I operated. Now, I cannot take credit for that all by myself. My background had not prepared me for that specific analysis, but I worked with professionals through student personnel and the university lawyer. I always had a good lawyer advising me so that I had some idea about students' rights.

Hubbard attributed his ideas about student responsibility to his own upbringing.

I graduated from high school in the spring and did not go to college until the fall of the next year; so I had a year and a half to just be a teenage citizen. During that period, I knew what freedom and responsibility meant because I did not have anyone looking over my shoulder. I felt that was part of growing up, learning to be responsible and taking responsibility for your own actions. I guess it was partly my own experience. I had very strong support from my family. They trusted me. It sounds strange, but they liked me and they wanted me to do right, and they helped me to do right. With that combination of freedom and strong support from people who cared about me, I developed a general philosophy as to the proper environment for people in the college years, especially in the first two years of college, because that is a critical period. That is when the dropouts occur. That is when students sometimes get into trouble. That is when students get the basic learning skills to carry them on through. So I emphasized the first two years.

THE CLIMATE FOR STUDENTS OF COLOR

Hubbard described the climate for students of color at the University of Iowa in the following way:

I came in on the wave of the Martin Luther King assassination, and that aroused the spirit of the community. King had been to our campus a few times to speak and always had a wonderful audience. When he was assassinated, people were just aghast that such a thing could happen to a person with such high ideals, who was so eloquent, and who had aroused the conscience of our community, just like he did throughout the country. I credit him as much as anyone for setting the environment so that, when people like me tried to do something, people understood that there was a serious problem and that there was something they could do. There were things not only that they can do, but that they should do in order to live in a way that was consistent with their expressed beliefs. People say they are Christians; they say they believe in democracy, and yet their actions do not always bear that out. So, that was the general environment. It was much better than if it had been 10 years earlier. Back then, people were discriminating and thought it was the right thing to do. They did not allow people of color to do certain things because, after all, they were not White. Ten years later they did not feel that way, but they did not quite know how to go about making changes. They needed help, and that is where I came in.

Hubbard's actions as he attempted to facilitate change at the University of Iowa in his work in student affairs were not focused on dramatic events; rather, on the product of gradual influence.

We would look for key issues or key points where we could have an influence. One of those, which is consistent with being in a university, was education. We knew that the educational opportunities for Blacks in the southeastern United States were inferior. First of all, they were excluded from White schools, and the Black elementary schools, to a certain extent, were starved. The Black schools were not adequately supported. The teachers were not adequately paid and the colleges available to Blacks in the Southeast had a great deal of trouble financially. We began working with Rust College in Holly Springs, Mississippi. Their president came here as part of a cooperative arrangement, and he gave a speech. In that speech he said, "Our problem at Rust College is how to boost students from an eighth grade education through college in four years. The schools simply didn't prepare students for college." So, we said "Let's do something about that." We collected things, like clothing, money and books, and sent them to Rust. Our librarian took a semester off and went down there to help get their library in shape. She was a very gentle lady in her 60s and she ended up staying there and making a whole lot less than she would have made here. She felt that was something she should do. The Rust College choir came up to this area quite frequently, and we would sponsor concerts for them so they could earn some money to get their music program going. We worked to help Rust with the kinds of things that a college or university can best provide.

Inviting civil rights leaders to campus had the effect of opening up students to the idea of protest.

The students kind of gained skills and learned tactics because of civil rights activists coming to campus. The work of the activists from off campus taught the students how to engage in their own kinds of demonstrations, the picketing and demanding of student rights. The students petitioned the university to correct some of the things they perceived to be problems. The students demanded that the rules be changed and that their relationship with the university be changed. Shortly after the first Black students were allowed to live in the residence halls, in 1956, these same students insisted on certain improvements. The Black athletes staged a protest that won national attention. I do not remember the details, but I think they threatened a walkout. They felt that they were getting unequal treatment and they had to be better than White players in order to get into the game. They complained that the coach would use White players if the victory was at stake. Further, a lot of our students went on Freedom Marches and participated in sit-ins at restaurants and so forth. There was an undercurrent of human rights sensitivity within the student body, and that was a very important factor that influenced all of campus.

One of the things that I do not think I mentioned in the book was about the Greek system. The Greek organizations had restrictive clauses in their constitutions, and we insisted that those had to go. There was a great deal of resistance from the alumni representatives that these clauses had to stay. But we insisted and we had quick cooperation from certain leaders among the Greeks and the presidents of the Greek organizations. That was another example of the fact that a group that is generally considered quite conservative, the Greeks, had among themselves leaders who took the challenge and educated their members, and educated their alumni, too. The key was identifying leaders in the Greek system to actually lead their peers rather than having the administrators telling them they should be different. Rebellion takes different forms. And, you can rebel against your peers, too. The Greek leaders were doing that, but in a way that did not jeopardize their positions as presidents of the organization. I do not think any of them were discharged or removed for that reason. This is a specific example of something that I was saying earlier, the motivating force for bringing people around, encouraging them to act, is leaders. Leaders are peers who have certain ideals and who have personalities and the verbal skills to goad others into action. I established some permanent friendships with some of the student leaders and presidents of the Greek organization. And as for sororities, they were more cooperative than the fraternities. Later, the student government leaders who made my life miserable became some of my best friends.

I looked upon women as being pretty much as oppressed as people of color were. They shared a great deal in common. Some people resented the fact that women were trying to ride on the backs of the advances made by the people of color, NAACP, Herbert Lee, and so forth. I felt they had a legitimate goal, that they were suppressed, held back, underpaid, and in various ways denied full status as citizens. So, I was supportive. I was a member of the founding chapter of the Society of Women Engineers. I worked with women and went out to the rural high schools to talk to girls to convince them that science-based careers are for them. When the women students at the university protested about the restrictions placed upon their sexual activities and so forth, I generally agreed with them that things needed to be improved.

According to Hubbard, until the war protests began, student activism surrounding civil rights had been rather peaceful and responsible.

The University of Iowa was a quiet community. It had a reputation for being a party school but not a politically active school. This environment was made possible by having a president and a vice president for academic affairs who cleared the obstacles and made it easier. I think it was the top-down empowerment that made it so effective.

THE WAR PROTESTS AND STUDENT LEADERS

When the war protests began, all that changed and Hubbard found himself in more difficult situations.

During the war protests, the student government tried to close the university. They really put a lot of pressure on the university. That is probably the point at which I had to oppose them the most. I insisted that a closed university was an oxymoron. In order to be effective in its role in society, the university has to be open and, by closing it, the students were really saying you have no more role to play. We finally reached a breaking point when the students were raising a fuss by demonstrating, setting fires, bomb threats, and marching on the highway. People in the state got worried. They were worried about the safety of their sons and daughters. We tried to assure them that things were not that bad. But, finally, we reached the point where we said if any student feels that his or her life is in danger, they can leave; they have a choice. Students could either leave and take whatever grade they had at that point, or they could stay and complete the semester. That happened in early May of 1970, which was the time when the juices were rising. Many of the students were happy to say well, "I'll drop out because I'm afraid." Some wanted to stay even after they had dropped out of their classes. We told them, "We're sorry, but the residence halls are for registered students and you canceled your registration."

According to Hubbard, students in the war protests had learned their skills in the civil rights movement. They moved from engaging in nonviolent, peaceful protest to being much more violent, a change which Hubbard attributed to the leaders.

In any community, there are certain people who assert their leadership and convince others to follow them. I had a lot of respect for those leaders because they were operating on principles of which I approved. But there were many conservative people in the community who said they were rabble rousers, that they were trouble makers. Some said they should not be there they wanted us to get rid of them because of their political activities. The leaders came up with ideas like blocking traffic on the interstate highway, but to carry that out requires a lot of people. Since they needed a lot of people, they would get them by throwing the fire alarms in residence halls. Then, when the students came out into the streets, the leaders would talk to them and get them carried away. There is this aura of excitement about such events that really appeals to many students. Students were not philosophically into it, necessarily, but this was a very exciting thing to do, and they wanted to be part of the action. Of course, the leaders knew that psychology very well. They knew how to get people to do what they wanted. I think that the basic philosophy expressed openly was that of democracy, of people being able to control their own futures, and so forth. But, there was also just kind of a rebellious attitude, a "They can't tell us what to do" attitude.

.

COULD HE HAVE DONE THINGS DIFFERENTLY?

Hubbard was an academic working in student affairs. He had had no formal training in the field. When asked about this and how it affected his work, he replied,

> There were at least four people who lost their jobs because they refused to cooperate with me. One of them went to the president and complained. I do not think it was my philosophy that bothered them as much as the fact that I was given a great deal of authority over an area that they perceived I was not prepared to handle. They believed I was using philosophy that was appropriate for academic affairs, but not for student affairs. Even my title caused some confusion. Initially I was given the title, dean of academic affairs, but people were upset because the title did not have the word "students" in it. So my position was eventually called vice president for student services.

Hubbard believed things could have been done better.

> We were amateurs. We were groping our way through strange territory, and there are probably things that we could have done, but our great ally in this was faculty. The faculty understood what we were trying to say. Even though the students were asking for concessions, which posed problems for the faculty, like canceling classes and so forth, the faculty understood; and when it was necessary to protect the institution, the faculty did the right thing. They stood guard all night in buildings to guard against the bomb threats and so forth. We had a great deal of support from the faculty.

> We were enlightened, and we did not think we had the absolute truth, either. Instead of chastising the students because they were not behaving the way we wanted them to, we emphasized the fact that, "You are preventing us from carrying out our primary mission, which is to educate you." So we put it on a basis of educational values rather than personal behavior. In response to the protests, we had the National Guard at the ready and the governor was meeting with the chief of the highway troopers. We had a little command post, as we called it, and we were in contact with people with walkie-talkies out in the crowd. We kept informed so we could keep the governor informed, because we did not want a rash decision being made that would bring in people with firearms. In fact, we made a deal with the highway patrol, which was unusual. The deal was that if they had to bring officers on campus, the officers would not carry side arms. Luckily, we had an enlightened commander, and he understood.

Hubbard thought the difference between the relatively peaceful protests of the earlier civil rights period and the later, more disruptive era can be explained:

> The students got fed up, not only the students of color, but the White students who had been fighting for certain ideals. The students saw that their ideals were being flaunted in the real world. It was a matter of students saying, "Things have to change. They can't go on the same way. It's grossly unfair to treat the people of color as they have been treated, and we're not going to take it anymore."

How Students Are Different Today

> Today, there seems to be a great deal of lethargy in the student body, and a great deal of party activity. That is, students are interested in having a good time and they are not too excited about trying to change the world. They just want to enjoy it. But, if you can get an issue that touches them where it really matters, then you can bring about action.

Hubbard had mixed feelings about special offices for minority affairs.

> I resisted establishing an office of minority affairs because I saw my role, not as creating an island where the minority could be accommodated, but rather changing the entire institution. If there was a problem with admissions, instead of setting up a minority recruitment program, we got the main admissions office to change its tactics. We took the directors of admissions, financial aid, and counseling services to Black churches and to community centers so that they could deliver their messages directly. Because they were in on the action, they felt that they had a responsibility to use their own skills. I did not know all the details of running an admissions office, or financial aid, but they did. I wanted to change their behavior and make the university a different place. America has a long tradition of a two-class system. The people in the upper class do not want the people in the lower class to go too far, to rise too high. So, when you establish a separate office that is concerned with minority affairs, there is kind of a tendency to make it second class, not to give it the same status, not to give it the same support. I think we avoided that to a certain extent.

The Role of the Civil Rights Era in His Life

> The civil rights era alerted me to the very important role that politics plays in our society. I had not appreciated that. I had thought politics

was something for someone else, and the less I had to do with it, the better. I realize now that that is not a very good philosophy. If you do not engage in political action, or utilize political instruments, you are not going to have the influence that you should have. Politics is where the action is. Politics differs from what I had been doing previously, which was science-based engineering. In engineering, the key to resolving problems, to learning about how the system works, is to consult science, to work with the mechanical system. The key to working with people is to work with people. To work with people, you have to form committees, which are looked down upon by many people. You have to communicate, and you have to have different points of view, and committees play a very important role. I used a combination of those two ideas. I would call my administrators into regular meetings, and hold regular meetings with the students, and so forth, but I did not go into those meetings just to ask them for their advice and recommendations. I went in with proposals, written pro- posals, and asked them, "What do you think of this? Do you have any suggestions?" I would take notes. Then, I would come back with a revised recommendation and acknowledge that they all had an impor- tant role to play. They had important experience. Even though I was the neophyte in student affairs, I appreciated their help, and I think that helped a great deal.

Hubbard learned from his involvement in the civil rights and student protest periods and carried that over to his views about principles.

I worked hard to advance certain principles, and one of those princi- ples is that a good educational environment is a diverse environment. You have people that came from wealthy families and people whose families are destitute. You have people from the East, from the West, North, and South and people who have dark skin and people who have an accent that is different than the prevailing accent in the com- munity. We want people to develop an appreciation for the fact that universities are very heterogeneous communities. On the other hand, we are not trying to turn out clones. We want people to retain their identity, their traditions, and to appreciate the values that others have, but also appreciate their own heritage, to be proud of themselves and their families, proud of the way they live, they look. I put it this way: We were not trying to turn out a puree, put everyone into a mixer and turn out a uniform product. We are working on creating something like a jambalaya, where you can pick out a shrimp or a sausage or some other tidbit and appreciate it by itself. But, it all goes together to make a delightful mix, which is better than either alone.

It is very apparent that Hubbard never approached the discrimination he faced personally as a victim.

> I looked upon the people who were trying to block me as violating their own principles. They should be ashamed of themselves. It was not my job to help them. I simply pushed them aside. It helped that I was always at the honors level in the work that I undertook. It helps to be a leader academically if you are trying to convince people to do a certain thing. They can't say, "Well, he's not too hot himself."

As an African American, Hubbard believed his own identity played a role in the way he navigated through these difficult times.

> The students realized that I was speaking from experience and that I was not taking the distant view. I had walked the walk, and what I was saying made sense to them. It was consistent with what they had been taught about democracy and Christianity and other religions. So that helped. I was also somewhat more articulate then than I am now. I was able to put these ideas into words that the students and the faculty both understood, and give a rationale which made sense to them.

IMPACT OF CIVIL RIGHTS ON HIGHER EDUCATION

Hubbard believed the civil rights and student protest movements had a significant impact on higher education, although he attributed the primary motivation for change in higher education to external forces.

> I think that the principle motivation came from people outside of the educational community, people like Martin Luther King, Jr. and other leaders of the civil rights movement. They started the ball rolling, and in particular, the people like King, appealed to the conscience of people in universities. Once they were convinced that there was a need, that there was a problem, they knew how to go about using their resources educating students. I think the universities were not the initiators, but they were very strong allies. Once they got into motion, they made a great deal of difference and produced a generation of students who were much more sensitive and much more aware than previous students had been. So, universities produced people who had an idea of how to go about making the world a better place.

Today, institutions would not even think of doing some of the things they did before with reference to the people of color. The role of students has also changed. The way students are viewed is different. Students are now expected to take part in the institutional government, under rather limited conditions, but much more than before. Instead of being told, "Never mind that we're doing what we're doing. We're doing it for your benefit, and you'll appreciate this later. In the meantime, you behave yourself." I think the students who were in the civil rights movement, and some who have benefited from it, appreciate very much the gains that were made. This year, the Latino and Native American students are having a big celebration of the achievements that they have made. They are dedicating a center, which we have provided for them. The students have a sense of being a part of the action, of having pride in being part of the institution, and of having contributed to something that has changed the environment at the university. It is not just White people who feel that they have had an influence, but people of color too. I think this creates a sense of pride that permeates the institution. It is very important to have substantial representation of minorities in the faculty. It changes that environment too, both the viewpoint of how other professors view them, but also how the students view them. When I was teaching at first, students told me, "You were the first African American that I ever had a chance to really talk to. I came from a community where there were none."

EPILOGUE

Philip G. Hubbard passed away on January 10th, 2002 at the age of 80. He retired from working at the University of Iowa in 1991. His obituary in the Iowa City Press-Citizen talks about the impact that Hubbard made on the university and the community. The obituary notes that in 2001 Hubbard received the first ever Lifetime Achievement Award from the Iowa City Human Rights Commission. The author stated:

> Seldom can we point to a single person's efforts and say "Because he did this, we have that." But with Hubbard, that list goes on and on, from the university's human rights policy to his many accomplishments as an academic to his massive footprint on the university as an administrator.

The obituary continues:

> Today our collective efforts to ensure human rights for all still fall short of our dreams and aspirations. We hope in the spirit of the work and life of this great man, many others will come forward to make more progress and the kind of difference he did.

We believe that this obituary captures the essence of the man that we interviewed for this chapter and are pleased that we were able to share his story about his role in helping the University of Iowa struggle with civil rights concerns.

ROBERT H. SHAFFER
University of Indiana (1941-1969)

In the 1950s and 1960s, Robert Shaffer worked in student affairs at Indiana University (IU). He came to Indiana in 1941 as the assistant to the dean of the school of business in charge of student personnel matters. He held that position for one year and then served three years in the military. Upon his return to Indiana in 1945, Shaffer was put in charge of the Veterans' Guidance Center. He later became assistant dean of students and, in 1955, became dean of students. He held that position until 1969. This chapter represents Shaffer's memories of the civil rights events at Indiana University in the 1950s through the 1960s. He describes the factors that influenced how IU dealt with civil rights concerns and explains why the school did not have any major protests or riots like those on many other college campuses.

INSTITUTIONAL CONTEXT

IU was best described as a rather typical, Midwestern, conservative, coeducational university, rather large for its time, but still smaller than it is today. It had all the trappings of a large coed university. The institutional climate between 1955 and 1969 was, by rule, nondiscriminatory. Herman Wells, the president, removed any vestige of any discriminatory rule when he came in. The president was kind of a leader in the area of civil rights. Because of his backing, the staff was able to move very rapidly. We had Black residence hall residence assistants, and we had our first Black counselor in our counseling office by 1962. Hiring them didn't make a ripple on campus; nobody on campus had a problem with it.

At the same time, because Indiana University was in southern Indiana, and it was this typical state university, it had a lot of institutional lethargy in changing the actual mores and operational matters on the campus. For example, there was a lot of self-segregation because the students of color felt barriers. In the student union there was an area referred to as the "Black section." This separation was all voluntary. There weren't rules about segregation in the cafeteria or in the residence halls. However, early in the 1960s, the dean of students' office, through the residence hall system, worked with Black student leaders to very deliberately break up these islands of what we always termed "self-segregation." I believe such segregation increased the feelings of security for students of color. I remember that, in student government, we actively recruited Black student leaders to participate to help break that line. The university approached civil rights from all fronts, with the student government, counseling, resident advisors and student activities taking the lead. It wasn't until the 1970s, I believe, that the first Black student became a member of a traditionally and historically White fraternity. To put it bluntly, they aren't integrated yet. So there was and is institutional lethargy.

Much of what happened up North resulted from Northern colleges sending civil rights activists to the South to bring about change. They came home, and quickly saw, "Lord, we have these problems right here at home!" Then they said, "Well, we'll have to change right here and now before we go anywhere else." And, of course, that upset some people. Their attitude was "Go away and demonstrate elsewhere. Don't do it here."

At IU, we did not have any major protests or riots like many college campuses had. In 1962 or 1963, we had one protest when we had employment interviews in the school of business by firms that the Black students felt discriminated against Black applicants. We did not know the facts. The people representing those firms denied it, but, as we all know, just because you verbally deny something doesn't mean that you don't do it. The students demonstrated against the school of business placement office. The thing that made that so interesting and stand out in my mind was that the Black student leaders firmly and gently made the White students walk at the end of the parade, not up in front. I liked that because it showed that they wanted possession of that issue. This, I thought was very responsible.

One of the good things we were able to do is keep the line of communication open to the student activists. As a result, knowing that we were going to at least be neutral, if not actually aggressively supportive, the activists would tell us what they were going to do. Administratively, most of the trouble occurs when participants spring something in the way of a demonstration without preparation. We never tried to stop them. In fact, we named, Dunn Meadows, "Little Hyde Park," where literally any topic could be discussed in any way that any student chose. Now, that caused some trouble, but we had that and it worked for us. Eventually, the more radical students said, "We don't want to go out to Dunn Meadow and demonstrate, we want to demonstrate where the students are," in this case in a large class-room. They wanted to be there when students changed classes. That was a technique they learned from Wisconsin, to my knowledge. It was not a bad idea, clever from their point of view, but it sure upset some of us. We didn't want, if we could help it, major demonstrations in the lobby of a large classroom building at class change time.

By mixing the issues, sometimes the activists gained strength, because they got a lot more people with varied skills and different points of view. But, also by mixing the issues they sometimes got people involved that they themselves weren't too happy to have causing the trouble. For example, there were at least three students who publicly said, "I don't want a peaceful demonstration. To get attention, I want trouble." IU was really conservative, and even some student leaders said, "No, no, we don't want trouble if we don't have to." They would often throw those guys out, or attempt to relegate them to lesser roles.

At that time on our campus, the "average White student" was apathet-ic, lethargic, and conservative. Many of them were critical of the dean of students for "stirring students up." It made me madder than hell, really. We did not think of it as stirring them up. In one case, a repre-sentative of Young Americans for Freedom publicly stated that in some of the troubles at IU the dean of students' office was the instiga-tor. It was silly, of course. Nevertheless, if one was an ultraconserva-tive and thought the status quo was to be kept, you would be angry when the student activities office issued guidelines on how to organize a good demonstration, which we did. We suggested how to get public-ity, how to involve students, and how to make appeals. By doing this, we guided them, you might say, and most demonstrations were rela-tively orderly as a result. I feel we were discharging our obligation to the institution and to students in a more productive way than just try-ing to keep order. Many of the student staff members of the dean of students' office were also graduate students in student affairs working towards advanced degrees. We talked about proactive posture and proactive stands and all that in the classroom, so we pretty well had to practice what we preached.

We certainly could have done things differently. In the first place, we could have been more aggressive as an institution. There was a lot of institutional lethargy. In general, we were fortunate being where we were, with the president that we had. I think most observers thought most protests and demonstrations were handled pretty well, just about as well as could be done at a large, complex, state university. Our campus was dominated in part in those days by athletics and the Greek letter system. Often they wanted to solve the problems of the world by 4:00 o'clock and go have a tea dance. This cavalier attitude often made me angry because so many students weren't serious. Yet I found most student activists involved in the civil rights movement were dead serious. Such a laissez faire attitude represented a failure by the university, in my opinion, then and now!

THE EXTERNAL COMMUNITY CONTEXT

Part of understanding how IU responded to civil rights is rooted in the history and culture of the surrounding community.

Indiana was settled by Kentuckians from the South, and that is one of the reasons that we had considerable resistance to civil rights in the community. For example, barber shops would not cut Negro students' hair until President Wells and the dean of students' office worked with the union to hire a licensee who promised to cut all hair. The president handled it very well. He authorized me to tell any barber who claimed he did not know how to cut Black students' hair that the university would pay for him to take training at a barber college. When the barbers were told that, they usually said, "Oh, well, we can cut it." Also, we worked through the head of the barber's union. It was a coup d'etat in a way, because this guy was a southern Indiana barber and popular in the community. He was the licensee that took over the union barbershop. So when he started cutting the hair of Black students, it set a tone that convinced others to follow suit.

With less success, we tried the same tactics to integrate local restaurants. Actually the restaurants were not as well organized and, when we would individually talk to restaurant owners, they would say, "But my customers don't want it." The student union restaurant was absolutely desegregated as were the university dining halls. But it took several years into the 1960s for the community restaurants to be truly integrated, meaning that students of color would really feel comfortable eating there.

In town, we still had trouble because theatres up through the 1950s made Black students sit up in the balcony. Of course you know students; one day in 1959 a bunch of students, Black and White, just took over the downstairs, and they desegregated that theatre right then and there. Again, the community was slower than the university in integrating. For example, IU had many foreign students during this period also, and many townspeople confused foreign student of color with African Americans, much to our disgust.

According to Shaffer's accounts, the university administration, along with students, worked very hard to make significant changes in the surrounding community. Outward vestiges of discrimination slowly changed as community standards changed.

The community response to protest and civil rights had that 1950s' flavor of anticommunism. In 1964, when the democratic mayor created the Bloomington Human Relations Committee, and appointed me, a democrat, to chair that committee, the community thought that was a radical step towards all of us going to hell. Many people would write that members of the university administration had no business being on a city commission, and that they certainly had no right to impose their values on the city. Well, we did, and we should have. You couldn't separate the university from the town of Bloomington. It was just too small. During that period, with the support of the mayor and the local paper, the city and some firms hired their first Black fireman, their first Black uniformed policeman, their first Black mail carrier, and of all things, the first Black telephone lineman. Now, of course today or even 10, 15 years after that era, people said, "Ah, that was just tokenism, and those guys were just tokens." In a way that's true, but given the era, those were steps that had to be taken. They led to more appointments and acceptance. I believe most of the Black leaders of the city of Bloomington felt those were good steps, and backed us up.

All of the mainline churches in Bloomington catered to Black students after World War II. Segregation at the churches broke down fast, and the churches stood by us even though they had some troubles. The First Baptist Church lost many members when they started having Black members in their choir. I knew that pastor very well, and we worked closely. He just said, "Well, this is it." Objectors just went to other churches. Most churches, however, responded pretty effectively, which again was a great help to us. In other words, we had support from a major segment of the external community.

THE ROLE OF STUDENT AFFAIRS

Student affairs was really instrumental in shaping the attitudes and the policies about civil rights on the campus. In 1955, we adopted the American Civil Liberties Union guidelines for practically every constitutional right, except one—the right to face your accuser. Interestingly enough, it was the faculty that balked on that one, because you could not subpoena a faculty member who was accusing a student, let's say, of plagiarism. That was the only guideline I failed to get firmly established during that period of 1955 to 1968. About 1968 and immediately following, the constitutional application of the campus took care of those things, but even then, often, you could not get a faculty member to testify against a student, or for a student.

Many faculty members were supportive of our actions towards civil rights, but we got most of our organized support from church foundations. We approached each one, and had them represented, through their student arm, on committees and in special bodies. By involving them, it gave an aura of respectability to some of the activism that did take place. In other words, if your church leaders were up there, it was pretty hard for critics, of which we had a lot, comprised of students, parents, townspeople and alumni, to say, "Those guys are a bunch of Communists."

Until 1955, when I became dean of students, I viewed the dean of students as the institutional officer who kept order and maintained appropriate behavior. Our image was more or less the keeper of the morals and a lot of that stuff, back through history. Well, once I got the job, I realized that my job was to help students express themselves, not to suppress them. For example, I remember one heated argument, almost the first year I was dean, about the fact that students had plastered posters on trees throughout the campus. The business vice president, who was in charge of campus facilities, called me up and said I was to see that every one of those was removed and that it never happened again. Well, number one, I couldn't prevent it from happening again. And number two, I thought posting the fliers on trees was smarter than hell. They got more publicity than they usually got for this particular movement. The vice president commented, "Well, if this were a state park, you wouldn't do that." That is when my staff laughed because I raised my voice to a high falsetto and preceded to explain that it was not a state park, it was a college campus. My staff would sometimes put this incident in skits, poking fun at the dean of students.

Of course, the police just wanted to keep order. I remember we had a "Fair Play for Cuba" demonstration in 1962. Nineteen students put on quite a good demonstration just at the time of the Cuban missile crisis when the campus tenor was against Cuba and war seemed imminent. I tried to get the campus police to protect those students, because they were being heckled and bombarded with stuff. One police officer, actually a friend of mine, said "I protect only good, red-blooded Americans, not protesters." Well, we had to deal with such beliefs because we felt the university, and even the city, should not have a police force that felt that way. We had to have some good training sessions. It was a good lesson for all of us on how to help students voice their concerns without going that one step farther to incite violent action. Student activists had to be careful if they were going downtown to the Courthouse Square, for example, because down there they would have been attacked by the town "intelligentsia." We have many people in Bloomington who did not like college students demonstrating downtown.

PERSONAL VIEWS ON CIVIL RIGHTS

Shaffer's views about civil rights were shaped by a number of forces. As he explained:

> I had taken two courses taught by Roger Baldwin of the American Civil Liberties Union in 1937 and again in 1938, at the New School of Social Research in New York City. It is now called The New School. Personally, I was supportive of civil rights, but of course, in those days, one's individual personal views didn't change an institutional stance very much—particularly those of a young assistant dean. One had to be somewhat circumspect in the way he attempted to bring about change, even though he personally wanted it to come faster.

As for the Vietnam War, Shaffer's views were influenced by his own personal experiences.

> I had a son killed in Vietnam. Of course I was against that damn war, but you can't say, therefore, that the university was officially, as an institution, against it, which the activists demanded. They wanted the faculty council to formally condemn the war. I had to explain to them how I could put it before them, but I had no power to beg the faculty. The students said, "Well, we'll demonstrate until they do." We even had a sit-in at the president's office on that issue. The president at the time was Elvis Starr, who had been secretary of the army before he

261

came to IU. He was not about to involve the university in a formal stance on that issue at that time.

In terms of civil rights, politics and political activism often interfered with the goals that individuals wanted to achieve. In other words, one cannot rationally be against civil rights for all people. Yet, once one started getting activists involved, like the Young Socialist Alliance, particularly on our campus, or the Students for a Democratic Society in part, and the Fair Play for Cuba committee in part, they involved political issues, such as recognition and withdrawal from Cuba and a lot of things at a time when the protesters didn't have another 50 people who would agree with them. So when one was trying to change an institutional stance, these others issues interfered. I used to ask student leaders and my graduate students in student affairs to think about how they would go about changing an institution's views, as contrasted with changing an individual's view? Of course, they are two very different worlds. The students struggled with such questions.

LESSONS FOR TODAY

Student affairs has to change from their image as a custodial, keeper of the morals, supervisory role to one of actually facilitating the individual to develop informed views. The university, in all its aspects, should teach students to not only form open attitudes and informed views, but also encourage them to express themselves actively. The division of student affairs on any campus cannot be, and should not be, just a maintainer of order and keeper of morals. In a complex world like we have right this minute, you don't have order. Anybody who thinks that all is well is crazy.

One thing I learned was to keep channels of communication open. I worked with many other campuses during that period, and I'd often be called in when they had a particular negative or disturbing problem. Typically, an event would occur and their staff members would not even know it was going to happen. On our campus, we tried to say, "Come in and tell us what you're going to do. We'll try to make sure the police don't go off all crazy-like. We'll try to help you organize." On our campus, we actually told them some things they could do and keep channels of communication open with us. Otherwise, student leaders would work secretively and engage in underhanded, even violent or damaging, actions. Even my most radical student activists at IU would say that they never had to work undercover, because they could usually take open actions.

Students must be kept involved. We tried mightily not to let three or four students take over a cause. We had a problem there, once, when the Young Socialist Alliance was dominated by three students. You would have this big movement with the Young Socialist Alliance saying this and that, and it was really only three guys who were saying anything. So we tried to get more students involved. Whenever the student union, student activities office, or student government put on a leadership seminar, we went out of our way to recruit some of these antibureaucratic, anti-institution guys and girls to be in there.

I think a third lesson is to not personalize differences. I tried to tell my staff that often, perhaps to keep me from doing just that. I would really be indignant when student activists would double cross us and do things they had agreed not to do, such as activate fire alarms, cause damage, disrupt classes, and spread bomb threats. Personalizing differences often results in an attitude of "I'll be glad when that person graduates." We must remember that the cause will remain and there will always be a successor. I urge any dean these days and any activities director or union activities director to get acquainted with campus activists. A student affairs office, to be effective, has to know the "trouble makers" and has to be able to communicate with them. The campus and community are all in the same boat on these issues. The more an office practices that approach, the fewer are the demonstrators who feel suppressed and resort to violent acts.

Another lesson is that evaluation is important. After every minor or major problem, we would have a staff meeting. My staff used to laugh because it seemed like we were always meeting to evaluate what happened and what we could have done better. That paid off institutionally. Everybody was involved, including the staff members who thought they had not been supported, let's say, on a particular stance. They had the opportunity to say so. The idea was that such meetings and evaluation would help us be more skilled next time something happened.

EPILOGUE

When Shaffer stepped down from his position as senior student affairs officer at IU in 1969, he undertook a number of important jobs that continued to serve the field of student affairs. He had always held a faculty position in the higher education program at Indiana and was appointed as department chair of the department of college student personnel administration. During that time, from 1969 to 1972, he was editor of the *NASPA Journal*. In 1970, Shaffer founded and was dean of the Interfraternity Institute; he held that position until 1981. Shaffer has won numerous awards for his service to the profession, including the Scott Goodnight Award from NASPA for outstanding performance as a dean in 1973, and ACPA's Distinguished Service Award in 1979. In 1987, NASPA established the Robert H. Shaffer Award, presented annually to an outstanding faculty member in a higher education or student affairs graduate program.

Photo compliments of the La Grande
Observer.

HARRIS W. SHELTON
Florida State University (1968-1971)

arris Shelton, who is now the vice president for student affairs at Eastern Oregon University, began his career in student affairs at the age of 25. His first higher education position was at Florida State University (FSU), where between 1968 and 1971, he worked as the assistant dean of men, then the dean of men, and then the dean of student development. Shelton earned his doctorate in higher education from FSU and then left Florida to become dean of students and later vice chancellor for student affairs at the University of Alaska, Fairbanks. This chapter represents Shelton's perspectives and memories of civil rights concerns at Florida State during the turbulent times of the late 1960s and early 1970s.

THE CONTEXT AND BRIEF HISTORY OF FLORIDA STATE UNIVERSITY

> Florida State was, from the very beginning, a more liberal setting than the University of Florida. It was not the university of legacies, of politicians and judges and lawyers who were sending their boys on to college and then to law school so that one day they would run the government! Florida State was much more a learner-centered environment. At Florida State, I felt vibrancy. The faculty was inquisitive. There was a sense of mentorship, of unrestricted inquiry.

The first Black student enrolled at Florida State in 1962, and the first Black Ph.D. candidates graduated in 1970. Programs in African American studies and women's studies were established in the 1960s. By 1968, there were approximately 400 Black students and a student body of 13,000. The environment for Black students at FSU in the early 1960s was described by some as "not congenial" but also "not violent" (Rabby, 1999, p. 263). Shelton describes the population at FSU in general, and certain enclaves of Black students in particular, as "politically savvy, fearless, articulate and angry." FSU was so active in terms of protests that it was called "the

Berkeley of the South" (Rabby, p. 263). In 1970, the faculty senate at FSU established a recruitment program to increase the presence of Black students on campus. As a result, Black enrollment increased 500 percent between 1968 and 1970 (Rabby). The increasing numbers of African American students on campus, many of whom came from the urban North, created an environment ripe for change.

Shelton noted:

> Once the enrollment of Black students hit some level of critical mass where there was empowerment in numbers, it was easy as a staff person to observe that these were politically sophisticated students, for the most part. These were not students out of the Florida backwoods who were coming to higher education, but young people from urban centers such as New York City, Philadelphia, Cleveland, and Detroit. These were students who were recruited to FSU because of absolutely excellent academic potential; students who were very interested in some of the majors that Florida State offered; and also interested in pushing the system limits to achieve social change. So, you had, by day, a very talented population of students of color and, by night or weekend, especially on hot nights or weekends, empowered students who were angry and who had agendas for change. It was a magic moment, but not always a pleasant one.

Similar to other communities experiencing significant student activism, both students and nonstudents planned and participated in protests in Tallahassee.

> Early on there was no one, galvanizing issue, as there might have been at Jackson State University. Also, there had been Black students at Florida State for enough years that a counterculture of former students and nonstudents had formed. In some cases, these were stopouts who did not leave Tallahassee. Some had local jobs, and many were early activists in a town which viewed itself as genteel, sort of the epitome of White antebellum Southern ways and traditions. Sooner or later, there were bound to be clashes. And these nonstudents found ways to plug into campus issues, to join with students, often in protest. You had an interesting crossing-over there. The vibrant and dissatisfied group was much more determined by race than by enrollment status.

> Some of their issues were local, others external. And there was a residual anger regarding the Martin Luther King assassination, for example, as well as other civil rights issues. In reflection, I have a real admiration for the Southern born-and-bred Black students in relation

to their urban peers. Given the attitudes that surrounded them all their lives—the White establishment, the Leon County sheriff's office, the admonitions and role modeling provided by their parents—to participate in protests in Tallahassee, Florida was gutsy. They had grown up with some level of fear, with family stories of the past, maybe a grandfather's recollections of church burnings and stories of lynching. For them to have the courage to speak and act against segregation, against discrimination by the dominant, White culture made them just as brave as the marchers at Selma or Birmingham, with dogs and fire hoses and locals spitting on them. Although that was not the way of things in Tallahassee, those Southern Black children certainly experienced an element of fear when they spoke out against old ways, Jim Crow attitudes.

If our Southern students were afraid, they were at the same time surrounded by students who were not Southern, students from the urban North who had not experienced Bull Connor treatment (the notorious public safety commissioner in Birmingham). To that group, it was something they had seen on television; it was not a real part of their lives. When they came to Florida State, it was empowering to our local students, but at the same time I imagine that there was some fear by Southern Black students that they might be viewed as second-class citizens by the newcomers. However, the dynamics might have played out; there is no question that the local students owed a lot in the development of their own political strategies and activism to their new Northern friends.

As is the case with many communities in the South, Tallahassee had a strong history of racial segregation that was slow to erode. The community, under the leadership of students from Florida A&M University (FAMU), the historically Black university located in Tallahassee, organized a bus boycott in 1956. Sit-ins at local businesses, including theatres, occurred throughout the 1960s, and the public K-12 schools were not integrated until 1970. Most of the community protest strategies and activism was organized by the local branch of a group called CORE at FAMU in 1959. Some students and faculty from Florida State were active participants in CORE and in efforts to integrate the community. The community could be described as "hostile" to the efforts of those at FAMU and FSU to bring about racial integration (Rabby, 1999).

We had a sheriff, the Leon County sheriff, who did not like having a liberal university with liberal Black students in the middle of his beautiful, Tallahassee town. There were constant "Easy Rider" type conflicts—the hippie culture versus the locals, the Black students versus the locals, the Vietnam protestors who were not hippies or Blacks, just angry. Kent State and Jackson State both occurred during this time period, as did Earth Day, May Day, and a number of the national days of protest. A number of us participated in marches where we got off the campus and marched through downtown. It was frightening. This was an old, Southern town. As long as you were on campus, you felt somewhat insulated. But two blocks off campus and you were fair game, and that is the feeling we had. Some shop owners leaned out their windows during these marches, flipping us off with catcalls, and shaking their fists.

It was in this environmental context that FSU students participated in protests against the university, the government, and the local community.

THE BUILDING AND BURNING OF THE BLACK CULTURAL CENTER

The university bought a two-story house on the perimeter of the campus. It was bought with no original purpose other than it became available. A group of Black students made it clear that they were looking for a place to have a cultural center. It did not have to be a permanent assignment, but here was the house, and we thought, "Why don't we match them up?" It was a peaceful, reasonable request and it was not that difficult for the university to act on. With not a great deal of discussion or planning, we agreed. The students called the house the Black Students' Educational and Cultural Center. Students then decided that they needed some sound equipment. The university and student government came up with several thousand dollars for audio equipment. Then the students decided that they needed a resident manager to live there. Part of this was about loyalty to an older Black student, a returning Vietnam veteran who was married, who was very popular with these students, who did not have much money. The little organizing group selected him and asked us for some furniture for him and his family.

At that time, the president of the university was J. Stanley Marshall. His executive vice president was named Cecil Mackey. Cecil later became president at Michigan State University. Both of them were adamant that there would not be a resident in the house. They did not want it occupied at night. There still was a fear that when you cannot see the students and you are not sure what they are doing, it is probably no good. I took the other position because we had value in the house, valuable equipment in the house, and because this was, in fact, a very responsible, young man who was the candidate for resident manager. I believed that it would be in the university's best interests to have someone there who would be responsible and a liaison between the students and the university. This led to one of my first career lessons with respect to the organizational chart.

I received a call one Friday in the late afternoon. "President Stanley Marshall is on the phone for you," I was told. The president's voice was sharp and tense, and I sensed I was in some trouble. "You don't seem to understand certain realities," he said.

> You have been publicly advocating a position which is opposite to my instructions to you. I want to discuss this with you, face-to-face, and that will be first thing Monday morning. You will want to take some time over the weekend to reflect on how things are done here, how decisions are made. On Monday you will be free to exercise an option to continue employment, should you choose.

On Monday morning he explained, without rancor and very calmly, that he was the president, he, alone, was responsible for the success and control of the university, and that, if I did not support his position, then that would make me a freelancer; and the president made it abundantly clear that he did not sign paychecks for freelancers. Obviously a clear lesson learned at the time.

Saying "no" to the Black Student Union (BSU) on the issue of a live-in manager further weakened an already-strained relationship between us. "No" was not a word they had heard much lately, and it was not received well, at least by the student leadership. The several keys to the front door of the Cultural Center were duplicated a number of times, and students began to wander inside the place at night—clearly in defiance. Black Panther meetings were held there, as were Panther breakfasts for community children. Their actions amounted to a statement that said, "We are bigger than college students. We are humans, and we're going to do what we believe to be right, in spite of the rules."

As administrators, we dealt with the procedural issues, the protection issues, and not the civil rights or students' needs issues. I was told to patrol the house, and to remove anyone who violated university policy. The stated reason was that the things going on in there were not "university events." No more meetings of the Black Panthers. No more breakfasts for Black community children. In retaliation, some individuals twice attempted to burn the center down. The immediate reaction was that this was the work of local non-Blacks as a part of a racist agenda. Later, however, the BSU hinted that some of their members might have been responsible for the arson. The action was billed as a protest against a shift in the attitude of the administration. Instead of being cooperative and helpful, we were now throwing up roadblocks to progress and no longer being sensitive to their needs. I remember a feeling of betrayal. I had been their representative to the administration; I had been steadfast with them and truthful. In reflection, my approach was more of passion than of mature educational leadership.

EMERGENCY MEETINGS, DEMANDS, AND INTIMIDATION TACTICS

On January 20, 1970, thirty Black students barricaded themselves in a classroom building and demanded a meeting with the university president.

I actually had a call from the president at 3:30 or 4:00 in the morning saying, "I've just been summarily moved out of my bed and I'm going to go over there and meet them [the Black student group] at 5:00 a.m. this morning." And he said, "If I'm going, you're going too." So we met and went in together, and we did not quite get into the meeting room before we picked up escorts. We were essentially surrounded, each of us. And I think there were two other administrators there.

There were about 30 Black students and about four White administrators. We were isolated from each other, the administrators. The Black students had berets; they were very rehearsed. They marched in with small groups of bodyguards, with each White administrator in the center of a group. We were seated at distances, with several students in between us, so we were not able to communicate with each other. The student leader of the group rose and delivered their list of 31 demands, each one numbered number one.

The items on the list were really innocent and innocuous for the most part: Black greeting cards in the university bookstore, expanding the availability of cosmetics that were used by Black women. They were just simple things that should have never been issues in the first place, had we been more sensitive in anticipating Black student needs. At the end of the 31 demands being read, the president of the BSU, John Burt, looked at President Marshall and said, "We demand an answer now." The president said, "Nothing happens here and now. I'll take these under advisement." The student leader, John Burt said, "Well, you can do whatever you want, but we want an answer now." So, there were a couple of little exchanges, and when the president would not give in, on a signal from John, all of the Black students snapped to attention. They stood, and then marched out of the room. But they left four students in the room, sitting between each of us, so that we couldn't talk or strategize or summarize. After a short, couple of minutes, we were allowed to walk outside the building. It was barely light, sort of dusky and cloudy. The president and I turned the corner where there was a large hedge and I remember having this feeling of being out of danger. As we walked along the hedge, it rustled, and I realized that there were students in the hedge. They were behind it; they were in it; they were all the way down the sidewalk. You talk about an increase in the fear factor. "Why are they hiding; what's going to happen to us now?" This was new territory for most of us, and I suspect for the students as well.

I went to my car, the president walked to his. We had agreed to meet for breakfast, include a few more folks, and discuss the demands. That walk to the car was when I noticed students on rooftops, sort of shadowy figures watching us in the early dawn. They were crouched down, reminding me of snipers.

I talked with the leader of the BSU a little later about that. He was a wonderful guy because he could scare you with his anger and then you would see his lips twitch with a kind of a little smile. He was just really on top of how to relate to frightened, White administrators. I said something about the students watching us from the roofs of buildings, and he said, "We have no choice. We always have to have the higher ground." And I said, "Okay, I'm not sure what that means. We're not having an invasion." And he said, "For the rest of your life, you'll be in an invasion."

Sometimes problems are simple enough that the easiest solution is just to correct them. It should have been easy for the president to say,

> I can see 12 of these 31 demands that I am somewhat ashamed are on the list. These are things we can correct immediately. We'll get right on these. Some of the others might take a little time and thought. How about setting up a smaller meeting than this in, say, 10 days? We can make a report to you then on our progress.

If he had used a cooperative approach rather than the back of his hand, I am fairly sure the meeting would have ended differently. Generally speaking, the Black students did not like President Marshall; they were suspicious of his sincerity or willingness to improve their situation. I think they probably liked Cecil Mackey, the executive vice president, a little more. Cecil was less intransigent. He could give the impression that he was listening.

The preamble to the proposals warned the administration that a state of emergency existed due to university neglect. The list of demands started with the following paragraph:

This meeting has been called because past efforts of the BSU to deal with issues effecting the survival of Black students on this campus have proven themselves to be patently ineffectual and frustrating. Attempts to deal solely with the administrative arm of the university have resulted in characteristic responses—lack of trust and confidence in Black student leadership, and failure to respond in accord with the gravity of the issues. We have reached a point at which the prevalent mood among Blacks, struggling for dignified and productive existence on this campus, is severe frustration! The situation is rapidly deteriorating; the pressure is building.

The demands were then listed. Topics included:

- Increased recruitment of Black students and faculty

- Increased funding for "Black-oriented" programs

- Hiring of Black barbers, beauticians, coaches, nurses, and doctors

- Appointment of Blacks to all university committees

- Hiring of Black officials for athletics events

- Establishment of university day care for children of "nonacademic employees"

- Naming a university building after a prominent Black

- Stocking Black oriented products, e.g. cosmetics and greeting cards in bookstore

- Banning of all materials, including textbooks, which are found to contain racist material

Finally, the BSU requested that President Marshall convene the faculty senate of Florida State University and to charge that body with responding to these issues.

In a news article *(Marshall Berated by Blacks,* 1970), the president of the faculty senate attempted to deflect the initiative. Professor Wayne Minnick said he felt the students would have no trouble gaining the attention of the senate, but questioned what good it would do.

If it were a matter of increasing opportunities for Black students in graduate programs, or adoption of a Black studies program, we might be of some help. However, the issue of a resident manager for the cultural center and many of the issues you have raised are strictly administrative concerns.

Nonetheless, the Faculty Senate did call itself into special session just five days later. At that time, the 31 demands (renamed "proposals") were presented once again. John Burt of the BSU urged the Senate "to mobilize its resources and its constituency to assist the administration in the resolution of this emergency. We look to you now, for the hour is late." The immediate response was the creation of a Commission on Black Student Affairs, comprised of four members of the faculty, five Black students appointed by the BSU, a representative of student government, and Shelton, as the administration's representative.

Missing from the list of demands was a request regarding curricular issues.

It was not a burning issue at the time. The students probably believed that they had demanded enough for this first round. Within two years, however, an emphasis—although not yet a minor—was added to the curriculum in African American history and politics.

The university's response to the demands was generally thoughtful from this point on, albeit slow and deliberate. However, the demand to employ a residence counselor/manager in the Cultural Center was not agreed to, which infuriated the Black student leadership.

TAKING OVER BUILDINGS AND OTHER PROTESTS

While not an exhaustive chronicle of protests, here are some other events that helped to earn FSU the title of "Berkley of the South."

The Bellamy Building, which was the behavioral sciences and criminal justice building, was taken two, three or four times and occupied by students over a period of about 10 months. It seemed like occupation had a different message, and the building was just a vehicle for a variety of messages to be delivered.

There was a counterculture at work in the Tallahassee area. Some parts were students, some stop-outs, some dropouts, and some were just there—unaffiliated with the university. They were led by an astute, very sharp activist and organizer by the name of Raleigh Jugger Jr. Raleigh with a bullhorn was a juggernaut. He was good. Raleigh would typically take up a position in the center of campus at about noon. He could, in that place and at that time of day, garner more interest than at any other spot or time.

Raleigh would stand up on the edge of a fountain, single out this or that White administrator or faculty member who might be unfortunate enough to pass that way, and challenge him. I remember being challenged in front of about 150 people as to whether or not I would lay down my life for a "brother." I remember the president, as a matter of fact, being catcalled by Raleigh's bullhorn during a stroll on the sidewalk. He got sucked into the gathering, probably thinking that he could strike a blow for equality, but soon regretted going anywhere near the confrontation. The situation posed to him was, "So Mr. President, if there was a busload of Klansmen and rednecks on their way to break up a peaceful demonstration, would you lay down in front of that bus for me?" It was a nonsense situation to be in or to let them put you in. Trying to answer such a question just digs the hole deeper. But, we all had to learn the hard way. Some of us were slow learners.

The White students on campus were very sympathetic to all of this because that was the tenor of the moment. Issue by issue, White students and Black students might disagree or have different personal beliefs. But, the White students wanted to show their appreciation, wanted to share their support. White students were also angry at other things—mostly Vietnam. Black students had shown their support for the protests against Vietnam. I think there was a moment, a sort of dawning, where Black students realized that it was predominately Black soldiers who were dying. The strategy and focus began to shift. Instead of supporting White students regarding Southeast Asia, the Black cause became its own mission. Then you have to understand that just about the time the coals would start to die down, some member of Florida's legislature, or the governor, or the president of the United States would grab a can of lighter fluid.

One night, one hot Florida State, Tallahassee night, several hundred students were just milling—absolutely the perfect cauldron for something to happen. Suddenly, several Florida Highway Patrol cruisers appeared. Three or four trooper bodyguards escorted the Florida Governor, Claude Kirk, to an area right next to a large pod of students. Two of the troopers were carrying a rocking chair because the governor, unannounced, unknown to the university, had decided to have a dialogue with students on this hot night. Students just could not resist. There were catcalls. The governor got angry. The governor yelled things back, some of it very uncharitable, some of it marginally racial, and, by the time he left, he needed those trooper bodyguards.

One spring evening, there was to be a snake dance. Typically, students would come out of the residence halls or student union as the thing wound by, and would join the snake. Gerard Fowler and I (Fowler is now professor of higher education at St. Louis University) were assigned to be "out and about" during the evening. Fowler was the other assistant dean of men. The dance started on Landis Green in front of Strozier Library with about 200 students. It picked up size and steam, and it occurred to us that the head of the snake was leading a lot of students to the ROTC building. We knew this could be inflammatory, and we also knew we were unable to stop it. By the time the entire group reached the building, the numbers were estimated at 600-700. Students were just milling around on the lawn in front. Several people had been yelling things during the dance things like, "Shirts of brown, burn it down," but no such moves were made, at least in the early stage.

I noticed that, in a dark wooded area across the street, there was activity of some sort—light glinting off of metal objects and movement in a dark area that was usually lonely and inactive. Suddenly, the doors of police vans opened in the woods, and a large group of local police and sheriff's deputies dressed in full riot gear came, double-time, toward us. They skirted the crowd and formed a ring around the ROTC area in order to protect it. I would guess about 40 of them, Plexiglas facemasks and helmets, each carrying what appeared to be a shotgun. They assumed a "parade rest" position around the circle, guns held in front of them.

I walked over to one of them, a young man who appeared to be no more than 19 or 20 years of age. He stared through the Plexiglas mask, but would not make eye contact with me. I raised my ID card to his level of vision and said, "I am the dean of men. I need to know if that weapon is loaded." He maintained an erect and detached posture but gave no response. I said something like,

> I want you to understand something very clearly. You are about 10 steps from a large, angry group. They don't want you here. One of these guys is going to walk up here with a wrench and pop you on the kneecap. I want to know when you react with that weapon, if someone's going to die.

He made eye contact with me and just ever so slowly nodded his head yes. The gun is loaded and yes, he would react that way. There were a couple of rocks thrown but I don't even think there was a window broken. There was no fire lit, and no one got hurt that night.-

Richard Nixon's visit to Tallahassee stands out as a galvanizing moment for the protest movement at Florida State.

> The platform was wheeled out to Air Force One. For several hours before Air Force One landed, the city of Tallahassee was on its way to the airport. Students, townspeople, families with children wanted to see the president, as despised as he might have been by some. When you came through the airport gate, based on your appearance, based on your dress, you were either directed to the left or to the right. I was coming from the office in a coat and tie and my wife was dressed as a teacher, our cherubic children were lovely, so we were directed to the left. Tie-dyed T-shirts, long hair, and most Black students were herded to the right. It turned out that the right side of the viewing area could quickly be sealed off so as to contain the "undesirable" group, at least from the point of view of the organizers and Secret Service. Once Air Force One had landed and taxied over to this area on the tarmac, this area was sealed off by a ring of police who were armed, but not with riot gear. Probably 300 students were contained in such a way that they could not get out. My area, the folks who did not appear that they would make trouble, had only a few folding barricades to mark the area we were to stand in.

> I watched the students to see what the reaction was to this cordon. Claustrophobia was bound to set in as they were tightly packed, and it was a hot afternoon with direct sun on the hot pavement. As the event progressed and the president addressed the crowd, it became clear as to why there were two groups. The students were a target for Nixon. When he pointed at them, the cameras followed. At one point, he turned to face them, fist in the air, and said, "These young people are not the leaders of America's tomorrow. They are the bums of today."

After a short while of the heat, claustrophobia, and general targeting by Nixon, or maybe it was just because someone had to go to the bathroom, a couple of students tried to get out of their group. They were pushing against police, who would not let them leave. A sort of low-level panic erupted. Within minutes, students were beaten with batons by police. Some were knocked down and beaten on their backs, the backs of their legs and heads. White students and Black students together were getting a dose of old-fashioned, Southern justice, and not even the Secret Service attempted to stop it. It was all over pretty fast. Some of the students were bloodied. The president retreated into his airplane. I have a photograph somewhere that appeared in the Tallahassee Democrat the next morning. It shows the side of a uniformed police officer. His uniform shirt had a patch on the arm that read "Tallahassee...The Fair City" or something like that, and his baton was coming down in the face of our student government president. He was a graduate student, had been a social studies teacher, and was always a voice of reason. That day he got a bloody face.

ACTIVISTS HAD THE SAME DEVELOPMENTAL ISSUES AS ANY OTHER STUDENT

Amidst extraordinary political times and violent confrontations, FSU students still faced the personal challenges of typical college students.

The students who were participating in these events were postadolescent, but very young adults. These were people who needed to be cared for and cared about as human beings, more than just as students. This seemed especially true in relationships between Black students and White students. I watched the difficulty of romantic relationships between races. In the case of a young Black male who fell in love with a White female, the pressure from peers was intense on both of them. A "brother" who preferred the company of a White girl was quickly a target of anger by "sisters." Frequently the only way to interact together was to hide and to sneak. Rather than having the opportunity to grow in a natural, social way, the relationship was forced into the dark, literally.

We had some three-walled, outdoor, handball courts. Even with the streetlights shining at night, there were shadowed and dark areas, and I remember that this was the meeting place of one interracial couple. They just could not risk being seen or discovered. Another, similar couple used my office. They walked in one day and closed the door. They told me that they were in love, that they were in an impossible situation, and needed some help to get through it. Several evenings they would show up, we would close the door and chat for a short while—so as to appear to any observers that this was a legitimate meeting with two students and an administrator—and then I would excuse myself so that they could be alone and the relationship could develop in a protected and unexposed way.

Situations like this helped keep me grounded. I could stay busy all day just putting out brushfires—disputes of all sorts between students and the university. It was refreshing to attempt to help two young people such as these. Such experiences sort of returned me momentarily to the beginning, to the days when calling oneself an "educator" was not as confusing.

THE INSTITUTION'S RESPONSE TO CIVIL RIGHTS DEMANDS

Whether dealing with human problems or political unrest, FSU and other universities across the country had to respond. In many cases, the campus climate left institutions ill-equipped to handle volatile situations and disorderly conduct.

I am not sure that there was a unified or agreed-upon response. The type of response and the intensity depended upon the audience. For example, recruitment of African Americans was a clear direction for FSU by the mid-1960s. Another example is the appointment of a commission on Black student affairs by the faculty senate. On the other hand, many students and faculty did not want to be bothered by these issues. Some were afraid of a dialogue between races. And the environment was one of antebellum South and some of the old thinking that went on behind the magnolias and Spanish moss and plantation houses.

Probably the best way to explain the institutional climate is to profile the division of student affairs, which was looked to by the rest of the campus for direction in how to handle these "disruptive students." Our vice president was a full colonel, retired Air Force. Retired colonels occupied positions as assistant to the vice president, director of financial aid, and director of career services. The director of residence life was a retired Marine major. I am not suggesting that having a military background makes one less caring or hospitable. I do think there was a subtle message for students that, as long as things are orderly, as long as you are purposeful and goal oriented, as long as you understand that you are privileged to be at this institution, then everything will be fine. It was not an overt racial undertone or overtone. It was more about the perception of what good people did and how they did it, and what bad people did. Good people do not throw rocks and yell through bullhorns, or challenge people in broad daylight, or occupy buildings, or shout obscenities.

I think the administration in general was frightened, right from the top, even from the board of regents, and the fear manifested itself in protective and closed activities—meetings held in secret so that the wrong people would not listen. There is no question that one element of the staff of FSU, including faculty, wanted to retaliate against disruptive behavior. Some folks wanted to teach the culprit students a few lessons. At our best, we abandoned a position of educators in favor of one of defense of the university. There were many early morning meetings designed to discuss locking files procedures, escape routes for employees if a building was occupied, evacuation places for folks to go to. I do not recall much conversation about student development theory. Imagine cutting the teeth of a new career on all of this stuff. I suspect that the profession of student personnel, student affairs lost some very capable young professionals who just said "that's enough" and walked away.

At the system and board level the emphasis was on "strength and resistance."

After the resignation of John Champion as president, J. Stanley Marshall was named acting president. John was the first and highest administrator to fall victim to protest and activism. Stanley Marshall really wanted the appointment to the presidency, and he was aware that the board of regents wanted the campus to return to preactivism levels of "normalcy" and maybe a few students "put in their place." For Stan to be thoughtful and compassionate or to appear to be tolerant of disruptive behavior would certainly work against him in the appointment process. Stern and tough might get him the job.

There was, in 1969, an event held by a coalition of SDS, Weathermen, BSU, and other activist groups. In protest of the annual FSU Military Ball, the group held the "Anti-Military Ball." Admission might be a burned draft card or bra. Stan did not like the several messages that were generated from such an event, and pulled the plug on the music. Before the night was over, troops in riot gear were inside the student union to disperse the crowd. This became known as the "Night of the Bayonet" and served Stanley Marshall well. He was appointed to the presidency, for real, not too long afterward.

The campus could have handled student unrest differently, but that would have been out of character at that time for FSU, and for most other institutions. It was pretty predictable behavior—circle the wagons, protect the buildings, protect the institution, protect its reputation, protect the jobs of folks, and if a few students were the fallout, what the hell. I am sure that was typical of that time which was early in the very disruptive phase. Clearly the community-at-large, including the legislature, wanted students handled with strength and resistance.

THE ROLE OF NASPA

At that time, there were three basic means of communication within the NASPA structure: attendance at meetings, the *NASPA Journal*, and talking with folks as a result of networking—usually resulting from meetings. The organization, itself, did not communicate with its membership very effectively in 1969, 1970, 1971. Compared with today, NASPA of 30 years ago was a very different type of organization.

Other factors that influenced NASPA's role included the fact that not all campuses were involved in disruptive behavior, and those that were differed one to another, some significantly. Not many professionals in this business then felt equipped to publicly analyze the situation, or to make recommendations to peers for how to deal with this or that situation. I do remember that at several regional meetings there were sort of round table discussions where folks could throw out a situation for group comment. Actually, I learned a good deal from those sessions. In that setting, NASPA was a facilitator but not advisor or direct communicator.

Those NASPA years were a part of the patriarchy as well. Young professionals admired their heroes at national meetings—NASPA presidents, such as Jim Appleton at Oakland and later USC, Jim Rhatigan at Wichita State, John Blackburn at Alabama in Denver, Al Miles who ended up at Alabama, Channing Briggs, a New Englander who served the association as executive director, etc. Had any of their institutions been heavily involved in real destructive stuff, we probably would have heard a lot more from the leadership.

So, while NASPA folks were conducting research on "Aspirations of Freshmen in Residence Halls," or some similar topic, I was suspending students blocking the corridors of Bryan Hall while protesting the presence of Marine Corps recruiters. There was not much time to network or prepare, and there was not much of a connection with NASPA.

Naming those folks reminds me of a funny story. Florida State was advertising for a vice president for student affairs in 1971 and Jim Rhatigan was a finalist. During one of the interview sessions, our student body president sat across the table from Rhatigan. At one particularly tense moment in the examination of just how liberal and tolerant the candidate was, Jim Rhatigan packed his pipe with tobacco, looked across the table at the student and asked, "Got a match?" The student told him no, to which Rhatigan sort of chuckled and said "No matches? What kind of radical are you?"

PERSONAL LESSONS LEARNED

I suppose some lessons resulted from my particular upbringing. I grew up on Navy bases for the early years of school where there were virtually no Black people. Later, I was a Southern White boy in a segregated school system where there was really no contact between races in any segment of my life. However, by the time of the civil rights movement, I had traveled all over the country, and had at least some exposure to different ways of thinking and acting with regard to relations among different races and cultures.

Secondarily, I was a very young professional at Florida State, and a long way down the organizational chart. Coupled with a willingness to listen to students, I probably had more credibility than most administrators around me. Some were a little too old, a little too Southern. I was so young—I had good student trust and students wanted to talk, they wanted to converse with someone who would listen. They wanted me to approve of what they were doing, or to explain why I did not approve.

One thing that comes to mind is that, as an institution, we did not do well with things. Our approach was shallow, surface, and not always professional or educational. Instead of listening to students' concerns and frustrations, we circled the wagons—as I said earlier—so as to protect ourselves and the institution at all costs. We reacted as the keepers of FSU. There was no sense that there were human development issues woven into the disruptive acts, but rather that the disruptive individuals were outlaws committing crimes and robbing "good" students of a chance to learn in quiet and peace. We were very noble.

I can reflect now on how completely we are shaped by our culture and our immediate environment. Initially at Florida State, I had good exposure to Black students, but not Black students who spoke their minds to Whites. It was new to me and to others to encounter students with clearly formulated positions, strategies to accomplish their goals, and the courage to fly in the face of several hundred years of convention—to step over the boundaries of acceptable behavior. It was one thing to watch it all on television—from Selma and Mississippi to Memphis and the motel where Martin Luther King was assassinated. It was very different to me to realize that each of us as educators had a personal stake, a personal role in the battle for human rights. In place of Birmingham, my role was on my campus, making sure that a young man and woman had the opportunity to learn about each other and to explore their relationship without fear of reprisal.

There is an interesting and incorrect notion among some in higher education that students maintain a different, lesser class of citizenship. We not only act this out daily, we also teach it to students. For example, "student jobs" are of less importance and/or esteem than regular jobs. "Student wages" are less than other wages. "Student senate," "student government," "student newspapers" seem to have a connotation of transience, inexperience, lesser, not real, not real important. Without a doubt, this condescending treatment was a frustration to students in the 1960s who believed they had something to say and wanted the respect of honest dialogue. A lot of this thinking remains unchanged in 30 years. These are some lessons learned the hard way.

How Activism Is Different Today

For students arriving at college in the late 1960s, activism was virtually expected behavior. New freshmen had role models resulting from television coverage of demonstrations. Marches and protests were accepted as effective means of expressing opinions or grievances. The music of that time sort of glorified a sense of being antiestablishment.

Today and for a few years, I notice that where there is activism it is very goal oriented, as opposed to just the former generalities of "Peace and Love." Today's activist topics are largely financial— tuition costs, federal aid legislation, funding for the arts, how much money should go to athletics, what political causes can be funded by student fee dollars? This certainly might change, and change rather quickly, if the United States continues its threat of unilateral military action in the Middle East and elsewhere.

I also notice that there is more of a trust in leaders and administrators to listen and then to act responsively to student concerns—much more trust than existed 30 years ago. There is a nice sense of civility and responsibility that was not always there in former times. Having said all of that, I do sometimes miss the electricity, the feeling of vibrancy with a large group of students joining together against a perceived common enemy.

ADVICE FOR OTHERS IN STUDENT AFFAIRS

Listen carefully when students speak. Find a way of involving them in the solution, as opposed to adopting their concern and solving the problem for them. This approach encourages discovery, encourages ownership in the solution, and in the institution's willingness to listen and to deal with concerns.

Ensure that channels of communication are clearly known by students. This takes some designing and testing on occasion. I frequently ask students on campus, or at a lunch table in the dining hall, "How many faculty and staff do you speak with daily, on average?" "Which office is the easiest and most comfortable for you to take care of business?" "If a friend has a problem that needs addressing, do you feel comfortable in knowing where to refer them?" "Do you feel comfortable that your friend will be treated courteously and fairly when they get there?" It is important to take the temperature of your campus environment on a regular basis.

In my opinion, one of the great lessons of the 1960s and 1970s was that the colleges who were already "student centered" were those which had fewest problems. By student-centered, I mean that every staff member understands and accepts their responsibility to create and maintain a pleasant climate and learning environment. They all realize that each contact with a student can be a retention issue. Students are valued clients. Respect is mutual and evident. Students do not perceive the faculty or administration as enemy, but as helpful and facilitating. That type of institution had a head start with its students in the ability to communicate—especially to listen.

At Florida State we were not student centered. We really had no unity, no strategy. We were a loose confederation of professionals during that time. This is not to suggest that there was always dysfunction. We had very talented people in place. There was a good respect and communication within the staff, at least at my level. Many of the professionals reached out to students, attempted to mentor them, listen to them. We were all concerned with the safety and well-being of our students. My point is that we were not a cohesive team. The top administration sent mixed messages occasionally. We were in many ways left to our own devices and ingenuity in order to cope with the uncertainties we faced. And, in that process, there was no template. Reflection and retrospection are wonderful luxuries, and sometimes they stretch across both affective and cognitive domains.

EPILOGUE

Shelton left Florida State in 1971 to become dean of students at University of Alaska, Fairbanks (UAF). Before deciding whether he should move to Alaska, Shelton asked someone at UAF what kinds of activism they had experienced up there. They told him, "We did have a protest. About 50 students got a permit and they protested out in front of the student union building. However, a moose ran through and broke it up." Compared to the "heat" of FSU, Alaska must have provided a nice respite. During the 1984-85 academic year, Shelton received a sabbatical leave to New Zealand, and consulted with four of the public universities over a nine-month period on issues in and around student affairs and student development. When he returned to UAF in 1985, he was named vice chancellor for student affairs. During the years 1994 through 1999, Shelton "retired" from UAF. He wrote several books and articles, as well as serving as a consultant. He also traveled to Russia twice and authored the first US-Russian exchange agreement for intercollegiate athletics teams. In 1999, Shelton came out of retirement, moved to Oregon, and became the vice president for student affairs at Eastern Oregon University. He continues to hold that position today.

JO ANNE J. TROW
Oregon State University (1965-1995)

L ike most of the college administrators interviewed in this book, Jo
    Anne Trow has a long history in higher education and student affairs
    administration. Trow's recollection about the role of student affairs
during the civil rights era adds a unique perspective to this collection of stories because of her experiences as dean of women, dean of students, and
vice president for student affairs at a university on the West Coast of the
United States. She was the last dean of women at Oregon State University,
and one of few women to hold the title of vice president for student affairs
in the 1980s at a large university. Compared to universities on the East
Coast and in the South, Oregon State University's experience during the
civil rights movement was somewhat less turbulent, due to the low numbers
of underrepresented populations in the state and region. According to Trow,
the civil rights era at Oregon State wasn't really a period of unrest, "but an
opportunity for awakening."

Jo Anne Trow began her 30-year career at Oregon State University (OSU)
as assistant dean of women in 1965. Prior to coming to Oregon State, Trow
worked at Denison University from 1956 to 1959, Washington State
University from 1959 to 1963, and Michigan State University in 1964. She
earned her doctorate in student personnel administration from Michigan
State in 1965. In 1966, Trow became the dean of women at Oregon State
(this title was dropped in 1969) and associate dean of students. She held this
title until 1984, when she was named vice president for student affairs at
OSU. From 1993 until her retirement in 1995, she served as chief student
affairs officer at Oregon State.

CONTEXT FOR CIVIL RIGHTS IN OREGON AND CORVALLIS

The state of Oregon has had a spotty history in race relations and civil
rights. For many years, Asians and Blacks were not permitted to own

property and the Ku Klux Klan was active in the 1920s (although they were directed against Catholics as much as minorities). Many smaller, rural communities had few if any minorities. It was only during WWII that any number of African Americans came to the Portland area to work in the shipyards. Most stayed. Asian Americans have been here in large numbers, but many were interned during the war as well. Hispanics began to come after the war, mainly as migrants, but many stayed. (Today, Hispanics are the largest minority group in Oregon, followed by Asians and Native Americans.)

So with this background and with the knowledge that Corvallis is a relatively small community with a population of just over 50,000, the university had to work especially hard to educate our students and the community, and to support the minority students who came here. There are ongoing concerns with law enforcement profiling, housing discrimination issues, and other similar concerns. In addition, the city makes a concerted effort to celebrate and recognize diversity.

THE CLIMATE AT OREGON STATE UNIVERSITY

According to Trow, there was a very small African American population at Oregon State University.

Most of the African American students in the 1960s or 1970s who were either at the University of Oregon or Oregon State were from California. Most of them were athletes. Even at Oregon State, Black athletes were not necessarily welcome, even in the athletic department, until the late 1960s. Oregon was really conservative in many ways.

The conservative climate, coupled with the desire for equal rights and treatment of African Americans and other underrepresented groups, led to a number of confrontations at Oregon State University.

Let me give you one story. It happened a year before I came, and I think it precipitated an increased sensitivity on the part of students. There were a number of Asian American students at Oregon State. They were often engineering majors, good students, and well respected on the campus. In the spring of 1964, one of the fraternities asked a Japanese American, Gene, to be a member of Sigma Chi. I was not at the university then, but the man that I worked with for many years was the dean of students at the time and played an important role in this story.

One of the things that this fraternity does, as a matter of course, is send their chapter alumni a list of the new people they are going to initiate. Supposedly, if the alumnus happened to know anyone, he could send a letter of congratulations. Well, a couple of alumni saw Gene's name on the list and they said, "You can't initiate him; he's a Japanese American, and we don't do this." Well, the students went to the dean and said, "What are we going to do?" and the dean said, "You're going to initiate him." So that began a long series of conversations with Greek organizations on the influence of alumni, and whether or not they could veto what a chapter wanted to do, particularly in terms of who they wanted to initiate.

About a year later, this same issue came up with sororities on campus. Trow advised the Panhellenic Council at the time and worked hard to help them understand the importance of non discriminatory behavior.

Many sororities have a system where you have to have an alumna recommendation before you can be rushed. We told them we could do that no longer. I ended up in a lot of conversations with national officers, but we held our ground. We said, "The students insist we do not want discrimination from outside the institution to take place." There were a number of our sororities that wanted to have members who were Asian American. That was the beginning of developing some sensitivity on the part of students that you don't discriminate on the basis of race. If you want to have somebody be a part of your group, you have the right to ask them, and somebody else shouldn't tell you, "No, you can't."

As Oregon State became more diverse in terms of its student population, more race-related issues became prevalent on campus. Trow related this story:

An African American woman had been assigned to room with a White woman in the freshman residence hall. The parents of the White woman came in and said, "She can't live with her. We want her [the Black student] to be moved out." I said, "Well, it is not an option to move this other woman out. If your daughter wants to move to another hall or another room, she can do that." The daughter said, "No, I want to stay where I am; my friends are down the hall, and I won't do it." We responded that our policy states that if a person is unhappy with her roommate, the person who is unhappy must move, not the other one. So we went around and around on this. The parents went to the board members that they knew, and to the president, but the administration backed the dean of women's office on what we said.

The White student moved and eventually left school. I think her parents decided they weren't going to let her stay here. The Black student eventually moved out of the residence halls, but we did not make her move out of that room. I can't help but think in some ways that other students in the corridor might have made life uneasy for her. This was one of those teachable moments where we worked with the residence hall students to understand the importance of learning to live with people who are different. Of course the Black woman felt really put upon, and it was difficult for her anyway because there were very few Black students on the campus at the time. Most of the Black students were athletes, mostly football players and a few basketball players. Most of the Black women ran track. In fact, I think the Black student in this incident was a track athlete on scholarship. It was the kind of incident that didn't get a lot of publicity, but it did begin to indicate to me that we might eventually find things difficult. I was in my second year at Oregon State when this happened.

One of the most widely publicized incidents that focused on minority relations and civil rights occurred in the winter of 1969. A Black football player violated the existing team rule of having no facial hair by growing a beard. The coach's order to shave the beard and mustache was seen as a violation of that student's rights. The student eventually shaved his beard, but not the mustache, and was not allowed to play. Students in general, and particularly the Black community, took issue with the coach's decision. So, in the winter of 1969, the Black Student Union called for a boycott of classes to support the football player. Even though the coaching staff denied the allegation that they discriminated on the basis of race, students continued to agitate and rally. This all culminated in a march off the campus through a symbolic gate that leads to the downtown area. Led by the Black athlete, a large group of students of all races and a number of Black community leaders from Portland started at the student union and marched across the quad, through the campus, and out the gate. They "walked off the campus." Newspapers across the state carried the event, and the repercussions were felt for years in the athletic department and the campus in general. (An interesting note is that the football player graduated and went on to work for the City of Portland, and he and the coach, who recently passed away, remained in contact and were friends.) The faculty, for the most part, was very supportive of the walkout. Out of this concern grew the establishment of the Commission on Human Rights and Responsibilities, which still exists and deals with issues of alleged discrimination.

Since that time the university has achieved a great deal in providing more education, public forums, and coursework to promote diversity. The educational process continues to be important, as there seem to be one or two incidents a year, even now. For example, a White student who drank too much shouts a racial epitaph at another student or paints slurs on a resident hall door. Every time we had any kind of incident, any kind of racial harassment, people often bring up the incident of the athlete's beard and walk-out by the Black Student Union.

THE ROLE OF STUDENT AFFAIRS

In response to the protest in 1969, Trow supported the formation of the Commission on Human Rights and Responsibilities Commission initiated by the faculty senate. At an earlier time, she was also very involved in starting a Women's Commission.

In the late 1960s and early 1970s, as war protests increased, the staff in student affairs, working with the students, developed a structure to facilitate demonstrations on campus. Our students tended to do what they were supposed to do. When they wanted to demonstrate, they registered all of their information and took care of doing what they should in order to abide by the policies. We didn't tell anybody they couldn't do something. We didn't censor things or say, for example, "You can't put that in the newspaper." They printed what they wanted to print. If they wanted to hold a big demonstration in the middle of the quad we said, "Fine, just do it when we don't have classes." We didn't tell them they couldn't do anything, as long as they obeyed the law. In fact, in many ways, I remember a couple of times that we gave them advice on how to protest to get what they wanted.

As a result of concerns of minority students for more identity on campus and for increased support in what might be seen by them as an unfriendly environment, two things happened. A series of cultural centers, physical facilities, were set up and an academic support program, the Education Opportunities Program (EOP), was established.

The student affairs staff was instrumental in finding and furnishing the physical facilities, small houses on the edge of campus for the Black Cultural Center, the Hispanic (now Cesar Chavez) Center, the Native American Long House and the Asian American Center. While all these centers were not created at the same time, over the years they have become important parts of the university culture. In order to assure their continued existence, each one is supported financially through the Memorial Union fees budget. The union is also responsible for the upkeep of the buildings, for supervising the staff (who are paid from student fees), and for working with the student, fee-funded programs in each center. The centers have continued to be a tremendous asset to the campus in providing a place for students in the various ethic groups to gather, in creating educational programs and social events for the general student body, and for giving an identity to the particular cultural group.

In the late 1960s, the student affairs staff was instrumental in creating a program of academic support for minority students. Called the EOP, the program focused on individuals, particularly minorities, who might not otherwise come to college or, if they did, might have difficulty succeeding. The experience at the time showed that many minorities from the urban and rural areas of the state were often not sufficiently prepared for college, and EOP was prepared to help them overcome this. EOP over the years has been very successful in recruiting minorities, providing necessary remedial work, being a supporting mentor for the students and assuring graduation. The program has had a very high graduation rate, and reaches out to many students who might not ever venture on to a four-year campus. While there were some federal grants for the program, the support has come from the university general fund with students getting funding through the usual financial aid channels.

While the impetus for this program came primarily from student affairs, it ultimately was located in the academic affairs area. This move gave it more credibility with the faculty. Interestingly, in a recent reorganization at the university, the EOP is now supervised by student affairs and works closely with the four minority affairs/student affairs staff members.

THE EXTENT TO WHICH OSU HAS STAYED THE SAME

Despite the conservative culture of Oregon State University, initiatives have been implemented, in addition to the EOP, to promote diversity on campus.

I think the institution has changed a lot. There are special diversity programs that Larry Roper, the current chief student affairs officer, put into place. Every year, they bring in all kinds of diversity and educational opportunities for the campus as a whole and for the surrounding community.

In terms of offerings and opportunities for minority students, they were involved, and we made an effort to help them be involved, in the creation of cultural centers. We have a Cambodian student organization. The Japanese-American and Chinese-American students have their "nights" when they perform and serve food from their cultures. These students are good students and great folks, very loyal supporters of the institution. Not too many Asian-American students participated in the traditional campus activities. The students who have tended to be most involved in student activities and who have become the focus of the university are Black, Hispanic, and Native American students. It really depended on what kind of student leaders emerged from the ethnic groups. I can remember one student who was very vocal on the needs of Hispanic students. He graduated, went to graduate school, and earned a master's degree. Now he is working with the state on the needs of the Hispanic population in Oregon.

About 12 years ago, the university established the DPD programming, "Difference, Power, and Discrimination." It is an academic program, set up to be a part of our core requirements. Students are required to take a DPD course in order to graduate. Various members of the faculty, not necessarily in African American Studies, teach the courses. The courses look at the issues of difference, power, and discrimination. Each year there are a few new courses that faculty approve, and then others drop out of the series. This is part of the effort to sensitize all students to this whole issue of differences and how we can live and work with people of color.

I still think it is interesting how people still talk about the beard incident, because that happened 30 years ago. It wasn't too long after that when a Black student became very active in student government, serving as the president of student union. Oregon State University, as mentioned earlier, was a conservative campus. However, over time, the minority student population on campus increased. Athletes were not the only Black students on campus as was the case in previous years. Occasionally, the press would pickup on isolated racial incidents that occurred on campus, which would frustrate the student affairs staff. Whenever these things happened while I was still working there, I would say, "Oh, no! Let's hope this is the only one this year." There was always a call to expel the student, but often the infraction didn't fit the rules or discipline guidelines for expulsion. There is always a call for zero tolerance as well.

Every four years, you see a whole new group of people. They come with a great deal of predetermined ideas, prejudices, and ideas of what should and shouldn't be. Most of them have some prejudice to a degree, and they get involved in things they probably would never have gotten involved in otherwise. It is a never-ending process. Today, I think students are more tolerant, or at least they don't demonstrate their intolerance as much as they used to in the past. I really do think students are much more tolerant and accepting and have had more interaction with people of other races. I think people from the same circle of minority groups are becoming more understanding of nonminority groups. The racial incidents tend to be spawned by one or two individuals. The students who have been targets of racial incidents want something done. They are rarely physically hurt, but are hurt psychologically and feel demeaned. Now, I can think of a couple of students where every time someone looked at them sideways they complained that they were discriminated against.

THE RESPONSE AT OSU

The institution has promised to try to work with people, and we haven't said, "No, no, no, no!" It's been more like, "Let's try to work this out." My relationship with students in the 1960s thru the 1990s, I think was positive. Gaining the trust of some of the minorities was not always easy, and there were some successes as well as some failures in solving the issues to everyone's satisfaction.

Of course, I've been gone for eight years, but I think the staff really tries to work with the students. Our student affairs staff is a lot more diverse now that it was 10 years ago. We have an African American chief student affairs officer and other minority staff in activities and a few in counseling. The community has diversified the faculty also. More and more students are saying that they want more faculty of color.

In one effort to bring more support for the various minority communities at the university, a minority board of visitors was established in the late 1970 and early 1980s. Community members from across the state were recruited to serve on the board and to give the university ideas and insights on how to better the climate for minority students and faculty on the campus. They continue today as a vital element of the university's commitment to diversity and support for individual and group rights. They have made a valuable contribution. Corvallis, where OSU is located, has a very small minority community, especially African Americans, so finding support for the recruitment of minority faculty, who can serve as a role model for students, as well as fulfill the role of teacher/researcher is very important.

LESSONS LEARNED

I think the civil rights movement just reinforced my long-time belief that you can't let this kind of stuff [racial discrimination] go on. I don't think it changed my attitudes. I can remember a couple of incidents that occurred when I was in high school that just didn't make any sense—the way minorities were treated in particular—and I refused to let it happen here. One thing that I was really proud of in my association with NAWDAC was the involvement of minority women in that organization and their support for minority women. In some ways the experience has given me the impetus to really push some things and say, "Let's not ignore the issue." I've always tried to support students when they've wanted to move ahead in terms of integration and having people of color as a part of the ongoing programs at the institution.

I don't know whether we could have done anything differently. We might have done it quicker, but then, the campus tends to take a long time to decide to do something—working through all those committees. I think we probably could have done more in providing dollars to try to get more minority faculty, because that is what it takes. This is an important way to provide role models. I know that when I was trying to hire some counselors, we just didn't have the money available to pay what they wanted to be paid. On a different note, I think we could have perhaps taken the opportunity to become more aware of what might have been going on in the athletic department. I say this because in the late 1960s early 1970s I didn't realize how relatively few Black athletes were there. Until one basketball coach retired in the late 1950s, there were no Black men on the basketball team. I think it just took us a long time; however, once we began to devote resources to diversity, it began to pay off in terms of involvement from the minority community. There is still a lot to do. We certainly can't ignore issues that we still face today. Tomorrow, something may pop-up that needs to be done, but the institution has been willing in the last 10-15 years to put resources behind enhancing the experiences of minority students.

The environment that student affairs people work in is so different now from the 1960s and 1970s. Everything is more compartmentalized today compared to 30 years ago. I don't think there is necessarily anything learned from it, but I think one of the problems with compartmentalization is that you tend not to communicate with the rest the university or stay abreast of what is going on. This can be a real issue if you sense something beginning to happen, if there's unhappiness, if there's concern over something that happens in a student organization, or that counselors hear about in residence halls, and you don't have the kind of contact overall where someone can step in and provide advice and support and try to resolve the issue before it explodes into some kind of racial situation. Because we are so fragmented, it is hard to have a coordinated response. I think we need to take advantage of the opportunities that are presented when diversity occurs on a campus that does have the range of cultures, experiences, and background to help students recognize that everyone is not the same, nor should they be the same. Students need to accept and appreciate those differences and understand them as well.

EPILOGUE

Jo Anne Trow retired from Oregon State University in July 1995 as emeritus professor and vice provost emeritus. Trow has been an active member of NAWDAC since 1955, serving as president and on the executive board in the 1980s. She has also been an active member of ACPA and NASPA. In her retirement, Trow continues to play an active role in the Corvallis community. For example, she serves on the Corvallis Parks and Recreation Advisory Board, the Willamette Criminal Justice Council, the OSU-Corvallis Symphony Board, and the League of Women Voters. Trow has won numerous awards and distinctions, including the establishment of a campus-wide award named in her honor by Oregon State students in 1963. The Jo Anne J. Trow Award to Women of Distinction is bestowed annually on the OSU campus. She is also the recipient of NASPA's Scott Goodnight Award for Outstanding Performance as a Dean in 1989.

EMILY TAYLOR
University of Kansas, 1956-1975

E mily Taylor, included in the book *Woman of Influence, Women of Vision* by Astin and Leland (1991), was dean of women at the University of Kansas (KU) from 1956 to 1975. This chapter represents Taylor's experiences with civil rights, broadly defined to include both the rights of African Americans as well as women. Because of her long history in higher education and the availability of rich additional sources about Taylor's life, this chapter contains more paraphrasing and contextualization by the interviewees than some of the other chapters in this volume.

HOW PERSONAL BACKGROUND INFLUENCED TAYLOR'S VIEWS ON CIVIL RIGHTS

Emily Taylor was born on an Alabama cotton and pecan plantation in 1915. She was the daughter and granddaughter of strong Southern women—her grandmother, who had been orphaned in the Civil War, inherited the family plantation when she was only 14. Taylor moved to Ohio, her father's home state, as a child (Rix, 1988). Taylor was aware at an early age, growing up in Ohio in the 1920s and 1930s, that girls were treated differently from boys. Others were shocked when at the age of six or seven she announced she wanted to be a lawyer rather than a "mommy." Later, she was not awarded first place at a state speech contest because they "couldn't allow that nice boy to be beaten by a girl." When she was 12, she figured out that men were paid more than women at the local factory for the same work. So, when she had her first teaching job after graduating from college and learned that a male teacher with the same experience was making 50 percent more than she was, she vowed she would never take another job without ensuring she was not paid on a "female scale" and made the same amount as comparable males. "And I never did, never once."

It was always assumed that Taylor would go to college. She earned an associate's degree from Urbana University (then a two-year college) and a bachelor's degree in English and history from Ohio State University, and then took a job as a high school English teacher in a suburb of Cincinnati. The summer after her graduation, she enrolled in a master's program in counseling and guidance at Ohio State University. As she registered for classes, they asked about her field of study and, when she confessed she hadn't thought about that, they asked her what she wanted to be when she grew up. "And I said, 'I'd like to be a dean of women.'"

The associate dean of women, an economist who conducted research on consumer co-ops, influenced Taylor in her senior year of college. Taylor assisted her with a series of public radio programs on the topic, and she also learned archery golf from this multitalented woman administrator. The dean urged her to "be something...be a lawyer or a psychologist or an economist," and then add the dean of women role to that professional field. Taylor continued to teach and attend graduate school in the summer until she got her master's degree, and then went to Indiana University (IU) as an assistant to the dean of women in charge of one of the residence halls. At IU her mentor and chair of her doctoral committee was Kate Hevner Mueller, one time IU dean of women. Mueller was an important psychologist in the 1940s and 1950s who studied new roles for women, and predicted many of the important themes of the women's movement of the 1960s and 1970s (Tuttle, K. N., 1996; Mueller, 1954). Taylor describes Mueller as an exemplary mentor—she encouraged her to attend psychology and sociology colloquia, insisted that she join the University Women's Club, introduced her to numerous colleagues, and held a monthly seminar for staff members, which was more valuable than most graduate seminars, according to Taylor.

Taylor started her professional career as dean of women at Northern Montana College in 1946. After receiving her doctorate from IU, she served as associate dean of women at Miami University in Oxford, Ohio, from 1953-56. She came to KU as dean of women in 1956. Taylor's advocacy for women students was nationally recognized—she established the first commission on the status of women on a university campus in the United States in 1958, three years before a national commission was initiated. She pushed for changes in the parietal rules, such as reducing curfew hours for women, and initiated a senior women's key program in 1961, years before most institutions changed the rules. KU was the first institution in the country to progressively eliminate closing hours for women, from the senior to the freshman classes. As Taylor explained,

> Relaxing parental rules removed a windmill to fight. We could pay attention to the larger issue—sex discrimination. I believe in equality, and our sole function is to produce as many autonomous adults as we

can. Many deans of women typically tried to keep woman students in their place. I tried to tell them their place is wherever they choose (Moody, 1973).

Taylor admitted that she was "slower on the uptake" with racial issues than she was with the sexism and gender issues she dealt with throughout her life. But her advocacy and struggle for women's rights made her quickly see the injustice that African American students at KU faced in the mid-1960s when they staged a protest and took over the chancellor's office in 1965.

EARLY EXPERIENCES WITH DIVERSITY

Until my college years, I had never even met a minority person on my level. I had met some people who were working people, and people in the South where I was born, but none who were in my classes. This was also true when I went to Montana. There were no Black students. There were some American Indian students, but there were no Black students in the college at all. I came here from Miami [Ohio] where Black students were certainly a very small minority. But when I came to Kansas in 1956, the very first thing I noticed in town was the sign saying, "We reserve the right to refuse service to anyone."

I've remembered it particularly because it was such a surprise to me, as Kansas had the reputation of being quite the opposite, of being very much involved in the Civil War on the North side. So I was surprised to find out how much race discrimination there was here. I discovered that the sign was more than just pro forma. It really expressed the way things were.

During my last two years in college, although I came in so ignorant of racial concerns, I joined a group that really was trying to work on racial issues. We had a number of different programs where we would have both Black and White students talk. I was on several of those panels. On one of the panels was a football player, a very famous football player. It would have been sometime between '35 and '37. He said that the fellows on the football team tried to include him in the camaraderie, and invited him to parties and so forth. He said, "I don't go. I don't go because it's not available to anybody else. It is available to me because I play football, and that doesn't seem right." We also had a program with Central College which was all Black. The thing that I remember about the instructions before we went to the program was that we could eat with them, we could talk with them, but we could not dance with them. That was the one requirement, no interracial dancing.

I remember at Ohio State there was a Black woman in the law school, the only Black woman there. I was on a panel with her, and after the program, she came and asked me if I would go to a movie with her. This was not possible without being arrested in those days. I did a lot of soul-searching about the situation, and I decided against it. I've always felt guilty about this. I decided against it because I just could not, in the midst of the Depression, afford to be arrested for anything, and have that on my record. But I certainly understood her point of view. Here she was, a law student, an excellent citizen, and she couldn't even sit on the main floor of the theatres. This stands out in my mind for a number of reasons. One of them was that it showed how little progress had been made until fairly recent times — getting people to understand what a dreadful thing discrimination is.

When asked where she got her sense of justice regarding discrimination, Taylor replied that it came from her mother. She then related a story about how her mother stood up for a young Black woman in their hometown who should have been the high school valedictorian but was denied the honor because of her race. No valedictorian was announced that year. "I felt I came from a long line of women who didn't put up with nonsense from other people."

And when asked how she developed her ideas about the civil rights movement she responded:

Well, I don't know how much I thought it through. I just was being myself — that's just the way I felt about things, and I operated on that basis. I don't know that I ever sat down and said, "Now look, this is right and this is wrong." I think it's just kind of an unconscious thing. You either think something is right or it's wrong. But I think, mainly, I never liked to see people hurt. I couldn't understand any reason why people should be hurt because of something over which they had absolutely no control.

HOUSING ISSUES AT THE UNIVERSITY OF KANSAS

I found out after I got to KU that Black and White students were never placed in rooms together, even if they didn't ask for a particular roommate. In 1962, we had a test case of two women students who asked to room together. Under our system, seniors got the first choice of rooms anywhere on the campus, and there was a numbering system. Number one took whatever room she wanted and so forth on down the line. It was fair enough. Two students came in together, a Black student and a White student, and they asked to room together, and I said, "Fine." And the chancellor found out about it, and said, "No, it's not fine." I'm making him sound terrible, but he really was a wonderful person. I don't mean to demean him in any way, but I don't think he was quite as advanced on the racial issues as some were. You can imagine the situation we were put in to have to tell two women who asked to room together, and had a number that permitted them to choose a room together, that they couldn't do it.

This housing issue occurred shortly before what I consider the start of the civil rights movement on this campus. All over town, we had problems with Black students getting a place to live, and people saying that there weren't any rooms when there really were. There were a lot of test cases, where White students would go immediately afterwards and be offered a room. That shows that there were White students, even in the very early days, who were very much interested in correcting some of integration patterns. Our office also handled employment for students. One woman called in saying she needed someone who could type, and she said, "And I want someone who's White." So, the staff member who took this phone call told me, and I said, "Well, you just call her back and tell her that's not the way we operate, and that if she has requirements of that kind she's on her own. We're not going to help in any way." We never heard anything more from her, so I suppose she got someone whom she wanted.

I remember a graduation party for a fellow who just got his Ph.D. He had a little party and the next day his landlady asked him to leave. He said, "Mrs. Smith, what did I do that caused you to ask me to leave?" And she said, "Well, I just want you to leave." And he said, "Is it because one of the people that were here last night was Black?" And she said, "No." And he said, "Well, was it because one of them had a beard?" And she said, "Well, I don't like beards." And he said to her, "Mrs. Smith, you know Jesus had a beard." And she said, "Not my Jesus." I don't think she liked any part of it. She wasn't going to admit the one about the Black student; it was more appropriate to say you did or didn't like beards than it was to say you did or didn't like Blacks.

CAMPUS CIVIL RIGHTS ORGANIZATIONS

The first thing that I would consider to be a genuine movement, a civil rights movement, was in 1965, and it was right after the free speech movement in California, which I think may have interested some people in doing something about campus problems. The Black students had an organization of Black and White students. The White students had been the officers of this organization; every officer was White. And so the Black students decided they were going to run the organization themselves. I'll tell you the story as it was told to me by a Black student. He said, "We threw them all out last night. We threw them all out," referring to removing White students from leadership roles in the organization. And the reason they threw them out was, as they said, "All White students have to do is to shave and take a bath, and they're back; they're one of them. Now there's nothing we can do like that, where we would be accepted."

They didn't throw the White students out of the organization, just out of the leadership of the organization. What they said to them, specifically, was, "You can do us a lot more good by taking a bath and shaving and going back to your own people and helping them to understand what it is that they're doing." I thought that was very smart.

I was on a program a few years ago, on a "talk back" following the production of "Hair." There was a woman whom I had never seen before. I remember she was wearing a great big hat. And she said, concerning the same issues that I'm talking about, "Oh, no, they did-n't throw them out. It was a White suggestion that they leave and the Blacks take over." At any rate, that's how she viewed it. And, so, I don't know whose suggestion it was. All I know is that one of the Black leaders in the group told me, personally, that they asked the White officers to leave, and said exactly what I told you, how simple it was for Whites to become a part of their own group, an how much good they could do by helping there. The Black students decided that, as long as their White colleagues were viewed as part of the hippie crowd, they weren't influencing anybody. There were some White students who took up the Black student cause, but there were some White students that took up any cause that came along. So I'm not sure this cause permeated the campus in any significant way.

KU STUDENTS MAKE DEMANDS

In the spring of 1965, tensions at KU increased. Impatient with Chancellor Wescoe's response to their earlier calls for change, the Civil Rights Council, a student group, planned a sit-in at his office. The next day, 150 students, mostly African Americans and some Whites, crowded the Chancellor's office and waiting room. The students demanded an end to exclusive clauses in fraternity and sorority charters, an end to segregated student teacher placements, that discriminatory advertisements not be accepted by the student newspaper, that the housing office not list segregated housing, that a committee of faculty, students and administrators be formed to hear grievances, and that the student council and the chancellor sign a resolution supporting the Civil Rights Council's demands. Following arrests, jailing and release from jail, students demonstrated by marching to the Chancellor's residence (Griffin, 1974; Monhollon, 2002).

Emily Taylor described the chancellor's response:

> Chancellor Wescoe appointed me to chair a committee, which he called a "Committee to Deal with These People." They had eight leaders in the group, seven Black students and one White faculty woman who were from KU. I think they had seven demands that they were making. The chancellor appointed a group of people to get together to form a negotiating committee, but the chancellor didn't want to call it a negotiating committee. He made a big point of it, and he did not want to go rapidly. He wanted us to take our time. It went a lot more rapidly than he wanted. What I remember about the situations the Black students wanted corrected is that every one of them turned out to be true, even though they were all denied by those who were responsible. The chancellor said he had checked their demands out and that none of their accusations were true. As it turned out, he was obviously lied to, lied to by a lot of people.

> The first demand was that they stop marking the race of student teachers who applied to work in the Shawnee Mission [suburban area of Kansas City on Kansas side] schools. Shawnee Mission didn't want to hire Blacks. The school of education denied that it did this. Then a faculty member, who had been here before and had left, wrote back and told us what the key was for the secret marking. Sure enough, it was perfectly plain once it was seen. It was a private arrangement. And even more disgraceful is the fact that the dean of the school denied it to the chancellor, and certainly to us. Applications were coded so that no Black student ever ended up there where they were

not wanted. It was obvious that something was going on. The school claimed that it just was happenstance, but it wasn't.

The negotiating committee appointed a committee of three to write a statement of affirmation of policy. That was actually the term that they used. The chancellor asked that we change that to "reaffirmation." So we agreed, although obviously it was not a reaffirmation because it hadn't yet been made. And that was when the university made the statement that there would be no discrimination on the basis of race, national origin, or ethnicity in our affairs. I wanted to add sex. And the other two committee members said, "If you'll just go along with us now, we'll help you get that put in, but this is the Blacks' thing, and so we shouldn't interfere with it." I stupidly fell for that. And I've always regretted it and resented it, because it took eight years from then to get the inclusion of sex in the statement that appeared in all KU publications. I think the reaffirmation of policy was a good statement; it just wasn't good enough because it left out gender. But I did try to get it in.

One of the demands was the creation of the Human Relations Council, and this was done. I think the Black students actually got all their demands. I'm not sure. I remember one of them dealt with off-campus housing. The university agreed not to approve any house that discriminated. But of course, we were already trying not to do that. Whenever we knew it, we told the landlady that she couldn't discriminate and be on our list. Now, there was nothing to prevent her choosing renters some other way, and I suspect there was a lot of that.

DIVERSIFYING THE CHEERLEADING SQUAD

Taylor's recounting of the challenges of diversifying KU's cheerleading and pom-pom squad is an excellent example of the lack of a level playing field and "affirmative action" for special groups in the know.

The one which really created the most difficulty, I think, was that the students wanted Black cheerleaders, and pom-pom girls. The funny and sad part of it was that some of us, including me, had been on the judging committees to choose these people through the years, and we had sat there, being taken in by all this, without any knowledge that what we were doing was making sure that there weren't any Blacks in these groups. We were given a form which was about a page long—it seemed like a hundred items on it. Applicants came in by groups of four, and did their thing, and then they left, and we marked how good they were. Then another group of four would come in. Well, the people who were good were so obvious, that they always ended up as the cheerleaders and the pom-pom girls.

The advisor to this group was incensed by the Black students' demands, and he made sure that all the pom-pom girls and cheerleaders were incensed too. They kept saying, "But you were on the committee that made the choices," and I really didn't know at that time how to answer. I didn't understand what had happened. Then one night at an orientation dinner, I was sitting with a group of high school seniors who had come from Shawnee Mission, and they were telling me what they were going to do when they got here. And one of them said, "I'm going to be a cheerleader." And so I said, "You know, that's a competitive thing; you have to compete for those jobs." And she said, "Oh, that's not the way it's done. The cheerleaders choose the people that they want, and then they teach them the routines, and so of course, when we go before the committee, we're better than the others." So I learned at an orientation dinner, from a high school senior, how cheerleaders were chosen and how we'd been taken in through all those years. I really felt bad that I hadn't been able to catch on sooner. And I wasn't the only one. Don Alderson (dean of men) was just as opposed as I was to any kind of discrimination; he was there every night, and so were a number of faculty members. And I don't think any of us really understood. So, one of the things that those demanding Black cheerleaders kept saying was, "If we're going to have Black athletes, we're going to have Black legs flying." That was it.

We had some outstanding Black women who were very much a part of campus affairs. One woman I remember was in a sophomore honorary society, now called Lambda Sigma. She had taken dance lessons, and she was the one we turned to when we wanted to get Blacks started as cheerleaders. We got a former cheerleader who was on our side to teach her all the routines, and then she could compete with the best. She didn't have to be chosen, she competed with the best and she was the best. We would have taken even more if we'd had any other logical candidates, but we didn't know anyone that was as good as she was. She was already prepared as a dancer.

There were some very superior Black women students, and one of my reasons for being interested in the problems of Blacks was that half of the Blacks were women. We used the same approach in the work that we did for the office of women in higher education to prepare women for high-level, administrative positions.

The Importance of a Name

As civil rights efforts changed to Black empowerment, Taylor and other student affairs administrators dealt with what students wanted to be called.

> There was a young Black man who really became my confidant. He came to my house many times. He was sort of a leader of the group. I asked him, "What do you want to be called?" And he said, "If you say Caucasian, then you should say Negro. If you say White, you should say Black." That made sense to me. But very few people said "Caucasian." It was always "White" and "Negro," but that turned out to be not the way the majority of Black students wanted. At that time, they were becoming very militant, and they liked the word, "Black." They had some people who were leaders of the group who wore what they believed to be native African clothing. One of them in particular stands out in my mind, and he made no bones about it that he did not want to be called a Negro under any circumstances.

> At the same time, in 1965, I went to a meeting of NASPA. The women deans met at the same time, but most of our program was together, and I was in charge of the program here. I had to prepare this program concerning the very issues we're talking about now. So I wrote the word "Negro" on the blackboard. I had thought about it for quite awhile, but nobody was saying "Black," and the term "African American" hadn't even come into the language. I put "Negro" and a man from Wichita who had been asked to speak, who had been hired to run Wichita State University's minorities program (they were way ahead of us), came in and the first thing he did was take the chalk and slash through that word Negro and put "Black" in large letters.

> When KU finally hired somebody to establish a program, the person we hired wanted the office called "minority affairs." It was a new term to many of us.

Fraternities and Sororities

> Only one of the Black sororities had a house, and I went there frequently the same as I did to everybody else's house. They asked me to give their initiation speech once. I really worked on that speech, more than I had on any other. This is long ago, and I would never make the

same speech now. But I remember telling them that they had to make up their minds about what was most important to them, and if they had some particular goal in mind, then what they needed to do was to look at the people who were successful in that particular field and follow them, just do what they did. And I think that some of the things that I was suggesting were not things that they were real happy to be doing. They didn't say anything. They were very polite, but really I was basically saying that if you want to succeed, you're going to have to do things the way White people do, the way the majority does. And I suppose that, to some extent, that's still true. I knew that any old English teacher could tell you that you can correct the same error a thousand times in the course of 12 years, and it may not have any effect on that people's language. What changes language is when they decide they want to be like somebody they admire. Then they start emulating them, and that's how they get from "ain't got no" to "ain't got any" to "don't have any." And I think it's the only way

HIRING OF BLACK FACULTY

By the end of the 1960s, the university started to try to hire Black faculty. By that time, everybody was trying to find qualified Black faculty. They used Black women as a kind of a lure, claiming they got double credit for hiring both a woman and a Black. I remember the first Black woman who was hired as a professor in sociology. She was very superior. One of the members of the sociology department, whom I knew very well, said to me, "You know, it's great to be doing the 'right' thing, but it's a terrible toll on a department." I asked, "What do you mean?" He said,

> Well, it's just looked down on; if you take a Black person, and particularly a Black woman, then that means you couldn't attract any of the really good sociologists, and so you lower the value of the department by having them.

That was somewhere in the late 1960s that he told me that. This woman didn't stay very long.

We didn't have very many women faculty, Black or White. One woman graduate student told me that she had a seven-year-old daughter and that she had been assigned to teach a class at 7:30 in the morning and at 4:30 in the afternoon, so that she could not get the child ready for school, get her to school, and she couldn't pick her up. And that when she talked to the chair of the department about it, he said, "Well, none of the men want to teach in those hours."

I was doing a little study on graduate women and the problems that they were having. I wrote to all of them saying, "I'd like to talk to you, and if you'd like to talk with me, we can get together." I think I didn't use the word "appointment," because I didn't want to make it sound like a command performance. Many of them came. We saw dozens of them, and they just had one story after the other to tell. One of the interesting things about the stories is that the woman with the child and the 7:30 and the 4:30 classes, said that the department chair called her in and asked her what this meeting was going to be about with me, and what she intended to tell me. He was concerned enough about our meeting to make an issue of it. Well, I didn't do anything through the department—I probably should have. What I did do was tell her what she ought to do. She also told me that one time the chair called them together and said the department secretary was ill, and, "You men had better get your test questions in early, because we're going to have to send it to the typing pool," and one of the women said, "Well, what do you mean by you men?" And he said, "Well, you women can type your own."

ROLE OF STUDENT AFFAIRS ADMINISTRATORS

Taylor was asked if she thought that student affairs administrators were really on the front line with key areas—such as housing and employment—and that classroom issues were separate. Deans had to deal with things early on, and faculty and others could ignore them for a while.

We had people who had a very clear demarcation as to whose job various things were. I remember a man in the history department came over one day, with a woman student in tow. He had a very loud voice, and he was kind of shouting at the top of his voice saying, "She's got a problem, and it's not my job. My job is to teach history. It's your job to solve problems." We could hardly wait to get her out of his clutches long enough to talk with her.

She confirmed that student affairs administrators are the one who have to solve the problems.

I think there's some lack of knowledge, really, about what those who are responsible for out-of-class life really do, among the faculty. And I think that the idea that all faculty members can understand immediately or deal with any problem in these days, as complex as it's gotten with financial aid and all these various areas, doesn't make sense.

ISSUES WITH PROFESSIONAL CONFERENCES

Taylor was asked how she thought KU or other universities could have handled the issues related to the civil rights movement better.

> I don't know just exactly where other people were. I know that I was advisor for the Intercollegiate Association of Women Students (IAWS), so I did know people from many, many different colleges. One time in the mid 1960s somebody asked us to come to the University of Tennessee. They bid for the next convention, but they also made clear that they could not house any Black students in the same places they housed the White students. And so we refused to go. Our students thought that was an appalling idea, that they would even suggest such a thing, that they couldn't house them together. We had that problem in everything, even in the professional organizations. We still had professional organizations that went to these places. They wouldn't even put Blacks and Whites in the same residence halls or hotels. Sometimes, what they picked out for Black students wasn't really too satisfactory. We really did put up with a lot. When you look back on it, it doesn't really seem possible, that people were so stupid, or so prejudiced. What would be the point of it? If something bad happened to you as a result of what somebody did to you, I can understand your hesitance to take them into your bosom. But for somebody who has never done you any harm whatsoever, and seems like a perfectly decent kind of person, such behavior is truly pointless.

LESSONS LEARNED

As she looked back on this era, Taylor reflected on the lessons student affairs administrators can learn from dealing with the issues of racism and sexism.

> I think we have to continue working along the same lines. The goal remains the same, I'm sure. It's to eliminate all forms of discrimination against anyone. I think that people have to be encouraged to fulfill their potential and, if they do, then they should have the same opportunity to make it that anybody else does. But I don't know exactly where we learn anything. I think the whole thing just moves in a disorderly fashion, but ultimately gets to an appropriate destination.

Nobody talked about Jackson State as they did about Kent State. And this really annoyed the Black students. It annoyed me, too, because there were more Black students killed there than there were at Kent, but at Kent the victims were White and at Jackson State they were Black. At Jackson State, some of those students were shot in their own residence halls, through the windows. I often think of these matters in terms of what would I do if I were Black?

EPILOGUE

The women's resource and career planning center Taylor established at KU was renamed the Emily Taylor Women's Resource Center in 1974, her final year as dean of women at KU. In 1975 she was named the director of the office of women in higher education of the American Council on Education (ACE). One of her major projects there was the development of the National Identification Program, which identified and supported women who were qualified to be college presidents. She served as director for seven years, became senior associate for the ACE, and then returned to Lawrence, Kansas, in 1986 where she retired. Taylor has remained active in local, state, and national initiatives. She served for eight years on the Kansas Board of Healing Arts. She is the current chair of the Lawrence Caring Community Council, the local unit of the LIFE Project (Living Initiatives for End of Life Care). She serves on the Senior Council for the Lawrence Chamber of Commerce and received the chamber's Citizen of the Year Award. She was recently named as the first inductee of Urbana University's Hall of Fame. She is the recipient of numerous other professional awards, including: the NAWE Esther Lloyd Jones Distinguished Service Award; ACPA Diamond Honoree Award; NASPA Outstanding Contribution to Higher Education Award; and the NASPA Foundation Pillar of the Profession Award.

M. LEE UPCRAFT
Michigan State University (1963-1969)
Pennsylvania State University (1969-1974)

Lee Upcraft's experience as a student affairs practitioner in the civil rights era went on to shape his career.

> My involvement had an enormous impact on me personally, and the way I think about students and think about civil rights. I came into this profession at the same time the whole civil fights movement was beginning. I had my first student affairs job in 1963 and lived through the next 10 or 12 years while all this was going on. I was a very young professional who was probably more sympathetic to the student point of view than perhaps I should have been.

For Upcraft, the years 1963 to 1974 were all about student and civil rights. His experience was shaped first by his career at Michigan State University (1963-1969) and later by his work at Pennsylvania State University.

> From 1969 to1974 at Penn State, every day of my life was spent in some way dealing with student activism. In retrospect, that time looks wonderful, but while I was going through it was a mixed blessing of excitement and challenges and also just fatigue, as it just kept going on and on and on.

This chapter is Upcraft's recollection of how things evolved and went "on and on and on." An important part of his story is not only what transpired in the civil rights years but also how his involvement went on to shape his career.

STUDENT RIGHTS AND CIVIL RIGHTS

While the civil rights movement was distinct in many ways from other campus movements, there were also commonalities. Upcraft's interview focused on civil rights, but students were beginning to be empowered at this time that cut across all areas.

> There was this sort of student rights movement where students were trying to get rid of *in loco parentis* and establish that one didn't have to leave one's constitutional rights at the door when they went to college. Then there was the antiwar activism, and then civil rights—the rights of various groups, mainly focused on race/ethnicity. The issues kind of all blended together. For example, our Black students were at the forefront of the antiwar movement because it was Blacks who were dying in the war more than anybody else. This was also the era where students first discovered drugs and marched in demonstrations and gave administrators a hard time. Collectively, these movements shaped how I thought about students, my career, and how institutions reacted to students.

> Students exercised their rights in many ways. The first demonstration I was ever involved in at Penn State was when Black students took over the vice president for student affairs' office and started building a wall with a bunch of bricks at the doorstep to the office. The wall was symbolic of the barrier that the institution was putting up. Students had rights and I thought they had the right to see them upheld.

INSTITUTIONAL CONTEXT

When asked to describe the racial/ethnic environment at Michigan State and Penn State, Upcraft explained:

> At both institutions there weren't many African American students. So, those that were there began to raise questions about how committed the institution was, not only to getting more Black students to come to both Michigan State and Penn State, but also in helping them succeed once they got there. But having said all that, it is difficult for a place like Penn State to recruit African Americans. In the middle of Pennsylvania, there are not a substantial number of middle class African American families. There aren't community cultural opportunities available for Black students who decide to come here. I don't know what it's like to be an African American parent, but my guess is I wouldn't want my kid to go to Penn State or any other large research university that only had three percent African American students. All of this made the climate always tense. At Penn State as director of student activities, I had a lot of African American students hanging out in my office. They just were not satisfied with the extent

to which the institution was being responsive to their needs as African American students.

Given the national dimension of the civil rights movement and student connections to the NAACP, some African American students would participate in civil rights work in the summer and then bring the energy back to the campus. As a middle man, I would help direct student energies from the national arena to the campus one. What this led to for some students was fighting at the national level and then coming back to Penn State to see things they didn't see before regarding discrimination, prejudice, and racism.

MAN IN THE MIDDLE

In this era, friction often emerged between what students thought was right and what the institution thought was right. Upcraft's recollection was particularly poignant when he talked about students doing the right thing. With regard to the wall mentioned above, Upcraft remembered this was a "high risk" situation for students and he was impressed with their commitment.

They knew they were doing the right thing, but they were scared to death of what the institution might do to them or what might happen to them, personally. My position as a young professional placed me in an empathy position with students, although I didn't always agree with their tactics. Many times, the students were fearful of their lives. I recall one African American student who was in the midst of being arrested for blockading a building, and he said to me, "I know I'm doing the right thing, but my mother's going to kill me." One of the defining moments at Penn State was when we arrested a bunch of Black students. It was in the era when hair meant something, and all the African American students had huge Afros. They were arrested, taken to Rockview Prison, and had their heads shaved. When they came back on campus after being bailed out of prison, I really wasn't sure what was going to happen. I had very strong, positive feelings about these students and what they were going through, even though there were times when I thought the way they did things was making things worse.

I often felt like I was in the middle of the students and the other administrators on most issues. I would attend meetings with Black students when they discussed their demands, and I would go to administrative meetings where I was the person who was most relied upon to tell the administration what the students were all about. And, so I served a mediating role between the administration and the students. I felt like somebody caught in the middle, like nobody was happy with me. But it was at a time when it was really very difficult for a very conservative administration and a very committed group of Black students to talk to each other. You would put them in a room, and either nothing would happen or everything happened. I spent the better part of two or three years just being in the middle, trying to help each side understand what the other was saying, and trying to prevent either side from doing something really dumb.

In the role of "middle man," Upcraft did a lot of work behind the scenes to establish credibility with both administrators and students.

I recall at one of the arrests in Old Main that included Black students; they were charged in our university discipline system. Since I witnessed a whole bunch of stuff, the discipline system wanted me to come and testify to what happened. I had a very, very savvy boss and he argued that, if I were to do that, I would totally destroy my credibility as a mediator ,and he excused me from being involved in the judiciary process so I could stay in communication with the students. The primary thing the institution expected of me was to stay involved in this stuff. The only thing that saved me was that nothing ever happened on the weekends! Still, I think my role as a mediator kept things from getting worse.

THE IMPACT OF CIVIL RIGHTS ON POLICY AND THE ORGANIZATION

I am kind of cynical about the progress that has been made in the whole civil rights area, particularly at Penn State. The juxtaposition of a recent campus incident over race and rights and that of the incidents that took place early on in my career leaves me wondering what's really changed. In the spring of 2002, our Black students took over the union building and set up a list of demands, demands that were essentially the same as when the Black students took over the vice president's office in 1968. There are still not enough Black students. There's still a lot evidence of discrimination and racism. It's not as safe an environment for Blacks as it is for Whites. There's still a very low representation of African Americans on the faculty. There is a better track record in student affairs and academic support, and, of course, an exemplary record in intercollegiate athletics.

One area of progress for African American students is in athletics. The issue of race in sports struck a chord for Upcraft. Penn State, like many campuses around the country, has enjoyed relative success in the area of diversity on its sports team. Upcraft recalled a recent event:

> I remember getting myself in a lot of trouble. I was at yet another meeting where the provost for the university was talking. He said,
>
> > We have to do something to increase Black enrollment and to maintain the retention of Blacks, and this time we're really serious...We're going to do whatever it takes to overcome the bad image that Penn State has for African American students.
>
> I raised my hand and said, "I don't think there's a problem. The way to solve this is to do for all students what we do for athletes, since the African American graduate rate among athletes is higher than White students." Needless to say, there wasn't a great deal of enthusiasm for my idea. The provost said, "Oh, my god, we could never afford that." Such a response makes a cynical person like me even more cynical. We know what to do; we just lack the will to do it.

Upcraft feels defeated by his over 30-year fight to help African American students.

> The university is run by a corporate structure that is, for the most part, conservative, male, and privileged, and is not always sympathetic to race-related policy issues. Anything that smacks of threatening the basic power structure of the university is not going to be dealt with, and I got some insight into that. It is not only those who are directly dealing with problems of inequity (e.g., director of the women's center, vice president for multicultural affairs) that are thinking about civil rights. In the upper levels of the administration, day to day, absence of crisis, there's not much conversation or thought from them about how to reduce racism or create a climate where all students can succeed. We can get more Black students here and graduated if we did what we did for the student athletes. We can provide academic support services to help them succeed. It is a matter of the will, not the way. The Penn State way is not to do any more than necessary to solve a particular crisis.

> The things that do make a difference at places like Penn State are leadership—some presidents have made a real difference—and also the attitude of White students. About a dozen years ago, I conducted some focus groups of White students and their attitudes toward race relations, and it was very discouraging. They see affirmative action as special treatment. They believe that African Americans get into Penn

State with lower credentials than White students. They believe that African Americans get all the aid. There's just a litany of "this isn't a level playing field and race ought not to be considered in admissions, grades, or anything else." White students resent the fact that they believe that African American students are getting special treatment. I've always said the solution to the race problem on campus is more a function of White students than of Black students.

A few years later, I was involved in a study of African American women. We followed a cohort of 20 women from the time they enrolled until the time most of them graduated, and the stories they tell are just amazing…you wonder how they ever made it through because of the racism they perceived they were subjected to. The students talked about the support they received from their church, through fraternities and sororities, and through involvement with each other, but they had little good to say about all the "special programs" that Penn State has to enhance African American student success. These programs were irrelevant to them. All in all, we may have a slightly better climate today, but the fundamental system has not changed. It has opened its doors a little bit, but it has not changed.

Upcraft's first-hand experience as the mediator between students and the administration during the civil rights era made him an intimate student of higher education organizations, their policies, and their administrations. Upcraft learned a lot sitting in the meetings where administrators were talking about students.

I was in actual conversations where the gist of the discussions was at the administrative level with administrators saying, "What do we need to do to get these students off our backs? What do we need to do to work our way out of this particular crisis?" or implicitly, "What's the least that we can do that would work our way out of this crisis?" There was no real discussion of "how can we deal with the issue of racism on this campus in a way that prevents this from happening again?" It was crisis management mode; it was a political mode. "If we do this, then this will score us points with these people and not with these people."

An interesting twist that Upcraft talked about was the larger arena of civil rights in the state of Pennsylvania where:

The Black legislative caucus was a force to be reckoned with. Much of what the administration did to address students concerns on campus in the 1960s and 1970s was to satisfy the Black caucus.

Administrators asked, "What's the least we can do to satisfy their interest in Penn State and their concerns?"

More often than not, Upcraft's sympathies resided with the Black students and their constituents rather than the administration.

I felt the students were right and the administration was wrong, and I said so. It's tough for administrators in general, who are sympathetic to the civil rights concerns of students, but also even more difficult for people of color to function within that system. The students, with their idealism, are likely to say, "If you had any core values, you wouldn't even work for these racist bastards." And a typical response of an administrator who cares about creating change might be, "This is a system that you've got to deal with, and you better be thankful that we're here, advocating for you and trying to do the best we can to make things better here." I believe that, and I think that's an important function. But the students, of course, don't buy it. African American administrators work tirelessly to advocate for students, but they are ultimately part of the system, and that dual role is often difficult for students to understand.

IMPACT OF THE STUDENT AFFAIRS PROFESSION

The civil rights movement and the work that emerged out of it affected the larger student affairs profession in major ways. First, the crisis management aspect of the daily lives of student affairs practitioners in the civil rights era became a focal point of national meetings. Administrators would come to national meetings of groups like NASPA to get ideas on how to handle situations that were new to campuses. Conversations at NASPA during this time period revolved around "How do we manage this situation? There's all this stuff going on and student affairs is caught in the middle, and how do we do this?" There were discussions at conferences were vice president after vice president was saying, "Here's what happened at my institution. All hell broke lose and here's how I handled it." So NASPA, in particular, became an opportunity for us to talk to each other about how to cope with these things. If somebody went though something we anticipated but we hadn't yet experienced, we wanted to know about that. What do you do when students take over your office or lock you in your office? Or, what do you do when the police come on campus? Or what should be done to discipline students who, out of conscience, take a stand and get arrested but who are really not criminals? These weren't the "normal acting-outers" with whom the discipline system typically dealt. All of sudden, the discipline system was flooded with people of conscience, instead of your garden variety drinkers and academic dishonesty folks. What we found was that our old systems of discipline weren't capable of dealing with these new problems.

NASPA and other national organizations of student affairs practitioners became opportunities to learn what to do with new kinds or problems. If you were to go back and look, you would find that the discipline systems got revamped quicker and faster during that time period than another other, because we found that our old systems just weren't capable of dealing with new problems. The dialogue on the national level was, "How do we manage this and what can we do to find out more about students and their environments?"

This leads to another impact that Upcraft sees the civil rights movement had on the field of student affairs: student development research.

Activism and the student rights movement really jump-started the research on college students. When I entered the profession in 1963, college students and college environments were not subjects of research. I remember the excitement of reading Nevitt Sanford's *American College* because it was the first thing that was ever written about students and environment. Initially, a lot of the research on students had to do with why they were acting up. Here are these nice, middle- class students that come from good families who are throwing bricks through windows. The civil rights time period was when student development came into use as a phrase.

Finally, Upcraft sees that another major impact of the civil rights movement was to legitimize the field of student affairs.

It was the student affairs practitioners who were on the front lines of the civil rights movement with students. I felt like there were days that, if it weren't for student affairs, the whole place would have blown up. My colleagues and I, as a student affairs collective, were holding the center together and keeping it from flying apart. There's a lot of talk about the "poor me, student affairs doesn't get any respect" kind of stuff which I've never felt, I never bought it. I think in a lot of ways our involvement in these kinds of things legitimize the very important role in helping institutions better understand students and helping students better understand institutions. It is in this way that student affairs as a division is essentially the middleman in helping institutions, as a whole, interface with their students. I came out of the civil rights movement feeling like "Hey, I'm really part of the profession that's even more important that I thought it was."

IMPACT ON UPCRAFT'S CAREER

Perhaps the greatest impact of Upcraft's professional involvement during the civil rights movement was on Upcraft as a person and a professional. Upcraft has established himself nationally, as an expert on many issues related to student development. He has authored and edited over 100 publications, including 10 books. His work is focused on students and student affairs, and his research is always purposeful to incorporate issues of race. Upcraft's start on campus at a time of racial upheaval has shaped how he has answered research questions, taught classes, and responded to administrative dilemmas.

As was suggested earlier, Upcraft's involvement made him somewhat cynical about change in higher education, and about higher education as an organization that confronts and deals with the difficult dialogues of racism. This made Upcraft more realistic about organizational change.

> There are limits to what a system can do to change, to be more responsive to people's rights. I also learned what buttons to push to facilitate and navigate change. I learned a lot about how to deal with the system, what the "hot buttons" were to the extent that it was going to change, how they were going to do it. Penn State, for example, is very sensitive to public relations, so I would confidently play the public relations card. "If you don't want to do this, it's going to look really bad for the university and you don't want that."

Another hot button that Upcraft found that didn't work as well was appealing to the conscience of the organization.

> I tried to convince the powers-that-be that institutions do the right thing because it's simply the right thing. That got me nowhere. I had to be more politically astute; I had to work behind the scenes; I had to figure out who the people were that were more likely to be agreeable to what I was arguing and whose values are more consistent with mine. But I discovered that marching into a meeting and confronting the president, provost, or dean didn't work. You work behind the scenes; you work on individual people who have some power and influence. I became a more politically savvy administrator in that regard.

Part of being a politically savvy administrator meant that Upcraft gained credibility with various groups on campus.

I had a fairly decent reputation as an administrator who would get things done. The other administrators didn't really like my liberal views, but they tolerated them because they relied on me to communicate with students. I think, prior to my involvement, civil rights were for me sort of an abstract thing out there that, as a knee-jerk liberal, I was committed to, you know, equality and all that kind of stuff. But what affected me profoundly was when I spent time with African American students and other minorities who were affected by all of this. All of a sudden, an abstract idea became a very real thing and that had an enormous impact on me as a student affairs professional and on me as a person. I am fortunate that I had an opportunity to spend time with the victims of our society or with people who were personally affected by the racism in our country and the racism in our institution. I found myself far more in sympathy with the students and what they were demanding than I did with a conservative administration whose primary goals seemed to be the preservation of its own self. My involvement in civil rights put a human face on my values and made my antennas especially sensitive to any group that was getting the shaft, either by society or the university.

EPILOGUE

In concluding the interview, Upcraft noted that his cynicism about actual change should not be viewed as negativity about the profession.

I feel very fortunate to have cut my teeth in this profession, in the midst of all this stuff. It was challenging and exciting. I got to know students in ways that I didn't before, but mostly I was tired. I just longed for the day I didn't have to deal with all these crises, when I could actually sit down and think about what I was doing. It was a time when you just had to make decisions instinctively and hope for the best. Still, it was very exciting, and I am glad to have been a part of it.

Upcraft continued in student affairs administration at Penn State until his retirement in 1994. His positions in higher education included assistant vice president for counseling and health services, director of residence life programs, director of the student assistance center, dean of students, and director of student activities. When he retired, he was the assistant vice president for student affairs. He now holds emeritus titles in student affairs and the college of education. In his retirement, Upcraft continued to advise doctoral students, consult around the country, and write articles and books. Upcraft has written on such topics as residence halls, student retention, assessment in student affairs, student demographics, and the first-year experience. His work has been noted nationally by several professional organizations, including recognition as a senior scholar diplomat of the American College Personnel Association. He is currently finishing one more book, *Challenging and Supporting the First Year Student: A Handbook for Improving the First Year of College,* which should be out in the spring. Since his "second" retirement in 2001, Upcraft writes that he has "contented myself with spending time with my grandchildren, messing around in my wood shop, vacationing at our cottage in Maine, traveling around the country and Europe, and doing other 'stuff.'"

REFLECTING BACK:
THEMES FROM THE CASES

T he experiences of the individual student affairs professionals whose
stories are told in this book are unique to the individual, his or her college and its location. There are, however, common patterns or themes
that cut across the individual stories. In this chapter we attempt to identify
some of these patterns. First, we discuss the commonalities and differences
in context—the campuses and the types of civil rights issues on different
types of campuses. Next, we discuss the roles student affairs administrators
played in response to the contexts in which they found themselves. Then,
because student affairs administrators necessarily interacted with others, we
examine their relationships with several key constituent groups. Lastly, we
present their views about some of the lessons they learned.

CONTEXT

As we note in chapter one, student affairs administrators have a long history
of advocating for students' civil rights and for racial equality. However,
despite early warning signs (e.g., the free speech movement at Berkeley and
the failed integration attempt at the University of Alabama in the 1950s), few
could have predicted in advance how the struggle for civil rights for African
Americans would intersect with a newfound sense of freedom to speak one's
mind. Among other things, students were influenced by the demise of Joseph
McCarthy and his House Un-American Activities Committee, resurgence of
the women's movement, and resistance to an escalating war in Vietnam that
produced an indigenous student protest movement.

The intersection of these various movements led most of the student affairs
administrators featured in this book to agree with James Lyons who stated,
"The power of the civil rights movement on the American college campus is
more thoroughly appreciated and understood by also knowing the context of

those times. Those times were exciting, productive, troublesome, energizing, agonizing, socially powerful, and politically dramatic." Lyons listed the various events or movements that intersected with the civil rights movement: the psychedelic movement, Vietnam, Cambodia, the draft, the drop in voting age, the Rights and Responsibilities of Students document, the "pill", and curriculum reform.

The confluence of movements created challenges for administrators. As Rhatigan noted:

> Bear in mind, the different groups didn't wear signs. Advocates would come together on some issues, or act separately, then come back together again. You saw different people at different events. There was a lot of cross-fertilization, which created a very difficult problem for administrators.

Students have been protesting on U.S. campuses since the founding of Harvard (Johnston, 1998) but most authors of the period agree that the 1960s and early 1970s were different (e.g., Astin, Astin, Bayer, & Bisconti, 1997). Rather than protesting irrelevant curricula, although perhaps a part of the problem, or mimicking adult protest movements of the 1920s and 1930s, students of this era idealistically set out to change the country through student-initiated protest. Civil rights for African Americans were among the earliest and most volatile challenges students undertook. College students, both Black and White, began to protest with lunch counter sit-ins, freedom marches, and freedom rides, and risked life and limb doing so. In fact, many of the methods of civil disobedience used by students at Berkeley and other Northern colleges were learned through association with, if not direct participation in, voter registration drives and freedom marches in the South organized by the Student Nonviolent Coordinating Committee (Astin et al., 1997).

Following national trends, the nature of student activism on behalf of civil rights and racial equality differed between small, private colleges and large, public universities, by region, and by time period. In this section, we set the context by describing the nature of the issues regarding civil rights faced by the individuals in this book, and also the form that the issues and related protests took.

LARGE, PUBLIC, RESEARCH UNIVERSITIES

In the case of Southern, public universities, the first issue was simply access. As we note in chapter one, most Southern universities had not integrated by 1963, nine years after *Brown v. Board of Education of Topeka, Kansas.* Even when access was not prohibited, as at Midwestern universities (University of Kansas, Indiana University, Penn State, University of Iowa), African American students frequently encountered unofficially segregated environments both on and off campus. Although access and equal treatment were of concern to both Black and White students, when Black students first entered Southern, segregated universities they were few in number and were instructed to, as Charles Witten said, "Conduct themselves in a manner which will not lead to criticism by other students of their dress, manner, actions, and public statements." At the University of South Carolina (USC), Black students were told that the university would do everything it could to treat them fairly—as long as the Black students behaved. Eventually, USC began to get more and more Black students. Later, feeling that not enough had been done for them, Black student leaders routinely presented lists of grievances to administrators. The grievances at USC were similar to those at every other college in the country: more Black faculty, Black studies programs, more support services, etc. However, there was no indication by Witten that these grievances elevated to violent interactions at USC during his term as dean.

The situation at University of Alabama mirrored that at South Carolina. As with Witten, one of Blackburn's main concerns was insuring the safety of Jimmy Hood, the first African American male to register at the University of Alabama. Alabama as a state went to great lengths to prevent him, and other Black students, from enrolling. In addition, Blackburn worked with the community to find local services for Hood. Although Blackburn struggled with issues of climate for Alabama's small, Black, student population, he did not report large-scale protests or building takeovers during his tenure there as dean of men. Rather, he dealt with problems of a smaller though serious nature. For example, an incident occurred in the fall of 1964 when, during orientation, a group of first-year students lit a cross in front of the residence hall door of some African American students. When Blackburn learned that the graduate advisor in the hall had done nothing in response because he didn't want to "affect his rapport with the students," Blackburn found out who had done it, and forcefully told the students that such behavior would not be condoned at the University.

Florida State University, although quiet early in the period, went on to earn the nickname the "Berkeley of the South" (Rabby, 1999), exemplifying how the nature of protest changed over the decade. By 1968, African American students at Florida State had become more aggressive in their confrontations with the administration. Harris Shelton noted that once enrollment of Black students reached a critical mass at Florida State, they engaged in a number of quite violent protests over such issues as the curriculum, a Black student cultural center, Black power, representation of African Americans on the faculty, staff, and within the student body, and other campus climate concerns.

Although there were civil rights movements at other research universities at which the administrators in this book worked, they were typically less dramatic than those at Florida State, while being about the same issues. At the University of Iowa, Black students were allowed to live in the residence halls as early as 1956, and were described by Philip Hubbard as being relatively peaceful about issues of civil rights. Hubbard worked quietly within the system—identifying points where influence could be achieved. In contrast to the experience of others in this book, Hubbard took on Greek organizations insisting that restrictive clauses had to go. He was somewhat successful. Although recalling a walkout by Black athletes that gained national attention, he described civil rights activism as being purposeful but not destructive until the civil rights movement met the antiwar movement. At that point, students did attempt to close down the university.

Despite Kansas' reputation as a free state, Emily Taylor recalled a sit-in at the University of Kansas (KU) over civil rights as early as 1965. That sit-in resulted in arrests and a subsequent march on the Chancellor's residence. Among the demands made by the students were integration of fraternities and sororities; an end to discriminatory ads in the student newspaper; an end to segregated student teacher placements; an end to the university housing office's practice of listing segregated off-campus housing; establishment of a committee of faculty, students, and administrators to hear grievances; and support of these demands by the chancellor (Monhollon, 2002). Taylor also dealt with other issues such as a segregated cheerleading squad. Like many other universities, protests turned more violent when civil rights mixed with antiwar protests in the late 1960s and early 1970s.

David Ambler's experiences at the University of Kansas in the 1970s and 1980s reveal that issues facing African American students—and resulting demonstrations—did not end in the early 1970s; they just became more subtle. Resulting demonstrations were usually peaceful.

Even students at Oregon State in the late 1960s, who were described as being cooperative, protested. "Our students tended to do what they were supposed to do," noted Jo Anne Trow. "When they wanted to demonstrate, they registered all of their information and took care of doing what they should in order to abide by the policies." Nevertheless, students did demonstrate. In one 1969 incident, students participated in a walkout in protest over a coach's decision to prohibit a Black football player from playing because he refused to shave his moustache. As Trow said, "They walked off campus. It was a symbolic walkout. It was interesting because there were all kinds of students who participated."

According to Robert Shaffer, Indiana University (IU) did not have major riots over civil rights. Administrators there had taken a proactive stance toward civil rights at least since 1955. Residence hall staffs were integrated and efforts were made to integrate the Greek system. That's not to say that civil rights activists did not exist on the IU campus. However, located in what Shaffer described as a conservative community, which was much more likely to be resistant to integration than the campus, protests were much more muted than at some of the other campuses featured in this book.

Lee Upcraft described the situation for African American students at Penn State as tense. Penn State students would go off to work in national civil rights activities, and, upon return to campus, would notice discrimination and racism they had not seen before. The picture Upcraft paints of Penn State is one of a series of sit-ins and arrests of Black students and a situation of constant tension, rather than big dramatic confrontations. He commented, "I felt like somebody caught in the middle...But it was a time when it was really very difficult for a very conservative administration and a very committed group of Black students to talk to each other."

Howard University has had a long tradition of student protest; however, until the late 1960s, most of Howard's protest efforts had been directed toward bringing about change in Washington, D.C. Carl Anderson noted:

> Students at Howard protested segregated street cars and buses in Washington, D.C. back in the late 1920s and early 1930s. They also protested the segregated restaurant situation and the movie houses. In the early 1960s they were in the forefront of efforts to integrate what was then known as Glen Echo Amusement Park.

But by the late 1960s, students at Howard were also taking over the campus administration buildings. Some students brought charges of racism against professors, and students demanded Black studies programs. As Anderson said, "Meetings with students and protests occurred simultaneously. Sometimes we thought we had reached an understanding; however, that was not reflected in the next move that the students made."

PRIVATE LIBERAL ARTS COLLEGES

The issues—more students of color, more faculty of color, addition of ethnic studies programs to the curriculum, and general respect—were the same at smaller, private colleges, although protest activity tended not to be as confrontational. These colleges tended to have very small contingents of Black students, were located in rural areas, and were described as not being very comfortable places for Black students. For example, according to Judith Chambers at Pacific University, in 1969 a Japanese student led a demonstration demanding more support for minority students. Chambers stated,

> Out of that demonstration came what was called the Community Involvement Program. The program provided 200 tuition-free scholarships to minority students living in the Stockton community....An Asian student led the protest, but clearly in the beginning it was the Blacks who benefited the most.

At Denison, civil rights concerns progressed from issues of access to confrontation about campus climate. Mark Smith indicated that when he arrived at Denison the only "significant Black presence was on the female housekeeping staff....The student body was essentially White." Even following recruiting efforts, Smith noted that there were not sufficient numbers of Black students for them to have a comfortable, rewarding experience. Black students reacted to this:

> Presenting a list of demands was a tactic used by the Black students to call attention to their needs and discomfort, and to embarrass the administration; it was never expected that these demands would be met. While some things on the list were more possible than others, the Black students intentionally included things that we were unlikely or unable to do.

The car incident recounted in Smith's chapter is a dramatic example of the types of demands Black students at Denison made. Smith made the important point that the climate of many liberal arts colleges was different from that of large public universities; in his view students didn't need to make demands to get attention. But as concern about the war in Vietnam escalated, antiwar protest grew at liberal arts colleges. Often the protests were as much about exercising power as they were about specific issues.

At Haverford, a Quaker college, students got involved with integration activities within the local community. Then, as James Lyons described it, "One day we got a critical mass. I don't know how many Black students we had at the college then, probably 25 or so, which for Haverford's small size was a lot." Black students protested by co-opting a Quaker tradition: a silent protest to gain some respect for their situation. "They didn't say a word; there were no signs, posters, or handouts. At Haverford, this was devastating. That was the first time that the issue changed from admissions, from numbers, to climate." The use of the silent protest was exceedingly clever.

> The experience of the silent protest led us to hold up a mirror to look at ourselves and our college, and try to begin the much harder task of understanding how we appeared to Black students. "What is wrong with us?" We began to look much more clearly at what we were doing.

REGIONAL COLLEGES AND UNIVERSITIES

Wichita State, University of Nebraska-Omaha, Kent State, and Oakland University were medium-sized universities with large percentages of commuter students. Kent and Oakland were more volatile than Wichita State and Nebraska at Omaha. Before it became the site of one of the most sadly memorable events of the student protests of the 1970s, Kent State had faced demands of its Black students for better treatment. According to Ron Beer,

> Before the antiwar demonstrations, there were a lot of demonstrations by the Black students, particularly from the Cleveland/Akron area. There were some very, very vocal Black students. We had a number of the organizations—Black Panthers, Black Student Coalition—various organizations of that nature on campus.

As a result, Kent had a number of sit-ins and protests in which students demanded that Kent recruit more Black students, faculty, and staff, and provide a more comfortable environment for African American students. Other demands at Kent State included requests for services for Black students, a Black cultural center, and an African American studies academic program. Having somewhat different perspectives on Kent State than Ron Beer, Ambler concluded:

> Because of what we had done in the late 1960s in making Kent a more positive environment for racial minorities, we had pretty good relationships with the Black students. And, as we got to those ugly days of 1970, I felt pretty good about our ability to work with Black students, compared to our relationships with the White student protesters.

Beer contrasted his experiences at Kent State with those at the University of Nebraska-Omaha, recalling no civil rights demonstrations at the latter. Instead, civil rights at Nebraska involved reaching out, not only to the Black community, but to the Native American population as well. James Rhatigan also described Wichita State as comparatively quiet. However, there were some intense protests over discrimination in cheerleader selection and several other hot-button incidents. Further, Rhatigan observed:

> ...Black students were not experienced in self-governance. They had not been in the center of things. Now they were franchised in a hurry, but they didn't always know what to do with this power, so they squandered some very good things that they actually started.

Also of importance at open-access institutions like Wichita State was providing programs and opportunities for poorly prepared students to be successful in college.

In 1970, in an effort to bring about an improvement in campus climate at Oakland University, a suburban university near Detroit, African American students scheduled a meeting with the president. When they learned that the president was not in, they proceeded to remove the American flag from the campus flagpole. Then, the following day, they took over the cafeteria. James Appleton, who was dean of students, and Augustine Pounds, who was the advisor to the African American student group, have somewhat differing memories of the nature of the event. Both agree, however, with James Appleton's assertion that the "demands were not outrageous. Instead, they were focused on student recruitment, support services, the curriculum, advising, and campus climate issues." This takeover led to some important changes at Oakland and opened up dialogue between Black students and campus administrators.

Two-Year College

At the only two-year school in this study, located in a relatively urban and diverse area, Harrison Morson reported minor disturbances. In one incident, the Black Panthers wanted to come on campus to recruit new members and convey their message to those interested in hearing it. In a second request "several of the African American students recruited through the Educational Opportunity Fund program approached the student government association with a petition to form a minority student union," which was supported by some faculty. Morson noted that college was offering courses in African American history without student prompting, thus avoiding a point of potential tension. When the Black Student Union formed and attempted to exclude White students, Morson intervened to convince the Black students that it was in their best interest to include White students. Students at Union County Community College frequently participated in community marches and protests, often with Morson at the lead. A potentially more serious event occurred when an underground publication surfaced that was racist in nature. Morson dealt with this by working with the legitimate campus press outlets, and by supporting anyone who wished to file a civil suit.

THE OVERLAP OF CONCERNS

At all of the institutions associated with the individuals featured in this book, civil rights became entwined with the antiwar movement toward the end of the 1960s. Often this intermingling served to deflate civil rights issues. Upcraft summarized the confluence of issues.

> The issues kind of all blended together. For example, our Black students were at the forefront of the antiwar movement because it was the Blacks who were dying in the war more than anybody else. This was also the era when students first discovered drugs and marched in demonstrations and gave administrators a hard time.

Ron Beer believed the antiwar, the women's, and civil rights movements were all intertwined at Kent State. He summarized the sentiments of most.

> The Black student leadership felt, if they were sucked into the system of protest in general, that they would be lost, that they would be overwhelmed, and that people would lose what they were all about.

In fact, he noted that, the day of the shootings on the Kent State campus, Black students had organized their own protest in the morning separate from that of the White students.

PREPARATION TO DEAL WITH TURMOIL

Although somewhat of a generalization, it is not too much of a stretch to say that the individuals included in this book were in no way prepared to deal with the issues described above. What constituted adequate preparation in such situations is debatable because not only did student participants change over time, so did their concerns. As administrators became accustomed to certain student grievances and ways of expressing them, the issues changed. Most notably, student tactics changed from ones of peaceful negotiation to strategies employing angry confrontation and even violence. Inexplicably to many, by the late 1960s, colleges and universities, themselves, became the targets of student anger (Astin, et. al, 1997). The stories told in this book suggest several relevant aspects of preparation.

Early Experiences with Blacks/Civil Rights

Many of the individuals featured in this book were shaped by encounters with issues of race very early in their lives. These experiences undoubtedly had an impact on their views on civil rights. For example, Emily Taylor was born on an Alabama cotton plantation in 1915. Though she moved to Ohio at an early age, the Southern family influence remained. She admitted to being "slower on the uptake" with regards to racial justice than she was on gender equality. She had never met "a minority person on my level" until she went to college where there were few.

David Ambler drew a more explicit link between his early exposure to civil rights and the shaping of his progressive views on race.

> I grew up in northwest Indiana, which was one of the "true melting pots" of America. Long before it was called "integration," we had it there. Even though housing was segregated, both my grade school and high school were integrated. My parents were not wide-eyed liberals, but they did invest me with a respect for the rights of others and a sense of fairness and justice. It served me well in my commitment to civil rights which was an issue throughout the 40 years of my professional career.

Ambler went on to describe his experiences as a member of a racially mixed singing group being turned away from a country club engagement because of the Black members. "I was shocked," he noted.

> Not only could five of us not do the program without the other three, but also I remember the five of us said, "That's crazy. We're out of here." That was my first involvement with racial prejudice and it deeply affected my commitment to this issue.

James Lyons' first awareness of racism came in 1953 when he was a resident assistant. One Friday evening, he received a call from his dean who was writing him a letter of recommendation. The dean asked Lyons, "What is your view on civil rights?" Lyons responded, "Well, you know we've had all kinds of discussions about this." The dean then asked Lyons about his membership in a fraternity and whether there were any Blacks in the fraternity. Lyons replied, "There's only one in the college and he and I are good friends, but no, he's not a Phi Delt." The dean continued to question Lyons about the fraternity's clause that excludes Black students. At the end of the conversation, the dean asked again, "Well, how do I answer this question, then?" Lyons believed this to be an amazing, teachable moment.

It was powerful. I mean, he just drove an icicle into me and let it melt. That led me to organize a group of people to start a national movement, and raise money to change the clause in the national fraternity. Our efforts got soundly walloped the first time it went up. The clause was finally changed. That was my introduction to the sharper edge of civil rights.

Military experience had some impact on several of the student affairs administrators in this book. Hubbard, Shaffer, Ambler, and Witten served in the military. Charles Witten attended undergraduate and graduate school at the University of North Carolina, but he talks more about the influence of his military experience as a captain in the Navy than he does about his early educational experiences. For him, as an ex-naval officer, he did what he was told to do. If that meant integrating the university, then that's what he would do. He couched most of what he did as "treating everyone equally."

Of the four African American contributors to this book, Hubbard and Pounds spoke at length about the role of their backgrounds in shaping their administrative perspectives. Given the times, it is reasonable to assume that Anderson and Morson had some of the same experiences as Hubbard and Pounds. Although Hubbard grew up in Des Moines, Iowa where the schools were integrated, almost every other aspect of his family's life was segregated. School was the one place where Hubbard felt accepted and could excel on his own merits. His efforts at the University of Iowa and in Iowa City to confront discriminatory housing practices were a direct result of his own, personal experiences with "red-lining," the practice of identifying neighborhoods where Blacks could live. In his memoir, Hubbard pondered the question, "Why did African Americans endure unfair treatment without protest or petitioning for reform?" He answered the question by suggesting that the university would tell the complainant they were free to go elsewhere. Furthermore, he argued, "We took the view that our misery was transitory—we could endure it for a few years because an education was seen as the way to a better future" (Hubbard & Stone, 1999, p. 42). All along the way, Hubbard described himself as being lucky to have had mentors who supported him and who made sure that he was given opportunities to succeed. His involvement in civil rights at the University of Iowa began while he was a professor in the quest to end discriminatory housing practices and to desegregate some local restaurants. His commitment to fair practices extended to his appointment as dean of academic affairs and is seen in his efforts to end exclusionary practices in the Greek system.

Augustine Pounds' experiences were compounded by the fact that she is a woman. Having graduated from Pontiac High School, she applied to and was rejected by nearby Oakland University, despite having excellent grades. Not willing to give up, Pounds got a job at Oakland "in order to learn how students gained admission." What she learned was that "the most common career plan for African American students in Pontiac was to gain employment at General Motors." As an employee, Pounds asked for and was given permission to take classes. Although given permission to take only one course, Pounds continued to register until she had accumulated enough credits to graduate. Then, "When the other secretaries learned that I had completed most of the required course work for my degree, they filed a grievance against me for being a full-time student who received a salary rather than earning student wages." A favorable ruling allowed her to continue and graduate, winning the highest student award given to an Oakland student. Pounds spoke for many other African Americans of the time when she said,

> However, when I gained employment at Oakland University in the early 1960s, it was not easy or pleasant. Coming to Oakland changed my life forever. The belief and value system that I had grown up with was challenged daily. Racism was visible daily, but I had to decide what I could live with and challenge what was unacceptable. I had to decide how I would support students and how I would support my job responsibilities in order to keep my job. I knew, early, that I could not be part of a system that denied me freedoms.

ACADEMIC PREPARATION

Most of the individuals we feature held at least a master's degree in student personnel administration or a related field, such as counseling and guidance, when they began their careers. Some held a doctorate or had earned one since the 1970s. Thus, we can assume that most were versed in the latest and most current student personnel theories of the day when they encountered the student protests. Some had academic backgrounds in other fields. Judith Chambers had a master's degree in speech. Both Hubbard and Witten had undergraduate and graduate degrees in sciences and had significant military experience. Witten later earned a doctorate in education and started a student personnel program at USC.

RAPID PROMOTIONS

What is most remarkable about the careers of these individuals is their rapid ascension in the ranks of administration, many at a very young age. It is important to note that this was the era when the student affairs profession, as a whole, was elevated to a higher status within higher education. Specifically, the chief student affairs position moved from that of dean to that of vice president at many institutions, as presidents looked to student affairs professionals to guide the institution on how to deal with student unrest (Laliberte, 2003). As such, not only did the individuals in the book receive rapid promotions, but so did the profession as a whole.

Although they mostly described themselves as "flying by the seats of their pants," the individuals featured in this book were all promoted rapidly. In this sense, they were at the right place at the right time. John Blackburn went to the University of Alabama as assistant dean of men and within a year he was promoted to dean of men. The president of USC liked Witten's performance as director of NROTC and made him dean of students. David Ambler was promoted before even setting foot on Kent's campus. He was hired as assistant dean of men in 1966 and had been promoted to acting dean of men by the time he arrived on campus. Later in his first year, he was given the title associate dean of students. After the events of 1970, Ambler was appointed chief student affairs officer at Kent. He said, "At that time, it was a real buyer's market in this profession, and opportunities were many and promotions came fast—much too fast." Appleton was appointed dean of students fresh out of a doctoral program at Michigan State. Rhatigan was hired as dean of students at Wichita State in 1965, at the age of 30, and was the youngest person to occupy a position of that level at an institution of Wichita State's size. Hubbard was appointed academic dean based largely on his experience with Iowa City civil rights activities.

Carl Anderson was promoted from associate dean of students, a position he had held for three years, to dean of students when the dean at Howard had a stroke. At Florida State University, Harris Shelton progressed from assistant dean of men, to dean of men, and to dean of student development in a span of four years from 1968 to 1971. With only experience as a resident assistant, a master's degree in speech, and the support of the University of the Pacific's president, Judith Chambers was hired as dean of women at Mt. Union College in 1960. She was 23 years old. She returned to the University of the Pacific in 1968, where she worked for the president for three years before being appointed dean of students. Pounds came to the profession while earning her bachelors degree at Oakland University. She worked as an administrative assistant to the president before being appointed assistant director of commuter services in 1971, and as assistant director of Oakland's student center in 1973.

In summary, while some of the administrators in this book—Jo Anne Trow, for example—followed a more traditional path of serving in a position for a few years before being promoted and/or moving to a more senior position at a new institution, for many, their induction to increasing administrative responsibility came quickly and without much warning. Some, such as Robert Shaffer and Lee Upcraft, have had long careers at the same institution.

ROLES

In response to the conditions on their campuses, the student affairs professionals highlighted in this book undertook a number of roles—often simultaneously. Cowley (1940), writing from the vantage point of a simpler time on college campuses, described three roles for student affairs administrators: humanitarians, administrators and psychologists. The stories of the individuals in this book illustrate the more expansive role that emerged during the 1960s and 1970s (Laliberte, 2003). We identified the following roles: disciplinarian, counselor, educator, advocate, mediator, initiator, and humanitarian. Each of these roles is discussed separately below.

DISCIPLINARIAN: OUR LEGACY

Maintaining order on the campus and meting out discipline were the least favorite roles of student affairs administrators. These were roles, however, that were strongly identified with the profession, especially in relation to the civil rights movement. As Robert Shaffer affirmed, the traditional role of student affairs was to be the "institutional officer who kept order and maintained appropriate behavior...the keeper of the morals." He added, "Once I got the job, I realized that my job was to help students express themselves, not to suppress them."

Most believed that students ought to be held accountable for their actions, and many believed that student protesters ought not to disrupt the educational mission of the institution to further their aims. David Ambler, for example, stated that one of his guiding philosophies was that students ought to "take responsibility for themselves...that, regardless of your age, behavior has consequences and you will be held accountable for your behavior." As an extension of this idea, John Blackburn affirmed, "In those days, I kicked a lot of students out of school but I kept a good relationship with them. I even corresponded with them after they were out and encouraged them to come back." Under most circumstances, student affairs professionals did their best to warn students of the ramifications of certain actions. As James Appleton said, "It was necessary to make clear that, if an illegal protest continued, the university was going to act to clear the blocked hallway and the disruption of business." He further stated:

> However, if at all possible, we were also not going to back students into a situation where they had to defend a position that could lead to police hauling them out. There is a huge amount of space between being laissez faire saying, "Oh, what the hell, let them sit in" on one hand, and on the other end of this continuum calling the police. Patience to establish the dialogue, if possible, and in implementing sanctions paid off.

Many of the individuals we interviewed, however, were quite bothered by what they saw as the edict by higher-level administrators to keep the peace and maintain order at all costs. Philip Hubbard, for example, stated that "the president looked to student affairs to keep things under control so that the students did not embarrass the university or college and did not offend the trustees." In contrast to this approach, Hubbard insisted that a more effective way of affecting student behavior was to appeal to students' sense of educational values rather than chastising their behavior.

Harris Shelton, who, because of his junior position, was called upon to do things such as patrol the Black cultural center at night looking for students who were defying the administration by living there, declared his frustration with having to deal with the "procedural issues, the protection issues, and not the civil rights or students' need issues." He added,

> There is no question that one element of the staff of FSU, including faculty, wanted to retaliate against disruptive behavior. Some folks wanted to teach the culprit students a few lessons. At our best, we abandoned a position of educators in favor of one of defense of the university.

Augustine Pounds also expressed frustration with this, arguing,

> Those in student affairs were clearly the enforcers of the student conduct code. There is little in the history to show our role as advocates. When students were upset about the campus environment, the student affairs administrators expected them to manage their anger and deal with the issues that they faced. Our role was more to maintain order and serve as judges rather than focus on student development. It is surprising that students trusted and worked with us as well as they did.

Lee Upcraft noted an important change in the approach to discipline. He believed that the discipline system that was being utilized in the 1960s and 1970s was in need of an overhaul because it was designed to deal with "normal acting-outers" rather than responding to "students, who, out of conscience, take a stand and get arrested but who are really not criminals." He added,

> All of sudden, the discipline system was flooded with people of conscience instead of your garden variety drinkers and academic dishonesty folks. What we found was that our old systems of discipline weren't capable of dealing with these new problems.

Upcraft and many others represented in this book saw the need for student affairs officers to look differently upon their role as disciplinarians, to view behavior in a more contextual light that looks at both the kind of "infraction" as well as the "intent of the perpetrator" when determining consequences. There was also a general sentiment that student affairs administrators, while needing to maintain some sort of order at the institution, ought not to abandon the more lofty goals of helping students to learn and grow.

COUNSELOR: CARING IS IMPORTANT

Few talked about the counseling role, which was surprising given the fact that many of the individuals featured in this book had academic backgrounds in counseling. Some, like John Blackburn, rejected the role of counselor. Blackburn said that in his first housing position at Florida State University he expected to make use of his counseling training. He stated,

> I sat in my office and waited for the students to come to me. I was ready to help them. "Hi, I'm here to help you. What's your problem? Tell me your problem." No one came, except to tell me that the stereo or the plumbing didn't work. I decided that Senior Hall did not need a counselor. It needed someone to make the place work and it needed someone to make the environment more attractive and educational.

While others didn't overtly reject counseling, it did seem that their attentions were on other facets of their position. Nonetheless, the interviewees believed that it was important to establish good, solid relationships with all their students, regardless of racial background. They also expressed an intense degree of caring and empathy for their students. Judith Chambers and Harris Shelton, for example, both described the heartache experienced by students who were involved in interracial dating situations. Both described spending significant amounts of time with these couples, trying to help them problem solve and deal with the negative perceptions of parents, friends, and community members. As Shelton commented, "These were people who needed to be cared for and cared about as human beings, more than just as students." Several mentioned their role vis-à-vis women and new measures of contraception, which undoubtedly put them in a counseling role at least on occasion.

Befriending students was another form of caring. Mark Smith was among the many deans in this book who developed very close, personal relationships with his students. He described how, on a typical day, two or three African American students would come visit him in his office and talk about their personal and academic concerns. Smith elucidated, "As a dean, I was always dealing simultaneously with a large number of emotional situations involving young people and each situation demanded my undivided attention and clear thinking."

The contributors to this book talked about the importance of being a good listener and caring for students. As Rhatigan stated,

> People want to be successful, and you do this first of all through a genuine ethic of caring. If caring isn't there, you're doomed. If it is there, you've got a chance to succeed. You need skill to accompany it; you just can't care and leave your brain at home.

Harrison Morson added,

> One of the major lessons learned and carried forward from this experience was you have to listen and do not expect to have the answers in your hip pocket. You cannot pretend to be listening. You really have to make a concerted effort to focus upon what students are saying. Like it or not, you have to hear them. You cannot tune them out.

ADVOCATE: SUPPORT STUDENT GOALS, WITHIN REASON

Serving as an advocate for students was a role that all of the individuals in this book learned as a result of their experiences in the civil rights era. Many felt like Judith Chambers, who indicated that she "wanted to be an advocate for students." She added,

> I tried to support their points of view when they were reasonable...Student affairs professionals are not in the business to be police officers, even though at certain times we may need to act like one. We are there to be advocates for students. We are there to make sure the out-of-class life is a positive experience.

James Rhatigan also believed that his job was to advocate for student needs. He commented,

> I believed that you should look for ways to say yes to students, not ways to say no. Finding ways to say yes to students has been the

theme song of my entire professional life, really. When you can say yes, then students will recognize that they are being heard. Now they could turn to making their ideas work.

He clarified further:

> I wasn't a patsy, but I was an advocate. I went to work when others said no to a student. When people said no to a student, this was often infuriating to me. Usually I took the view that the student's issue was legitimate, unless proven otherwise. Maybe we were not accommodating the student because we were just too damn lazy or set in our ways. Now occasionally, of course, I was conned, and I always let the students know, "You got your dean. Congratulations."

Harrison Morson described that, at Union County Community College, the position of dean of students was created because the student leaders believed that they did not have an advocate or spokesperson at the administrative organizational table. As such, they petitioned the president to establish a new position of dean of student affairs. The position was created and Morson was hired with the express purpose of being an advocate for students and their concerns. He took this role seriously.

Still, most recognized that advocacy has its limits. James Appleton was clear that he was not an advocate for students, but that he "was in a position where I ought to be most sensitive to students and their needs and perspectives." He added, "Student affairs professionals were in a difficult position because students expected us to be their advocate, but the presidents and chancellors also rightfully expected us to be on their team." Further, there were clearly times when student affairs administrators could not satisfy student demands. In these cases, administrators made it clear that their job was to listen, support, and explain how and why they could not respond affirmatively. Judith Chambers stated,

> I would not have advocated for everything, particularly if I did not think it was reasonable. I would have been reluctant to support a battle I did not think we could win. One needs to carefully select the hill one is going to go down on.

There were some tangible benefits to being seen as a student advocate—the least of which involved the trust that was bestowed upon administrators by students. Harris Shelton stated,

> Coupled with a willingness to listen to students, I probably had more credibility than most administrators around me....I had good student trust and students wanted to talk, they wanted to converse with

someone who would listen. They wanted me to approve of what they were doing, or to explain why I did not approve.

Robert Shaffer added,

Knowing that we were going to at least be neutral, if not actually aggressively supportive, the activists would tell us what they were going to do. Administratively, most of the trouble occurs when participants spring something in the way of a demonstration without preparation.

EDUCATOR: THE ESSENCE OF OUR WORK

Educating students was the primary purpose, and most favored role, of all of the student affairs administrators whose stories we tell, regardless of their position at the time. Examples abound in the interviews of student affairs professionals trying to teach students how to be leaders, how to bring about change, and how to make the most of the educational experience. From John Blackburn's and Charles Witten's attempts to prepare student leaders for integration, to the frank manner in which individuals like Mark Smith and James Rhatigan talked to their students about "bad decisions," student affairs professionals clearly saw their primary role as educating students. The work of an educator took several forms.

- Providing a Supportive Educational Environment

  The interviewees were eloquent when it came to describing their responsibilities in creating environments that facilitated student learning. James Lyons, for example, stated, "We should be sensitive to the need for nurturing learning environments. As long as we can get beyond regulating students and taking care of the bureaucratic trivia, we can move to creating an environment that supports learning." John Blackburn concurred, "I think the students' attitudes ought to be influenced and changed, and it is our job to work at making that happen." Charles Witten was proud of the fact that the president at South Carolina introduced him as "my vice president in charge of all education outside the classroom." He added, "The role of student affairs was to facilitate the education of students and provide for the education with such things that they didn't get in the classroom." Further, Harrison Morson noted that higher education is an ideal venue to have such an effect. He elucidated:

  > This environment promotes one of the richest opportunities to influence others, especially those seeking direction and clarification

of life's issues....I envisioned my role as a facilitator—someone to assist students in developing an understanding and appreciation of the available opportunities for personal growth that were within their grasp. This commitment was the bedrock of my extension of service to students, and any other responsibility that I can think of held a lower priority.

● Teaching the Tools of Effective Protests

The role of educator took on a very specific function during the 1960s and 1970s: that of preparing students to protest effectively. For example, Augustine Pounds helped the students during the cafeteria takeover at Oakland to refine their concerns into specific requests. She worked with them to identify appropriate decision makers to consult and to identify appropriate solutions to their concerns. Judith Chambers also saw her job as "helping students behind the scenes. I can remember working with the students helping them to frame statements and questions in such a way, that the president or the board would not find them offensive." Harrison Morson added:

> Many students were unable to present their views in a manner that avoided being received as confrontational by those already operating from a seat of power....I urged student spokespersons to present themselves in a posture that promoted a search for positive outcomes through mediation and tolerance. I advised them to think through their presentation, as opposed to letting it seem like a spontaneous, spiritual, and/or emotional outlet....I talked to them about whom to approach first using the chain of command. I explained to them that you do not always want to skip people because, if you do, then you alienate them in the process of getting what you want done.

Not everyone was happy when student affairs administrators took on this particular educational role. Robert Shaffer recalls being accused by more conservative students of stirring up trouble for his work in helping activists to organize an effective protest. Nonetheless, he believed strongly in providing such assistance:

> We suggested how to get publicity, how to involve students and how to make appeals. By doing this we guided them, you might say, and most demonstrations were relatively orderly as a result. I feel we were discharging our obligation to the institution and

to students in a more productive way than just trying to keep order....Student affairs has to change from their image as a custodial, keeper of the morals, supervisory role to one of actually facilitating the individual to develop informed views. The university, in all its aspects, should teach students to not only form open attitudes and informed views, but also to encourage them to express themselves actively.

- Capitalizing on Teachable Moments

All of the student affairs professionals in this book took the opportunity to capitalize on "teachable moments." A few notable examples included the story told by David Ambler, who felt compelled to talk to student leaders at the University of Kansas before they voted to oust the African American student body president. He commented:

> I wanted the students to examine their hearts and minds before taking any actions they might later regret. I took the approach of talking informally to many of them and asking them "'to look yourself in the mirror and tell me that, if he was a White person, this would be going down the same track as it is now." It was my way of suggesting that there might be some racism at work here.

Ambler felt strongly that he needed to have them think about the ramifications of their actions, even if he alienated some of these student leaders. Similarly, Jo Anne Trow utilized a conflict between an African American and White roommate as a teachable moment. She declared, "We worked with the residence hall students to understand the importance of learning to live with people who are different." A final example comes from James Rhatigan who described how part of being an educator was helping different groups of students communicate with one another. He remembered telling opposing student groups, "You two talk about it. Don't tell me there's no resolution there. The reason you can't find one is because you're yelling at each other." He added that in some cases,

> I would have to jump in and try to get the Black student to modify his anger a little bit so that the White students could be permitted to do the right thing, not look like they'd just collapsed like a deck of cards....Then I might go over to the student government and say,
>
> > Look, talk to the Black students frankly. Do the right thing. They're waiting to see what happens, so let's put

your best foot forward. Let's frame that in such a way they can see that we're trying, even while we have our values, we're trying to help them achieve what they would like.

Students, almost without fail, would say yes to that approach.

MEDIATOR: ALWAYS IN THE MIDDLE

One of the most important roles played by student affairs professionals was that of mediator—either between opposing student groups or between students and administrators or students and faculty. Every single contributor to this book talked about the need to translate the demands and concerns of students to others, and to translate the concerns of the university to students. They used terms like "middleman," "conduit," "mediator," "negotiator," and "translator" to describe how they worked with students, faculty, and other administrators. James Appleton avowed, "Student affairs professionals across the country were the persons who were at the intersection between the students, faculty, and the administration." Similarly, Lee Upcraft captured this "middleman" relationship well. He stated:

> I often felt like I was in the middle of the students and the other administrators on most issues. I would attend meetings with Black students when they discussed their demands, and I would go to administrative meetings where I was the person who was most relied upon to tell the administration what the students were all about. And, so I served a mediating role between the administration and the students. I felt like somebody caught in the middle, like nobody was happy with me….Our involvement in these kinds of things legitimize a very important role in helping institutions better understand students, and helping students better understand institutions.

As mediator, student affairs professionals had to be able to communicate with multiple constituencies and serve as translators from one group to another. Sometimes this involved working with administrators and faculty to help them see that student demands were not going to disappear and merited a constructive response. Carl Anderson eloquently described:

> Part of the role of student affairs administrators was to help faculty and staff understand the students, interpret their views, perceptions, goals, and aspirations. We tried to help them appreciate the fact that not every demand was intended to be a challenge to their authority. Instead, it was a challenge to their way of thinking.

He continued:

> We supported the students, but at the same time, it was the student
> unrest that led to the point where change actually occurred. We were
> sort of like mediators. We helped the students to maintain balance,
> and communicated with students with respect to what the university
> would or could not be expected to do. At the same time, we communi-
> cated to faculty and administrators that it was essential for them to
> listen and respond to legitimate concerns. I think we played an
> extremely pivotal role.

On the other hand, student affairs professionals needed to communicate with
students and let them know that not all their demands would be met. Judith
Chambers captured this idea when she commented:

> It was also our job to try to interpret the positions the university had
> taken on certain issues that were not what the students wanted. Often
> times we were explaining to students why change couldn't take place,
> even though we didn't support the decision that had been made. On a
> daily basis I found myself in the middle of some argument. That was
> the result of feeling that I could be totally honest with the president in
> private, but I needed to be supportive of him and the actions that the
> board had taken in public. They were often exactly what the students
> did not want to hear.

Constant, honest communication with students and with other constituents
was essential for student affairs professionals if they were going to satisfac-
torily fulfill their role as mediators. This lesson was learned the hard way
for folks like Lee Upcraft and Harris Shelton, who both described the need
to be more politically astute with administrative peers and superiors in order
to get them to consider making institutional changes.

HUMANITARIAN: WORKING TO BRING ABOUT CHANGE

As mentioned in chapter one, Cowley (1940), used the term humanitarian to
describe student affairs professionals who tried to make institutions of higher education less depersonalized and more responsive to students' concerns.
We saw this role mirrored in the student affairs professionals highlighted in
this book who saw themselves as "change agents," working towards making
higher education a better place for students. They were not content with the
status quo and felt that it was important for their institutions to respond
positively to the challenges raised during the civil rights era. Even Charles
Witten, who claimed to be engaged in integration only because the law

dictated that he do so, eventually came to realize that a major component of his job was to create a positive educational climate that allowed all students at the University of South Carolina to be successful. The student affairs professionals in this book saw the need for institutions to respond proactively to the concerns raised by students. David Ambler, for example, admonished the field saying,

> If we do not make it possible for change to occur in our institutions, then students will once again use inappropriate methods to achieve justice and equity. It is a fundamental responsibility of student affairs to make the processes of change in our institutions work for students.

The individuals in this book saw most of the students' desires as legitimate aspirations that, while difficult to achieve, were worth doing. Carl Anderson stressed, "If it meant making some changes, then they [the institution] were prepared to do that." Some of the individuals, like Harrison Morson and Augustine Pounds, actively participated in student-led protests, while others were supportive from afar. Yet, while the approach followed by different student affairs administrators in bringing about change varied, the passion to see change occur and to support students was unified. Harris Shelton seemed to speak for everyone when he said, "Each of us as educators had a personal stake, a personal role in the battle for human rights." Similarly, Emily Taylor agreed, saying "I believe in equality, and our sole function is to produce as many autonomous adults as we can." Finally, Augustine Pounds expressed this belief,

> Integrity, fairness, equity, and hope, are perhaps the words most often associated with my memory of the Oakland experience. We never lost hope that the increased activism and criticism by students would make the institution take a look at itself and change.

INITIATOR: CREATING PROGRAMS TO FACILITATE STUDENT SUCCESS

Part of the humanitarian role fulfilled by student affairs administrators was directly related to the actions undertaken to bring about change. Not content to merely mediate problems, student affairs professionals created and initiated programs and policies that responded to the concerns raised by students. These programs and policies took a number of different forms, but they all served to meet the needs of students. The creation of TRIO programs, for example, was a popular response to serving the needs of historically underrepresented students. John Blackburn's creation of Mallett Hall stands as an example of the kind of forethought and planning undertaken by student affairs administrators during the civil rights era. Blackburn recognized the need to be proactive in teaching future leaders how to create community and think about values as a means to facilitate integration of African Americans at the University of Alabama. Blackburn summed up his philosophy in this way: "I had to be doing things: organizing students and creating sorts of (things), which now I would call communities, but at the time I just called it creating functions and so forth—achieving and doing things."

The other contributors to this book also created programs and policies that were responsive to student needs. Many of these, like Camp Serendipity at Haverford, the Community Involvement Program at the University of the Pacific, and the Commission on Human Rights and Responsibilities at Oregon State University, still exist today. Their continued existence is a testament not only to the creativity of their founders and the initial need for such programs, but also to the continued need to respond proactively to student concerns.

RELATIONSHIPS

Student affairs administrators did not operate in a vacuum. They faced the challenges of civil rights along with presidents, boards of trustees, students, faculty, and various external groups. These stakeholders had their own competing responsibilities and perspectives that acted in concert with, and sometimes in opposition to, those of student affairs administrators. As such, student affairs administrators' responses were both facilitated and constrained by the relationships they had with those around them. Below, we discuss the relationships between student affairs and students, presidents, faculty, the local community, and professional associations like NASPA.

RELATIONSHIPS WITH STUDENTS: FROM ROLES TO RESPECT

Perhaps because we focused on civil rights rather than student rights in general, few of the administrators whose stories are told in this book specifically labeled the shift that occurred in student-college relationships during the 1960s and 1970s as a shift from *in loco parentis* to legal rights, and those that did were administrators later in the time period. Nevertheless, almost to a person, they described a shift in the relationship between students and the institution. David Ambler spoke for nearly everyone in this book when he described the role of student affairs prior to the 1970s:

> Student affairs, particularly prior to 1970, was seen as the keeper of the gate for the institution, and in spite of the fact that it had some

pretty radical people in its mix, it always was in that position of representing the institution to students and yet professionally seeing itself as somebody to advocate for students, and that tension was always there. We were in charge of maintaining law and order, as we used to call it, on campus all the time. We were the people who frequently were initiating change to make things better for students, so you had this kind of schizophrenic personality in yourself. Our job was to keep students in line but help them get out of line.

In the shift from *in loco parentis*, where university officials, in particular student affairs administrators, acted as moral supervisors of students and as disciplinarians, to today's view of students as legally responsible adults who should be held accountable for their actions, the individuals in this book can be seen as transitional figures. They were transitional in that each of them was called upon to see students in a different light—as maturing adults who wanted to have a say in the way the university and the world worked, rather than as adolescents incapable of exercising good judgment over whom the university had complete control. At the same time, as Judith Chambers saw it,

> The job, on the one hand, was to help students be heard, and to try to connect them with the people who needed to hear what they had to say. On the other hand, it was also our job to try to interpret the positions the university had taken on certain issues that were not what the students wanted.

- Eliminating an Obsolete Concept

  Many of the stories told in this book relate situations in which student affairs professionals worked actively to move away from *in loco parentis* to treating students more like adults. At the University of Iowa, for example, Philip Hubbard's goal for student services was to do away with *in loco parentis*, which he termed an obsolete concept. He explained that, while the president looked to student affairs to keep things under control, he favored a view in which, "A student's continuation as a student should depend on his academic performance and, of course, paying his bills. The exceptions would be if the student was a hazard to himself or to other people or to property." Hubbard and others in this book eliminated the last vestiges of parietal roles and began to empower students. Hubbard observed, "The role of students has also changed. The way students are viewed is different. Students are now expected to take a part in the institutional government, under rather limited conditions, but much more than before." This represented a sharp change from the previous attitude that the university always knew what was best for the student.

• Participation in Leadership Opportunities and Decision Making

John Blackburn, Charles Witten, Robert Shaffer, Emily Taylor, and Mark Smith, some of the most senior student affairs professionals featured in this book, were at the forefront of providing leadership opportunities for students. They not only recognized that they had to provide leadership opportunities, but that it was in the students' and institutions' best interests to do so. They all saw students as responsible adults who had much to contribute to the decision-making process. Smith noted that, when he first became dean, students were the "student personnel staff of the college." In the early days of American higher education, students made leadership positions for themselves; by the 1950s and early 1960s, it seemed that student affairs professionals were training students to be leaders. Nowhere was this more evident that at the University of Alabama where John Blackburn appealed to students' leadership abilities to make integration of the university possible. As Blackburn recounted,

> I always told the student leaders that they were teachers. "You're a teacher; you're a student leader and that has teaching responsibilities that you have to fulfill if you're gonna be a leader." I still believe that today, that student affairs people should work with the student leaders as though they were teachers and let the student leader assume some responsibility.

With administrators who began their careers a little later, the discussion turns more directly to meeting student needs for greater freedoms and for power. As Augustine Pounds said, "The most important change, according to the students, was that students became more directly involved in the decision-making process at the institution." "At Pacific, we had students clamoring for freedom, being against the war, and wanting controversial speakers on the campus," said Judith Chambers. Accommodations to student demands for a seat at the decision-making table did not come easily, as Carl Anderson noted:

> I think eventually the university came to the recognition that somehow they had to find a way to mediate in order to be able to conduct the basic mission of the institution, namely, teaching, research, and service. But at the same time, the university had to recognize that these dynamics were not going to go away.

The challenge for student affairs administrators was stated well
by Anderson,

> We had to find ways to support those aspirations that were legit-
> imate, but at the same time, not compromise the university's
> basic mission—providing instruction and service to the stu-
> dents….Somehow, we had to establish a relationship that
> allowed us to communicate with the young people, and for them
> to communicate with us, even though we may not have seen
> things eye-to-eye.

This was not always easy. According to Ron Beer,

> There was the sense on behalf of some student affairs adminis-
> trators that "They are students. Don't listen to them. Don't do
> anything," leaving students adamant about wanting to meet with
> the president instead of the student affairs personnel, as was the
> norm on many campuses.

Respecting students' rights and needs to participate in decision making did not mean that student affairs administrators completely turned
over the reins to students. As Rhatigan asserted,

> There were demands we could not meet. Students would say,
> "We want to have this issue addressed and resolved and you
> have until September of next year." So I'd say to those students,
> "Well, throw up the barricades because I can't meet that kind
> of deadline."

Judith Chambers also stated,

> I think one of the lessons we didn't learn from the 1970s is that if
> a student exhibits behavior that is not acceptable, then you deal
> with that student. If 10 students exhibit behavior that is not accept-
> able, then you deal with those 10 students. The unacceptable
> behavior does not warrant a new rule for the whole community.

● Students and Administrators as Friends

One of the more interesting aspects of the relationship between the
student affairs administrators featured in this book and the students
with whom they worked was the fact that many formed close personal
relationships. The nature of these friendships is interesting in light of
the fact that the 1960s and 1970s are generally viewed as the period in
which the relationship between the institution and its administrators
was highly contentious, with administrators often cast as the enemies

of the students. Many of the administrators in this book talked about the importance of being friends with the students and of knowing them by name. The loss of this relationship in more recent years was bemoaned by several. Examples of the close relationship between administrators and students abound. Augustine Pounds described how she used to invite the African American students at Oakland to her house to "meet and talk and have a good meal." She used these meetings to learn more about the students and to allow them a safe space to vent their concerns. She added,

> I do not think that the students ever requested anything from me that I could not deliver. At times, when I was with students, they would ask me to leave their meetings. I respected that, but often reminded them that I could only support their behavior if it did not violate campus codes.

Mark Smith's relationship with students at Denison was such that at a reunion for the classes of 1957 to 1959, Smith remembered the names of all the students. He suggested, "Genuine partnerships are ageless." In a conversation with his wife, who was a student at Denison in the late 1960s, Smith asked, "'Why in the world did women students come to me with such unbelievable personal stuff?' And she said, "Because you couldn't be shocked and because we knew we could trust you completely and that you'd either help us or find somebody who could. Most of all, we knew you wouldn't be judgmental." Such was the kind of relationship that the student affairs professionals in this book seemed to have with their students.

In a similar vein, Charles Witten recounted the story of a student he clashed with:

> We had one Black real revolutionary who even altered his name....I don't know if he ever graduated, but when I was getting out of the car to go to church a couple of weeks ago...a car going by jammed on the brakes. They squealed and a man ran out, threw his arms around me and said, "Dean Witten!" He was that former Black revolutionary, now a respectable middle class minister.

Blackburn told a similar story.

> Not too long ago, I went down to the Chamber of Commerce; I was walking down and was starting to cross the street when a guy in a big, white, pickup truck stopped in the middle of the

street, jumped out, grabbed me and said, "I am so and so. " He said, "You kicked me out of school and it was the best thing that ever happened to me. I thought I could do any damn thing I wanted to do." He said, "I just want you to know that I have done well and I owe you a lot for that."

Many of the contributors to this book still keep in touch with former students and know where many others are and what they are doing.

- An Honest, Open Relationship

A "side-effect" of having a close relationship with students is the ability to be honest with them. It was clear that few student affairs professionals featured in this book had any hesitancy about calling students on the carpet if they did something wrong. In fact, they were straightforward in speech and action, in a way that current student affairs administrators might frown upon. Charles Witten described telling a nonstudent agitator to "Get the hell off this campus." A police officer who witnessed this told Witten, "I never saw a group of Black students talk to a White dean that respectfully as they talked to you." In response Witten said, "Well, these kids all know me." In another incident Witten recalled grabbing a White student by the collar and telling him, "If this parade goes, you go; you're out of school." He admitted that today he would not be able to do that.

Other stories highlighted in this book involve student affairs professionals being brutally honest with their students—something that would be more difficult to do if they didn't already have a close relationship with their students. James Rhatigan captured the essence of this honesty when he said that sometimes he would tell students, "That is the most stupid damn thing I've ever heard of," in relationship to a request the students had made or a position they had taken. He added, "If you didn't have a relationship with them, you couldn't say that because it would just make them angry. I spoke my mind to them at all times, but not brutally or condescendingly." The way that student affairs professionals talked to their students seems a bit strange in today's context, as their words were often blunt and to the point. Still, to a person, those in this book suggested that brutal honesty is acceptable when it occurs within a strong relationship.

The contributors to this book also expressed general agreement that a close relationship between students and administrators reduced the likelihood of unresolvable campus unrest. Robert Shaffer, for example, was among many who declared that one of the reasons that Indiana was so calm was because of the solid communication with students.

> We tried to say, "Come in and tell us what you're going to do. We'll try to make sure the police don't go off all crazy-like. We'll try to help you organize." On our campus we actually told them some things they could do and keep channels of communication open with us. Otherwise, student leaders would work secretively and engage in underhanded, even violent or damaging, actions.

He added, "Even my most radical student activists at IU would say that they never had to work undercover because they could usually take open actions." Similarly, David Ambler was convinced that the reason that no African American students were killed in the May 1970 protest at Kent State was because of the positive working relationships that were established between the Black students and those in student affairs. Others in this book expressed very similar sentiments.

- Has *In Loco Parentis* Disappeared?

Ambler, while at Kent State, noted with great optimism:

> The new dean of students was committed to the transition from the old dean of men and dean of women model with a heavy emphasis on behavioral control and social monitoring, to a comprehensive set of student affairs programs to respond to the contemporary needs of the new Kent students. The excitement for me and the other new student affairs staff was that we were going to be involved in developing them.

Later he commented on how happy he was when *in loco parentis* died. Despite the hopes of individuals like Ambler, not all of the administrators we interviewed agreed that student affairs has changed significantly in their approach to students. Or perhaps they thought that student affairs had regressed.

Although Robert Shaffer argued that student affairs had come to see itself somewhat differently by the end of the student protest era, he still saw room for change:

> Student affairs has to change from their image as a custodial, keeper of the morals, supervisory role to one of actually facilitating the individual to develop informed views. The university,

in all its aspects, should teach students to not only form open attitudes and informed views, but also encourage them to express themselves actively.

Some complained that student affairs had regressed. Mark Smith noted:

> Students wanted badly to be members of the administrative team. Much of that is gone, in part because of the emphasis in student affairs on policing and discipline. Former students who were at Denison in the 1950s and 1960s marvel today at how important and respected they felt, how proud they were to be the primary citizens of the campus community (and they were). These feelings created high morale, intense loyalty, and strong identification with the institution.

James Lyons agreed,

> For example, conduct issues are more important now in part because of the way we are treating students once they arrive. We are back to treating them like children again. The guiding principle seems to be "keep the waters calm, don't allow disturbances, and don't upset the parents."

WORKING AT THE PLEASURE OF THE PRESIDENT

Many of the student affairs administrators we interviewed had a great deal of respect and admiration for the presidents with whom they worked. Describing their presidents as "humane in the truest sense of the word," "as a kind of a leader in the area of civil rights," and as "outstanding and socially conscious," many of the interviewees credited their presidents with making the campus climate more welcoming to African American students. These individuals told stories of their presidents creating task forces to deal with racism and diversity, of being encouraged to apply for federal TRIO program grants, and of how their presidents were leaders in the local community in terms of educating the general public about the university's stance on civil rights. The general sentiment on the positive role of presidents, according to our interviewees, is captured eloquently by Hubbard who stated that the positive outcomes achieved on campus were "made possible by having a president and a vice president for academic affairs who cleared the obstacles and made it easier. I think it was the top-down empowerment that made [diversity efforts] so effective." Morson echoed the comments of others when he stated, "I attribute much of our stability to the character and political astuteness of the president."

In the most positive cases, presidents empowered their student affairs leaders to work with students to help bring about institutional change. As Shaffer commented, "because of his backing [the president's], the staff was able to move very rapidly." In some cases, the presidents themselves actually helped to facilitate student protest. Chambers, for example, described how the president at University of the Pacific supported an open speaker policy, even though the board of trustees "did not always understand why the students had to hear from Angela Davis, or why there had to be nude dancers from Berkeley dancing on the chapel lawn." When trustees and alumni threatened to withdraw financial support, Chambers credited the president with strongly defending keeping the campus as "open as possible." Chambers added that this level and type of presidential support was the "primary reason we did not have as much trouble as other schools." Such presidential support changed the nature of student affairs work from being one of "reigning in disruptive students" to "empowering students to help bring about institutional change."

Others recognized, however, that presidents did not always have the freedom to be on the forefront of institutional change—especially in light of the attitudes of conservative boards of trustees and community members. For example, Blackburn stated that at the University of Alabama the president was in no position to "be out in front" when it came to integrating the university. He went on to explain that the president was supportive of the integration efforts, but that he looked to student affairs to make the integration of African Americans into the university a successful experience. Similarly, Witten described his president at "a good ol' boy" who "could not get out too far in front of his trustees." This was also the case for the presidents at Florida State, Alabama, and USC who were reflective of strong state cultures.

Indeed, some presidents seemed to be very concerned about the public image of their institution. At institutions where the president seemed particularly concerned with institutional image, the role of student affairs administrators was to "keep things under control so that the students did not embarrass the university or college and did not offend the trustees." The extreme of this view was expressed by a couple of those we interviewed, who described working with presidents and boards who were "frightened" and that "fear manifested itself in protective and closed activities."

All of the student affairs officers we interviewed recognized that they worked "at the pleasure of the president." In many respects, they saw their role as being supportive of their president's perspectives regarding civil rights concerns and saw their job as carrying out the goals of the institution in this regard. As Anderson confirmed, "The presidents and chancellors also rightfully expected us to be on their team." Yet, in many cases the student affairs professionals found themselves empathizing with the students, and saw part of their job as "translating" what the students wanted to the president. In the cases where the student affairs personnel had a positive relationship with their president, they typically believed it was their job to be honest and forthright with him about such issues (at that time, all of the presidents were men). As Lyons declared,

> I have a responsibility to argue with the president, to check the president, to disagree with the president, to inform the president. You don't disagree publicly, obviously, but behind closed doors, the president could count on me to challenge him

Upcraft added, "I discovered that marching into a meeting and confronting the president, provost, or dean didn't work. You work behind the scenes; you work on individual people who have some power and influence." Relatedly, Ambler admits, "There are times when I wanted to argue stronger with the presidents and provosts with whom I worked, and maybe I didn't argue as strongly as I should, because I didn't want to jeopardize our position in the hierarchy." This fear was real, as folks like Harris Shelton discovered when he publicly disagreed with his president. On that occasion, Shelton received a phone call, in which the president explained that, as the president,

> He, alone, was responsible for the success and control of the university, and that if I did not support his position then that would make me a freelancer. The president made it abundantly clear that he did not sign paychecks of freelancers.

The kind of president to whom they reported clearly shaped the experiences of student affairs administrators during the civil rights era. Whether the top-down mandate was to "quell dissent" or "encourage student protest" was largely dictated by the views of the president. Being "one of the president's men" was typically seen in a positive light when the president was supportive of student affairs and of student needs. It was a much more difficult position when the president's views did not jibe with those of the student affairs administrator. Especially in the turbulent times of the civil rights era, when there was a mismatch between the president and the student affairs staff, the latter was likely to find him or her self looking for a new job.

RELATIONSHIPS WITH FACULTY: NECESSARY, BUT NOT AS HELPFUL AS HOPED

In general, faculty played a small role in experiences recounted by the student affairs administrators interviewed for this book. The two views expressed most frequently were of faculty as liberal in theory but resistant to change in practice, in which case student affairs sometimes played a role in calling their bluff, and of student affairs as a resource for faculty who wanted to make positive change but didn't know how. John Blackburn set the context when he observed, "It was obvious that, if the university was going to be successfully integrated, then student affairs administrators were going to play a prominent role." Its role, he said, was "to fill vacuums that exist on campus. That's the way to have an impact, to fill vacuums." Implied in this statement was that faculty played a secondary role in civil rights activities on campus. Of course, Philip Hubbard, who oversaw student affairs from a post as academic dean, worked closely with faculty. In fact, he credited faculty with being an essential ally.

David Ambler, Charles Witten, and Mark Smith each described faculty who were liberal in views, and who sometimes even criticized the administration for not doing enough, but who, when asked to change academic policy, were resistant. As example, Witten recounted his efforts to create an Opportunity Scholars Program. As he said,

> I remember a lot of the faculty who wanted to do something...but we started a program where the president could admit 100 students a year who didn't come up to normal academic standards if they were outstanding in other ways. It came up for discussion at a faculty meeting, and the faculty was hesitant. They looked it as a way to admit academically unqualified athletes.

Witten's response was to say, "Hey, look. You guys wanted to do something. We've got our eye on a bunch of kids who are artists, writers, actors, etc., really talented and we have a program for them." The faculty did eventually approve the program.

Mark Smith's recollection of faculty involvement was not so positive. "We tried hard to make the situation better, but again and again the faculty would turn on us....But what hurt us the most was that faculty leaders who claimed to be antiracist and pro-civil rights wouldn't support us." Smith went on, "Few faculty members had experience with Black students from urban areas and most had no clue about Black feelings and sensitivities, not to mention the abilities of educationally underprivileged Blacks."

Likewise, Ambler saw the faculty at Kent as being somewhat hypocritical (our word not his).

> This was an interesting case [request to start an African American Studies Program] in that you always have a lot of faculty that are whipping the administration for not doing what ought to be done, but when the tables were turned on the Kent State faculty, they were the ones who were resistant to setting up an African Studies program.

According to Harris Shelton at Florida State,

> Many students and faculty did not want to be bothered by these issues. Some were afraid of a dialogue between races. And the environment was one of antebellum South and some of the old thinking that went on behind the magnolias and Spanish moss and plantation houses.

When pressed by the Black Student Union, the Florida State faculty senate did create a Commission on Black Student Affairs, to which Harris Shelton was appointed. Several others talked about conservative faculty and board members who were generally opposed to student affairs efforts to listen to protesting students. For example, Judith Chambers commented:

> Like others, I wanted to be an advocate for students....but the tension between members of our board, some of the conservative faculty, and even some of the conservative students also put the student affairs staff members in a position where they never felt they were either doing the right thing, or enough of the right thing.

Others experienced a faculty that was concerned but uncertain how to respond. As Smith noted, few faculty had had experiences with Black students and their backgrounds. In this case, student affairs saw an opportunity to serve as a resource. James Appleton expressed this view best when he said,

> The faculty was not resistant, but had difficulty understanding what this meant....So, the best of our student affairs professionals became resources for faculty as much as for students. Part of our job was helping the faculty understand the meaning and reasons behind these disruptions, while we also tried to convince students to be more patient and understand some of the traditional values of the academy that could make a difference in their ability to succeed in the years ahead.

Likewise, Anderson noted,

> The role of student affairs administrators was to help faculty and staff understand the students, interpret their views, perceptions, goals, and aspirations. We tried to help them appreciate the fact that not every

demand was intended to be a challenge to their authority. Instead, it was a challenge to their way of thinking.

The student affairs administrators expressed some frustration with the slowness of the faculty governance process but may have benefited from student affairs' marginal status. Blackburn argued,

> Nobody really gives a damn what you're going to do in student affairs. If you want to do something in the academic world, you've got to go through all these committees and the departments and approval, and by the time you finally get it approved, you've lost interest in what you originally were proposing. In student affairs and housing, if you can keep behavior to the point that it can be rationalized and don't lose money, nobody particularly cares what you do in housing. So, student affairs people have all this opportunity to do things.

It should be noted that several of the student affairs administrators we interviewed indicated, as did Robert Shaffer, that "many faculty members were supportive of our actions towards civil rights." Harrison Morson agreed,

> Many faculty members went well out of their way to support the fundamental needs of those who came to campus lacking basic college survival skills. Study groups and related support services were established within the classroom and through the professional counseling department.

Hubbard found faculty to be an essential ally.

> We were groping our way through strange territory, and there are probably things that we could have done, but our great ally in this was faculty. The faculty understood what we were trying to say. Even though the students were asking for concessions, which posed problems for the faculty, like canceling classes and so forth, the faculty understood, and when it was necessary to protect the institution, the faculty did the right thing.

RELATIONSHIPS WITH THE LOCAL COMMUNITY: A SOURCE OF TENSION

The colleges in which these individuals worked were deeply affected by the external climate of U.S. society in general, as well as of their host communities. The nature and degree to which the external climate affected campuses and the experiences of student affairs administrators varied by institutional type, location, and time period. However, the nature of the specific context of each college affected the kind of interaction the college had with its larger community and thus affected the role of the student affairs administrator.

● A More Liberal Environment

One of the themes that emerges from the stories is that the colleges and universities in which these administrators worked were generally more liberal than the towns in which they are located. John Blackburn described the University of Alabama as "an oasis of integration in an otherwise burning state." Although most communities were not burning, the general principle applied to all. Injustice in the larger communities often created the conditions for protest or activism on many campuses. As Augustine Pounds noted, "Tensions in Pontiac added to the tension on campus." This was particularly true for those who worked at some urban and Southern universities. Likewise, a more liberal campus climate often created tension between the college and its surrounding community as Judith Chambers noted.

> In the 1960s and 1970s, Pacific was greatly misunderstood by members of the Stockton community. They did not understand our liberal policy on campus speakers. Any controversial action on the part of a student or a faculty member found its way to the front page of the paper, and of course, protests were also misunderstood and not supported by the community.

In other cases, such as the case of Haverford where students worked to integrate barber shops in nearby Ardmore, student affairs administrators saw external conditions as a vehicle for raising student awareness and for bringing about change. Common problems were discriminatory housing practices, such as "red-lining" in Iowa City, and lack of places where African Americans could get their hair cut in Bloomington, Indiana, eat in Washington, DC, or watch movies in Tuscaloosa, Alabama. Of course, in Alabama, South Carolina, Florida, and Washington, D.C. discrimination off campus, as well as on, was less than subtle. Howard students had been actively engaged in integrating the public transportation system in Washington, DC since the 1920s and 1930s.

In many cases, students protested against these discriminatory practices in their larger communities at great personal risk. Jail was one potential consequence, but so, too, was physical attack, particularly in the South. Robert Shaffer summed up the attitude of Northern cities:

Student activists had to be careful if they were going downtown, to the Courthouse Square, for example, because down there they would have been attacked by the town "intelligentsia." We had many people in Bloomington who did not like college students demonstrating downtown.

In the South, the situation was even worse. As Harris Shelton noted,

A number of us participated in marches where we got off campus and marched through downtown (Tallahassee). It was frightening. This was an old, Southern town. As long as you were on campus you felt somewhat insulated. But two blocks off campus and you were fair game, and that is the feeling we had.

- Relationships with the Local Police

In these contexts, student affairs administrators dealt with the police frequently. Indeed, having a good relationship with the local police was important. Ron Beer described, one lesson he learned was "to develop an open and candid relationship with key authority figures in the community—police, fire, mayor, city manager, sheriff, district attorney, constable, state police, national guard, etc." Police and National Guard protection for the first African American students at the Universities of Alabama and South Carolina was essential to ensure their safety.

Student affairs administrators were often the key to liberating students from jail, as John Blackburn recounted: "I spent my weekends getting students out of jail. It's amazing how popular you become on Saturday night when they're in the tank down there. When I walk in they say, 'Dean, hey do you remember me?'" In another incident, described by Charles Witten, the city manager asked Witten to get a parade permit back from students. Witten negotiated with the students, and the permit was returned. Witten was respected by the Columbia police because they had witnessed him confront Black students during a demonstration at USC. However, relationships were not always positive ones. As James Rhatigan noted, "We worked very hard at improving student relationship with the police....We had our own campus police force, and that relationship was not always good, especially in the 1960s."

A portent of things to come, Kent State actually called on the State Patrol to enforce calm in civil rights activities. As Beer said:

> At times, Black students tried to take over buildings and we called in the Ohio State Patrol because the students were interfering with the normal functions of the institution....We asked the patrol to provide clear instruction when they walked into the classroom or office. They said, "Here's what you're doing and it is unacceptable. You've got five minutes to move. Failure to do that will result in the following." When we articulated that, we were gently firm, if you know what I mean. We did not mess around. But, the patrol did not kick people.

Beer believed that the Black students at Kent expected the police to be involved, as that was just part of engaging in the civil rights movement. It was the only way, short of violence, to drive home the point, and it worked.

● Building Bridges and Upholding Reputation

Student affairs administrators also played a part in building bridges between various local communities, particularly with the African American community. For example, Ron Beer described recruiting Hispanic and Black students by visiting local churches, or to pow-wows to recruit Native American students. At Haverford, Indiana, and Howard, students were involved in protest activity directed to opening up barbershops and public transportation to Black students. As Lyons recounted, "Just like going to Mississippi, it wasn't in our backyard, but it was wrong, and we felt good because we tried to help—and did." Haverford engaged in a number of meetings with Black churches and attempted to hire some people from the community. "We wanted to create some bridges, a presence." According to Lyons, Haverford created a camp which "involved the coming together of two groups with great cultural differences—a Quaker meeting and two local Black churches." Several talked about their role in initiating programs, such as Upward Bound designed to serve local populations. The Upward Bound program at the University of South Carolina and TRIO programs at Wichita State are two examples. Students at the University of Iowa, under the leadership of Philip Hubbard, established a relationship with Rust University, a historically Black college located in the Southeast. These programs helped to build bridges to local communities and to demonstrate a commitment to African Americans. And, as James Rhatigan noted, the Black community often kept the pressure on the university to insure that the university would keep trying to improve the situation for Black students.

Student Affairs administrators were also in the position of upholding the reputation of the college or university. Jo Anne Trow (and the comment from Judith Chambers quoted above) illustrated this well when she said,

> Occasionally, the press would pickup on isolated, racial incidents that occurred on campus, which would frustrate the student affairs staff. Whenever these things happened while I was still working there, I would say, "Oh, no! Let's hope this is the only one this year."

As the stories of each of the individuals in this book demonstrates, student affairs administrators walked a fine line between supporting and managing student unrest, even if that unrest spilled over into the local community, and maintaining good relations with the local police.

RELATIONSHIPS WITH NASPA: A PLACE TO NETWORK

At best, NASPA and other professional organizations of its kind were able to provide student affairs professionals with a network of colleagues who were experiencing similar things. Such networking was essential when campuses seemed to be literally exploding from student protest and unrest. As Carl Anderson described, NASPA made people feel like they weren't "isolated and alone" in having to respond to such difficult times. He continued, "I think we served as sounding boards—as catalysts for sharing strategies to respond to these issues and concerns." Similarly, Judith Chambers confirmed that NASPA provided a forum.

> What I believe it did provide, which was most valuable, was a forum for us to get together and talk about how each of us was handling the problems we were dealing with. Through my involvement with NASPA, I was able to develop some very strong friendships with colleagues across the country who were an enormous help to me when I was dealing with very difficult issues. I'd like to think that the reverse was also true.

The positive aspects of organizations like NASPA were captured by Jim Lyons who observed:

> NASPA's local, regional and national meetings were where you got to know other colleagues and their situations. It was where information was exchanged. It was where issues and practices were analyzed and presented systematically. It was the vehicle whereby clusters of nearby schools facing new winds and tides could gather to learn from each

other. This was terribly important because so much was new during those times.

Upcraft reiterated this point, stating,

> The dialogue on the national level was, "How do we manage this and what can we do to find out more about students and their environments?"...If somebody went though something we anticipated but we hadn't yet experienced, we wanted to know about that.

At the same time, there was some disagreement about the extent to which NASPA served as a true change agent in this difficult period. Augustine Pounds, for example, noted:

> I cannot recall coming away feeling empowered to handle a campus disruption. I do not recall being provided information that would help a university take steps to prevent a disruption. If there were "how to" guides or resources on how other campuses handle their issues, I don't recall ever being provided with that sort of resource.

Harris Shelton agreed.

> While NASPA folks were conducting research on "Aspirations of Freshmen in Residence Halls," or some similar topic, I was suspending students blocking the corridors of Bryan Hall while protesting the presence of Marine Corps recruiters. There was not much time to network or prepare, and there was not much of a connection with NASPA.

Similarly, Harrison Morson noted that NASPA "did not appear to be a professional group interested in reaching out to two-year colleges." He added, however, that "once 'inside' the association, I found numerous support components, especially the promising network of veteran peers." One explanation for these discrepant findings is that NASPA, in those days, was designed to serve the chief student affairs officer more so than the junior student affairs personnel. As such, while deans and vice presidents were networking and engaging in dialogue about how to respond to campus unrest, those in lower level positions often felt like they were left to fend for themselves. Appleton alluded to this when he stated that as a member of the NASPA executive committee he remembers sitting in hotel rooms with colleagues sharing advice. He explained, "I admit I hardly ever went to the formally scheduled conference sessions." It was in these informal sessions that NASPA members discussed "why Kent State blew up and why Denver did not."

Many who held leadership positions at NASPA were adamant that the organization did more than just try to "keep a lid on campuses." Instead,

James Appleton insisted that NASPA was concerned with "how to enable our colleges and universities to become more effective in educating a new student generation." Blackburn added that in 1967, in his work as director of professional development and standards for NASPA, they developed a policy on confidentiality of student records. In conjunction with the Research and Higher Education program at Berkeley, they organized a symposium about campus innovations. In evaluating the program, Blackburn suggested:

> Most of those innovations were not really innovations as you or I would do it, but in their particular campus, it was an innovation.... At first, I was kind of disappointed but then I saw how excited these people were to talk about what they were doing. That was the whole idea! We wanted to stimulate people to become innovators in higher education. I don't think we do enough of that now.

Lamenting some changes in the organization, Ron Beer added, "People used to be a lot more vocal than they are now about some of these issues." Still, Charles Witten insisted,

> What student affairs at the University of South Carolina did in the way of facilitating desegregation was to follow the old guidance set forth by the ACPA and NASPA many years before the problems of desegregation in the South ever appeared.

In effect, he credited the work of organizations like NASPA with facilitating integration.

MISTAKES MADE, LESSONS LEARNED

None of the administrators interviewed for this book was prepared to deal with the situations they found themselves in although some, such as Witten and Blackburn, were hired because someone believed they were suited to handle a tough situation (integration). Many were young and were promoted rapidly without much experience. Needless to say, they all learned significant lessons as a result of their experiences dealing with civil rights.

Although student affairs administrators saw themselves as filling a vacuum, as providing important resources for faculty, and as serving on the front line in the institutions' efforts to successfully navigate the complicated waters of the civil rights movement, they tended not to see themselves as heroes. In fact, they often made mistakes. Although some, such as David Ambler had clearly been involved in civil rights activities before they assumed their administrative positions, others had not thought much about civil rights.

Charles Witten admitted, "I did it [integration] because the law said to do it. I was a retired captain in the United States Navy and when legitimate authority told me to do something, I did it." For him, "I never called what we did the civil rights movement.....the state university had a job to educate everybody in some way or another." Witten's later actions to improve the situation for African Americans suggest that he was understating his actual commitment to civil rights. It is difficult to separate mistakes made from lessons learned. In fact, the individuals included in this book did not all specifically admit to having made mistakes, but they all did talk about lessons learned. One can assume that many of these lessons came as the result of mistakes, or if not mistakes, at least in response to an assessment that things could have been done better.

We Were Amateurs

These administrators found themselves in particularly difficult situations. They certainly were not experienced in dealing with student protests, many were very young, and others did not come from a background in student affairs. In fact, they were amateurs. As Phil Hubbard stated, "We were amateurs. We were groping our way through strange territory, and there are probably things that we could have done." Others noted, as did David Ambler, that they were "flying by the seat of our pants." Both John Blackburn and Charles Witten recalled telling their presidents that they would deal with a situation regardless of whether or not they had a clue as to how they would do so. Phil Hubbard summarized the view of most, "We were enlightened, and we did not think we had the absolute truth either." And, as noted earlier, they were young and were promoted rapidly.

Mistakes Made

The mistakes identified by our contributors varied widely. One noted by several was regret at not having integrated the fraternities and sororities. As John Blackburn admitted,

> I think if I made one mistake, I should have integrated the fraternities and sororities, but there were many other things to deal with at that time. But it was probably easier then than it would be now....We should have created something new; we should have built it fresh.

In fact, when we interviewed Blackburn in Tuscaloosa in the summer of 2002, almost 40 years after integration, the University of Alabama was still dealing with the issue of integrating fraternities and sororities. Jim Rhatigan echoed this sentiment regarding Greek life at Wichita State and concluded, "This situation exists to this day. You can't count this one as a success, even though there are statements of nondiscrimination on the books everywhere."

There was some admission that their colleges did not handle student protest particularly well. Both Harris Shelton and Carl Anderson indicated that the administrations of Florida State University and Howard could have done things differently. Although Shelton separated himself somewhat from the top administration at Florida State with regard to their actions in response to protests, he noted, "Instead of being cooperative and helpful, we were now throwing up roadblocks to progress." But he acknowledged that a more cooperative approach "would have been out of character at that time for Florida State University, and for most other institutions." Likewise, Anderson noted that Howard attempted to suppress student protests resulting in expulsion of 38 students. Reflecting on that incident, he mused, "I think eventually the university came to the recognition that somehow they had to find a way to mediate in order to be able to conduct the basic mission of the institution, namely, teaching, research, and service." Appleton, spoke for most when he said, "Most of what we did in the 1960s and 1970s was by trial and error. We made a lot of mistakes. We were not as sensitive as we should have been."

Others observed that they, themselves being young, were perhaps too sym-pathetic to the student cause. As Lee Upcraft admitted, "I was a very young professional who was probably more sympathetic to the student point of view than perhaps I should have been." Ambler concurred, "But I also have to say, we were the young and enough personally committed to civil rights that a lot of us were really caught emotionally, philosophically in dealing with this situation. We had to be the ones enforcing the standards of the uni-versity and on the other hand we understood what Black students were expressing." Such youth often put lower level administrators such as Harris Shelton in a bad position. They had student trust—until the administration took a more forceful position.

Reflection also led these well-meaning administrators to conclude that some of their efforts on behalf of Black students were not well thought out. For example, Jim Lyons commented,

> At Haverford, we had an abundance of discussions about attaining a critical mass of minority students. The term "minority" was unexam-ined back then. We didn't realize how limiting and dumb that term was. The other term that we would cast about was "disadvantaged." That became not only a useless term, but a destructive one because it

equated color with disadvantage. We weren't defining things very well. We saw our main job back then as increasing the presence of students of color at the college. It was about access and numbers, it was an admissions issue. We didn't worry about climate because that was what we knew best, that sense of community that is a part of Quaker tradition.

Dave Ambler admitted that demands for a Black cultural center at Kent resulted in the same kind of short-term thinking. The demand was met, but with unexpected results.

The problem was we didn't think the issue through as well as we should have. We didn't ask, "What is the purpose of a cultural center? How will it be used as part of student life or an academic program?" As a result, it became a clubhouse that soon was viewed as a hotbed of radical and criminal activity

Jo Anne Trow commented,

We might have done it [hire Black faculty, etc.] quicker, but then, the campus tends to take a long time to decide to do something—working through all of those committees. I think we probably could have done more in providing dollars to try to get more minority faculty, because that is what it takes.

As a way of transitioning into a discussion of lessons learned, James Appleton probably expressed best the experiences of most when he recounted the following dialogue:

Q: My, you exercise such good judgment. How did you get such good judgment?

R: Well, I've had a lot of experiences.

Q: Well, how did you get all those experiences?

R: Bad judgment, man, bad judgment.

PERSONAL LESSONS LEARNED

One general theme that characterizes the individual contributors to this book, for example, is that they learned how to listen to students and also that it was essential to keep channels of communication open. Chambers noted, "They [students] learned how to protest and we learned how to listen. But sometimes we forgot the lessons we learned."

Occasionally, administrators such as David Ambler came to learn that "protest is effective. It was difficult for me because my own childrearing was such that you either obeyed the rules or you got in trouble." James Rhatigan agreed. "What we learned was that protest works. It worked then and still does today. Protest is better than trying to negotiate your way along; it's a shortcut because the university is so slow." However, he also learned that colleges and universities need to have a strategy for dealing with protest.

Although some of the administrators in this book had been exposed to concerns of Black students before assuming their roles, others admitted to becoming aware because of their administrative experiences. The lesson learned here was that student affairs work was a positive means by which to bring about societal change. As Harris Shelton confessed:

> Initially at Florida State I had good exposure to Black students, but not Black students who spoke their minds to Whites. It was new to me and to others to encounter students with clearly formulated positions, strategies to accomplish their goals, and the courage to fly in the face of several hundred years of convention—to step over the boundaries of acceptable behavior. It was one thing to watch it all on television— from Selma and Mississippi to Memphis and the motel where Martin Luther King was assassinated. It was very different to me to realize that each of us as educators had a personal stake, a personal role in the battle for human rights. In place of Birmingham, my role was on my campus, making sure that a young man and woman had the opportunity to learn about each other and to explore their relationship without fear of reprisal.

This lesson was important because it involved student affairs professionals as individuals learning that they needed to understand themselves and their own backgrounds before they could understand others and work to bring about change.

The lasting influence student affairs professionals can have on students was another important personal lesson learned by several profiled in this book. Student contacts outside of the classroom are often more important to students than in-class experiences with faculty. We learned from this project that many administrators have maintained contact with students long after the college experience is over. Such relationships were a personal testament to the positive impact that student affairs practitioners can have on their students. James Rhatigan captured this sentiment when he said:

What really counts in my view is the single student, sitting in front of you, with a single problem, issue or hope, and you have one chance to do something. You succeed with that student or you don't. It doesn't require knowledge of theory. What is required is sound judgment and total commitment. When you do that, your chances of succeeding are good...Most of my life experiences have centered on the small picture—one student, one issue. Rarely did I have a long history with students who came to see me. They appeared at a point in time; our lives converged perhaps only that one time. I learned a long time ago that it was not the depth of those encounters that made a difference, it was the timing.

The final person lesson worth noting here was expressed by James Appleton who, after dealing with the cafeteria takeover at Oakland, closed his door and sighed. An African American colleague asked him "How do you feel?" To which Appleton replied, "I feel really good." His colleague, with compassion in his voice and not meaning to criticize noted, "Well, nobody's going to thank you." Appleton then asked what he meant by that, to which the colleague replied "This kind of attention should have been given 100 years ago. Why should you get credit for it?" Appleton noted that this was an important lesson that forever changed him.

CONCLUSION

Student affairs administrators in the civil rights era played a crucial role in addressing the various constituencies demanding attention during the civil rights era. The stories in this book demonstrate the effect of the times on the variety of roles, relationships, and the personal lessons learned. In addition, these stories provide lessons for today's student affairs professionals or anyone concerned about civil rights on college campuses. In some ways, the civil rights period served as a transitional time for the student affairs profession, symbolized by the elevation of the position to the vice presidential level. Yet, we find that many of the concerns expressed in that era remain with us today. This is the topic we address in our final chapter.

LOOKING FORWARD:
LESSONS LEARNED

What are the lessons learned from an examination of these interviews? Some may ask how it is possible to draw lessons from experiences that happened over 30 years ago. After all, higher education is very different today than it was then. Although it is true that much has changed, the lessons generated from our reading of the experiences of various individuals who occupied student affairs roles in the 1960s and 1970s provide an important historical perspective for today's practitioners—especially when it comes to dealing with issues of diversity and activism on campus.

While higher education has made some progress in terms of equity issues since the civil rights era, in many respects the concerns of today mirror the concerns expressed by students of color in the 1960s and 1970s. Lee Upcraft, in comparing a list of African American student demands from the 1960s with those of today, for example, noted that both lists asked institutions to respond to the underrepresentation of students of color, the need for more faculty and staff of color, more inclusion of minority perspectives in the curriculum, a more supportive campus climate, and the need for more academic and social support services.

Some of the most important lessons learned by the student affairs professionals in this book centered on their understandings of how campuses can best be responsive to students from diverse backgrounds. They learned that merely having a certain number of students of color on a campus would not, in and of itself, provide an environment that was conducive to the success of those students. Providing access to historically underrepresented student groups is only a first step. Student affairs administrators learned that creating a positive campus climate requires several components. Change, they suggested, must begin at the individual level, with student affairs professionals educating and sensitizing themselves to issues of diversity, privilege, and difference. Furthermore, they realized the importance of hiring institutional personnel (faculty, staff, and administrators) from different racial/ethnic groups who offer different perspectives on academic concerns and who can serve as mentors, role models, and educators for the student body. Perhaps most importantly, they learned that the successful integration of campuses involved more than just offering a smattering of diversity-related programming. It required transforming the entire campus climate to one that is supportive of students from diverse backgrounds and perspectives—an opportunity and challenge that continues to this day. Part of this challenge involves reaching out to members of the local community because climate is important both on and off campus. Student affairs professionals were and are in a position to help create a campus environment (both academic and social) that promotes the success of all students.

To this end, one of the most profound changes that occurred for student affairs administrators during the 1960s and 1970s was that they became more valued by presidents and faculty, who looked to them to help manage student unrest and to help bring peace to the institution. As was made clear in this book, student affairs professionals served an important role of mediating conflicts between students and faculty, students and the administration, and between students and other students. They also served as resources in helping all constituent groups to better understand one another. The success with which student affairs professionals handled these challenges resulted in the elevation of the senior student affairs officer from dean to vice president (Laliberte, 2003).

This promotion, both in name and in the eyes of academic peers, reflects the importance and responsibility of the student affairs role. However, some of the interviewees highlighted in this book worry that the current generation of student affairs professionals, especially those at the highest levels, might have lost focus on this purpose of the profession: heeding the needs of the individual student. Student affairs programs are often million-dollar enterprises with large numbers of responsibilities and huge staffs hired to carry out a wide array of duties. The student affairs professionals in this book warn us about letting the administrative functions of our positions stand in the way of assisting that individual student, the student upon which our mission is based.

One of the major lessons learned is that the relationship between students and institutions ought to be one that empowers students and treats them like adults, and this duty transcends concerns about institutional image and politics. To accomplish this, student affairs professionals, at all levels, need to know what students are thinking and doing; they must be in a position to listen to students and respond to their concerns in a respectful manner. Keeping lines of communication open between students and the institution is essential to minimize discontent and avoid dissent. Such respectful communication also will facilitate student growth and learning. We learned during the civil rights era that the more open and student-oriented campuses were less likely to experience crises.

As such, the student affairs mission must not be to only maintain order, but also to educate students. Likewise, education cannot be narrowly based upon only the academic concepts of the institution. The student affairs profession is rooted in certain fundamental beliefs, among them that higher education needs to focus on educating the whole student—physically, socially, emotionally, and spiritually. Additionally, we believe that students ought to be treated as unique individuals, each with worth and dignity. For student affairs professionals who survived the turbulent times of the 1960s and 1970s, this guiding framework kept them and continues to keep today's student affairs professionals centered, focused, and committed to the cause of helping students and their institutions achieve their goals.

Many of the student affairs professionals in this book suggested that, while protest can be an effective way to bring about institutional change, institutions of higher education do not need to wait for students to submit a list of demands before engaging in institutional improvements. Student affairs professionals should be in a position to know what institutional changes ought to occur (by means of assessment, for example) and be willing to undertake proactive change. Evidence of proactive change is prevalent throughout this book, as when Charles Witten and John Blackburn helped to prepare their campuses for integration. Student affairs professionals need to think about whom their students are (and will be) and what those students will need to be successful. This involves being creative and proactive in determining what changes are necessary to bring about desired outcomes.

FINAL THOUGHTS

On the 50th anniversary of *Brown v. Board of Education of Topeka, Kansas*, we are reminded that colleges and universities played a key role in the struggle for civil rights in the 1960s and early 1970s. On college campuses across the country, student affairs professionals found themselves at the center of this struggle. Although they do not see themselves as heroes, student affairs professionals played the role of advocate, educator, mediator, protector, and change-agent. They worked with constituency groups both on and off campus to help bring about positive change. Of course, important civil rights concerns continue to exist—a close examination demonstrates that we have made progress on many fronts, but that in many areas we still have a ways to go to provide true equity and equality. There is much to be learned about the experiences of student affairs professionals in the 1960s and 1970s, an era when student affairs came of age. The stories in this book go a long way to illuminate this critical period, highlighting unique aspects of the civil rights struggle as well as the very nature of our profession.

REFERENCES

Adelman, C. (1972). *Generations: A Collage on Youth Culture*. New York: Praeger.

Altbach. P. B. (1973). *Student politics in America: A historical analysis*. New York: McGraw-Hill.

Anderson, J. D. (2002). Race in American higher education. In W.A. Smith, P.G. Altbach, & K. Lomotey, (Eds.), *The racial crisis in American higher education*. (Rev.Ed.), (pp. 3-21). Albany, NY: State University of New York Press.

Anthony, B. M. (1978). Educational concerns of Black Americans. *Journal of NAWDAC, 41,* 148-152.

Appleton, J. R., Briggs, C. M., & Rhatigan, J. J. (1978). *Pieces of eight: The rites, roles, and styles of the dean by eight who have been there*. Portland, OR: National Association of Student Personnel Administrators Institute of Research and Development.

Astin, A., Astin, H., Bayer, A., & Bisconti, A. (1997). Overview of the Unrest Era. In L. Goodchild & H. Wechsler, (Eds.), *The History of Higher Education*, (2nd ed. pp. 724-738). Needham, MA: Simon & Schuster Custom Publishing.

Astin, H. S. and Leland, C. (1991). *Women of influence, women of vision: A cross-generational study of leaders and social change*. San Francisco: Jossey-Bass.

Branch, T. (1988). *Parting the Waters: America in the King Years, 1954-63*. New York: Simon & Schuster.

Brett, R., Calhoun, E., Piggott, L., Davis, H., & Scott, P. (1979). A symposium, our living history: Reminiscences of Black participation in NAWDAC. *Journal of NAWDAC, 42,* 3-13.

Clark, E. C. (1995). *The school house door: Segregation's last stand at the University of Alabama*. New York: Oxford University Press.

Cohodas, N. (1997). *The band played Dixie.* New York: The Free Press.

Cowley, W. H. (1940). The history and philosophy of student personnel work. *Journal of the National Association of Deans of Women, 3,* 153-162.

Crookston, B. B. and Atkyns, G. C. (1974, April). *A study of student affairs: The principal student affairs officer, the functions, the organization at American colleges and universities, 1967-1972.* Technical report. No. 3 presented at the National Association of Student Personnel Administrators National Convention, Chicago, IL.

Cuthbert, M. (1930, March). The training and personality of the dean. *Minutes of the Meeting of Deans and Advisors to Women in Colored Schools,* Nashville, TN, Box 90-8, Folder 169, Lucy D. Slowe Papers, Moorland-Spingarn Research Center, Manuscript Division, Howard University, Washington, DC.

Exum, W. H. (1985). *Paradoxes of protest: Black student activism in a White university.* Philadelphia: Temple University Press.

Fley, J. A. (1963). Discipline in student personnel work: The changing views of deans and personnel workers. (Doctoral dissertation, University of Illinois, UMI No 63-3157).

Greenleaf, E. A. (1968). How others see us. *The Journal of College Student Personnel 9,* 226.

Griffin, C. S. (1974). *The University of Kansas: A history.* Lawrence: The University of Kansas Press.

Halberstam, D. (1998). *The children.* New York: Random House.

Hollis, D. W. (1956). *University of South Carolina (Volume II): College to university.* Columbia: University of South Carolina Press.

Hubbard, P. G. & Stone, A. E. (1999). *My Iowa journey: The life story of the University of Iowa's first tenured African American professor.* Iowa City: University of Iowa Press.

Johnston, J. A. (1998). Student Activism before 1960. In G. De Groot, *Student Protest: The Sixties and After* (pp. 12-26). NY: Longman.

Kaplin, W. A. (1986). *The law of higher education: A comprehensive guide to legal implications of administrative decision making* (2nd. ed). San Francisco: Jossey-Bass.

Laliberte, M. R. (2003). The student affairs profession transformed: Catalytic events of 1968 to 1972. Unpublished Doctoral dissertation, Johnson & Wales University.

Lowery, J. (2002). Dr. Charles Witten: A conversation about a remarkable life and career. *Palmetto practitioner: Issues in student affairs.* Retrieved on January 26, 2002, from www.http://sa.sc.edu//sccpa/palmetto/A2002.htm.

Marshall Berated by Blacks. (1970, January 28) *Tallahassee Democrat*, A7.

Meyers, E. M. & Sandeen, A. (1973). Survey of minority and women student affairs staff members employed in National Association of Student Personnel Administrators' member institutions. *National Association of Student Personnel Administrators Journal, 11*, 2-4.

Monhollon, R. L. (2002). *"This is America?" The sixties in Lawrence, Kansas.* New York: Palgrave.

Moody, S. (1973, May 13). K.U.'s class of '73 matured in troubled years. *Kansas City Star*, p. 51.

Moore, G. (1967, May 19). Who says college kids have changed? *Life*, 90-100.

Morrison, M. A. 1990. A sentimental journey across campus with John L. Blackburn. *Alumni Magazine*, University of Alabama, pp. 3-7.

Mueller, K. H. (1954). *Educating women for a changing world.* Minneapolis: University of Minnesota Press.

National Association of Deans and Advisors of Men. (1949, April). *Proceedings of the Thirty-First Anniversary Conference of the National Association of Deans and Advisors of Men.* Highland Park, IL, 37-40.

National Association of Student Personnel Administrators. (1954, May). *Proceedings of the Thirty-Sixth Anniversary Conference of the National Association of Student Personnel Administrators.* Roanoke, VA, 189-197.

National Association of Student Personnel Administrators. (1965, April). *Proceedings of the Forty-Seventh Anniversary Conference of the National Association of Student Personnel Administrators.* Washington, DC, iv-vii, 35-40, 186.

National Association of Student Personnel Administrators. (1989). *Points of view*. Washington, DC: National Association of Student Personnel Administrators.

National Civil Rights Museum. (2004). Permanent Exhibits. Memphis, TN.

Nichols, D. D. (1990). *The delirious decade, 1965-1975: A social history of a community college*. Farmington, MI: Tri-Nic Press.

Noble, J. (1969). The Black student movement: A search for identity. *Journal of NAWDAC, 32*, 49-54.

Rabby, G.A. (1999). The pain and the promise: The struggle for civil rights in Tallahassee, Florida. Athens: University of Georgia Press.

Rhatigan, J. J. (1978). A Corrective Look Back. In *Pieces of eight: The rites, roles, and styles of the dean by eight who have been there* (pp. 12-13). Portland, OR: National Association of Student Personnel Administrators Institute of Research and Development.

Rix, H., (1988, April 4). A guru to women of influence: Emily Taylor offers voice of optimism. *Kansas City Star*, pp. 1C, 6C.

Sanford, N., (Ed.) (1962). *The American college: A psychological and social interpretation of higher learning*. New York: John Wiley & Sons.

Sanford, N. (1967). *Where colleges fail*. San Francisco: Jossey-Bass.

Schwartz, R. A. (1990). The feminization of a profession: Student affairs work in American education, 1890-1945. Doctoral dissertation, Indiana University. DAI, 51, no. 05A.

Strauss, W., & Howe, N. (1997). *The fourth turning: An American prophecy*. New York: Broadway Books.

Student rights and freedoms: Joint statement on rights and freedoms of students. (1992) Washington, DC: National Association of Student Personnel Administrators.

Tautfest, P. B. (1969): The joint statement on rights and freedoms of students. *Journal of NAWDAC, 33*, 27-30.

Teddlie, C. & Freeman, J. A. (2002). Twentieth-century desegregation in U.S. higher education. In W. A. Smith, P. G, Altbach, & K. Lomotey (Eds.), *The racial crisis in American higher education* (rev. ed.). Albany: State University of New York Press.

Towle, K. A. (1966). Comments on the Berkeley situation. In Ruth Strang, et. al, NAWDAC, Perspective and Prospectus: A Symposium. *NAWDAC Journal, 29*, 101-103.

Tuttle, K. N. (1996). What became of the dean of women? Changing roles for women administrators in American higher education, 1940-1980. Doctoral dissertation, University of Kansas. UMI No. 963751

Tuttle, W. M. (2001). Separate but not equal: African Americans and the 100-year struggle for equality in Lawrence and at the University of Kansas, 1850s-1960. In Domer, D. & Watkins, B. (Eds.), *Embattled Lawrence: Conflict and community*, pp. 139-151. Lawrence: University of Kansas Division of Continuing Education.

Wallenstein, P. (1999). Black Southerners and non-Black universities: Desegregating higher education, 1935-1967. *History of Higher Education 9*, 121-148.

(1/15/2002). Saying goodbye to a good man: Obituary for Philip G. Hubbard. Retrieved 11/20/03 from http://www.press-citizen.com/opinion/pceditorials/staffedit011502.htm.

APPENDIX A

Oral Interview Questions for
NASPA Study Participants

Role of student affairs practitioners in the civil rights movement (focusing on the struggle of African Americans and other students of color for access, integration, campus support, access to resources and services, and curricular change).

Personal Experiences (ask for vita)

1. Walk through your professional path for us?
    What were your institution, position, and role (in relationship to students) during the period under question?

2. What was the institutional climate for students of color as this era began?

3. Tell me about your experiences in dealing with civil rights issues.
    * What was your role?
    * What did you do?
    * What was the outcome?

4. How did your involvement in civil rights on campus shape the direction of policy in this area (on campus and in society as a whole)?

5. What change came about as the result of your involvement in the civil rights movement?

6. How did those experiences affect your views about:
    * civil rights?
    * your institution?
    * your profession?
    * your personal feelings?

7. How would you describe this period of "unrest" with others that you have experienced throughout your career?
   In what ways was the civil rights era unique?

8. Looking back, how do you think your campus handled the civil rights movement on campus? What could have/should have been done differently?

9. What role did the student affairs staff play in implementing and continuing to monitor issues raised in the civil rights movement?

10. What kind of lessons did you learn from those experiences?

11. When looking at your career as a whole, how does your role in civil rights movement fit into the big picture?

APPENDIX B

Written Response Questions for
NASPA Study Participants

1. Pick one incident with which you were involved and describe it in detail.
   • Tell us how you were involved, what you did, why you did it.
   • Paint a picture of what that event was like.

2. What did higher education contribute to the larger civil rights movement?

3. How would you characterize student involvement in the civil rights movement? How does this compare to student involvement today?

4. What should higher education do to cultivate interest and participation in larger social issues?

5. What impact did higher education have on the civil rights movement and what impact did the civil rights movement have on higher education?